"When's the last time someone whispered love words to you, Ami?"

She stared at him. "We aren't talking about me."

"I am. When?" Jeff straightened against the desk and, arms folded, watched her through narrowed eyes.

She returned his gaze, her eyes going to his mouth. The wayward tingling she remembered each time she thought of him returned, and she swallowed hard.

"Well?" he asked. She shook her head.

He moved, covering the steps between them in seconds, and his hands spanned her slim waist. He pulled her against him, placing his mouth over hers. None too gently, he forced her lips apart, pressed her head back, playing havoc with her breath. He raised his head enough to look into her wide, shocked eyes, unaware of the feelings he aroused in her....

ABOUT THE AUTHOR

Zelma Orr had a most interesting career before turning to writing full-time. She was a U.S. Customs Officer for the Treasury Department in her home state of Texas. Zelma loves to travel, and keeps a diary of the places she has been to use for story ideas in future books.

Books by Zelma Orr

HARLEQUIN AMERICAN ROMANCES
 7—MIRACLES TAKE LONGER
18—IN THE EYES OF LOVE
55—LOVE IS A FAIRY TALE

These books may be available at your local bookseller.

For a free catalog listing all titles currently available, send your name and address to:

Harlequin Reader Service
P.O. Box 52040, Phoenix, AZ 85072-2040
Canadian address: P.O. Box 2800, Postal Station A, 5170 Yonge Street, Willowdale, Ontario M2N 5T5

Love Is
a Fairy Tale

ZELMA ORR

Harlequin Books

TORONTO • NEW YORK • LONDON
AMSTERDAM • PARIS • SYDNEY • HAMBURG
STOCKHOLM • ATHENS • TOKYO • MILAN

Published May 1984

First printing March 1984

ISBN 0-373-16055-0

Printed in Canada

Chapter One

She couldn't see the flaming rays of the setting sun behind the Franklin Mountains, but Ami knew it was there. It reflected in the tiny windows of the old adobe building across the street from her animal clinic, and she stared at the crimson-lined clouds lying on top of the dark rocks, the end of the Rocky Mountain chain in Texas. To her, it was a restful view and, tired as she was, she sat still, relaxing her body and mind at the same time. It was after normal office hours, and she had just finished operating on a small Yorkshire terrier, wanting to wait awhile to see how he came through the anesthesia before she went home. Wearily she pulled her stained smock off and threw it into the hamper.

"Tell them we're closed, Rio," she called when she heard the bell at the front of the clinic.

A moment later her young charge stood in the doorway. "Mr. Hilton wants to talk to you, Ami."

She looked around, startled, seeing the two men behind Rio. The man in front grinned. "I'm Steve Hilton, Miss Whitelake. This is Jeff Wagner, owner of Wagner Ranch."

Ami took the outstretched hand, looking into light blue eyes topped by sun-bleached blond hair. He was a bit over six feet tall for her to have to look up at him from her five feet eight inches of height.

"We should have called, since it's so late," he apologized.

"That's quite all right," she said, taking the hand extended by Jeff Wagner. He was taller than Steve Hilton, his dark gray eyes set in a deeply tanned face, and he had dark brown—almost black—hair. He smiled politely, showing even white teeth.

She walked behind her small metal desk and motioned them to the remaining two folding chairs that made up the furniture in her office. It had been several weeks since she answered an advertisement in the *Veterinarian's Association Gazette* for the position as veterinarian at Wagner Ranch in southeastern Arizona. In the Christmas rush she had forgotten about it until last week, when Steve Hilton, the foreman from Wagner's, called to see if she was still interested in the position. She had assured him she was, and he had promised to call later to arrange a time he could come to see her to discuss it.

Instead of calling, he showed up in person, bringing the owner of the ranch with him.

The foreman looked around the room and back at Ami. "Miss Whitelake," he began, "Jeff has been out of town a lot lately, and since he was home, we took the opportunity to come out to talk to you. I hope we haven't caught you at a bad time."

"I understand," she said, glancing at Jeff Wagner, who studied her with an almost angry expression on his face. She stiffened, and a nerve in her temple quivered as an unfamiliar wariness filled her, wondering if he blamed her for being called away from whatever duties he was bound to.

Steve Hilton went on. "Wagner Ranch is about seventy-five thousand acres, with several breed of cattle: Hereford, Brahma, Charolais; horses, of course, and a few sheep. Our vet covers all territories, and in all fairness, it's a big and lonely job, since you spend most of your time in the line camps, which, I must say, are not modern motels.'' He smiled at Ami and sent a look at Jeff before he looked back at her. "It will be rough on a woman.''

Ami expected hesitation over hiring a female for such a job as veterinarian at a big ranch would be, and was surprised they had gone this far. She had no intention of arguing the male point of view, but he wasn't going to get away with pushing her out of the picture before she had her say. He was going to have to tell her bluntly that he didn't think she was qualified before she would accept it.

"Any veterinary job is hard, whether it's filled by a male or a female, Mr. Hilton." Her voice was quietly determined. "If you prefer to have a man on this job, why are you here?"

Steve Hilton's eyes widened at her unexpected question, and Jeff Wagner straightened in his chair, which seemed too small for him. It was he who answered her, his voice just this side of cool.

"Your qualifications are as good as we've seen, Miss Whitelake. We merely want you to know the situation before you decide anything."

Ami nodded and waited. Steve leaned forward. "We'd really like you to see the ranch, and then let's discuss it some more. We can determine from that if you'd be satisfied, and I believe seeing you in those surroundings would help our decision, too.''

It had to be some operation to warrant such precaution, Ami thought. "I think that would be a good idea," she said and stood up. "Have you had dinner?"

Steve answered. "Well, no, we were trying to catch you before you left work."

"I've had a long day and I'm hungry." She grinned without apology, the dimple in her left cheek showing briefly. "I'm not much of a cook, but there are some excellent restaurants on this side of town. Give me a few minutes to change, and we'll check out one of them.''

A few minutes later she emerged from another room at the back of the clinic, in clean jeans and shirt, and called Rio, introducing him to the two men. ''You want anything to eat?'' she asked him.

''A hamburger,'' he said.

Her smile at the young man was indulgent at the typical teenaged request for food. ''We won't be long,'' she told him.

Over dinner Ami asked quesitons about the ranch. ''What happened to your vet?''

''Hammett is still with us, but he'd like to retire. He has arthritis in his legs and isn't able to ride as much as he needs to. He'll be there to help out when there's too much for one person. We also have an excellent school in Tucson that we call on when we're short.''

Ami was conscious of Jeff Wagner's dark eyes on her each time she asked or answered a question, as if judging her. She met his gaze without flinching, but her heart did a swift upturn for no accountable reason as his eyes went from hers to her mouth as she touched it with her napkin.

With difficulty she turned her mind away from the odd feeling and asked, ''How long will you be in El Paso?''

We plan to head back tomorrow. The ranch is about six hours drive from here, and we want to stop in Las Cruces.'' Steve Hilton did most of the talking, but his boss was taking in all the conversation, his gray eyes seeming to bore deep into Ami's private thoughts. Strange stirrings began again in her chest, and she was unsure if they came from the man's constant attention or from her own failure to recognize the feelings.

Keeping her voice carefully level, she said, ''Before you leave, I'd like you to meet Dr. North. I bought the clinic from him about two years ago, and he can advise you on my working habits and the operation I have here. It's very small compared to what you've described at the ranch.''

"We'd like that." Steve glanced at his watch. "Are there motels nearby?"

"Yes. Right on the interstate."

When they left the restaurant, Ami pointed out two of the nicer ones to them. She told them good night as they dropped her at the office, and gave Rio his hamburger and french fries before going on to her apartment. She prowled restlessly. If they made the trip that far, perhaps she was being considered for the job, although it could be only a token visit so they could report to labor organizations and equal rights advocates that they had looked for a female but found her unqualified. She thought about it a few more minutes, shrugged, and went to bed.

Dr. North was puttering in his workshop behind his home when Wagner and Hilton paid an early morning visit to him. He eyed his visitors and grumbled. "I get somebody who knows how to handle my animals, and she goes looking for another job." The faded eyes twinkled at Ami, then he turned to the two men.

"Ami has one fault, gentlemen. Or maybe it isn't a fault. She has a much stronger preference for animals than for humans, possibly justified." He looked at Ami, leaning against the doorframe, her long body relaxed, a half-smile tilting her upper lip. "She'll make you a good employee; outstanding, as a matter of fact. I prefer to have her here, but—" He let the sentence dangle. They had discussed the job at Wagner's before she applied for it, and Dr. North encouraged her to answer the advertisement. As much as she loved animals and enjoyed working with them, he was sure she'd be an asset to the ranch owners.

Ami couldn't resist her next statement. "Doc, they

seem to have some doubts about hiring a female. Did you ever have any qualms about working with a woman veterinarian?''

Bushy white brows quirked upward for a quick glance at the two men, then his eyes went back to Ami. "Certainly did." He shook his head and laughed out loud. "I was scared to death, but my pioneering spirit won out and I've never been sorry."

They talked about the widespread rabies on the border and the mild El Paso weather, then took their leave of Dr. North and returned to the clinic. Rio had already fed the animals and gone to school, leaving Ami's office door open to the bright sunlight.

"Do you have any family that would object to moving from El Paso to the Arizona wilderness, Ami?" Steve asked. "It's very different from living in the city."

She smiled. "No. Rio and Remus are all I have. I'm Rio's legal guardian, and Remus is an old rebuilt mongrel, not worth much, but all mine." She added, "Both of them."

Steve studied the tall girl in front of him. "When could you come out to look over the ranch?"

Ami looked from Steve to Jeff Wagner, meeting a dark, almost unfriendly gaze that gave her a thorough once-over. Butterflies fluttered in her stomach, and she stiffened under his scrutiny as she turned back to the foreman.

"Anytime, really. I could be there early on any Monday and back here by Tuesday night, so I wouldn't have to be closed more than a couple of days. Dr. North will keep an eye on the office and Rio for me."

Steve watched her for a moment, a thoughtful look in his eyes. Jeff's eyes narrowed as he listened to the exchange. "How about next Monday? We'll have someone pick you up at the airport."

She nodded her agreement. "I'll call to let you know

the flight schedules before I leave." Good-byes said, the two men left her, and Ami watched the car as it turned the corner at the end of the next block, grinning to herself.

I'd love to be a fly on the roof of the car and listen to their conversation between here and their ranch, she thought. She shook her head. Or maybe she wouldn't, she amended, thinking of Jeff Wagner's distant expression and obvious misgivings about her ability to cope as a veterinarian on a big ranch. He talked very little, and perhaps that caused her curiosity about him. It had been a long time since she had been exposed to the strong silent type, or any type of male, for that matter.

Ami went about the chores that always needed doing at an animal clinic, her thoughts moving in a wide-ranging circle as she kept busy. Her mind was full of Jeff Wagner and Steve Hilton, and her thoughts scurried from past to present and back again.

There wasn't really anything to keep her in El Paso, should she get the job at Wagner's. She enjoyed the clinic, and Rio was happy in his school and with the friends he had made here in the lower valley on El Paso's east side. But they could adjust to living elsewhere. Dr. North urged her to move on to bigger and better things if she could, telling her she could always come back to El Paso if she wanted to.

"Any diversified experience will be to your benefit, Ami," he told her when they discussed her application to Wagner's. "I'll miss you and Rio, but you can come visit me anytime." Dr. North smiled at her, and she hugged him affectionately.

Two years ago, just out of graduate school for veterinarian training and running from a broken marriage, Ami had arrived in El Paso, looking for a suitable location for a small animal clinic. All she had left behind her was the man she thought would be her husband till the end of time. Losing him through no fault of her own, she had determined to pick up the pieces of her life, and in order to do that, she had left Laramie, Wyoming, where she had finished college, married and settled down, turning to a strange place where she could start over alone. From childhood she had been a loner, and that never bothered her.

Lon and Roma Whitelake were the only parents she had ever known, adopting her after she was abandoned by her birth mother in an alley back of a bar in Cody. Before she died the young unmarried woman managed to put the small girl in the alley where people passed at all hours, and lucky for Ami, it was Lon and Roma who passed first. They didn't stay on a reservation but lived with and worked for a rancher who helped them cut through red tape to adopt the tiny baby and keep her as their own, even though they were already old.

Roma was deaf, and she and Lon had developed their own system of sign language. Before she could speak any words of the English language, Ami could communicate with her adoptive mother through lightning-quick hand signs learned from the two people she loved dearly. Her playmates were the animals in the forests and high desert, and she sang in tune with the birds that flocked to the fields to feed. She was five when old Lon made her a guitar and taught her how to play it.

The old Indian couple loved her, raised her to enjoy life, and taught her to survive in an alien world few Indians near them cared to know. It wasn't easy for them, she realized in later years, and she knew she was a curiosity to her schoolmates, with her odd turquoise-colored eyes in a smoothly tanned face, capped by hair the color of wild hickory nuts she gathered from the forests she roamed as a child.

Ami was in her first year of college when a flu epidemic hit, and Lon and Roma died within days of each other. Hurt and lonely, Ami still knew they would never have had it any other way, neither wanting to

survive without the other. During her senior year she
met and dated Tim Stanton, transferring all her love to
him, and they were married after she was graduated.
Tim was already a successful coach with two Olympic
hopefuls on his track team. Deliriously happy and in
love with him, she settled down to make him happy,
not even following the vocation she had set her sights
on all the past years.

"Let's start our family now, honey," Tim said one
night as he held her. "Have at least two children before
we get too old to enjoy them."

Happily, she agreed, and when after a reasonable period of time she failed to get pregnant, she went to her
doctor. She still shivered at Tim's reaction to the doctor's verdict that she would never have children. He
couldn't visualize a healthy young female body failing
to produce the children he wanted, and her pleas for
adoption fell on deaf ears. Tim wanted his own flesh
and blood, not someone else's. After weeks of silent,
cold hostility, they were separated, and she was left
alone again to live with her failure as a wife. With nothing to settle in a divorce court, she gave him back his
name and took back the one given her by the old Indian couple she had loved as her own parents. In the
wild loneliness that followed the divorce she grieved
anew for the only family she had ever had.

Running from the hurt, she reached El Paso, looking
for a job or a small clinic she could manage on her own.
Dr. Joe North was the first veterinarian she visited.

He had eyed the girl sitting in front of him, tall with
odd-colored eyes, a few freckles scattered across the
tilted nose, lips turned up in a half-smile that never
seemed to leave her mouth, becoming a quick grin at
regular intervals, showing a small dimple in her left
cheek. Her shining dark hair, sun-streaked, was cut
short to frame her face.

"I'll tell you, Ami, I'm thinking about retiring. If

you'd care to work here with me, let me make up my mind, then if I decide to retire, you can have the clinic. If not, you'll have some experience behind you and can look around."

It was an unexpected offer, and she accepted unhesitatingly. A while later a near-fatal heart attack made Dr. North's decision for him, and she acquired the clinic as her own. The hard work helped heal the hurt inside of her, and as time passed she was able to think of Tim without pain, and she knew she was on the road to recovery that she had thought she'd never find.

The slam of the side door brought her back to the present, and she heard Rio talking to the animals as he made his way through the pens, knowing he would find her in the small office at the back of the clinic.

Ami smiled at him as he stopped in the doorway. The black eyes met hers squarely, and she knew he had been thinking about the new job all during the day.

When she had first applied for the veterinary job at the Wagner Ranch, Rio hadn't said much, perhaps because her own attitude had been one of only mild interest, believing as she did that there would be many applicants for the job a lot more qualified than she was—and men, at that.

"Are you going to take the job?" Rio's question interrupted her musings.

She took a deep breath, watching him as she spoke carefully. "I'll go out to Wagner's and see how the ranch is run, but I imagine they have several more people to see. I didn't ask, but a vet for a big outfit like theirs is never selected just from one interview. Besides that, I want to see for myself what goes on." When he didn't say any more, she continued. "Dr. North will look out for you and Remus for a couple of days while I'm gone."

"And if they decide to hire you, what then?" he persisted.

"Rio, I have about as much chance of getting that job as being elected president. Women are not encouraged to look for jobs that big in a man's world. Too bad you're not qualified—you'd have an excellent chance."

He eyed her uncertainly. "You're good. Why wouldn't they hire you?"

Rio was still innocent in the ways of the world, but he would have to learn that things didn't always happen as they should—or the way he had them figured out. In two years he had forgotten how it felt to be abandoned with little hope for the future; Ami had helped him forget.

"Women are supposed to stay at home and raise kids, Rio." Her statement uncovered a bad memory, and she hurried on. "Or go out and work at some low-paying job a man wouldn't have, then go home and take care of everything and everybody." She stopped, not interested in showing any bitterness to Rio. The world was confusing enough without her adding to it, she decided.

Rio dropped into the chair in front of her desk, staring out the window over her shoulder. He had matured in the two years they had been together, and a smile softened her features as she remembered their first encounter as though it had happened yesterday.

She had worked late that night and locked the door of the clinic behind her, careful to leave a night-light on for the animals.

She was hungry, and as she turned the corner to the area where the dusty Subaru Brat truck sat, she paused, listening. Distinct sounds came from the darkened spot. Her heart thumped as she made out a shadow bending near the wheel of the truck.

"What are you doing?" she asked.

The figure whirled. Ami saw a dark face, straight black hair over startled dark eyes, before the boy bolted. She went after him, her long legs covering ground in a hurry. She gained on him, and the two bodies hit the ground, rolling over and over with Ami coming out on top, one knee in the boy's chest, the other pinning his arm. He had hit harder than she had and, breathless for a moment, didn't fight her.

"All right, amigo. Before I call the cops, what were you doing?"

Sullen defiance answered her. She shoved her knee into his chest. "I asked you a question. Answer me."

"I wanted the wheel covers."

"What for?"

"Vende."

She pressed her knee downward. "Speak English."

"I sell."

"How much would you get for them?"

The dark eyes closed as he waited a second to answer.

"How much?" she demanded.

"Dollar. Dollar and a half."

The boy suddenly found himself free of the knee pinning him as Ami looked down at him. "Get up."

He sat up but made no effort to stand.

"What's your name?"

"Rio."

"Rio what?"

He shrugged.

"You hungry?"

No answer.

"Come on and let's find something to eat. I'm starved."

The look on Rio's face was as though she looked into a mirror: scared, hungry, and lost—the way she had been enough times to recognize desperation. Dr. North would chew her out royally for what she was doing, but she smiled, turning back toward the deli.

"Come on, Rio. I haven't got all night." She looked back at him as he got up to follow.

She kept him. A check with local police and immigration officials disclosed only that he was a native-born United States citizen. A faded card he carried in a ragged wallet gave his name as Rio Lawson. Lawson? An odd name for a Mexican-American, but there the trail ended. She was informed by disinterested officials that there were many cases of lost children close to the southwestern borders, and her best bet was to turn him over to the welfare agencies experienced in dealing with that type of problem.

Dr. North thought she was out of her mind, but he helped her clear through all the red tape and legal jargon to have her appointed as Rio's legal guardian.

"You have to go to school and you have to work," Ami told him.

She was twenty-seven and he was fifteen, and sometimes he resented being told what to do by someone just enough older than he was to assert authority. They worked out their problems, and Ami considered him an outstanding investment, finding to her delight that he was intelligent with no problems, once they placed him in a grade with children of his age.

Her apartment was too small for both of them, so they redecorated a small room at the back of the clinic and furnished it in simple furniture he chose himself. That way he could be independent and still close enough for Ami to keep an eye on him.

Not long after Ami acquired Rio as her legal ward, they found an old dog near the clinic who had been hit by a car and left for dead. They dragged the animal into her small operating room and spent two hours rebuilding the bones.

"Will he live?" Rio asked, his big dark eyes wide with fright.

She shook her head. "Maybe not, but we tried." They nursed him back to health and they became an odd trio familiar to the neighborhood. She named him

Remus from her memory of Brer Rabbit and Brer Fox fairy-tale books, and Rio laughingly adopted him as his guard dog to share his room at the animal clinic.

"I'm hungry. Can we eat at Leo's?" Rio's voice startled her back into the present, and she smiled at the normal growing boy's request.

"Sure," she agreed. "Let's go." For the moment the question of the new job could rest.

Chapter Two

As the orange-and-silver Continental 727 circled over Tucson, Ami watched the desert coming up to meet them. Flying was a convenience she could well do without, she decided, never having reconciled herself to being seven miles above the earth with only space to support her. It seemed ridiculous to put people on the moon when she had a great desire to keep her feet on solid ground. Over one hundred people shared her flight, and she felt less uneasy as she looked at other passengers calmly waiting for the huge machine to land. It touched down on the runway with only a slight bump, and she breathed easily again.

It was early, the airport uncrowded. As she entered the long hallway from the plane exit, an announcement came over the loudspeaker: "Miss Whitelake, meet your party at the information booth."

Curious, she made her way to the counter, where several people were gathered.

"Miss Whitelake?" At the sound of her name, Ami turned to face a tall suntanned cowboy, Stetson in hand, silvery strands mixed in dark hair cut above the collar of a denim shirt. Levi jeans completed the well-recognized uniform of the working southwesterner.

"Yes."

"I'm Jasper Clayton from Wagner's." He grinned, white teeth slashing the darkness of his skin.

She smiled back at him. "How did you recognize me?"

"Steve told me you were young and tall, and I was gambling you were pretty. I won."

"I tried to tell Mr. Hilton I'd rent a car, but he wouldn't hear of it."

Jasper shook his head. "Takes too much time to drive that distance. This is easier on everybody." He led her to the baggage claim area and picked up the small overnight bag she indicated on the conveyor.

Feeling a slight uneasiness, Ami asked, "We're not driving?"

"No. Wagner's has its own plane, and I'm part-time pilot, part-time cowboy." He eyed her. "You afraid of flying?"

She shook her head. "Not exactly afraid, Mr. Clayton, but I'd rather keep my feet on solid ground. Or at least no higher than a eighteen-hand-span horse."

"Call me Jasper." His smile was sympathetic. "I'll try not to scare you."

The plane they approached was a sleek silver-and-green four-passenger Convair. He strapped her in, climbed into the pilot's seat, and talked into the radio. In moments they were taxiing to a takeoff position.

Ami closed her eyes, her head braced against the back of the seat. Almost before she let out her breath he was saying, "About twenty minutes now.

"That's Wagner's below," he said after a short time, pointing to his right.

The razorbacks of the rocky mountains below them rose in splendor, protecting the desert and valleys between. The perfect geometric design of the earth from the air surprised her, like a blueprint with perfectly lined squares and rectangles. She swallowed over the dryness in her throat as the plane began to drop, watching the ground rushing toward them. The wheels hit, and they bounced once, rolling smoothly to a stop.

"That wasn't too bad, eh?" Jasper reached for her and swung her to the ground.

Ami let her breath go. "Now that we're down safely, I must agree it's better than hours of driving."

Jasper's truck was parked near a small building at the end of the private landing strip, and as they drove toward the houses in the distance, Ami took in the passing landscape. Elevation at this point was almost a mile high, but mountains rose thousands of feet over them, many miles distant. As far as she could see was cultivated grazing land, a scattered herd of several breed of cattle much in evidence. She stared at strange-looking cattle she recognized as the Charolais, a breed without horns that she had read about but had never seen up close.

"Those cattle are experimental, aren't they?" she asked.

The man beside her nodded. "Jeff's had some a few years, and they've done well here. He's planning to start breeding them soon."

"Are they strong?"

"Exceptionally so." He grinned. "And expensive."

Ami studied Jasper's profile as he drove, thoroughly relaxed behind the wheel of the truck as he had been at the controls of the small plane. He didn't talk like the usual cowboy with a western drawl, but sounded more like a schoolteacher. He was quite good-looking, too. Her lips curved. *One of these days that characteristic might interest me,* she thought, *but then, he's probably married. I guess they're all married,* she amended her thoughts, and felt a small unidentified thrill as she thought of Jeff's dark gray eyes boring into her. She looked away from Jasper. Of course, they all had families.

They turned from the gravel road onto a lane that led toward a grove of cottonwood trees. As they got closer Ami saw the low building of adobe and cedar logs sprawled across the end of the lane and rambling back some distance. She fell in love with the simple architecture blending into the desert landscaping, with the purple mountains, miles away, forming a perfect backdrop for the setting.

She drew in her breath. "Beautiful."

Jasper followed her gaze and agreed. "Yes, it is." He pointed to her left. "The foreman's home is there. You remember Steve? And his wife, Janie. The veterinarian's house is just the other side. The bunkhouses are behind the big house, and the home corrals are beyond them."

He stopped the truck and climbed out to come around to her side. She was standing on the ground when he got there and found that, even with her lanky height, he was still six inches taller. Ami had always been self-conscious of her height because extra-tall men were not easy to find. Already she had met three men from Wagner's taller than she.

"I'll take you to meet the household first. You met Jeff, the boss. He has his daughter, Amanda, in Baltimore for tests." Jasper stood for a moment, gazing away from her. "She's six years old." He took a deep breath as if making a decision and looked down at her. "She's deaf." His eyes narrowed as though against pain.

Ami swung around to face him as the statement sunk in. She waited, but he didn't say anything more. "Is she completely deaf?" she asked finally.

He nodded. "Accident when she was two. Jeff has had her to every clinic and expert that he thought would help. Nothing. I think this is his last hope." He took a deep breath and added, "They'll be gone another week or two."

Ami was right about Jeff's being married, then, and in addition to the errant thoughts she had entertained about him, she felt sympathy for the family, remembering Roma. Roma had never asked for sympathy and managed without problems with her own set of hand languages, but a six-year-old child had a long way to go in a different world than Roma and Lon lived in.

There were more questions she would have liked to ask, but Jasper was walking toward a door on the long side porch. He opened the screen and stood aside as she entered. It was the kitchen—a huge sunny area that had to be the biggest working kitchen she had ever seen. Near the double sinks stood a dark-skinned woman of ample size who smiled at Ami, looking her over at the same time.

"Ami, this is Lily, our chief food ambassador. Her husband, Harris, is her assistant. They do the almost impossible job of feeding our hungry crew when they're in the local area. Lots of hungry mouths at Wagner's."

"How are you, Lily?" she asked.

"Fine, Miss Whitelake. You're too pretty to be a cow doctor."

Ami's eyes flashed to Jasper. "Your chief cook might become my favorite person."

Jasper laughed with her and led her on through the big house. "Hazel is Lily's daughter, and she looks after Amanda most of the time and, of course, helps with all the jobs that have to be done."

The house was simply furnished with heavy oak pieces, elegantly male. You could tell who the boss was here, Ami thought. Where was Mrs. Wagner's female individuality?

The image of Jeff's face came to her, and she felt again the tremulous flutter under her ribs. *Watch it, Ami. You're thinking about your boss, who just happens to be married.*

Then they were outside, walking a quarter mile toward the attractive rock-and-log house that belonged to Steve and Janie Hilton.

Jasper knocked lightly, and a friendly, gamine face appeared. "Jasper, come on in." Janie leaned a little toward overweight, but her pleasant, outgoing personality drew Ami to her.

"Hello, Ami," she said, hand outstretched. "Steve, Jasper and Ami are here."

Steve ambled in. He and Janie looked enough alike to be brother and sister, features and coloring the same, except Steve was lean and almost as tall as Jasper.

"Good to see you again, Ami."

The four of them sat down, and as they drank coffee Janie had poured, Steve went into detail about the ranch, and Ami asked more questions. "It's even bigger than I imagined," she told Steve.

He nodded. "It's a lot of territory," he agreed. "Let's go take a look around," he said, and Jasper walked with them to the corral. She noted the sturdy workhorses, the clean roomy stables. Near a gate was a miniature gray burro, nuzzling a small goat, pushing it to the fence with playful nudges.

Ami laughed delightedly. "What's that?"

"That's Charlie, Amanda's burro. Janie and I found him in the mountains. He aggravates everything and everyone within miles, especially when Amanda's gone and can't pet him every day."

"He's adorable." Ami watched the antics of the tiny animal and could picture a six-year-old leading him around. She sobered, realizing Amanda could not hear him make his peculiar noise that was so like a laugh.

Jasper, standing near her, said, "I'd better get on to my work. See you all later." He strode away from them, whistling a lively rendition of "Cotton-Eyed Joe."

Steve watched him go, then said to her, "Jasper is also the family lawyer and looks after all of us to see we don't get into too much trouble."

"Family? Are all of you related?"

Steve laughed. "Well, not really. Jeff, Jasper, and I were all in the same outfit in Vietnam. We swore if we came out of it alive, we'd stick together. We made it, so Jeff brought me and Jasper back here and gave us jobs. Jasper and Jeff were pilots; I was their navigator."

Ami was thoughtful, seeing the three of them plotting to get themselves out of the hell of Vietnam and back to really living.

"Are you all from this area?" she asked.

Steve shook his head. "I'm from Washington state, originally. I worked for Boeing Aircraft before the war. Jasper is from Colorado. He was just starting out as a lawyer when he was drafted."

A straight-backed figure limped toward them from one of the stables. "Ami, this is Claude Hammett, our retiring vet. Claude, Ami Whitelake."

"Ami," the gravelly voice acknowledged. His faded blue eyes meeting hers held a wealth of knowledge that deteriorating health couldn't take away. The rough hand that grasped hers was firm, and she wondered if he had trouble holding instruments a vet needed. She smiled as she met his speculative glance, taking in his possible replacement. Jeff probably told him the lady in question would never be able to fill his shoes. *But I'll try, given the chance,* she decided as she walked on with Steve.

Next in their line of the tour was the house reserved for the veterinarian. As they started in she said, "I really don't want to intrude in Mr. Hammett's home."

"He hasn't lived here in six months. When his wife died last year, it got to be too big for him and he moved into the bunkhouse, where he has lots of company."

It was a lovely house, almost as big as Janie and Steve's, furnished the same with very simple heavy oak furniture. Ami, impressed by the people she had met, could see successful business in capital letters.

"I've never handled anything anywhere as big as this," she told Steve.

"You run a clinic."

"Yes, a small one," she admitted.

"Basically they're run the same, Ami. As I said before, Hammett still helps out around the home corral, and the school in Tucson is very dependable." He studied her face as she gazed around.

The blue of the late afternoon sky darkened as it lay across the ragged mountain peaks that stretched as far as the eye could see. The desert, as much an enemy as armed troops unless you respected it, lay in its own splendor across the thousands of acres between the ranch house and the mountains. Ami couldn't decide which of the two scenes she loved the most, for both had been her world as long as she could remember.

They ate the big evening meal in Lily's kitchen, and Ami, usually a light eater, was miserable. Her cooking efforts left much to be desired, and she took full advantage of Lily's expertise. Pork chops, cabbage that tasted fresh from a garden, corn on the cob, mixed salad, fresh baked rolls, and corn bread. She should have left the huge helping of apple cobbler alone.

"How can you eat like this and stay so slim?" she said, groaning.

"Isn't easy, as you can see," Janie said, looking at her not-too-slender figure.

Back in Janie and Steve's house, they sat, talking about weather comparisons. "It's dry in El Paso, Ami, but we have the same climate here. It's high desert, low humidity," Steve said.

She nodded, looking around the comfortable living room. Two walls were paneled in light oak and one wall was covered with a pale yellow flowered wallpaper. The fourth wall was solid bookcases. Unexpectedly Ami yawned, and then blushed as she apologized.

Janie laughed. "It's getting late, and you've been on the go all day. Let's get some sleep."

In the large airy bedroom she stood at the window, looking toward the rugged mountain ranges she could see only as distant shadows. She liked the people she had met today, and the ranch was like nothing she had ever seen in its vast dimensions. The slight uneasiness she felt when she thought of Jeff Wagner was the only question she didn't get answered to her satisfaction. Undressing, she slid between cool sheets, drifting easily into sleep.

Ami was up early the next morning, out at the corral as the sun peeped over the eastern mountain range. Old Hammett was there, feeding, brushing, and fussing at Charlie.

"Little pest," he said, his voice gentle.

As they talked Ami asked more questions. "Good job here, good people to work for," he said. "If you don't miss city ways." He eyed Ami's slim figure, her ringless fingers. "Not much social activity out here."

She grinned. "Cowboys must have entertainment, Mr. Hammett. How about grange dances?"

"You dance?"

"Well, I used to, but it's been awhile. You mean square dances?" The laughing eyes showed interest. "Do you have good callers?"

"Yes, they have a monthly dance in Tucson, and there's one every week at the grange hall in Tombstone. Jeff's a regular caller. Good, too."

"Jeff?"

"He'll be your boss if you take the job," he said.

She nodded, picturing again the silent, stern-faced Mr. Wagner. "Do you know what my competition is for the job? I haven't asked how many others are being considered."

Hammett snorted inelegantly. "There've been several people out here, but Steve's mighty hard to

please." He went on after a moment. "He's pretty particular about who he selects because of our isolation.
You have to be able to get along with everyone and you
spend a lot of time alone, too."

Recalling Steve's remarks about the loneliness, Ami
said, "I can see that. It's such a modern ranch, though.
I wouldn't call it isolated, except geographically. All
those windmills must make you pretty self-sufficient as
far as water and power, right?"

"Yes, Jeff's grandfather was way ahead of his time
when he built this place. Chet, Jeff's dad, followed in
his footsteps, and Jeff is just as smart and as hard a
worker."

At that moment Steve joined them. "Sleep okay,
Ami?"

"Oh, yes, thanks."

"Let's get some breakfast, then ride around, and I'll
show you some of the stock."

She waved good-bye to Hammett and, after one
more look around the corral, followed Steve.

Hours later they stopped at Camp 20 near the ragged
line of the Dragoon Mountains, where she met Carue,
the chief camp boss. Carue was mostly Indian, Ami
guessed, and he looked at her with dark-eyed suspicion
as Steve introduced her.

"Rough job for a girl," he grumbled.

Ami's eyes danced at the echo of Steve's remarks
earlier. It was the first word spoken against her as a
female since her arrival and even to her it seemed a
halfhearted protest, as if they had already been warned.
"Why more rough on a girl than a boy?" she asked.

He looked her over. "No modern conveniences in
the line shacks and camps. No mirrors to see how purty
you look."

Steve watched and listened to the exchange with a
grin on his face, recalling Ami's quick retort when he
had mentioned it being a hard job for a woman. He also

knew Carue disapproved of a woman in this very much male-dominated domain.

"Mr. Carue, you should see where I was brought up. Your camp looks like Radio City by comparison." Ami grinned, then stepped closer to him and whispered, "Don't worry, I don't have the job yet." As she walked away with Steve she was conscious of Carue's gaze following them.

Steve continued to explain the layout of the ranch. "We have several camps that we work from, and they're numbered for reporting purposes. There're a lot of isolated places, so we have a radio system for reporting in at regular intervals. That way, if you have to be out of range, we know about where you are and how long you'll be there. If someone should get hurt, or in trouble of any kind, he won't be missing long before someone goes looking for him."

Ami nodded in approval. As they drove back to the big house Steve asked, "What time's your plane leave, Ami?"

"Eight forty-five."

"I'll alert Jasper. You'd better leave here about six thirty."

They rode in silence, Ami's eyes busy with the scenes around her, interested particularly in the huge portable irrigation systems, looking like monstrous granddaddy longlegs. Silos and windmills dotted the rolling acres of land.

"It's beautiful," she said.

Steve glanced at her, taking in the curving mouth, wide eyes, strange-colored and searching, beneath the tousled cap of dark hair. He grinned, appreciating anyone who could see beauty in the wild, untamed desert. "I'd like you to take the job, Ami."

Her heart jumped and she caught her breath, unable to answer him for a moment.

At her silence Steve asked, "Any doubts? I'll have

to tell you in all fairness that I'm not kidding when I say it's a lonely job and you'll be on your own and working alone most of the time. Sometimes we go a couple of weeks without seeing Jasper or Jeff." He smiled at her. "Janie's hoping you'll take the job; she'd love having you around."

Ami swallowed hard. "Rio and Remus? Can I bring them with me?"

"Of course. There's plenty of room. How old is the boy?"

"Seventeen. He graduates from high school in May. I've had him for two years." She met his gaze directly. "I'm quite bad about picking up strays, Steve. I'd better warn you now."

He laughed. "We're all strays of a sort, I guess."

"What about Mr. and Mrs. Wagner? Do you just hire, or do they have to approve?"

"There's only Jeff," Steve told her. "Myra died when Amanda was two."

Shock kept Ami silent as he went on. "Jeff leaves the hiring to me. Would you rather call me after you've thought it over?"

She smiled. "Give me till we get to the house. I can make up my mind by then." Her mind was having a hard time realizing Jeff Wagner was a widower; a young, good-looking widower. How very sad.

Steve agreed as he again took in the tall boyish figure, the odd-colored eyes, the long slender fingers.

They had almost reached the house when Ami asked, "Can Amanda talk?"

"No. She's good at using sign language, and most of us can understand her. Jeff and Hazel are both excellent in the language, and Amanda doesn't let it slow her down at all."

"What happened to her mother? She must have been awfully young."

"Yes. She was twenty-six. It was one of those freak

car accidents. About twenty miles west of here." He was silent, thinking back. "We thought Jeff would go crazy. Wife killed and child badly injured. It was doubly hard once he found out that Amanda was deaf."

Ami was quiet. Tragedy strikes indiscriminately and is always impossible to understand. When she realized the truck had stopped, she sighed, opened the door, and slid to the ground. Her eyes took in the house once more, the clean, well-kept area as far as the eye could see. She thought of Rio. It would be a good life if he would accept it.

Maybe that was a selfish slant, she thought as she turned to Steve. "I'll take the job."

"Great." Steve put out his hand, and she took it.

Jeff was a widower. That was her first solidly conscious thought as her flight lifted into the darkening sky. At least he had Amanda, she thought, and remembered the dark gaze, almost angry, as he had listened to her discussions with Steve, saying little. Her curiosity where he was concerned was strictly boss and employee, she told herself not too convincingly. Jeff Wagner was good-looking, and the magnetic pull she felt caused her to move restlessly in the seat.

But Steve said she wouldn't see any of them often, and it would be to her benefit to stay away from Mr. Wagner.

Chapter Three

Settling into her new home was a pleasant job, with Janie, Steve, and Jasper there to help. Janie, delighted to have another young female in a heretofore practically all-male kingdom, was an instant friend. Jasper, of all things, was a bachelor and evidently enjoyed that status with no mind to change things, according to Janie.

On Friday, after arriving at Wagner's, Ami accepted Janie's invitation for dinner, along with Jasper. She sat, feet curled under her on the couch, satisfyingly full of good food, half listening to Steve and Jasper reminiscing about their Vietnam experiences with Jeff. Some of their tales were comical, but she shivered at the close calls they remembered and the utter disregard for human life they had faced.

A light knock sounded at the door, and Steve went to answer it. "Jeff," he said. "Come on in."

Ami got to her feet. Jeff had stayed on the east coast with Mandy longer than he had planned, and this was the first time she had seen him after her arrival at Wagner's. As she faced him the tremor under her ribs that she had ignored for weeks was back, and she bit her lip, silently telling her body to behave.

"Jeff, you remember Ami."

Jeff extended his hand, and Ami smiled up at him as she took it. "Of course. Are you settled all right,

Ami?'' he asked, dark gray eyes looking her over thoroughly. Perhaps he thought she might have changed after becoming his veterinarian. Her hand tingled as he continued to look at her without releasing his hold.

"Yes, thank you.'' He let go of her fingers, and she put her hands behind her to hide their shaking.

"Any answers, Jeff?'' Janie asked.

He shook his head. "Nothing.'' Disappointment showing, he explained about the tests. "I'm not surprised, of course, but—'' Here he shrugged.

"And Amanda?'' Jasper asked.

"She's tired. Hazel's putting her to bed.'' He grinned a little. "She's better off than I am.''

After a few minutes, Ami took her leave. "Thanks for dinner, Janie. It's a good thing I won't be around here very much. Between you and Lily, I'd soon waddle instead of walk.''

She said good-bye and left, but not before promising to meet them in Tucson at the motel Janie named on Saturday afternoon. They had enthusiastically invited her to the monthly grange dance, and she found herself looking forward to going.

"No jeans,'' Steve told her.

She smiled to herself, wondering where she'd come up with anything other than jeans. Maybe in the old trunk, she thought.

For long moments she stood looking at the midnight blue of the sky, with the stars sparkling white, seeming near enough to touch. A cool desert wind carried the fragrance of sagebrush and mesquite bushes, and the friendly animal sounds were familiar music to her. Humming an old western tune, she walked the quarter mile to her cottage, thinking of Jeff and his disappointment over Amanda's hearing tests.

Maybe she should talk to him about Linda and Dave, she thought. She and Linda had graduated from the University of Wyoming the same year, and Linda and her husband had gone on to study medicine, specializing in hearing problems. She would trust their opinion above any other expert on ear troubles.

The trunk didn't yield much in the way of square dance clothing, but memories crowded their way in, try as she would to keep them out. She had only a few items left from her college days and two-year marriage, and the picture she found at the bottom was the last one she had. They were on bicycles, laughing, on a picnic in Laramie; young, carefree, and in love. She and Tim had shared a happy two years, the dark ending a shock to both their systems. Her fingers moved over the glossy surface of the snapshot. Tim was handsome; a healthy specimen who would make some woman happy if she could reciprocate by bearing his children.

Ami knew she should have thrown that picture away, but she didn't.

Pushing the sudden emptiness away, she reached into the trunk and pulled a black skirt from underneath everything else, frowning as she tried to remember what she had worn with it. The red print top would have to do.

She had to do something about her clothes, she thought. Anything would be an improvement. She had never been much for dressy clothes and, since Tim, she had gone from bad to impossible. After repacking the odd lot of items into the trunk, she went to bed.

Ami met Amanda the next morning as she stood watching Hammett and Remus herding a stubborn calf into the corral. The little girl came flying around the corner of the stables, colliding against her.

"Whoa!" Ami said, holding the slight figure steady. She looked into clear gray eyes, wide spaced in a thin suntanned face. The puzzled look in the gray depths caused Ami to remember the child's deafness. Setting her on her feet, she stepped back and, using the sign language learned years ago, she said, "You must be Amanda. My name is Ami."

Serious eyes regarded her steadily, and a grin crossed

the face, wrinkling the small nose. Tiny fingers moved in answer.

"Hey, you're good." Stooping so that she was on a level with Amanda, she asked, "Where did you get Charlie?"

Amy understood by Amanda's signing that Steve and Janie had found him in the mountains. "He's a year old," Amanda signed. The intense gray eyes sparkled. "I'm six."

Ami took her hand and led her back to the corral, where she found Charlie loping back and forth between Hammett and Remus, trying to get their attention. She and Mandy sat on the fence, laughing at the antics of the tiny burro and conversing like old friends. As she left them, Ami signed to Mandy, "Come to see me at my house, okay?"

Amanda grinned her agreement and turned back to the animals. Ami headed toward the cottage, anger stirring in her chest at doctors who would give up on the tiny girl and say there was no hope at all.

I'd certainly argue with them if she were mine, she vowed.

At six o'clock Saturday morning Ami called Linda in New Jersey. "Hello, Dr. Monroe."

"Ami. Where are you?"

She smiled as she heard the familiar voice. "In the wilds of Arizona. How's everything in the east?"

"Fine. Dave's already at the clinic, and I was on my way out. When are you visiting us again?"

"I need a favor, Linda." She told the story briefly and got the answer she wanted.

"You know we'll try, Ami. Talk Mr. Wagner into letting us have a look at Amanda and call me back."

As the connection was broken Ami sat back in relief and felt confidence in Linda and Dave that she would have to transmit to Jeff...Somehow. Mandy must have another chance to hear.

Perhaps Jeff was right; perhaps all the experts were

right in thinking there was no chance that Mandy would ever hear again. When she heard it from Linda, she would believe it.

Ami's thoughts went back to when Linda was only a speaking acquaintance at the University of Wyoming in Laramie, where Linda was in premed and Ami was taking the animal husbandry courses, preparing for her veterinary career. She had started across the street as a car careened around the corner, hitting the curb and coming straight at her, and the other girl had just stepped into the crosswalk. Even as she stared, horrified, she had made a flying tackle, taking the girl with her, rolling into the street and from under the car. The damage had amounted to Linda's broken arm, multiple scratches and bruises on both of them, and the shock suffered by the driver of the car when his brakes failed. She and Linda had become the best of friends and remained as such through the years.

Feeling satisfied that she was right in initiating a campaign to give Amanda at least another fighting chance to hear, Ami went about her work, making sure all the chores around the home corral were finished up for the weekend. It would be a lot easier for her when Rio was graduated from school and came out to join her.

Upon her decision to take the job at Wagner's, Dr. North had agreed to let Rio stay with him till his graduation from high school in May, not too many weeks away. The new owners of the clinic were glad to have him help them with the animals for the remaining few weeks.

It was early in the afternoon when she left the ranch to drive into Tucson alone and checked into the motel, reserving an adjoining room for Janie and Steve. On the front seat of the truck beside her was her old Giannini guitar she had lugged around with her for years. In the years since old Lon made her first guitar from pine, she had never been without one, entertaining herself as well as her classmates when they cared to listen.

Downtown, she found new jeans and a T-shirt and a set of strings for the Giannini, ate a sandwich at the drugstore, and went back to the motel. She finished restringing the guitar and let her fingers slide over the new strings. Softly, she murmured the words of a current love ballad.

Her hands grew still. Almost two years, and some of the hurt left over from losing Tim was still there. Not often, not deep, but there. Unbidden, Jeff Wagner's face came between her and the guitar, dark gray eyes probing into her thoughts. Shaking her head, she stretched on the bed and was instantly asleep.

She woke suddenly, wondering where she was. A loud knock startled her. Sluggish, she sat up, looking at the door of her room.

"Ami, it's us. Are you there?" It was Janie.

"Yep, just a minute." She glanced at her watch as she moved to the door. Five o'clock. She had slept a long time.

"Where've you been?" Ami asked as she opened the door.

"We waited for Jeff. He wanted to ride with us." She smiled as Jeff stepped into sight behind Steve.

"Were you asleep?" Janie asked as she flopped across the bed.

"I sure was. Now I'm ready for tonight."

They chatted awhile, and Janie said, "We'd better get going. Are our rooms next door?"

"Yes, but I only got one." She looked at Jeff.

"No problem," he assured her. "The owner's an old friend. He'll find something for me." His eyes told her, "You don't have to worry about me." She turned away from him.

A few minutes later Janie called to her, and Ami joined the group to pile into Steve's six-passenger, long-bed truck for the short drive to the grange hall.

It was a good group: the band was excellent and the square dance callers were in great form. Jeff called two dances, and Ami liked his voice, clear and easy to follow. She saw Steve near the band, talking animatedly with his hand going full time, and she remembered Janie saying he loved country-and-western music and all the instruments the band used.

"Going with me, Janie?" she asked, heading for the rest-rooms she had seen earlier.

"I'll wait here for Jeff. I think he's through calling."

Returning on the opposite side of the stage, Ami saw Steve, guitar in hand, talking to the piano player. Picking up the Giannini resembling her own, she stood beside Steve, letting her long fingers slide across the strings. Surprise showed in Steve's eyes as he watched her, leaning relaxed against the piano.

He grinned. "Can you play that thing?"

"A little," she admitted.

"You wouldn't, by any remote chance, sing, too?"

The turquoise eyes smiled. "Some."

"How up-to-date is El Paso on country-and western standings?" Steve's eyes showed increased interest.

"Very much so."

"Ever hear 'Old Flames'? Joe Sun has a great recording of it."

Ami fingered the strings, blending with Steve's key, and she heard the piano player join them. On the second chorus her husky voice picked up the words, and as she sang she forgot she had an audience.

Steve nodded as the song was finished, and they went on into "Even Cowgirls Get the Blues." They kept up their playing and singing till the regular band came back from their break. The audience, quiet until now, gave them a spontaneous round of applause.

On the way back to the table Ami wiped her sweaty palms on the folds of her skirt. "I was scared."

Jeff was standing by her chair. "You didn't look scared," he said. "Ever sing professionally?"

She shook her head. "Not me. I don't have any training and not enough nerve."

Gray eyes dark and unsmiling watched her. "You could do it."

"No, thanks. I like my job at Wagner's."

Tom Pardue from Kingston's Ranch, on the other side of the mountain from Wagner's, had wangled an introduction to Ami earlier, and now he came to claim her for the next dance. She went from his to several pairs of arms, then found herself dancing with Jeff.

"Trust these cowboys to find a pretty new girl around." He swung her expertly across the floor.

Ami smiled up at him. "This is one time that being a minority is definitely in my favor." She didn't add that his arms around her felt just the way they should and was glad he couldn't tell her heart had sped up at the touch of his hands. She found herself suddenly wondering if he had a girlfriend and, if not, why not. He had to be among the top eligibles in their corner of Arizona.

As they left the dance Jeff said, "I'm hungry. Is that little café with the good Mexican food still open, Steve? The one near the old airport road?"

"Yes. Shall we try it?"

Everyone agreed, although Ami would rather have waited for breakfast. The food was good as promised, and she enjoyed it, but riding back to the motel, sharing the backseat of Steve's truck with Jeff, she groaned, "I ate too much."

A muffled chorus answered her. Jeff said, "You don't look like you ever eat too much."

"Frequently," she said, turning her head to smile at him. "I run it off, chasing erring cattle."

"The usual question: Why a veterinarian?"

"I ran wild with the animals up near Cody while I

was growing up, always patching up the hurt ones and crying over the ones I couldn't help.'' She smiled, remembering. ''I still do.''

''Still patch them up?''

''And cry over the ones I can't.''

Jeff looked at her, but her eyes were closed, a smile turning up the corners of her mouth, with the short upper lip accentuating the fullness of the lower one. She was unaware of his gaze lingering on her mouth. They separated at the motel, agreeing to meet for breakfast before starting home the next day.

Ami slept fitfully and she blamed it on the late-night meal. At five thirty she got up, took a barely warm shower, then turned the water to stinging cold. As she stepped from the shower and reached for a towel, she thought of Jeff and met her own startled eyes in the mirror, letting the towel drop, and looked at the reflection of her long slim body. It had been a long time since a man had held her, and she felt Jeff's touch again as she dressed.

That would never do, she decided, shaking her head resolutely, and headed for the coffee shop, hoping it was open. It was. An older couple sat in one of the booths and a young couple with two bright-eyed boys were at a table. Ami headed for a booth and slid across the red Leatherette seat.

''Good morning.''

Her head came up at the familiar voice. ''Good morning.'' Jeff looked fresh and wide awake as he joined her. He, in turn, noticed the faint lavender tint of shadow beneath her odd-colored eyes.

''Would you like a menu?'' The young waitress flashed a fresh smile at them, but her gaze lingered on Jeff. Ami took a long look at her boss and silently agreed that he was worth looking at.

''Coffee for me,'' Ami told her. Jeff, too, refused breakfast in favor of coffee.

When the coffees came, Ami said, "I'm still full from our midnight feast—or one o'clock, or whenever."

"So am I. Our friends still asleep?"

"Anyone with any sense at all would be," Ami said.

"Thanks." Jeff grinned.

She smiled back at him, wondering briefly where he had slept, but had better sense than to ask. "Amanda gets her eyes from you. Other than that she must favor her mother." No one had mentioned Myra's name around Jeff, and she wasn't sure he would talk about her, but he answered easily.

"Yes, she's small like her mother and has her turned-up nose and blond hair."

Ami leaned forward, elbows on the table. "You weren't able to get anyone to offer you any hope at all of her ever hearing?"

His lips tightened and he hunched his shoulders as if against an attack. "No."

"Jeff, listen, I know you've been to the best-known doctors and—"

He broke in. "And the last one. No more tests. The same rhetoric over and over."

"I was in college with a girl who went on to be a pediatrician. She and her husband specialize in hearing problems. Let me call them and ask about Mandy."

"No. Thanks, anyway."

"They might—"

"No." He looked at her, his eyes hard and uncompromising. They finished their coffees without speaking.

Ami broke the awkward silence. "I think I'll go on home. Steve and Janie may sleep all day."

"Mind if I ride with you?"

A bit startled at the question, she said, "Of course not. My things are in the truck. All I need do is check out."

"Be with you in ten minutes. I'll leave a note on their door."

The sun was coming up as Ami pulled the little Subaru Brat out onto Interstate 10. Jeff was quiet, and she made no effort to speak.

"What's the name of that song?" His question broke in on her thoughts, and she glanced at him, wondering. "You've been humming the same one off and on for miles."

She thought a moment, and the words came to her. "'Years,'" she said. She had been thinking of the words of a song about years of hanging on to dreams that were gone. But she had stopped hanging on to her dreams, although they had died hard. At least she had let them go.

Ami drew in a deep breath. "It's a beautiful day," she said and heard the man beside her murmur his agreement.

Chapter Four

An early morning breeze kicked tumbleweeds down the narrow street of the small desert town as Ami leaned her long body against a post outside the café where she and Rio had breakfasted. From her stance she could see the low horizon running south from Douglas and over into old Mexico, to her right the route she would soon follow to the Wagner Ranch. She could see the long jagged outline of the end of the Dragoon Mountain chain, looking deceptively near, but long acquaintance with desert distortions told her they were many miles in the distance.

Leaving El Paso after Rio's graduation from high school, they took the long way to the ranch, dropping south of I-10 below Lordsburg, New Mexico, through the sparsely settled corner of the state of Arizona, coming out just east of Douglas. She wanted Rio to get an idea of the type of isolation they would be living in.

A movement down the street caught her eye and, turning, she took in the scene some fifty yards away from her. Three cowboys, dressed in dusty jeans and sweat-stained shirts, blocked the sidewalk. Rio was the center of their attention. Separated just enough, they formed a barrier designed to keep him from passing.

"Ah, amigo," the taller of the three addressed him. "Why the hurry?"

Rio stepped aside with a murmured good morning,

but the second man stood in his way, grinning down at him. It was plain the boy wanted no part of the three and equally plain they were bent on harassment.

Ami's eyes took in the scene and, before it was completely engraved as an image, she straightened away from the post, moving before she gained her full height. In seconds she stopped outside the circle of men.

"Everything okay, Rio?" The question was directed at him, but her eyes watched the closest bearded cowboy.

"*Sí, señora.*"

"Hey, look, Hank, he belongs to the pretty lady." The cowboy, enjoying his role, grinned to show a tobacco-stained, broken tooth behind thin lips. Pale blue eyes shifted from Rio to Ami, lingering on her figure.

The man addressed as Hank turned to look at Ami, taking in the oddly smiling eyes, curving lips, and tousled head almost even with his own.

"I'm ready to leave, if you are, Rio." Her eyes never left the group as she spoke.

Hank grinned. "How about that, Luke? She's taking Rio with her, not even polite enough to introduce herself."

As he finished the sentence his arm snaked out and caught the slim figure around the waist, sweeping her against him. Ami looked into the grinning face, dark eyes close to her own, smelling tobacco and sour sweat.

The curving lips tilted a little more, the eyes darkened a trifle, and suddenly she relaxed against the imprisoning arm, forcing Hank to shift his weight to hold her. As he did Ami brought the heel of her right boot to his instep and, as he yelped and partially released her, she slammed her left knee into his groin. With a grunt of pain he let her go, only to catch her elbow just above his ear. She was free as he staggered and sat hard on the concrete. She stepped away from him and, as the other two started toward her, hooked her thumbs in her belt and said in a soft voice, "Touch me and I'll yell rape so loud, they'll hear me in Tucson."

The men hesitated, glancing from her strange eyes to their fallen companion.

"Let's go, Rio." Rio glanced at the three, turned, and followed her. The incident had taken only a few minutes, and no one appeared to have noticed the altercation.

A few parking places down the street Ami and Rio stopped at the dusty pickup, where Remus waited in the front seat, wagging his tail in a hearty welcome. Ami patted the huge head as she swung up behind the wheel, and Rio, entering from the passenger side, added his touch of affection. Neither of them looked back nor spoke as she started the truck, heading toward U.S. 80, which would put them near their destination.

In the back of the pickup, covered with tarpaulins, were all of Rio's belongings and a few she had left behind on her first move. There were still boxes of her medical and animal care books, and Rio's books on painting and charcoal drawing, his hobby at which he was quite good.

Ami was thoughtful as the little truck gained speed outside the city limits. Already enjoying her new job in the isolated Arizona desert, she was hoping Rio would adjust to the loneliness and hard work, a world away from the small animal clinic and neighborhoods he was used to.

They couldn't have asked for a more perfect end-of-May day for traveling. The desert unfolded around them as the miles added to the speedometer, and it was still morning as she turned down the gravel lane leading to the big ranch house.

Rio stared with wide eyes at his surroundings. "Where's your house?"

"Ours," she corrected. "Unless you want to stay in the bunkhouse."

He turned to her. "Would you mind?"

She grinned. "You'll soon be eighteen, Rio. It's your choice. Let's look."

There was no one in sight as they walked to the corral, where they found Hammett polishing a leather saddle. As Ami introduced Rio, Charlie came loping with his sideways gait from around the stable.

Rio laughed, remembering Ami's description of the small animal. "This must be Charlie. Is Amanda around, too?"

"No. She and Hazel are in Tucson with Jeff. They'll be back in a couple of days." Hammett put the saddle aside as Ami explained that Rio was interested in the bunkhouses. "Come on, Rio, and I'll show you some of the quarters." As they started away he looked at Ami and said, "We missed you, girl."

Ami stared after him in surprise, and a warm glow flushed her cheeks. She liked the old man, but he wasn't one to show much outward feeling, and pleasure brought a big grin to her face. He had accepted her as veterinarian, replacing him in a job he had held for many years, and never showed any resentment toward her.

They were back in a short while with Rio enthused about moving into the bunkhouse, and they set about unloading the truck. The books were the hardest but, packed in sturdy boxes, they could be unpacked as needed.

Her worry over Rio adapting to the new life was unfounded, and they fitted themselves into a hardworking routine for the hot, dry summer. In the line shacks and camps more than at the ranch, the trio, including Remus, of course, who accompanied Ami on every trip, was a closely knit family. Rio loved the wild desert and mountains as she did, missing only the hamburgers from their daily fare. They took their books with them, studying some each day, sometimes by the oil lamp late in the evening.

It was on one of these evenings that Ami mentioned more schooling to Rio. "It's too late to get you into any of the colleges for the fall semester, but what do you think of starting some classes for the spring term?"

Rio looked up from the book he was reading. "I want to be a veterinarian."

"Is that right?" she asked, feeling a thrill of pleasure.

He put the book down. "Yes." His voice was firm, and he sounded sure of himself as he talked. "I know it will cost a lot of money, but I'll work and pay you back." He smiled at her.

Her mind went back to the evening they had met, and her features softened, remembering the past years, their good times and bad times. "That's a good choice, Rio, but it's a lot of studying and hard work."

"I know," he said simply, "but it's what I want if you think we can manage."

"We'll manage," she told him and made a mental note to send off for catalogs they could look through. And she did, in her spare moments, though they were few with all the work to be done on the ranch.

The young heifers and spindly leg newborn colts were a full-time job for weeks, getting them shots and marked, the system she liked better than branding, since clips in the ear were faster and not painful to the animals. At the end of the month they headed back to the home corral, where paperwork had to be taken care of and supplies ordered. Ami had the entertainment of the grange dances to enjoy with Janie and Steve, sometimes Jasper and Jeff, but Rio spent most of his spare time with the Sandovals, the family of the big chief foreman. There were six children, one of whom was Nada, a lovely seventeen-year-old with liquid brown eyes, black hair to her waist, and a shy smile that fascinated Rio.

Wagner's held their annual barbecue around Labor Day, a big, well-celebrated holiday for all employees. The affair had been postponed until mid-September because of trips taking Jeff and Jasper away from the ranch.

Ami, working alone far away from the ranch house, was late getting back on Friday afternoon, and the shindig was well underway as she stopped her truck behind the house. She eyed the colorful crowd, listened for a moment to the laughter and voices calling above the noise, then turned and went inside.

A shower first, she thought, wrinkling her nose. She smelled like cows.

Feeling better with a definite improvement in emanations, she pulled on jeans and a sleeveless red terry cloth T-shirt. Outside again, she looked at the crowd and shook her head, directing her steps toward the kitchen. Rio would be with the Sandovals, who seemed to have more or less adopted him, and she no longer worried about his being lonesome. Life after many months on the ranch was great as far as they were both concerned.

Lily turned, frowning, as Ami opened the screen door. "It's time you—" she started, then saw Ami.

"Oh, honey, I thought you were that no-good Harris. I guess he's in the beer barrel, and I need some climbing."

Ami laughed. "Let him enjoy his beer, Lily. Tell me what you need."

A moment later she had the step stool in the huge pantry and was climbing through the trapdoor to the giant storage loft. She found the items Lily named and started down.

"What the hell are you doing up there?"

Ami looked down into Jeff's upturned face, and the

small dimple flashed in her cheek. "I may get hungry sometime and I was checking out the goodies."

"Where's Harris? That's his job."

"Mr. Jeff," Lily broke in. "Ami offered to help. You know where Harris is."

It was Jeff's turn to laugh. "Yes, I do, Lily. But you could have yelled for help. Ami should be at the barbecue, eating, since you're the one who's always trying to fatten her up." He stopped and looked back at Ami. "Pass those things to me."

A few minutes later she turned and backed down the ladder, only to be caught by the waist and swung to the floor. Big hands held her a moment longer, and she was forced to look straight at him. Quizzical gray eyes searched her face, then he let her go.

Ami was aware of an odd sensation in her stomach as she turned away. "Anything else, Lily?"

"No, thanks, Ami. Go enjoy the party before Mr. Jeff has a fit."

As they walked side by side through the hallway, Ami turned to Jeff. "Can I talk to you a minute?"

"Sure. In here." Jeff turned into his study, and she followed him. He walked to the huge desk, sat on it with one leg swinging, and motioned her to a chair. She shook her head. She looked around the big room she had never been in, hesitating to voice her question now that she was alone with him.

"Any problems with your job?" he asked.

"No. Everything's going very well." She drew in a deep breath and plunged. "Jeff, I'd like you to reconsider talking to Linda and Dave about Mandy. They're the friends I mentioned, doctors who specialize in diseases of the ears."

"No." It was a flat, uncompromising statement.

Even though she had expected that reaction, her heart sank. She wet her lips. "Can you really pass up the chance that they may be able to help her?"

"If there was a chance, but there isn't. I've told you, Amanda has been through enough tests, and the best medical sources say she'll never hear." He sounded as though he were gritting his teeth. "Why does it matter to you, Ami? Do you get a percentage out of recruiting patients for your friends?"

She refused to be baited, and persisted. "Mandy is an adorable, intelligent child, and I know she can manage the deafness and not being able to talk, but she should have the chance, slim though you think it is, to hear someone say I love you and be able to say that aloud to someone she loves." She took another deep breath. "Are you satisfied with her saying I love you this way?" Her fingers went to her lips, to her chest, then extended toward Jeff in the sign language she knew so well. With her hands out to him, she suddenly forgot she was talking about Mandy and her I love you wasn't repeated with feelings a small girl would have.

He regarded her intently. "When's the last time someone whispered love words to you, Ami?"

She stared at him. "We aren't talking about me."

"I am. When?" He straightened against the desk and, with arms folded, watched her through narrowed eyes.

She returned his gaze, her eyes going to his mouth. The wayward tingling she remembered each time she thought of him returned, and she swallowed hard.

"Well?" he asked. She shook her head.

He moved, covering the steps between them in seconds, his hands spanning her slim waist. He pulled her up against him, placing his mouth over hers. None too gently he forced her lips apart, pressed her head back into his shoulder, playing havoc with her breath. He raised his head enough to look into her wide shocked eyes, unaware of the feelings he roused in her.

"Kiss me back, Ami," he demanded, his mouth still touching hers.

She tried to shake her head. "No, please."

"Yes, or we'll stay right here until someone comes looking for us." She could see her reflection in his eyes. "That could be awhile."

Sensing danger to her peace of mind, she tried to think of a way out, but he held her tightly. She stood on tiptoe and her hands went to his shoulders and, tilting her head back, she found his smiling mouth with hers. A warning light flashed somewhere as a sharp thrill shot all the way to her toes and his mouth took possession of hers once more. She slid one hand behind his head while the kiss held, taking her breath and sending a warm glow through her body. She pulled back a little to look at him through half-closed lids. Their lips were a whisper apart when, suddenly, the tip of her tongue seared a path across his mouth and, as she felt him draw a sharp breath, her hand brought his head down, crushing her lips against his. The surprised response of his body to the unexpected byplay was immediate as his hand moved flat over her hips, his metal belt buckle pressing hard into her middle. Ami stood on tiptoe, stretched to his tall slimness, the thoroughness of the kiss sending electric waves shimmering through her.

She waited for him to make the first move and, as he lifted his head, she reluctantly stepped away, staring up at him, one hand touching her throbbing mouth. Her voice was soft, almost a whisper, as she said, "I don't remember the last time someone said I love you but that's the first kiss in a long time."

She turned blindly to the door. With one hand on the knob she looked back at him, standing where she had left him, his arms again folded, gray eyes unreadable.

"Please call Linda and talk to her and Dave."

"You never give up, do you?" he asked. "After that outstanding performance, you think you can get your way."

"You started it; I just responded." She shrugged, a

casual move far from what she was feeling. "Rather a natural reaction, don't you think?"

"Touché," he said, smiling a little.

"Will you call?" she persisted.

"No, Ami."

She returned his steady gaze a moment, opened the door, and walked out. *I sure didn't win that battle,* she thought, her emotions trying to sort themselves out and failing.

Making her way around the outskirts of the crowd, she called responses to greetings and waved to others as she moved. The band was a real cowboy band, all right. They were in the middle of a square dance, and she stopped to watch the dancers whirling on the improvised board floor.

Across from her, she saw Eileen McKane, Jeff's girlfriend of long standing. Her white peasant-necked blouse, tucked into a billowing green checked skirt, set off the smooth honey-tanned skin and upswept blond hair to utmost perfection. The McKanes and Wagners had been neighbors for a lifetime, and rumor had it that Eileen would be the next mistress of Wagner's.

She hadn't known about Eileen when she wondered about Jeff's girlfriends, but wasn't at all surprised to find he had a very special one. For a long moment she allowed herself to remember Jeff's hard kiss, which had made her forget all her sensible warnings to her own heart. The best thing to do was beat a fast retreat out of the line of fire if she didn't want to get burned again.

"How about a song?" It was Steve beside her.

"Why not? A real captive audience." She grinned and took the guitar one of the men in the band handed her.

A couple of ballads later she asked Steve, "Heard that new one 'Old Habits'?"

"No. How's it go?"

"Give me a straight E, and we'll have it," she told him.

Games of horseshoe went on around them, but most of the crowd turned to listen as Ami sang. She got to the last verse, conscious of the crowd's attention, when she turned her head to meet Jeff's gaze. Impudently she kept her eyes on him as she sang.

It wasn't at all hard to sing to him, she realized as, finally, she put the guitar down, waved to Steve, and made her way through the group in the opposite direction from where Jeff stood. She spotted Rio with the Sandovals, being attentive to Nada. She smiled; Rio was growing up.

Rounding the corner of the fence around the corral, she came upon a group of the children jumping rope. Mandy was with them, blond pigtails bouncing, gray eyes sparkling. She saw Ami, broke away from the others, and ran to meet her. Ami stooped to hug the little girl.

"Having a good time, Mandy?"

Mandy signed "yes", then she took Ami's hand, pulling her to the jump rope, and they ran in, jumping easily together.

Finally out of breath, Ami waved good-bye and walked toward her cottage. She still hadn't eaten, but it didn't matter. Her disappointment at not being able to convince Jeff he should take Mandy to see Linda and Dave rankled deep. She couldn't really blame him for his doubt, because of so many negative reports and disappointments, but surely Mandy deserved one more chance, and Ami had confidence that if anyone could help, it would be Linda and Dave.

Mandy took her up on her first invitation to visit, and they had got to know each other. She enjoyed the small girl's silent company—silent, but friendly and outgoing with her. They understood each others' sign language most of the time, and she grinned, remembering once when they didn't.

They had been drinking lemonade in Ami's kitchen one hot August afternoon when Mandy asked a question Ami didn't understand. Impatiently Mandy left her chair and came around to her side of the table. She reached up to place tiny fingers over Ami's eyes and withdrew them to repeat her question, making her signs slowly and distinctly as she might to a dim-witted individual.

Ami laughed aloud as she understood. Mandy had asked, "Where did you get your funny-colored eyes?"

"I don't know what my parents looked like, Mandy," she told her. "But the color of my eyes probably came from one of them. Yours are like your dad's, so maybe my dad had funny-colored eyes and I look like him." The answer had satisfied Mandy, and she went back to drink her lemonade.

Rounding the corner of her house near the back door, Ami looked off to the western ridge of mountains. Clouds bumped over the jagged outline, drifting toward Tombstone. The usual September rainy season had not reached Wagner property, and unless the winds changed, the clouds she was watching would be too far south to help them.

Sounds of merriment from the barbecue activity came faintly as she sat on the step, enjoying the cooler air as the sun lowered behind the mountains. It hung on a golden thread for a moment and disappeared beind a purple curtain, putting on a spectacular display for her.

Remus rounded the corner of the house, stopped to wag his tail, and came to sit beside her. She patted the big head, hair divided in places where she had stitched him back together. Aside from his scars he seemed totally healthy again.

She looked up as Jeff came across the yard, carrying

Mandy. His tanned face looked even darker than usual against the sun-streaked blond head on his shoulder.

He sat beside her as she made room, and Mandy gave her a sleepy grin. Jeff looked her over and said, "Don't you like celebrations?" She wondered if it was her imagination that his eyes lingered a bit on her mouth as he spoke.

"I like the short workday and long weekend that goes with this one," she said, conscious of her own feelings as she remembered his hard kiss. In spite of trying to control it, her heart accelerated its beat.

"Do you need some time off?" he asked.

"No. I needed a chance to bring our supplies up to date, and Rio needed to catch up on hamburgers."

Jeff looked down at the quiet child on the step near him and said, "I want you to hear how Amanda feels about more tests." He looked back at Ami, eyes narrowed. "She's the one who has to endure all the shots, tubes, poking, and questions."

Ami stiffened. "I would never do anything to hurt her. Linda and Dave are—"

"Doctors," he said. "And doctors don't think much beyond the guinea pig status of their patients they don't know what to do about."

"It's not true," she protested. "They've done some wonderful things with children who could hear no better than Mandy." He had no right to put her on the defensive, and she felt anger building inside.

Ignoring her, he turned to Amanda, and she read the question he asked. "Ami knows a doctor who might help you hear, Amanda. She can get an appointment for us if you'll go talk to him."

In the gathering dusk Amanda stared at Jeff, turning questioning eyes to Ami, who smiled, hiding the uneasiness she felt inside. To her dismay tears filled Mandy's dark gray eyes and her lip trembled.

Ami made a move toward her, but Amanda stood up

and took a step forward. She looked at Jeff, and her tiny hands moved. "Can Ami go with me?"

"You want to go?" Jeff asked Amanda.

The pigtails swung in a negative movement. "No, but if Ami goes, I'll go."

Her heart hammered as she met Jeff's dark gaze across Mandy's head. His mouth tightened. "You have your answer," he said. "If you want her to go, you'll have to go, too."

"I can't do that," Ami told him, surprised at the turn of events.

"I thought you had such great faith in your friends." He stood, picking up a yawning Amanda.

"Yes, but—"

"But not enough to be bothered going through tests with her, is that it?" He shifted Mandy so her head rested on his shoulder. "In that case, we won't bother." He strode away from her.

"Wait," she said, running to catch him. "Can we talk after Mandy's in bed?"

He gave her a brief glance, nodded, and said, "I'll be back in half an hour."

In her bedroom she searched briefly for the packet of clippings in a flat folder and pulled them out to look, the first time in months. It showed a small graduating class on a stage with an inset picture of a pretty blond girl smiling shyly at the camera. Attached to the picture was a clipping headed "University of Wyoming graduate cited for work in hearing defects." It went on to say: "Linda Garson Monroe was given a prestigious scientific award for her extended research into hearing defects, which has resulted in the revolutionary use of the patient's own body material to repair damaged tissues and nerves." It gave Linda's year of graduation and the doctorates she had received since that time. "Dr. Monroe and her husband, David, also a hearing specialist, have recently opened their own clinic in Newark, New

Jersey, specializing in diseases of the eyes, ears, nose, and throat.''

Smoothing the clipping with her fingers, she smiled at the pretty girl, remembering how close they had become after the accident and how Linda and Dave had taken her under their wings when her marriage to Tim broke up. She had gone, blindly, not knowing where else to turn, and they had been there when she needed them and applauded when she finally decided she could survive without Tim. For a long time she had been doubtful that she could.

A brief knock brought her back to the present, and she went through the short hallway to the already-opened front door.

''Come in, Jeff,'' she invited, and as he walked past her, he gave her a hard look. She motioned him to a chair and she sat opposite him on a big hassock, the clippings beside her.

She wet her lips as he continued to look at her and felt again his kiss from the afternoon. ''I—it's an unusual request for me to go with Mandy,'' she began. ''Perhaps Miss McKane would prefer to go with her, since—since—'' She stopped.

He looked slightly amused. ''Since what, Ami?''

She linked her hands together over her knees and said, ''She might not appreciate having me travel alone with you.'' *I wouldn't hear of it if I were in her place,* her thoughts continued silently.

''Is that your only objection to going?'' he asked.

''It's a busy time here.''

He nodded. ''I know, but Hammett and Rio can handle it. Any serious problems, and they can call the school,'' he said.

She remained quiet, searching for words to use to explain that he and Mandy should go alone. In truth, she was afraid to go with Jeff Wagner, and for the life of her, she couldn't decide why. She had never been afraid of anything that she could recall, except facing life without Tim, and she had managed that, too, after all. Surely one kiss could be forgotten without any trouble. It didn't seem to affect Jeff, still...

Ami picked up the clippings, handing them to Jeff. "This might make you feel a little easier about trusting Linda and Dave," she said and sat still as he read through the articles.

He gave them back to her. "I'll take her because she's willing to go and she'll go only if you go with her. It's up to you." His mouth was a straight line, but she could feel the curve of it over her own.

This is ridiculous, she thought. *You'd think I'd never been kissed before.* "Suppose I call Linda tomorrow and see how soon we can get an appointment?"

"You'll go, then?" he asked.

She nodded. "They'll want to do complete tests before they decide if an operation will help. It could take a week."

"We have a week," he said and stood up to leave. "Let me know what Linda says." He smiled briefly, said "Good night," and went out.

Jeff well knew how long tests would take; he had been through enough of them with his tiny daughter in the past four and a half years. She winced at the idea that she had reminded him how often he had gone with high hopes for examinations and tests.

Uneasy dreams about Mandy's tear-filled eyes disturbed her sleep, and Ami awoke early, placing her call to Linda at six o'clock, eight o'clock on the east coast.

On the third ring Linda spoke into the phone. "Dr. Monroe."

"Linda, it's Ami."

"Ami. I didn't really expect to hear from you so soon. Did you convince Mr. Wagner?"

"Well, he wanted me to set up a date with you for

the tests when you have an opening.'' She looked down at her crossed fingers.

"How about next Thursday? If he can check Mandy in real early, we can start on her right away.'' Linda hesitated. "We'd like her to come prepared to stay a week while we check tissue compatibility.''

"Yes, I'm sure that will be all right. And, Linda, I'll be with them.''

"Oh, Ami, that's just great. It's been so long.'' Linda's laugh was delighted. "You can stay with us.''

"I'd better stay near the clinic. Mandy's going because I'm going with her, so I can't disappoint her.''

"I'm disappointed, but just so we can see you. Dave will be happy about it, too.'' Linda took a deep breath. "I'll reserve rooms for you at the motel close to the clinic for Wednesday evening, and if you have a change of plans, call me.''

"Thanks, Linda. I'll see you on Thursday morning.'' She hung up the phone, conscious of trembling fingers. With lots of luck, Dave and Linda's sure hands, Mandy would have a good chance to hear the night calls of her beloved desert.

Jeff's Bronco Jeep was gone when she went outside, and she reasoned he'd be at the regular Saturday night grange dance; plenty of time to tell him about the appointment. She took her list of supplies to Lily, leaving them for Harris to collect when he came in.

It was late afternoon when she whistled for Remus and watched him come loping toward her. He still favored the leg she had rebuilt, causing him to roll a little to the right. It didn't bother him as he jumped into the front seat after she opened the door for him.

Ami pulled into the parking lot at the grange hall minutes ahead of Steve and Janie. "Okay, Remus. Take care of everything. Blow the horn if you need me.'' She rolled the window down a bit and locked the truck. The dog watched her leave, then settled down to wait. She swung into step with Steve and Janie, waving at some of the regular crowd that called greetings to them.

"Hey, look who's with Jeff." Ami turned at Steve's comment to see Jeff talking with the Howards from a neighboring ranch. Next to him stood Eileen McKane, blond head only to Jeff's shoulder. The dress she wore would cost two months of Ami's salary. The palest of lavenders, caught at the tiny waist with a cummerbund of matching print, it hugged Eileen's petite shape at just the right places. Very much self-assured, she didn't look overly enthused to be in the hall. Brown eyes swept the crowd with studied indifference.

"Eileen, as I live and breathe," Janie said. "How did he accomplish that miracle?"

"I saw a dress like that while I was shopping in Tucson. I was afraid they'd charge me just for looking." Ami's voice held grudging admiration.

"Yes, and doesn't she wish she was anywhere but here!" Janie smiled.

"Why?"

"Well, now, this here is for cowboys and such, not enough uptown for her ladyship," Janie drawled.

"Isn't she a ranch owner?"

"You said it right—owner. Not to be confused with worker, as such."

"Oh." Ami wasn't sure she understood that at all.

"Jeff usually leaves her at home when he comes here, but guess she figured if he wouldn't stay with her, she'd bless us with her presence. I'm impressed." Steve looked anything but impressed, his grin wide and devilish. "Let's dance, Janie, my sweet." He turned to Ami. "I'll be back for you. Fight off any predators who might venture around."

Ami laughed and looked around. All the usual grange crowd was there.

"Hello, Ami." She looked up.

"Hello, Jeff."

"You know Eileen?" he asked.

Ami smiled at the woman by his side. "I saw her at the barbecue yesterday."

Eileen gave her a small smile. "Yes, of course, the new veterinarian." She made it sound equal to being employed to shovel manure.

"Yes, I work at Wagner's. Nice place." Her eyebrows went up as she eyed the woman's insolent expression. What did Jeff see in her, she wondered, aside from the fact that she was gorgeous and owned half of Arizona?

Jeff pulled a chair out for Eileen and settled into the one opposite Ami. "Were you able to contact Linda?"

Ami leaned forward. "Yes. You have an appointment Thursday morning at nine. Linda will take care of motel reservations for you." She glanced at Eileen to see her sit up with a jerk, eyes narrowed.

Jeff, too, looked at Eileen and back at Ami as he recalled her hesitation about the other woman's reception of the idea that Ami accompany them to Newark. "Did she indicate how long we'd be there?" he asked.

"She'd like you to come prepared to stay a week. Something about different parts of the body having different tissue compatibility." Jeff nodded. He had heard all that before.

"What are you talking about?" Eileen demanded to know.

Jeff explained. "Ami has friends who are doctors specializing in hearing problems, especially children."

She interrupted. "I thought you were through wasting time on those quacks. Hasn't Amanda been through enough? Why don't you admit she'll never be normal and put her in that special school in Tucson, where she can learn as others like her do?"

Ami stiffened, lips parted to lash out at her, but Jeff

spoke first, his voice quiet. "I'm not ready to give up completely, Eileen. Perhaps—"

She broke in. "Always one more chance, throwing money away." She was furious, her full lips pouting, her eyes shooting sparks at Ami.

Angry at the woman's unthinking remarks and uncomfortable at the exchange between her and Jeff, Ami wished she were anywhere but witnessing the quarrel, and was glad to see Janie and Steve return to the table. They talked ranch talk with Jeff while Eileen sat in stiff silence.

"Come on, Ami," Steve said, "it's our turn." He pulled her through the crowd, and she heard Eileen say, "Must we stay for this?"

"Are we 'this'?" she asked Steve.

"Afraid so. Miss Eileen isn't a country-and-western fan." Steve wasn't disturbed at all by that knowledge.

"Is she a fan of anything?"

"Well, she likes Jeff. Doesn't care to share him, however."

I don't think I would, either, Ami thought, remembering a strange kiss that turned her knees to water. She was still shaken by the outraged anger in Eileen. Whatever her private feelings, she should support Jeff in his search for relief for Mandy. They must be close to marriage if he allowed her to express opinions like that.

They were at the stage. The band had already deserted except for Ben Caskey, the piano player. They talked for a minute, and Ben said, "Hey, Ami, sing 'Broken Down in Tiny Pieces' for me."

"Sure thing."

Closing her eyes to the crowd and her mind to the words of the song, she picked up a guitar and blended her key with Steve's.

The author of the words she sang decreed that if you analyzed the value of love, broke it into pieces to really

look at it, you wasted your time. As she sang the philo-
sophical words of the ballad, Ami realized more than
ever that time had nothing whatsoever to do with
love's worth.

From that, they swung into a lively, lilting tune designed to lift everyone out of the dumps, and the crowd
joined in. Even with Eileen around, it still turned out to
be an enjoyable evening.

Driving back to the ranch alone, she was aware that
it didn't hurt anymore to sing the love songs. Tim was
in her past and, bittersweet as the memories were, she
no longer wished things were different.

*I hope you're happy, wherever you are. May you have
ten kids; five for each of us.* Feeling an emptiness for a
moment, she shrugged the feeling away. *No way I can
change; maybe I can finally accept it.* Her thoughts went
to Mandy, left without a mother; and Jeff, losing his
love so young. She felt a new impatience with Eileen
and her adamant refusal to realize possibilities existed
to help Mandy gain at least partial hearing.

"No one ever told us life would be all roses and
moonlight, huh, Remus?" The old dog snored softly
beside her.

The following morning she left word with Hammett
for Rio to join her at Camp 20 on Monday and took
Remus along with her on the ten-mile trip, stopping by
to have coffee with Carue and Ed Sparks, one of his
crew of cowhands in the isolated camp. Carue, after his
first outburst against a woman veterinarian, had taken
her under his wing, and anyone would have thought
she was his own private acquisition.

Jasper and Rio found her at the line camp on Monday, and she shared a cup of camp coffee with Jasper
before he went back to the ranch house. "We'll be in
late tomorrow, Jasper," she told him. "And Rio will
be helping Hammett while we're in Newark with
Mandy."

Rio echoed her own thoughts. "Will Mandy be all right?"

"I hope so. It would be wonderful if she could hear, wouldn't it?"

"*Sí,*" he said, and she smiled at the soft sound of the Spanish word.

Chapter Five

Wednesday morning she packed her suitcase, trying to remember what late September was like in New Jersey. No matter. Ami had little beside jeans, but as she rummaged through the closet she discovered a mauve-colored pantsuit she couldn't remember wearing. She pulled it from the hanger and surveyed it with critical eyes. It would do.

The phone rang, and she put the pantsuit on the bed to answer it. "Ami here."

"It's Jeff." As though she wouldn't recognize the deep voice. Surprised, she stared at the goose bumps on her arm. "Jasper will fly us into Tucson. We should leave about noon."

"All right."

When he knocked on the door a few minutes before twelve she was ready. She opened the door to see Mandy smiling up at her. Dressed in yellow overalls and a long-sleeved yellow shirt, she looked like a gray-eyed buttercup. Ami smiled at Jeff and stooped to hug Mandy.

Jeff drove the Bronco to the airstrip, where Jasper waited to transfer their luggage, and strap Mandy in the seat behind his.

"I wish I had a tranquilizer to last till we get to Newark," Ami told him as they readied for takeoff.

He laughed at her. "Don't you trust me yet, Ami?"

"You more than the big ones, Jasper. Jeff would kill you if anything happened to his plane." She relaxed a little as both men laughed.

Mandy peeked around her seat and grinned. She had no fear of flying and trusted Jasper anywhere.

They didn't have long to wait in Tucson, and the big airliner took off right on schedule, landing in Newark at eight o'clock, Newark time. It was already dark.

As they waited for their luggage Ami took out the paper with the name of the motel on it. Linda had called Jeff to confirm the reservations for him while Ami was still out at the camp.

Mandy nodded as they rode in the taxi to the motel, and Ami pulled her close, turning to look out the window as they moved along. In the dim streetlights she gazed at the full-leaved trees, thick and dark. It was too early for the leaves to have fallen, and even in darkness she could feel the differences from their Arizona climate in the damp air. The taxi slowed and turned into the driveway of a dimly lighted motel. The driver took their bags, and Ami waited as Jeff got their keys to the adjoining rooms, then picked up the sleeping child from her side.

"Let Mandy stay with me," she said as he unlocked the door.

He gave her a long look and nodded, placing the little girl on one of the twin beds. "Do you want me to put her pajamas on?"

She shook her head. "I'll do it."

Jeff brought in their bags and opened Mandy's, and after saying good night went into his room. The child yawned and smiled as Ami wiggled her out of her overalls and into the pyjamas. Ami picked her up and took her to the bathroom, kneeling beside her to let the little girl lean on her shoulder. She tucked her in bed, undressed, and slipped beneath the sheets in the other bed. She stretched, trying to relax, and her thoughts went to Jeff next door.

Eileen was crazy, she decided. Ami wouldn't let Jeff out of her sight, especially with another woman. She smiled to herself. Eileen was so sure of herself, she assumed there was nothing to worry about, which was probably true.

She called Linda at six thirty the next morning. "I was afraid I might wake someone," she said.

Linda laughed. "We've been up for ages. Dave is already in surgery. We'll meet you at the office at nine. Will that be all right?"

"Yes, of course." Jeff had already gone to rent a car, and Ami was expecting him back at any time. Mandy was at the window, watching for his return.

"Oh, Ami. I can hardly wait to see you and talk to you." Linda sounded the same as always. "It'll be so good."

"Yes, it will. See you about nine."

By the time Jeff returned with the rented car, they were dressed and hungry. They had breakfast at the motel restaurant, with Mandy bright-eyed and signing away, giving no indication that she was worried. Ami was conscious of the attention they received from other diners. The tall man, slender woman, and small girl all using sign language, so that there was no indication who was deaf until Jeff turned to speak to the waitress and then to Ami in a normal voice.

Linda had furnished directions the short distance to the clinic, and Jeff drove down Winters Avenue, turning at Langtry, and immediately pulled into a parking lot behind a low brick building. A sign at the side heralded the Monroe Clinic.

Mandy stood by Ami, holding tightly to her hand, as Jeff locked the car and took her other hand. He looked down at the child and, as she met his glance, he smiled and winked at her. Mandy skipped between them as they crossed the parking lot to the entrance. A sign said: DO NOT KNOCK. PLEASE ENTER.

Jeff pushed the door open and waited for Mandy and Ami to walk inside.

"Ami," a voice called, and she looked up to see Linda hurrying toward them.

"Hello, Linda." Ami was caught tightly, and after a moment, Linda held her away. Linda looked up, searching the smoothly tanned features.

"You look wonderful," she said and turned to face Jeff.

"Jeff, Dr. Monroe," Ami said, and to Linda, "This is Amanda," and signed for the child. "This is Dr. Monroe."

Linda shook hands with Jeff, then stooped to Amanda's level. "Hello, Amanda," she signed.

Solemn gray eyes looked Dr. Monroe over. Mandy looked at Jeff, who nodded, and she smiled, dipping her head a little as she did so.

Linda took her hand and led them into the inner office. "Dave will be here shortly. The operation took longer than expected, which happens frequently." She sighed. "We don't care how long it takes, just so it works." She pulled a chart to the center of her desk. "Let me get this filled out before we start any discussions."

The next several minutes were spent with Jeff answering questions and Linda recording the information. Ami played a game with Mandy, asking her the questions, and Mandy gave her own version of the answers, giggling when Ami called her a smarty-pants. Linda didn't miss the exchange between the two and smiled at them several times as she wrote on the chart.

"I'd like Amanda to stay in the hospital during the tests. Except Sunday, when we want all of you out for

dinner.'' Jeff translated for Mandy this time, and Ami
saw a look of doubt come into the child's eyes. Ami
reached for her hand and squeezed it and was rewarded
with an uncertain smile. She forced herself not to give
in to the urge to pick her up to reassure her.

After checking Mandy in, Linda led them down the
hallway to double doors that stood open. It was a big
room with four beds, each by a window. Three of the
beds were occupied, and a young nurse came by and
smiled at Amanda, walking ahead of them to turn back
the bright yellow spread from the pillows.

She turned and, with sign language, said, "I'm Ellen.
You must be Amanda."

Mandy nodded and lifted her arms to Ellen to be
helped onto the bed. Ami bit her lip, realizing Mandy
knew what was coming and was reconciled to it. She
looked at Jeff, wishing she could apologize for being
pushy, accusing him of not wanting to give Mandy
another chance to hear. He looked at her as if aware of
her thoughts and, suddenly, he smiled as though he
knew what she was thinking and accepted her apology.

A hand on her arm turned her to face Dave, who
laughed and said, "My favorite vet, as lovely as ever."
He bent a little to kiss her cheek and held a hand out to
Jeff. The men exchanged pleasantries, and Dave explained in depth the steps they would take to determine
what they could do for Mandy.

Hours later Jeff drove them back to the motel. "You
must be starved," he said.

"I am hungry," she admitted with a smile.

They ate in the motel restaurant, both quiet as they
thought of the day behind them and all the ones to
come. She looked up to find Jeff watching her and
smiled at him.

"You're very quiet," he said.

Ami was glad he couldn't read her mind, because
she was remembering the feel of his mouth on hers.

"Hospitals aren't my favorite places to visit," she told him.

"Nor mine." He reached and touched her fingers lightly. "I'm glad you came. Amanda has been much easier to deal with this time."

"I'm glad, too, although I do feel guilty leaving Rio and Hammett alone."

Jeff leaned forward. "They'll manage." He continued to look at her, his eyes going over her face until they rested on her lips, and she wet them with a flick of her tongue. When he looked up to meet her own gaze, his eyes darkened before he smiled and went back to eating.

It was nine o'clock before they stood in front of her room. Jeff opened the door and turned to her, blocking her entrance into the room. His hand came out to lift her chin so that she was forced to look up at him and watch as he leaned to place his mouth on hers. She stood still, hoping the tremors throughout her body didn't show. As his lips lingered on hers, hers parted involuntarily as the pressure increased.

He lifted his head, his hand still under her chin, and said softly, "Good night, Ami," standing aside to allow her to enter the room. She went inside without answering him and leaned against the door as he closed it behind her.

"This will never do," she murmured aloud to the empty room, and had a feeling she was in for a lot of talking common sense to herself.

Friday and Saturday till noon were spent in much the same way, tests and talks but no decisions. On Monday Mandy was scheduled for tissue to be removed from her inner ear for biopsy examination, but they had the weekend ahead of them. It was one o'clock Saturday afternoon when they checked her out of the clinic with an overnight pass.

"Would you like to see the water, Ami? The upper bay comes between New Jersey and New York about an hour's drive from us," Jeff said as they left the parking lot.

She turned to Mandy sitting between them, asking her the question, receiving an enthusiastic yes.

The day was warm and sticky with a breeze coming directly off the water. They passed an amusement park, shuttered and locked, with a sign indicating CLOSED TILL SUMMER.

"It's different," Ami observed, enjoying the heavy leaves of the trees along the sidewalk, just beginning to show a touch of autumn gold.

The last time she was in Newark it was different, she remembered, when Tim divorced her and she ran to Linda and Dave in their small apartment, licking her wounds and pulling herself back together. They had been her support, helping her to find her way back to living again. She shivered. No one should be allowed to hurt that way.

The car stopped, and she realized they had reached the water. "Too bad it's foggy. We could probably see ships coming up the water," Jeff said.

Strain as she would, Ami couldn't see past the thin gray curtain of fog over the water. She turned to Mandy, who was sitting forward, staring at more water than she had ever seen in Arizona. Jeff stopped the car at a lookout point, and they got out to go stand by the rock wall. The mournful sound of a ship's blast of warning echoed through the mist, and they saw it coming toward them in the middle of the river.

Jeff stooped and lifted Amanda to the top of the wall, and Ami smiled at her as the child's eyes widened.

"It's a freighter," she told her. "A ship that carries things from one country to another."

Mandy nodded and continued to watch the progress

of the ship. As it passed by them, Jeff put her down,
and held between them, she skipped on the sand. Ami
looked down as Mandy pulled her hand away and
looked up at Jeff.

"I'm hungry. Can I have a hot dog?" the child
signed.

He laughed. "It's dinner time. Let's find a place and
all of us can eat."

Back in the car, Jeff headed toward their motel. Ami
and Mandy watched the neat rows of homes pass and
occasionally smiled at each other. Ami looked around
when the car stopped to see they had reached the
restaurant that Linda and Dave had recommended.
Mandy was able to get her hot dog.

It was dark when they finally left the restaurant, and
Ami gathered Mandy to her as she leaned against her in
the car. By the time they reached the motel, she was
asleep.

Jeff came around to open her door and said, "Wait
till I unlock the room, and I'll come back for her." He
came back and bent to take the sleeping child from her,
and his hair brushed her cheek as he straightened. He
still smelled of the outdoors. Ami locked the car door
and followed him into the room, conscious of a fluttering in her stomach. *Well,* she argued to herself, *he's an
attractive man, and it's been a long time since I've been this
close to one. And it had better be as close as I get,* she
concluded, thinking of the fire in Eileen's brown eyes.

Jeff placed the sleeping Mandy on the bed she had
slept in on Wednesday night and removed her slippers.
With movements learned from long practice, he undressed her and took the gown Ami handed him, slipping it over the blond pigtails. He turned the covers
back and lifted Mandy to place her on the pillow. The
little girl sighed and slept on. Jeff stood a moment looking down at her and moved away. Ami was watching
his every move and was surprised at the tightness of his

mouth, realizing again the worry he was going through alone as he had so many times before. She touched his arm, and he turned to look at her and reached to pull her into his arms, holding her tightly against him for a moment before he pushed her away.

"Good night, Ami," he said and walked through the connecting door to his room.

She undressed slowly, getting ready for bed, glancing at the tiny girl, who didn't stir. When she turned out the lights, she went to look out the window at the thick shadows all around. It had been a long four days for her; what must it seem like to Jeff and Mandy? Her sympathy was with Mandy; the feeling for Jeff was more than that, and she was filled with uncertainty.

They had breakfast late and took out the map Dave had drawn for them to use to locate the house. It was easy, only a mile from the clinic, and near the small apartment they had lived in before buying the larger town house.

The house was like Linda: organized and lovely. The sour beef and dumplings were done to perfection, as was the homemade strawberry shortcake. Dave and Jeff retired to the patio, and Mandy went to sleep with no urging. Ami leaned against the sink, watching Linda put everything in its place.

She asked the question uppermost in her mind. "Does Mandy have a good chance?"

"Excellent, as a matter of fact. Think success, Ami. When have you let insurmountable odds bother you?"

"The odds were never for Mandy before."

Linda stopped what she was doing and turned to face her. "How about Tim, Ami? Are you over him?"

Ami considered the question. "After two years, I think it's time, don't you."

Linda nodded. "But I asked if you are, not if you should be."

"Yes." And, suddenly, she knew it was true.

"Hooray for you." Linda hugged her. "Now, what about Jeff?"

Startled, Ami asked, "What about Jeff?"

"Are you in love with him?"

She stared at her friend. "Are you crazy? Eileen has a capital claim staked there. You don't think I'd be foolish enough to get into competition with her? I only tangle with domesticated animals—not wildcats." Even as she denied loving Jeff, she couldn't help but wonder at the odd feelings about him, and the kisses she couldn't treat as casual touches.

"Well, I don't know Eileen, but I do know you, and you've got her beat all the way."

Ami laughed. "You're prejudiced."

"No prejudice allowed here." It was Dave. "Who is, in this day and age?"

"Your wife, sir. You should talk to her." Ami was still laughing. Inside, a weight had lifted. She was free of Tim. How wonderful, she thought, feeling exhilaration building. She never thought it would happen. She turned to find Jeff towering in the doorway with Mandy smiling sleepily in his arms.

"As much as I hate to eat and run, we promised to have Amanda back before eight. We'll see you in the morning."

In the car Mandy, still cuddly from her nap, sat in Ami's lap. She allowed them to check her into the clinic with no fuss, but Ami felt her throat constrict as they left her.

"Let's stop for a drink. Our last chance to relax for a while."

"All right." Ami watched his profile as he drove. His lips were drawn tight, matching the guarded look in his eyes.

The small bar where they stopped was almost empty. Possibly it was early, or people were off enjoying the last of the good weather before the onset of a long, cold winter.

"You'd better tell me what you want. I've never seen you drink."

"A piña colada sounds good."

Jeff grinned as he gave their order. "Sounds terrible."

Neither of them attempted to make conversation, but their silence was shared companionship without having to talk. As he left her at her room he bent to kiss her as naturally as he would if it were an everyday occurrence, and left her with her thoughts tangling around the feelings he brought to the surface.

Ami shook her head as she undressed, pushing her unruly thoughts into the back of her mind as she slid between the cool sheets. Tomorrow promised to be a very long day.

Chapter Six

They sat in the audio room of the clinic with Dave, Linda, and two other doctors who were consulting on the case.

Dave spoke first. "We've isolated Amanda's problem, Jeff, and Dr. Herbert, here, agrees with us that it's one that we can be confident of a great deal of success in if we operate. Dr. Herbert is from Boston, where they've done extensive research in traumatic hearing impairment. Since you were at Johns Hopkins with Amanda, you probably recognize Dr. Maldin as a prominent surgeon in the same field."

Jeff nodded, leaning forward. "What was your final evaluation?" His voice was tense as he asked the question.

It was Tuesday afternoon. Monday had been a gruelling battery of more tests, more talks, more waiting, and Ami was feeling uncertain about the entire procedure, fully realizing now Jeff's reluctance to put Amanda through all of this. She wanted to touch him, let him know she was there, but she sat still, listening.

"We'd like to operate. We wouldn't be using her as a guinea pig, Jeff," Linda said, her soft voice intense as she tried to convince him of the possible results of the operation. "We've done this type of operation with great success. It's usually on older people, but Amanda has a very good chance of hearing. Not as good as you or I, but as well as a lot of people who aren't even aware they have a hearing problem.''

Jeff stared from one face to the other, his glance finally resting on Ami. She looked back, hoping he couldn't see how her heart reacted. He stood up and walked to a table where a coffee pot had been set up for them, but he didn't touch the cups there. Instead, he turned and looked at the faces watching him.

''All right. If you think she has a fighting chance, go ahead.''

The operation took place early Wednesday, and Mandy was back in her room at one o'clock. Ami left to get them a sandwich and coffee. She bit her lip to keep the tears back, thinking of the tiny, still figure, her blond hair shaved two inches above each ear.

They took turns sitting with her until ten that night. Mandy was awake and fretful when the night nurse came by.

''I'll give her something for the pain, and she'll sleep. You should go home. I'll stay with her.''

Groggy from worry and exhaustion, they accepted the offer. They didn't talk on the way to the motel, and Jeff left her immediately with a quiet ''Thanks, and good night.''

Thursday morning it was raining; a slow, chilling rain that caused Ami to shiver as she looked outside. End of Indian summer, she thought.

While Jeff went to see Mandy, Ami stayed with Linda, sympathetic but confident. ''I know you think you're neglecting your job, Ami, and I understand your wanting to get back. Amanda is on the way to healing very well, and all we need is a week, maybe ten days, to see that the grafts take and there'll be no infection. I'll call you Saturday morning after we run the first hearing tests on Mandy.''

Ami had decided to return to the ranch on Friday,

since Mandy was doing so well. Jeff had agreed with her decision, knowing she was reluctant to leave Mandy.

Linda looked around at her. "It's been so good having you here." She hesitated, then asked, "Wonder why he had you come rather than Eileen?"

Ami laughed. "Stop thinking, Linda. It was Mandy, not Jeff, who wanted me to come with her."

"All right. Wonder why Mandy asked for you, not Eileen?"

"The way I understand it, Eileen not only thinks children shouldn't be seen or heard, but any illness disturbs her. She refers to Mandy's not hearing as an affliction."

"And Jeff lets her?" Linda was furious.

"I'm sure he's never heard that reference, or he might wash her mouth out with soap." Ami's voice was dry.

A few minutes later Linda dropped Ami at the motel, promising again to call her on Saturday.

It was twelve thirty, and Jeff was still at the clinic, telling her to rest while he stayed with Mandy. They were going to dress the operation to examine it, and Mandy would be sedated.

She undressed, folded the mauve-colored suit carefully, put it in her bag, dragged out her faithful jeans and plain white shirt, then headed for the shower, trailing the pale yellow terry robe behind her. She stayed a long time, shampooing her hair and letting the warm water soothe the tension from her neck and shoulders. It had been a hard week for her, but what about Jeff? He must be tied in knots.

Belting the robe around her, Ami went to stand by the window. The sky was a smooth dark gray, rain pouring steadily, and streetlamps were already on, even though it was just a few minutes past one o'clock. She shivered and pulled her robe tighter when a knock sounded on the door. She brushed her damp hair from her face as the knock was repeated, and Jeff called, "Ami, are you home?"

Smiling, she opened the door, forgetting she wore only the yellow robe. Jeff's hair was even darker with the rain on it. He shook his head. "The monsoons have arrived." He glanced at the robe, the still-damp hair. "I thought we could both use a drink and picked up some brandy. Will that be all right?"

"A small drink, Jeff. I guess it's going to be a long, long evening. Were they satisfied with the way the healing was progressing?"

"Yes, it looks good." He poured brandy in their water glasses, handing the smaller drink to her. "They're optimistic, and I'd like to be, but I can't help but remember all the other times it looked good." He stretched out in the armchair and sighed. He lifted his glass toward her. "Here's hoping this is the miracle we've been searching for."

She lifted hers back and sat in the chair opposite him.

"No real boyfriends, Ami?" The question out of the silence was unexpected.

She smiled at his emphasis on *real.* "No. No real ones."

"Why not?" Jeff sipped the brandy. "And why is a lovely girl like you stuck out in the desert with a raggedy dog and an orphaned Mexican?"

"I'm a vet. Remember?"

"You could have brought a husband or a boyfriend with you."

"I just told you, I don't have one."

"And I just asked why not?"

She could stop this type of fencing right now. Bluntly she said, "I'm getting over a broken marriage."

That stopped him for a moment, and he studied her over his glass. "What happened?"

Ami shrugged. "The divorce papers said incompatibility."

Your fault or his?" He was still watching her.

"Mine," she told him.

"You assume the blame mighty quick."

She sipped the brandy but didn't answer. The drink was warm down to her stomach. This was the most conversation they had managed in private the entire week. The subject was disturbing, and the direct questioning more than she needed.

"Where is he now?" Jeff had his head back against the chair, eyeing her through half-closed lids.

"I don't know."

"How long since the divorce?"

"Two years."

"You still love him?"

The inquisition was getting out of hand. Ami got up and walked to the window. Trees were bending with the heavy rain and wind, and as she watched, orange and blue lightning flashed, outlining the trees in silhouette. A heavy rumble of thunder followed.

"I wonder if Mandy will like thunderstorms when she can hear all the noise."

"Do you?" he asked.

"Yes, especially our southwestern storms. They're wild and beautiful, even if we don't get much rain with them. Here they seem sad and lonely."

They were silent, listening to the pouring rain. "You didn't answer me. Do you still love him?"

"No." She turned away from the window. "Do you need another drink?"

Jeff looked at his glass, drained the little left in it, and handed it to her. She filled it, adding a little to her own. Passing his chair, she handed him the glass and kept walking to the window and pulled the draperies closed, turned the lamp on, and returned to her chair.

"Did you have lunch?" Jeff asked.

She thought about it. "No, we had rolls and coffee. Linda was due in surgery. You?"

He grinned. "I ate some of Amanda's." He stretched.

"Maybe the rain will let up and we'll go out. I don't much want motel food, do you?"

"No, but I'm not hungry."

"By the time we get out, you may be starved."

They were quiet, and she was beginning to think he had gone to sleep when he groaned and sat up.

"What's wrong?"

"What will I do if this doesn't work?" His voice was uncertain, and he gave her a hard look. "I think I'll hate you."

She was beside him, kneeling by the chair. "She'll be able to hear. I know she will, so she can hear Charlie laugh."

He shook his head. "You told her Charlie laughs?"

"Yes."

"Of course. That's why she loves you so much. You see the world through her eyes."

Bright turquoise eyes laughed up at him. "It's prettier than through mine." She was still kneeling beside him, her face almost level with his. The dark gray eyes, clouded with worry, widened as he searched her features, and it required only a slight move on his part to cover her mouth with his, fingers beneath her chin to keep her there. In her unsteady position her body swayed, and he reached, pulling her into the chair with him. One arm held her close; the other hand slid beneath the folds of her robe. He drew in his breath as his hand touched the warm bare flesh.

I'd better move before this goes any further, she thought, but she didn't, watching as his face lowered to hers. There was an instant's hesitation before his mouth touched hers and, with a sigh, she relaxed against his shoulder. Her hands slid up his arms, pulling him closer, and his arms tightened, crushing her to him. Her head slipped back and her mouth shaped to his kiss, answering the need she felt in him. Lips parted, she felt his teeth against hers as warm, forgotten feelings stirred inside her. How long it lasted she didn't know, till he lifted his head, watching her through black lashes. Lightly his lips brushed her cheek, then found her parted lips again. His kiss was gentle this time, tracing the full lower lip, the curve of her cheek, then back to her waiting mouth. They sighed in unison, and she felt him slide forward in the chair, one arm beneath her legs as he lifted her. The bed gave with their combined weight, his hands pushed the robe from her shoulders, and his lips brushed against the rushing pulse in her throat.

"Jeff." It was only a whisper. She heard the sound of a word, not knowing if he had said anything. "We can't—" she started, but he silenced her as he found her mouth again. His hands beneath her brought her fully into his embrace, and she stretched her long legs against the hard length of him. Suddenly she was a woman, too long denied the demands of her young, healthy body, with no wish to stop their headlong move toward the fulfillment they both wanted. Her hand touched his cheek, his firm lips. Her eyes, searching the rugged features, found his looking straight at her.

"Move your hand, Ami," he whispered. "Undress me."

She did, unbuttoning his shirt and unfastening his belt as he twisted to slide his pants from his hips. His hand went down her body, slowly over the contour of her hips to her thighs to push her backward, caressing across her flat stomach, curving over her small high breasts. Hungry desire caught at him as she responded with slow movements against him. His lips parted over hers as he moaned deep in his throat, taking her with his powerful thighs, bringing a shattering, explosive breath from both of them. His mouth grew gentle on hers as he cradled her to him until both were breathing evenly again.

Time was lost as they lay close together, then she felt

his hands move over her, touching her breasts, trailing fingers across her flat stomach. She heard him whisper "Ami?"

It was a question she answered by turning, outlining her body to his, moving her head back so that he found her lips. They moved together until he took her breath with a soaring sweetness, his arms imprisoning her willing body. She was vaguely aware of the storm still raging outside, no less than the one inside the room.

When she awakened, the lights were still on and, for a moment, she wasn't sure where she was. Realization came as she turned her head to see Jeff asleep beside her. Black lashes against the tanned cheek didn't hide the shadows under his eyes. It had been a rough week for him, and she felt a rush of tenderness for him, compassion for Mandy, who was going through so much she didn't understand. Then it dawned on her what had happened as she studied Jeff's face. Knowledge that she was in love with him hit her, constricting her throat, bringing tears to her eyes, with not a chance in the world that it was returned.

Jeff's eyes opened and widened as they took in the face so near his. His glance moved over her face to her lips, back to her rumpled hair. Their eyes met. His hand moved to follow the curve of her hip, teasingly across her stomach to cup her breast. She drew in her breath, and Jeff's eyes darkened as he raised himself on one elbow, leaning to touch her lips. Her eyes were wide, and he saw the sparkle of tears.

"Why?" was all he said as his kiss closed her lids.

"Why what?" Her throat hurt.

"You're crying. Did I hurt you?"

"No."

"Then why?" His lips moved away and he was watching her. She shook her head, not knowing how to answer him.

His arms cradled her to him as his lips, warm and searching, moved across her face to her throat. He pulled the lobe of her ear between his teeth, nibbling gently, and went back to her mouth. He pushed her back against the pillow and propped himself up on one arm, looking down at her. His finger traced the lips like warm rose satin, the curve of her cheek, the tilted nose with five freckles he counted one by one. He followed the line of her jaw to the hollow of her throat, down to the cleft between the small breasts. A gentle caress across her breast hardened the brown tip, and he lowered his head to tease it with his lips. Warmth spread through her body as he moved to the other breast, rubbing the mound with his lips, his tongue closing over the hard nipple. Her breath came quick and warm, then stopped completely as her explosive feelings threatened, waiting to be released by his movements.

Both her hands went behind his head, holding him to her, relinquishing her hold only to allow his mouth to return to hers, where he whispered "Darling Ami" as he took possession of her once more. His measured movements were gentle, his hunger not as demanding as before.

He came out of the shower, saw her still stretched full length on the bed, her nude body clearly outlined by the thin sheet. He stood over her. "I can come back to bed."

She smiled. "I'm hungry." Then, as she realized he was fully dressed, she said, "You aren't going out, are you? It's too nasty."

Jeff sat beside her, not touching her, concentrating on her body beneath the cover. "There's a Chinese restaurant a couple of blocks away. I called, while you were sleeping and it's ready to be picked up." He smiled. "You do like Chinese food?"

She laughed. "I wouldn't dare not to after that, would I?"

He bent to kiss the laughing mouth. "No." He stood up. "I'll be back shortly."

Ami lay still after he had gone, realizing her life was in for some changes. Hurt lay just a kiss away. And she thought she was doing so well. She left the bed they had shared, took a shower, and dressed. When she heard his key in the door, she crossed to open it for him.

"Whew, you're right, it's nasty out there. Hope the food's worth it." His eyes went over her jeans and shirt, and her freshly brushed sun-streaked hair. "I like the other outfit better," he said, watching the color flare in her cheeks.

They were hungry and ate in companionable silence. "Your plane leaves at ten forty-five in the morning, so, if you want to, you can see Amanda before you go."

"Yes, you know I do." She leaned back, looking at her watch. It was ten thirty, almost ten hours since they had the first drink. She was cooking up years of heartache, she thought, feeling lonely. Eileen would never give up her possession. Not that Jeff would want her to; he had needed someone, and Ami was available.

"A penny?" he asked.

"Not worth it." She smiled at him, and rubbed her stomach. "I'll have to diet after this, or I can stay at the shack a couple of weeks on C rations."

Jeff was silent a moment. "I wasn't thinking, Ami." She waited as he hesitated. "I wouldn't want to be responsible for your being pregnant."

She stiffened and stared at him. He couldn't be expected to know he had nothing to worry about. "Would it help if I said don't worry?"

He looked at her sitting with her long legs across the chair arms. The gray eyes changed, and his voice was withdrawn as he said, "Yes, I should have known you could take care of yourself."

The intonation hurt for an instant, then Ami remembered her willing response in his arms, not blaming him for his suspicions. She said nothing.

He got up and walked to the window, opening the drapes she had closed hours ago. It was pitch dark and the sound of wind and rain seemed louder than before. "Turn the light out and come here."

Ami did as she was told, walking slowly in the darkness to stand beside him.

"More rain than we see in a year." She could hear the smile in his voice.

"I love the rain, but nothing beats our climate."

"Not everyone feels that way, you know."

"I guess not."

He pulled her closer, and with the same thought, they sat on the floor, leaning against the low windowsill. "Tell me how you came to be good friends with Linda." His tone was conversational.

"I met her when we were both in graduate school; she was in med and I was in animal husbandry training."

"All of it. Dave only told me a little about it. You saved her life, didn't you?" His glance covered her face, the strange-colored eyes, dark tumbled hair. "Dave would do anything for you. That's why I was able to get Amanda into the clinic so quickly."

"I was there when the car skidded and headed for Linda. I tackled her and broke her arm. A surgeon's arm." She laughed. "Some rescue."

"Arms heal; necks usually don't." Jeff was nuzzling against her throat, and she could feel the rough beard scraping her cheek. She wanted to run, hide from the heartache she could see coming. Too late, a voice reminded her. Much too late.

"Who are you, Ami? No one owns you. You're free

as the desert breeze." His lips traced her palm and he folded her fingers around his kiss. "Oddest eyes I've ever seen." His arms tightened. "There were tears before. Why? You said I didn't hurt you."

She turned her face so that her mouth was against his. She whispered, "No, you didn't hurt me." That would come later, she was certain.

Their lips caught and held, and, slowly, he turned her until they lay side by side on the carpeted floor. She made no objection as he unbuttoned her shirt. Her hands moved over the rough hair of his chest, holding him, and long moments later she lay close to him as he slept in her arms. It was a long time before she, too, slept.

Sometime during the early morning hours Jeff moved in her arms and left, returning with a blanket to cover her. She watched him go through the connecting door, and the memory of what happened came to haunt her.

What a mess. She lay still, eyes closed, refusing to believe she could be so gullible. *That's what I get for thinking I'm immune to loving anyone.* Dread of what was to come filled her.

Mind and body protested every move as she got up and dressed. Six thirty; four hours till plane time. A quiet knock brought her abruptly to the time she had to face Jeff. She was not ready. She opened the door.

Dark gray eyes smiled at her. "Let's get some coffee." It was as though he had never touched her. He didn't mention the hours spent in her arms, nor did she. Let it be said she could take a cue when offered, she thought. So be it.

Mandy was subdued when they got to her, still under sedation. Ami hugged her. "I have to go back to work, Mandy," she said. "See you in a couple of weeks." The gray eyes, so like Jeff's, were hazy, but the smile was Mandy's. She nodded.

Then they were in the car and on their way to the

airport. Ami kept her hands clenched into fists in her lap as Jeff concentrated on driving through heavy traffic. She felt as desolate as the wet streets looked and fought the heaviness inside her as they pulled into the airport parking area.

"Ami?" She turned to face him. "I know what happened shouldn't have, but I can't really say I'm sorry." When she didn't answer him, Jeff tipped her chin so that she had to look at him. As their eyes met, his darkened. "Can we live with it?" he asked.

Ami said what he wanted her to say. "Yes." Not for one moment was she sure.

"Thanks for being here with Mandy. It made it much easier for me." He bent his head and kissed her and, for a moment, he held her close. At the gate he pulled her to him again as though reluctant to let her go, then she was on the plane, and Newark was a patterned, misty picture below her.

She didn't remember much of the flights but was glad when Jasper deposited her at her door. He listened with delight as she recounted the days with Mandy, shaking his head at the mere thought that she might hear. Jeff had already called and talked to everyone, and Ami had only to add her detailed account.

Talking to Janie, she sensed the jubilation in everyone, expecting the best for Mandy.

And I should be happy, but I feel like I lost someone—someone I never had. She sighed, turning her mind away from Jeff and Mandy and concentrating on the job at hand.

Chapter Seven

Linda called her at six Saturday morning. "Ami, I hate to call so early, but I have surgery at nine. Best news, my friend. Mandy has at least fifty percent of her hearing, and that will improve." Linda's voice was ecstatic.

At the sound of Linda's voice, Ami froze. The silence went on till Linda said, "Ami, are you there?"

She swallowed over the dryness in her throat. "Linda, did anyone ever call you an angel?"

Linda's laugh sparkled. "Among other things."

"Linda, what about speech? She has so much catching up to do."

"Dr. Mathers and Dr. Preston are our best audio therapy specialists for children, and they'll work with Mandy while she's here the next ten days or so. They'll contact their counterparts in Tucson and get Mandy enrolled in their programs. It will take a little while, Ami, but Mandy learns very quickly, and in no time she'll be talking away. Trust us."

"Oh, I do, Linda. If there's ever anything I can do for you and Dave—" She stopped.

"I'm alive, Ami, thanks to you. Visit us again soon?"

"Yes. Yes, I will. Thanks again." She sat silent as the connection was broken. Mandy could hear, at least some. Who said the age of miracles was over? Hugging herself, she did a whirling dance step across the floor and was confronted by Remus, who grinned at her as if to say "Ain't it a blast?"

She went outside, breathing in the first dawn breezes, looking toward Janie's. There was a light on, and she started on the run, detouring by the corral, where Hammett was already busy.

She skidded to a halt in front of the startled old man, then, with a whoop, wrapped her arms around him and danced a jig.

"She can hear, Hammett. Mandy can hear."

He stared. "Are you sure?"

"Linda just called."

Tears clouded the bright blue eyes. "Lord have mercy."

The old man eyed her, shaking his head. "I never dared dream. I just never dreamed."

"What's all the fuss?" Rio asked from behind her.

Ami went over the news, seeing Rio's face brighten, the dark eyes flash in disbelief. Then he was hugging her, swinging her around as though she weren't as big as he.

When they calmed down a little, she said, "I have to talk to Janie and Steve. See you two at breakfast."

The door swung inward as Ami raised her hand to knock, and Janie stood there, tawny brown eyes dark with shock. "Jeff's on the phone. Mandy can hear." It was like Christmas bells heard around the world.

Janie pulled her inside, and they stood arm in arm, listening to Steve's half of the conversation. Steve said, "Ami, Jeff wants to talk to you." He handed the phone to her and reached for Janie.

Her hand clenched around the receiver as she heard Jeff's voice. "Ami, how are you?" He sounded tired.

"Wonderful. And you?"

"No way to explain it, Ami. No words." There was a brief silence. "Ami, I want to thank you for everything, although that sounds bland for what I'm feeling." She stiffened at the polite words. He went on. "Mandy was better off for your being with her, and she already wants to come home."

"We can't wait to see her," Ami finally managed over the choking in her throat.

"We'll see all of you in about ten days, I guess." He was gone.

Ami took a deep breath and turned to face Janie and Steve. With one movement they were all hugging.

When they settled down a bit, Janie said, "Now, tell us what they did."

Ami shook her head. "I wish I could. Dave explained some of the techniques, but it's over my head. I know they replaced some part of her inner ears with her own body material from her wrist. She only has a tiny scar on the inside of her arm, and Linda says that will fade in time. Lord, I love those two." The other love was one she didn't mention.

Ami's heart was light as she took Rio and Remus and headed for the line camps early Monday morning, knowing there was plenty of work to do before the late fall rains came. The cattle in the flash flood areas had to be moved to higher ground, and they went with them, checking the water and feed troughs. As they moved Ami's eyes were alert for deep scratches or bloody spots that might be an injury that needed tending or for infected insect bites. The long hard hours sent them to bed at night tired, but content with their life.

Days turned into weeks, with Ami and Rio learning from their daily adventures and experiences. She worked her way through the crisis of cattle injuries and viruses, going to Hammett occasionally for advice. The old man was a good sounding board for ideas and, more often than not, he agreed with her, adding only some point she hadn't yet thought about. He was one of many good friends they had made at Wagner's.

Jeff followed Dave's advice and put Mandy in the special school for speech in Tucson. Ami's heart went out to the tiny girl, alone all week with strangers, learning a strange language. She came home weekends, and the times Ami was at the ranch, Mandy came to see her.

One Saturday afternoon they sat on the back steps, concentrating on the work Ami held in her hand. She touched Mandy's shoulder and, using a mixture of sound and sign language, she told her, "This is patchwork. You put the design on this square of material and stitch around it." She handed her the needle and a square of white with a cutout of material shaped like the head of a longhorn steer. The little fingers were clumsy as she attempted to draw a thread through, so Ami put her arms around the slight shoulders and took the needle from her, showing her how to make the tiny stitches through both pieces of material. Concentrating, they both started as Jeff spoke.

"Homework?" he asked.

Ami laughed. "No. Patchwork. Mandy couldn't understand what I was doing, so I was showing her."

He reached for Mandy, who went into his arms, holding around his neck. "We're going to Eileen's for dinner, and Hazel needs to bathe you."

Mandy shook her head vigorously. "I'll stay with Ami."

Jeff smiled. "She's having hot dogs especially for you."

"I'll stay with Ami," she repeated, looking straight at him.

Ami stood up. "I'd love to keep her, Jeff. She's no trouble."

He hesitated. "I'll be late getting home, but you can take her to Hazel about seven."

Ami turned to the little girl. "Want to stay all night with me?"

Mandy nodded, wiggling down from Jeff's arms, going back to the square they had been working on.

Ami smiled at Jeff as he stood there, his eyes going over her slim figure in the long-sleeved denim shirt and jeans. He had held her and made love to her not many weeks ago, and now it was as though it never happened. To him, perhaps. She remembered every day.

He bent to kiss Mandy's cheek, and she gave him a smile, waving as he turned to make his way across the yard toward the big ranch house. Pushing her feelings to the back of her mind as she always did, Ami sat back down with Mandy, watching the little girl tackle the patchwork in her hand.

There was no doubt the school was helping Mandy. The words she spoke were easily understood. Sometimes she squinted, trying to think of the right sound to go with a word, and would revert back to sign language to make herself understood. At these times they laughed together and figured out the words she wanted.

Ami fixed hot dogs for their supper and, when Mandy yawned, put the pajamas on that Hazel brought her and lay down with her until she went to sleep. After a short while, Ami got up and went to sit in the living room, staring into space. When Jeff and Eileen married, what would happen to Mandy? Mandy never mentioned Eileen, but she didn't stay around when Eileen came to see Jeff at the ranch, staying at the corral with Charlie and Hammett, unless Ami was at home, then she chose to stay with her. After she became mistress of Wagner's, Eileen would probably insist that Mandy go to school in Tucson full time to keep her out of the way, where there would be no competition for Jeff's attention.

The thought hurt her and she went to stand outside. The sky was full of stars, the cold air clear and scented with desert smells. Jeff would do what was best for

Mandy; it wasn't Ami's problem. She winced at the realization that she wished she did have a say in what happened to the little girl.

Time moved along, and Ami marked off the calendar, watching the holidays approach, wondering how to avoid staying around the home corral when she knew Jeff encouraged shorter hours for everyone. Through Janie and Steve, and sometimes a visit from Jasper in the camps, she kept up with Mandy's progress.

"She's something to watch these days, Ami," Jasper told her on one of his visits, laughing as he described Mandy's sudden awareness that she could hear and understand most of what was said in a normal conversation. "You should come in more often on the weekends when she's home. She misses you."

Ami answered him very carefully. "This is a busy time for us, Jasper. Maybe things will slow down after the holidays and the rainy season are behind us." She couldn't tell him it would be dangerous for her to be too near Mandy, since it would mean being close to Jeff, where she had no business to be.

Sometimes during the long nights, unable to sleep, Ami's thoughts were full of Jeff. His personal life was strictly apart from her, as it should be, and the fact that it included Eileen by the same token excluded her. The short hours in his arms left her with memories that haunted her, wanting more, knowing what he had taken from her was more than repaid. She needed him as much as he needed her, but falling in love was a side effect she hadn't counted on.

If you loved once, she thought with some bitterness, thereafter you should have immunity from the disease.

The quiet of the vast canyon she had driven into prompted her to get out of her truck and walk with Remus trotting nearby. Breathing in the clean air, she could feel the approach of colder weather definite in the late fall temperatures. The toe of her boot hit a clump of dried mesquite, and her arms flailed outward to balance herself. She gave a half glance at the offending stubble and stopped. An unfamiliar pattern in the hard soil was out of place, somehow, as though a giant armadillo had slept, then ambled toward the runoff gulch near the foot of the mountain. She had seen something similar last month over by Camp 19 when she had been looking for the cattle tagged in the spring. Sure that she had left a good number of the young Charolais in that area, she nevertheless couldn't locate them.

Her gaze followed the marks a few hundred feet where they disappeared into a wash. Whatever tracks went in the wash were wiped out by the water coming out of the higher elevations after the rains of a week ago. No rain had fallen here, so the odd impressions remained.

But there were high winds, she mused to herself. She would ask Steve about it. She looked upward over the six-thousand-foot mountain range that separated Wagner's and the O'Toole property, which had been up for sale a long time, since the old man died a couple of years back. She went back to the truck, puzzling over the indentations, turning toward the ranch again.

Wagner's celebrated all holidays by letting as many hands off as they could. She was caught up on her work, cattle and horses well taken care of for the time being, and she'd be able to do some paperwork. Over the long weekend she'd talk to Steve and Jasper about the unusual markings she found.

When the Sandovals invited Rio for Thanksgiving dinner, she accepted Janie's invitation to eat with them. Jasper was there, too.

"I don't think I could take two hours of listening to Eileen," Jasper said with a malicious grin.

Janie laughed. "Now, Jasper, most men would be

able to be around Eileen and never hear a word she said, enjoying the scenery.''

"My hearing's too sensitive, I guess," he told her and added, "Oh, she's nice, but not my type."

Steve put in his two cents worth. "What you're saying is, 'What in the world will we do when Jeff marries the girl?'—isn't it?''

Jasper glanced at Ami before he answered, and she felt her cheeks grow hot. Jasper wasn't stupid by any means; nor were Steve and Janie. "She isn't anything like Myra, that's for sure," he said.

Ami waited for a break in the conversation before she mentioned the missing cattle to Steve and the odd marks in the soil.

"Remember, Ami, Jasper and Scully moved some to the holding area. Probably that group if you're missing so many."

Jasper thought about it for a minute. "Yes, we did take some with us the last drive up there, but I don't think we had more than two dozen of the Charolais."

"Did you notice any tracks or marks that you didn't recognize?" She described the odd figures in the soil near the canyon.

"No, but the wind was really high and it makes tracks like that coming down those canyons at eighty miles per hour."

"You may be right," she admitted.

Janie changed the subject. "Did you know Amanda is going to school full time in Tucson after Christmas?"

"For how long?" There was a sudden misgiving inside her as she waited for Janie's answer.

"She'll be there for a semester and won't be home before June. Just in time for the big wedding."

Ami went still, feeling her face drain of color. Somehow she had known. She swallowed. "I thought they would have a tutor come here for Mandy once she had been through the elementary steps of the therapy."

"Eileen wants her to have the best care, you know. That includes getting her away from the lowly influence of the ranch hands." Janie was watching her. Ami was sure her friend guessed some of what happened in Newark, although it was never mentioned.

Ami stood up. "Is Jeff at home today?"

"Yes. They're all having dinner at the house."

"Thanks for the lovely dinner, Janie. I'll see you all later." Ami's long strides took her the quarter mile to the ranch house in a few minutes. She contained the anger inside her as she detoured through the kitchen.

"Lily, how are you?"

"Ami, why didn't you eat with us? It's been a long time." Lily's face beamed at her favorite veterinarian.

"Business before your fattening dinners, Lily. Rio was at Sandoval's, and I ate with Steve and Janie." After a moment, she asked, "Is the boss through eating?"

"Yes. He and Miss McKane are in the living room."

"See you, Lily." Ami found her way through the long hall to the living room. Through the open door she could see Jeff standing near the mantel, and she stared, taking in the tall slimness, remembering things she tried hard to forget. Eileen lounged on the couch, a drink in her hand, very much at home. For a moment she considered turning around and leaving, protecting herself from the hurt she was courting just by talking to Jeff.

Ami's anger disappeared. She knocked, and when Jeff glanced up, she smiled. "Can I see you a moment, Jeff?"

"Come in, Ami. Can I get you a drink?" The dark gray eyes swept her figure and came back to her face. She felt heat in her cheeks, remembering his statement: *"I wouldn't want to be responsible for your being pregnant."* Had it been long enough for him to put his mind at ease? If anything, she was more slender than ever, always losing a pound or two when she was working the camps.

"No, thanks. I wanted to ask about Mandy."

"Sure." His eyes on her were disquieting. Since the night Mandy stayed with her she had seen him only once at a dance and, after that, she didn't go to any more when she thought he would be attending. It hurt, and she wasn't tough enough to face him as though nothing had happened between them. He might be able to ignore it, but she couldn't.

After a glance at Eileen, who regarded her with ill-concealed annoyance, she asked, "Why did you decide to send Mandy to school full time in Tucson? Why not a tutor here? The school will help you find a good one."

Jeff's hands went still on the glass. "The doctors think she's ready to advance to a full-time schedule, and, for that, they prefer her to stay there."

"I disagree." She faced him, realizing he could tell her outright it was none of her business. But it was. "You know she'll be better off here with you."

"And you?" Eileen's laugh was silky. The pale green velveteen dress, worth a small fortune, pointed out the delicate beauty in the tiny face, fitted over her rounded hips, accentuating the small waist. Ami felt big and awkward, not at all dressed to face the boss in her jeans and long-sleeved white shirt.

She turned resolutely back to Jeff, but before she could say anything, Eileen went on. "She'll be better off at school with people just like her and away from your spoiling."

Fury at her careless "people just like her" brought words to Ami's mouth she didn't dare utter. She didn't bother to answer Eileen.

Jeff's voice was mocking as he watched her discomfort. "You don't really know better than the experts, Ami. Besides, where's your loyalty? These are the people you assured me I could have faith in to do the best for Amanda."

"Yes, but let her stay here. I don't want her to stay up there all the time, alone." She was aware that it wasn't what she wanted that counted here, but she couldn't keep the pleading out of her voice.

"She'll be back the first of June, but I'll visit her regularly. So can you and Rio."

"No, Jeff, don't." For a moment he remembered the turquoise eyes bright with tears that she had never explained, and he straightened away from the mantel, taking a step toward her.

"She'll be home in time for the wedding. We plan to announce our engagement on Christmas Eve." Eileen was obviously enjoying her news. "You had heard about it, hadn't you?"

Ami's eyes rested on Jeff's face an instant, then she turned to face the woman. "No, I hadn't heard," she lied. "Congratulations."

Ami went to the door, looking back at them to say quietly, "I can see why you'd want Mandy out of the way for all your preparations. A child can put a crimp in things." She caught a glimpse of Jeff's outraged expression as she closed the door and ran through the carpeted hall, outside into the early darkness. She took a deep breath, but the tears came anyway.

She couldn't remember the last time she had cried like that. When Tim accused her of lying? Their separation? The divorce? A long time ago when dreams died. She didn't try to control the tears as she ran all the way home, glad Rio was still at Sandoval's; glad she could cry all alone. Remus waited on the porch as she ran up the steps and, too late, she remembered the doggie bag Janie had made for him.

"Sorry, fella." She patted his head as he followed her inside and went to sit by the window without turning on a light. She hugged herself, feeling the pain and frustration, not knowing if she cried for Mandy or for herself. When she convinced herself that Mandy was none of her business, she'd get along much better. It served her right for daring to fall in love again, especially with her boss, who belonged to another woman. Love is a fairy tale, best left to competent storytellers.

Hours later she stumbled to her feet, stiff from sitting so long, her throat dry from crying. She ran hot water in the basin, bathing her burning, aching eyes. The rumble in Remus's throat sounded just before the knock on the door.

"Who is it?" she asked, her voice husky from the tears.

"Jeff. May I come in?"

She stood in the middle of the room, feet apart, hands clenched into fists, but she didn't answer him.

"Ami?" The knob turned on the unlocked door, and Jeff stood across the room from her. One glance told her he was furious as he pushed the door closed, looking her up and down.

"Who the hell do you think you are that you know better than anyone else what's good for Amanda? Just because I slept with you doesn't give you license to tell me what to do."

Her head jerked and her body flinched as though dodging a blow. She stared, unable to speak, seeing the sudden realization in his eyes that he had hurt her. If that was his intention, he succeeded. The pain in her chest was so sharp that her doubled-up fist went automatically there to press against it, and she stared at him through a mist.

"I don't believe I deserved that." Her voice was a whisper. "But if I did, then we're even and you can leave now. I promise no more interference with Mandy.'' She walked into the bedroom, closed the door, and slid the double-lock bolt.

There was a moment of complete silence, then his voice came low and demanding just the other side of the door she leaned against. "Ami, open the door.'' When she didn't answer him, he repeated the order, finally slamming the door behind him as he left.

The hurt that filled her was unbelievable, but what had she expected? Jeff had taken the love she gave so willingly and used it as a buffer against his worry over Mandy. Somehow she couldn't find it in her heart to blame him.

She found the pills the doctor had given her after her divorce, swallowed two from the almost-full bottle, and went to bed, sleeping the sleep of the damned, turbulent dreams that left her exhausted. At five the next morning she got up, emptied the pills into the garbage, and without making coffee, dressed, whistled for Remus, and left the house. There were no lights on in the big house, nor at Janie's. Everyone was sleeping in late for the holiday, but her heartache went along for a companion as she rode toward the mountains.

It was daylight when she reached the area where the odd patterns decorated the arid soil, and she sat studying the marks before she shook her head and gave up. Steve was probably right. The mountain passes could turn eighty-mile-an-hour winds into machines that ruffled everything, even rock-hard soil.

Between her and the designs she inspected, Jeff's face came into focus, anger shooting sparks from the gray eyes, his voice a dagger stabbing into her as he reminded her of the night they spent together in Newark. They had slept together—that was all it meant to him, and it was up to her to wipe out the memory for her own sake.

Pushing thoughts of Jeff away from her, she stood looking around the vastness of the open range surrounded by distant mountain peaks. It would take weeks to round up the Charolais she knew were in the outlying areas, and she would need help from Carue and his men, probably from Jasper, too, flying over the places he could scan from the air.

She didn't return to the ranch but went on into Tucson for the Saturday night dance. It had been weeks since she had gone, but she was certain Jeff wouldn't be attending. With the upcoming engagement announcement, Eileen wouldn't put up with that.

She waited outside the grange hall till she saw Steve's truck pull in. "Hi, stranger." Janie hugged her.

Ami laughed. "Yes, two whole days since I've seen you."

Steve eyed her, wondering if she could possibly get any thinner. "Found any more tracks?"

She shook her head. "No, I gave up. It probably wouldn't make a very good pet anyway." At least they laughed with her instead of at her.

When band intermission time came, she was reluctant to join Steve and Janie. Singing love songs had been her substitute for tears more than once, her way of giving voice to pain. But this pain was too new, too raw. She wasn't sure she could do it right now.

Janie urged her. "Come on. We've missed you." She gave in.

Steve asked, " 'Crying Time'?"

She was glad her face was turned from him, but she didn't hesitate as she said, "Sure." Janie's clear soprano joined her in harmony, and she had to admit it sounded good.

Someone called "Old Flames," and their voices carried the message that a long-ago love was in the past, where it belonged, and would never hold a candle to the current flame.

Somewhere there must be a totally enveloping old flame to burn out the pain of the new.

Back at their table, Janie said, "Are you staying over, Ami?"

"I think I'll go straight to camp. There isn't any need for me to go all the way back to the ranch. Ask Jasper to bring Rio out to Camp Nineteen tomorrow or Monday, whenever he'll be out that way."

Janie sighed. "Why must you be so dedicated to your job? Well, okay, but we'll see you before Christmas, won't we?"

She laughed. "Yes, I guess so." As she left them, she realized it had helped a little to go to the dance. She needed all the help she could get and a little was better than none at all.

A chilly full moon hung over the mountain range to the west as she pulled up to the line shack nearest Camp 19. Smoke came from the chimney, and beside her, Remus growled low in his throat. It was then she saw the Bronco Jeep on the far side of the small building. Jeff. Had something happened to Mandy? Or Rio?

She hit the ground running, Remus beside her. The door swung open before she reached it, and Jeff stood waiting for her.

"Where have you been?" The hard voice brought her up short.

"What's wrong?" She held her breath.

"Nothing's wrong, except I've been here four hours."

"I thought Mandy—or Rio—" She stopped, weak with relief. Then, surprise in her voice, "You've been here four hours? How did you know I'd be coming here?"

"A guess. You were at the dance, weren't you? I expected you back earlier."

She was conscious of shivering, whether or not from the cold she couldn't tell. "May I come in? It's cold out here."

He stepped aside, closing the door as she and Remus passed him. She stood near the potbellied stove, holding out her hands to the warmth. "Why were you looking for me?" Their last encounter was still fresh in her mind and the hurt just as sharp.

"To apologize. I know what I said was unforgivable, but I hope you'll consider it anyway." His voice was low, sending vibrations through her body.

She stiffened. "Why should you apologize? Everything you said is true."

"No, Ami, it isn't true. I wish I could take back all the things I said, but since I can't, please let me apologize. Believe me when I tell you I'm sorry." She swallowed hard at the tenderness in his voice and stiffened.

"You've apologized; I accept." She turned her back to him. "Please go."

"I want to stay with you, Ami," he said softly. "Let me hold you the way I held you before."

She whirled, turquoise eyes staring in disbelief. "You're engaged. You can't."

"The engagement isn't official." If Jeff was ever capable of being uncertain, it was at that moment. It showed in the total absorption of his plea for her to listen to him, in the gentle expression in his eyes.

She shook her head. "No."

He didn't argue but watched as she stood belligerently in front of him. "I see you were right. You aren't pregnant, are you?"

Her head came up. "No, but don't push your luck."

"I came prepared this time." He reached for her.

She backed away from him, wings of fright beating inside her. However Jeff might be prepared, she wasn't, unprepared to give love that wasn't returned in full.

"Are you that conscientious, Ami? You don't really like Eileen. I thought you might welcome the chance to take what belongs to her."

She bit hard on her lips, hurting them. "I don't want what belongs to her. Whatever I am, I'm not a thief."

"If it were given freely?" Jeff was leaning against the rough logs of the wall, his eyes taking in the tall figure a few feet from him.

I should tell him I love him, she thought. *That would get rid of him in a hurry.* "Leave me alone, Jeff. I'll stay out of your way or, if you prefer, I'll resign."

He smiled at her. "No, don't resign, Ami. I'd have the entire cowboy population in Arizona to fight. Besides, you're a good veterinarian whom I have neither the time nor inclination to replace."

Yes, she thought, *Eileen is pretty demanding on your time.*

Dark gray eyes searched bright turquoise, taking in the withdrawn look, tilted nose, the leanness of her that he still remembered against his bare body. Long slim fingers locked together were ringless, and they had been bare long enough that the sun had erased any indication rings had ever been worn.

"What about your husband, Ami? Incompatibility meaning what? Not enough sex? Too many women? Or men?"

She hoped the pain she felt at the questions didn't show. "None of the above."

"What, then?"

"I don't want to talk about it. I promised myself I'd forget him and I have." Her eyes closed as she flinched away from remembering the price she was paying to forget him.

"If you can't bear to talk about him, you must still love him."

She got up and filled the coffeepot with water from the five-gallon jug of drinking water, placing it over the eye of the stove. She took the can of instant coffee she used when in the shack, and measured out enough for two cups. Pushing the crate around she used for a table and another crate near the stove, she sat down, drawing her knees under her chin.

"It will take a few minutes," she told him. "But if you insist, at least let's have coffee."

She took a deep breath. "Tim and I met my senior year in college. I was on my way to being a veterinarian, and he was well-established as coach and physical education instructor. His team had a couple of Olympic contenders in swimming and track. We dated a year till I graduated, got married, and I went on to graduate school."

She paused, got up to get the coffee, and brought it back, handing him an old ceramic mug. She didn't look at him.

"No children?"

Keeping her mind carefully blank, she shook her head. "No children. We had two years together, then Tim wanted out." She was beginning to have trouble with her breathing, but she went on. "I went to El Paso. Last I heard, Tim was still in Cheyenne and had remarried." She took a swallow of the coffee, grimacing at the bitterness.

"It couldn't have been so sudden that you didn't see it coming."

"Haven't you ever heard the old cliché 'love is blind'? I was."

"You didn't want any children?"

She shrugged, swallowing more of the coffee. "It just never happened."

The nightmare scene she thought left well behind her surfaced: Tim's disbelief when given the doctor's verdict that she could never have children; his final accusation that she was intentionally not getting pregnant because she didn't want to ruin her fashionably slim figure and be tied down to the house and a child; the weeks and months they lived in deadly cold silence; the divorce. Had it been another woman, she might have understood, but to condemn her for something she had no control over had been more than she could take.

"Are you all right?" Jeff was regarding her with curiosity as she sat motionless, looking into her empty coffee mug.

"Yes." She got up. "Want some more coffee?"

He handed her the mug. "There are a lot of eligible men around these parts, Ami. You don't have to be lonesome. You're a very pretty minority."

She smiled as she handed him the cup. "I'm not lonesome, Jeff. Someone else in due time, but there's no hurry." *When all my wounds heal,* she thought, *but I keep getting new ones.*

Neither of them spoke for several minutes, although she knew his eyes were on her. "Are you sure you don't want me to stay?" he asked.

She looked up at him. "I'm sure."

It was just daylight as he rose to go, and she walked outside with him into the chilly dawn. "Jasper and I are flying to Abilene to a cattle auction tomorrow. We'll be gone about a week." They stood side by side, looking toward the mountains to the east, where the sun would appear in a few more minutes.

"You spend a lot of time in these wild mountains, Ami. Seems like a pretty girl would get lonesome away from all the action." He looked down at her and smiled. "How many cowboys have asked for dates in the grange halls?"

She shrugged. "A couple."

He laughed. "I can imagine." The quiet went on until he said, "Why aren't you interested in dating, Ami, or am I wrong in thinking you don't?"

She watched the sky brighten over the mountain before she answered him. "If loneliness is what causes the need for dating, then I don't need it. I never get lonely." She wondered at his reaction if she told him of the many nights she remembered Newark and the times her body yearned for him the same as her wayward heart.

"You really love the mountains and desert that much?" He, too, watched the mountain rim. "I thought you were a little odd to want this job and figured you'd last about thirty days before you ran back to the city."

"Why did you hire me, then, if you thought I'd only be temporary?"

He turned to face her and put his hands on her arms, pulling her close before he said quietly, "I didn't hire you; Steve did."

The questions in her eyes turned the turquoise to dark shadows, but before she could ask them, he bent to place his mouth on hers, bringing her blood alive to sing through her veins and cause her heart to triple its beat. With an effort she kept her hands lightly on his waist.

He raised his head, smiling a little. "Bye, Ami. See you in about ten days."

"Good-bye, Jeff." She stood watching the Jeep bounce across the desert and said aloud, "You sometimes give a body more than it can stand, don't you, Lord?"

There was no answer that she could hear.

Chapter Eight

Work for Ami and Rio slacked as Christmas holidays drew near. They made sure the cattle were in protected areas and kept a close watch on the horses in the piñon-dotted aroyos near Camp 10.

Jasper found them one morning as they checked a herd of Charolais for injuries that might need attention. He left the truck a few yards away and strode to where they stood. Stetson pushed back on the salt-and-pepper hair, he grinned at the two. He carried two envelopes in his hand.

"I need a topographical map to find you guys," he said. "How's it going?"

Ami smiled and nodded as Rio stepped forward, hand out to Jasper, whom he hadn't seen since the Thanksgiving holidays.

"Are these the missing Charolais, Ami?" Jasper asked, glancing around at the healthy looking cattle.

She shook her head. "I'm really not sure if this is part of that herd, Jasper. I thought there were at least a hundred and fifty head. There's about a hundred here."

He laughed. "You should know now you can't account for each one every time. There are too many places to play hide-and-seek in these canyons." His dark eyes swept the expanse of desert and mountains around them. "They'll show up before spring when they get good and hungry." He handed her an envelope and one to Rio. "Jeff said to tell you the holiday officially begins the twentieth, and requests the honor of your presence at the Christmas Ball on the twenty-third."

Ami looked at the envelope in her hands to hide the tightening around her mouth and the look of dread that must be in her eyes. "Is today the eighteenth?" she asked. She knew it was—she kept a calendar in the small notebook she always carried in her truck and marked off the days, because it was easy to lose track of days and dates when you moved to your own time schedule.

"Yes, it is," Jasper said. "Late on the eighteenth, Ami. Can I help you finish up here?"

She shook her head. "We've finished, and there's only one place left to check. I can do that. Take Rio back with you so he can get a hamburger from Lily before he has to start eating all the holiday feasts. Remus, too."

Jasper laughed. "Okay, but are you sure you don't need help?"

"No, thanks, I can manage."

"I don't want to leave you alone, Ami," Rio told her.

Her eyebrows went up. "Nonsense. I've been alone before."

"But we could do the job faster if I stayed," he protested.

She smiled at him, knowing he was looking forward to seeing Nada after almost a month. "Go with Jasper and Remus, Rio," she said. "I'll bring your paint supplies from the shack."

"All right, but don't open the flat case," he said.

"Secrets from me, Rio?"

He grinned. *"Si."*

Good-byes said, she turned back to the few remaining animals she needed to look over, her thoughts going to the party. She'd rather not go, but Janie had said Jeff almost demanded each and every hand be there, and she was one of the hands.

Hearts had to go, too, she thought, a wry grin touching her mouth as she sprayed antiseptic solution on the forelegs and hooves of a huge steer standing placidly near her. The announcement of the engagement had been moved up to the twenty-third, she guessed, to allow for separate Christmas Eve activities. It didn't matter; her heart was already looking for a place to hide, and one day would make no difference in its success or failure.

Moving quickly, she reached the last sector just at sunset and finished the spraying as darkness fell. The solution would keep away most of the biting flies that could cause an infection in the animals before she came this way again. She looked toward the dark canyons and the perimeter of mountains once more, wondering how she had missed a spot that could hide fifty or more head of cattle. She knew Jasper was right, though, the area was a vast playground for animals to wander around. She headed for the line shack.

Instead of turning the little Brat truck toward Wagner's the next morning, she went toward Tucson. The old female complaint "I have nothing to wear" certainly applied in reality to her as far as the Christmas Ball was concerned. A shop for tall women had caught her eye the last trip she made into the city, and she found it again without difficulty, examining the styles displayed in the window before stepping into the quietly elegant shop.

"May I help you?"

Ami turned to face a young lady, tall and slim in her soft silk shirtwaist dress and Gucci slippers, and almost laughed as the girl's eyes went from her sun-streaked dark hair to the flannel shirt, faded jeans, and dusty boots. Her expression indicated she thought there was little to be done for her.

"Yes," Ami told her, straight-faced, with effort. "I need a long gown suitable for the holidays if you have a size seven tall."

"This way, please," the well-modulated voice said.

Ami followed the gently swaying hips to a partially enclosed section and blinked at the dazzling array of garments.

"Do you have a color preference?"

Ami thought for a moment. Eileen would be in some one-of-a-kind sparkling red or white outfit, she decided. Janie had a light rose velveteen. She had no idea what other wives and girlfriends would wear. She watched the dresses move beneath the girl's well-manicured hands.

"May I see that one?"

The slender hand hesitated at the dress she indicated and removed the padded hanger. It was a heavy silk jersey, the top lemon yellow with a simple rounded neckline that fitted to a tight waist gathered onto a skirt with yards and yards of material that was the same pale yellow shot through with gold. The long full sleeves matched the skirt.

"I'll try that," she said.

In the dressing room she shed her work clothes and boots, slipped the dress over her head, and zipped the back as far as she could reach before stepping outside to let the saleslady finish pulling it up.

"Very nice," the young lady said in a surprised tone, adding quickly, "We have lovely gold sandals that would go well with it."

Ami nodded and stood gazing at her reflection until the woman returned with the size she requested. Fastening the sandals, Ami turned in front of the mirror, mentally shrugged a "Who cares?" and said, "I'll take them."

The girl hesitated. "Will this be cash or charge?"

In the process of removing the clothing, Ami glanced at her in surprise and smiled a little as she reached for the billfold in her back jeans pocket.

"Cash. How much?" she asked.

"Two hundred and thirty-two dollars."

She counted, handing the money to the girl, and went on with her dressing. Her thoughts went to Mandy. What would Hazel put on her to fit the occasion of her dad's engagement and the Christmas holidays? Mandy had plenty of clothes, but Ami had no way of knowing if formals were included. Well, they should be, she decided as she left the shop with her purchases.

She stood for a moment on the street, enjoying the colorful display of decorations. She had read about the parade with all the stars and celebrities who had attended the start of the holiday season, and shook her head at what the pretty baubles must have cost.

Taking her time to window-shop, stopping to gaze at some of the elaborate displays, she came to the Tots Thru Teens Shop and went in. The woman who approached her smiling resembled someone's pleasantly attractive grandmother.

"Good morning. May I help you?"

Ami returned her smile and greeting. "Yes, I'm shopping for a six-year-old who is rather small for her age. Something for a Christmas party."

"This way, please."

They stopped at a rack of street-length dresses, a riot of color. Ami shook her head. "Do you have any long dresses in her size?"

"Oh, yes, over here."

The older lady stood aside as she went over the small garments, some part wool, some polyester, and some velveteens. A royal-blue velveteen dress with a white lace Peter Pan collar and long sleeves with matching cuffs caught her eye, and she took it from the rack. It had princess lines with a slight flair at the hem.

"If it doesn't fit her, may I return it?"

"Of course, ma'am."

Outside again, she looked for a restaurant, seeing one just down the street, and went inside, depositing her purchases on the booth seat beside her, realizing she was tired.

She was used to chasing cattle, not pounding pavement, she thought, smiling at the young girl who took her order for breakfast, which she hadn't bothered with before leaving the shack. Someone brought coffee, which she accepted gratefully, and she thought about the party, four days away.

She could break a leg and get out of going, she thought, but she had too much to do, getting Rio ready to start classes at school and, after that, getting the shipments cataloged for spring, all without Rio's help. It would be a gigantic task, but keeping busy was her aim, her only target that would keep her mind off Jeff, who would be safely married to Eileen in another six months.

Her breakfast came and she ate as her mind went on thinking of how she would get through the announcement of the engagement at the party with all the congratulations and best wishes for a boss everyone appreciated.

Just like everyone, she decided, hunching her shoulders. She would grin and bear it, not looking forward to the occasion at all.

It was late when she reached her cottage, and as she opened the truck door, was forced to greet Remus before she could take her packages inside.

"I just saw you yesterday," she scolded affectionately. "Settle down." He did, but then followed her inside to make sure she wasn't leaving him again.

The house was cold, and she turned on the furnace to take the chill off, stopping to light the kindling she had left in the fireplace to add to the warmth. She took her dress from the box and shook the folds out, placing it in her near-empty closet, and put the delicate-looking sandals on the shelf.

"Let's go and find Lily or Hazel, Remus, and see if they think Mandy's dress will fit."

She put a big log on the fire that had started and closed the screen. Picking up the box with Mandy's dress in it, she debated whether to take the Christmas presents she had wrapped to put beneath the tree, and decided to wait.

As her long legs carried her the quarter mile to the big house, she surveyed the area. Lights were already on at Janie's, and she heard doors slamming at the bunkhouse and wondered if Rio was at Sandoval's. Probably.

Heading in the direction of the kitchen, she looked up as the Bronco came around the side of the house, stopping a few yards from her. Jeff swung down and turned to lift Mandy from the seat.

Ami stopped in surprise, then knelt to meet the small figure running toward her. She put the box on the ground as she hugged Mandy. "When did you get home?" she asked.

"Sunday. I came home Sunday." In her excitement her words weren't plain and she used her hands to show her meaning.

"Super," Ami told her, taking her hand as Jeff reached to pick up the box.

"We plan to have a snack," Jeff said. "Will you join us?" His eyes went over her, unsettling all the arguments she had resolved to herself about her reaction when she saw him again after his last visit to her camp.

The resolutions dissolved, leaving her defenseless against her feelings. "Yes, thanks," she said, and added, "Hot dogs?"

He shuddered. "I hope not."

Mandy skipped beside Ami and, as they got to the porch, let go her hand to run inside. She spoke quickly to Jeff to explain about the dress and keep the subject impersonal. "I wasn't sure what Mandy had for the ball, so while I was shopping I bought her a dress, too." He stopped to look around at her, holding the door open, and she went on. "If you already have one, I can return it."

His hand on her elbow kept her from moving inside. "That was very thoughtful, Ami. I think Hazel had decided to let her wear a red skirt and blouse." He looked at the box he held and asked, "What color?"

"Royal blue."

"She likes blue." He released her arm as they entered the house and went to put the box on the dining room table away from the kitchen, where they were going to snack. Mandy skipped beside him as he returned, and Jeff detoured by the cabinet to get another plate. The three of them sat down at the small kitchen table by the window, which had been set for two. A plate of cold sliced chicken with rolls in a warmer had been left there by Lily, of course. Cheeses and tomatoes were sliced, and a dressing in a glass server was nearby.

Mandy touched Jeff's hand. "I want a Coke."

He shook his head. "Not this late, honey. Water only."

"Okay," she agreed, and waited for him to fix her plate.

Ami covered her mouth to hide the smile she couldn't resist, listening to the two of them. The smile disappeared as she wondered what Eileen would think of eating a cold snack in the kitchen with Mandy sharing her attentions from Jeff.

As they ate, Mandy talked and, occasionally, Jeff would look at Ami and wink as he answered the little girl.

Mandy pushed her plate away and turned to Ami. "Are you coming to our Christmas party?"

"Yes, I am. How about you?"

Mandy gave her a quick grin. "Of course." She sounded so grown up. "I have to be there to make sure I have enough room for all the things Santa Claus will bring."

Ami feigned surprise. "How do you know he'll visit here?"

Mandy turned to Jeff. "He always does, doesn't he, Daddy?"

Jeff nodded. "But you don't need anything this year. He may not stop."

Mandy's gray eyes widened. "All my clothes are too small, and my boots have a skinned toe."

"I could buy those for you," Jeff told her, but she shook her head.

"Santa Claus knows where to get all the things I need. You can just pay him." She yawned.

"Perhaps you're right, Amanda." He stood and reached for her. "Let's go find Hazel." He looked at Ami. "I'll be right back."

Mandy gave her a sleepy smile and waved. Ami remained at the table, chin in her hands, feeling a wave of emotion, almost feeling sorry for herself. After Christmas, Mandy would be in Tucson full time, seldom home except for holidays. She didn't see her much now, but then she wouldn't see her at all. It would be better that way; with the wedding in June, she wouldn't be seeing anyone around the big house very much. Her best bet was in the endless desert with her cattle; she knew her place, at least. She stood up and began clearing the things from the table.

"Lily will be back to do that." He looked her over again, smiling as he said, "May I see the dress?"

"Oh, yes." They walked into the dining room, and Ami picked up the box to untie the ribbon, opening the top to lift out the small dress.

Jeff took it from her, his hands going over the soft material. "It's lovely, Ami. Looks like it will fit her." He grinned. "One thing Santa won't have to worry about."

She smiled, too, relieved that he didn't think her out of place buying something for Mandy to wear.

"Let me repay you."

She shook her head. "No."

Jeff didn't argue but continued to watch her. "Do you have a date for the ball?"

She smiled at him. "Well, Jim Summers did ask me to visit his ranch for the holidays, and since I couldn't take off that much time, I invited him to your party. I hope you don't mind." Jim, a rancher from around Apache Junction, north of Tucson, was a regular at the grange dances.

Jeff frowned. "Jim Summers? He's old enough to be your father. I didn't realize you knew him that well."

"Only from the dances, but we've talked."

"Evidently," he said, his voice dry.

Ami asked quickly, sensing disapproval. "Do you mind? I can cancel without any trouble." Jim Summers had been a widower for several years, but even though he had issued invitations to her before, Ami never had considered them to be dates. She took those to be as serious as his regular offers of a job as his foreman.

Jeff looked at her curiously. "At this late date? How would you explain that?"

She shrugged. "Jim and I understand each other."

"Is Summers why you never get lonely?"

"He doesn't visit me in camp, if that's what you mean," she said sharply. "This will be the first time I've seen him other than at the dances."

"I'm sorry, Ami. I have no right to complain about who you see. I guess I was just surprised it was Summers." He glanced at the watch on his wrist, and she straightened, realizing he must have a date with Eileen.

"Perhaps you'll have Hazel try the dress on Mandy, and if it needs any adjusting, I can do it before the party."

"All right."

"Thanks for the food. It was a lifesaver, considering what I have at home." She turned to walk out the kitchen door.

"Ami."

She glanced over her shoulder to find Jeff a step behind her. He turned her around to face him. "In case I don't get a chance at the party, Merry Christmas." He bent and kissed her, his mouth lingering, caressing gently as her lips parted in surprise. He lifted her to his body for an instant and let go.

The warmth of the brief kiss sent her pulses racing, and Ami backed away, looking up at him. "Thank you, Jeff." She turned to leave the house, running across the yard to her cottage, running from the memories the kiss brought back, running from certain heartbreak that lurked around the corner. Did he ever think of Newark?

The dance was in full swing as she went into the large room where furniture had been rearranged and couples sat and talked or stood around in groups. Ami stared, surprised at the men in tuxedos, all colors, from the formal black and white to the wild paisley sported by Carue, of all people.

She blinked. *I guess I assumed they'd all wear jeans,*

she thought. She grinned as Janie and Steve joined her. "I'm not sure I'll recognize anyone in these outfits," she said.

"They'll all know you," Steve said. "Except for Janie, you're the prettiest thing around."

Janie punched him lightly in the chest. "You'd better say that."

He grinned. "I know." He turned back to Ami. "Where's Jim? I thought you invited him?"

"I did, but his favorite horse died and he had to go to the funeral," she said with a straight face.

Steve laughed. "I'm sure he'd have preferred a maiden aunt as an excuse rather than his favorite horse."

"But what really happened?" Janie asked.

"He called last night and said he had such a bad cold, he'd better not spread his germs around. He sounded awful."

Jasper came up to them, handsome as could be in a navy blue tuxedo, lighter blue shirt, and cowboy boots. Ami never failed to wonder what was wrong with the women that Jasper still ran around unattached. When she mentioned such a handsome bachelor on the loose, Janie told a story about a lost love while he was still in the military service. It was a shame Jasper and she couldn't get together and solve their heartbreak together, she had thought on several occasions. But neither had been able to break away from their personal chains, and they were good friends, nothing more.

"Merry Christmas, beautiful ladies," Jasper said. "You, too, Steve." He looked at Ami. "How come you're footloose at a shindig like this?"

"The same reason as you are," Ami teased. "I didn't get asked."

"In that case, come on and let's be lonesome together." He pulled her into his arms and waltzed her across the open space, making their way around the other couples trying out the small dance floor. Near a table laden with all kinds of food and drink, Jasper stopped.

"Let's feed our sorrow."

"Okay, but not much, this dress leaves no room for expansion."

He looked down at her. "Thank goodness it fits where it's supposed to." He grinned. "It was made for you."

"Must be the Christmas spirit," she said, raising her eyebrows. "It's already loosened your tongue."

Jasper leered. "Wait till I've had a couple of these, then watch out." He held up a small glass of pretty liquid. "If Harris mixed this, it only takes one to liven up the party."

They took small sandwiches and their drinks and moved to an empty seat in a corner. Ami's gaze went over the crowd, and she immediately wished she had kept her eyes on her plate.

Eileen was dancing with Jeff, her blond head under his chin. As predicted, she wore a sparkling white gown that displayed her charms to the best advantage. Her hair had silver and blue stars tucked into the shining strands. She was lovely; a glamorous woman who looked just right in Jeff's arms. Ami turned back to her plate and ate without tasting.

I should have had a cold, too, and stayed home, where I belong, she thought.

A small hand touched her arm, and she looked up into Mandy's smiling face. The royal blue of the velveteen gown touched off a sparkle in her gray eyes, and excitement added a hint of color on her cheeks.

"You're beautiful, Mandy," she told the little girl and meant it.

"My dad said you picked out the dress. Thank you." The husky voice from such a little girl, some of her words still not spoken clearly, almost brought tears to

Ami's eyes. What a blessing that she could hear so well now, and the therapy, even as much as she hated for Mandy to be so far from home, was extending the miracle to her speech. She could only be thankful, thinking of what might have been had Linda and Dave not been able to help. She was about to say something else when Rio joined them. She looked way up, thinking in surprise he'd grown a foot since they came to Wagner's. He wasn't wearing a tux, but had on a white silk shirt with dark pants and well-polished boots.

He smiled at each of them and turned to Mandy and bowed. "May I?"

Mandy looked up at him, her mouth open, glanced back at Ami, grinned, curtsied from the waist, and went into Rio's outstretched arms. Ami watched in amazement as they circled the floor.

"They do grow up, don't they?" Jasper remarked beside her.

"Yes," she agreed, her eyes still on the couple as others, too, turned to watch. Pride was deep inside her; pride at what Rio had made of himself and at what had been done for Mandy. She tasted the drink and looked at Jasper in surprise.

"Whew! You're right. Two of these, and I could outfly your plane."

They were laughing as Jeff stopped in front of them. "I see you two are enjoying yourselves," he said, smiling. As Ami looked up at him the gray eyes met hers for a moment, then went over the room. "I haven't seen Jim," he said.

"No, he didn't make it," she told him. "Jasper rescued me."

He looked back at her. "If you're through eating, may I have this dance?"

Jasper reached for her plate and glass. "Go with the boss. It's almost payday."

With Jeff's arms around her, she lost herself to the

feeling of being held closely against him without having to make an excuse for it. The fact that it was just a dance didn't enter into her thoughts as she moved with him, her body intensely aware of his touch.

He held her a little away from him and said, "The dress you bought for Amanda is just right and very becoming." He smiled. "So is yours."

She nodded and put her cheek closer to his chest without answering him. His outfit was dark gray with a white shirt, and he could have been any business tycoon enjoying his employees' Christmas party. But seldom did business tycoons use this type of occasion to announce their engagement. She stumbled a little, and he held her tighter.

"What happened to Jim?" he asked.

Ami explained briefly and he nodded, guiding her between and around the other couples on the floor.

What in the world am I doing here? she wondered, and her eyes met the cold brown ones of Eileen McKane as she stood with Steve and Janie, her chin in the air a couple of inches higher than usual to indicate her displeasure. *That's what I'm doing here,* she decided, *aggravating one Miss McKane,* and she looked up to smile into Jeff's gray eyes, holding his glance for several seconds until she was forced to look away. She was punishing herself, not Eileen. His arms tightened just as the music ended and he led her back to where the three stood.

Ami could almost see the angry tap of Eileen's foot as the five of them talked. Actually, Steve and Jeff talked. Janie's eyes glinted with laughter as she met Ami's glance and she winked. Ami pretended not to notice. Eileen stood it as long as she could.

"May I have a drink, Jeff?" He turned away and as soon as he was out of hearing distance, Eileen looked at Ami. "Jeff tells me he's missing some cattle." The brown eyes went over Ami, dismissing the holiday clothing as chain-store variety before she went on. "If you've searched everywhere, perhaps they were just overlooked." She shrugged to show her disinterest. "Oh, well, I'm sure his hands will find them before spring." Thus having had her say about lowly ranch hands, she went to meet Jeff.

Before Janie could make the remark Ami was sure would be forthcoming, Carue touched her arm and she was back on the floor. Hours later, tired and carrying the feeling of dread she had earlier in the evening, she waited for the announcement of the engagement to be made.

Hurry it up so I can leave, she urged Jeff silently. *I don't know how much more I can stand.* Mandy had come to say good night long ago, and Rio had left with the Sandovals. The sinking feeling in her stomach couldn't be from the drinks; she had limited herself to the one she shared with Jasper. Maybe she was hungry, she decided, and said to Carue, who was standing nearby, "Is there anything left to eat? I need a midnight snack."

They went to the table, still loaded with enough food to feed another party, and she took some cheeses on a small plate and rye bread she knew Lily had baked.

"Is that all?" Carue asked, filling the plate he carried.

She laughed. "If I ate all that, I'd have nightmares and I need my sleep."

"Plenty of time to catch up on rest and sleep. You're off work till after New Year's Day, aren't you?"

"More or less. I have a few things to do and I have to take Rio into Tucson and get him into his apartment before classes start."

Carue looked at her with interest. "I heard Rio wants to be a vet. As much as he loves animals, he'll make a good one some day. He's had the right kind of teacher."

She turned to him. "Why, thank you, Carue. I remember once—"

He put his hand up in self-defense. "I know, I know." He grinned. "I'm not wrong very often, though." It was as close as he would come to apologizing for giving her a hard time when she had first come to Wagner's and he had no faith in a woman veterinarian. She laughed and went on with her snack.

The band struck up a "good night ladies" type square dance tune, and couples swung around the floor. Surprised, Ami looked up and met Jeff's glance from across the room. No engagement had been announced. She didn't see Eileen.

A moment later she saw Janie and Steve speak to Jeff, and she and Carue joined them to say good night. Over the cheerful Merry Christmases and best wishes from everyone, she said her own and moved away with Janie and Steve, recalling for an instant the kiss she had received a few days ago.

"Did you drive?" Janie asked her.

She nodded. "I couldn't see walking in these shoes." Moments later she was in the small truck, heading home alone, still puzzled that the engagement had not been mentioned.

Chapter Nine

Christmas Eve. Ami lay still without opening her eyes, her first thought that of Eileen's remark about the missing cattle. It didn't worry her that Eileen considered ranch hands lower than the desert squirrels, but what did remain was the anger at her remark that indicated Ami was somehow to blame for the missing cattle at Wagner's.

She heard from Jasper that Eileen had purchased the property across the mountain from the line shack near Camp 20, and wondered about it. Jeff talked about adding it to his but had reconsidered because the six-thousand-foot mountain would split his property, making it more difficult to feed and round up his cattle. He didn't need it, anyway, he told Steve one day when they were discussing it within her hearing. She agreed; seventy-five thousand acres of land was enough for anyone. And when the two ranches were combined, what in the world would they do with all that land?

She sighed and slid out of bed. The engagement announcement must have been postponed for tonight, so it could be a more private affair. If she were the one getting the proposal, she would want it to be just for her alone. But she wasn't Eileen.

After gathering the packages she had wrapped days ago, she placed them near the door to pick up as soon as the big house stirred. The huge Christmas tree in the wide foyer already had bundles and packages underneath it as it sparkled with the red and blue decorations Lily and Harris had arranged on it. The items she had made during long dark hours in the line camps would be added for her favorite people at Wagner's.

Well, not all her favorite people, she admitted to herself. She had nothing for Jeff. If he didn't want her heart, then nothing else she had would suit the occasion.

Outside, she stood in the early morning sunlight, coat collar turned up against the chill winds off the snow-capped mountains in the distance. There wasn't a cloud in the sky. She loaded the packages in the small truck, whistled for Remus, and drove near the kitchen door of the big house.

As she opened the door she smelled the fresh coffee, but there was no one in the kitchen. She helped herself to a cup of coffee, placed it on the table, and went back to lug in the packages, taking them through the hall to the tree. She placed them around the other brightly wrapped presents and went back to her coffee, wondering absently where everyone was. There were lots of things to do before the big day. She rinsed her coffee cup, let herself out the way she had come in, swung back in the truck seat, patting Remus's head as he sat waiting, and headed for the camps.

Most of the day was spent rambling from camp to camp, wishing everyone happy holidays, sharing camp coffee with them. Some of them had been at the dance; some had not. No one mentioned the engagement of their boss, and it was not a subject she cared to discuss.

But the thought stayed with her as she returned to her cottage at dusk. Janie called and invited her over for a late snack, and she accepted, walking the long quarter mile in the dark. Lights winked from bunkhouses as well as the big house.

"Wonder what happened?" Janie asked as they went into the living room.

"When?" Steve asked, winking at Ami.

"You know what I mean. Why didn't Eileen make her big announcement last night? I thought that was to be the big item of the party."

Ami didn't answer, but Steve, who usually smiled at women's gossip, was puzzled, too. "She must be saving it for something bigger. I don't understand how she missed such a glittering opportunity with a captive audience."

"Did you know she had bought the O'Toole property, Steve?" Ami asked.

He shook his head yes. "Jasper said it was just recently. All that land for cattle to get lost in, in addition to what she already has."

"I'd better find Wagner's cattle before they wander across that mountain and she gets me for trespassing."

Ami didn't stay late. She was restless, wanting to get back to work, where she could sort out her feelings for Jeff in an attempt to force her heart to accept the fact that he belonged to Eileen, away from watchful eyes that might see the sadness inside her. The thought of Mandy belonging to Eileen hurt almost as much as the thought of her owning Jeff. She winced at the fierce jealousy she couldn't hide from herself.

Boxes and papers scattered around her, she sat in the middle of the living room, separating things Rio would need to take with him and discarding surplus items she thought he could live without. Rio was due in from Sandoval's any minute, and she'd have to wait to ask about some of the things before getting rid of them. She smiled, thinking of the Christmas present he had given her. The flat box she had been warned not to open had contained a charcoal portrait of her and Mandy sitting on the corral fence and Remus lying nearby. It was amazing to her what he could do with a piece of charcoal and paper, and she was prouder of that picture than the generous check given her by Jeff

or Christmas. All his employees received bonuses for
Christmas, and she considered it a nice custom as well
s a good tax writeoff for Jeff. She would just as soon
ot have had it, but it would go far toward paying for
io's schooling, which was just what she planned to do
ith it. There was nothing she needed that money
ould buy.

When the knock sounded, she was glad. It was time
io got in so they could plan their time to leave and
hat they would take. She had taken his apartment on
ption, and, if he liked it, they would be able to get his
chedule and move into the apartment in one day or at
ast a day and a half. Then she could pick up a few
upplies and head back, returning to a normal routine.

"Come in," she called. "Happy New Year." She
oked up, smiling, to see Jeff standing in the doorway.

"Happy New Year, Ami," he said, looking around
he cluttered room. "Going someplace?"

Where have you been? she wondered, but said, "Rio
. He starts college in Tucson this semester for some
lasses as well as preveterinary field training."

He nodded and turned a straight chair around, strad-
ling it, to sit watching her as she went on with her
ork.

She smiled up at him. "Thank you for the check."

"You're welcome." He watched in silence a mo-
ent. "The quilt you gave Amanda is beautiful. She
ves it and the book."

"I'm glad."

"Where did you learn your handiwork?"

"I had a roommate in college who could do anything
ith her hands. She taught me. I had lots of time to get
he hang of it when we weren't in clases."

"Until you married?"

She glanced at him but didn't answer. He stood up.
How long do you plan to be in Tucson?"

"No more than three or four days—whatever it takes

to get Rio's schedule set up and him into the apart
ment. Why?"

"Curious." He bent to put his hands beneath he
arms, lifting her to her feet, and turned her to face him
His hands slid up her arms, pulling her closer.

"Don't do this to me, Jeff, please."

"What? I only want to wish you a Happy New Year.

Her hands came up between them, pushing away
but he caught them in his, holding her close as he ber
to find her lips. She turned her face to his shoulder. H
held her, bending to slip an arm behind her knees and
lifting her, walked toward the bedroom.

"No, Jeff, I'm expecting Rio." She struggled to ge
free.

He stood her on her feet, tilted her head, and caugh
her mouth against his. She stood, not moving, as h
took his time kissing her, his mouth quiet and warn
over hers, as gentle as if she were a child. When h
lifted his head, her wide eyes looked straight up int
his, hurt turning them dark.

He couldn't read her expression; couldn't know th
frustration deep inside as she waited for him to releas
her. "Lovely, Ami, but cold," he said softly. He hel
her a moment longer, then let her go. "I'll be takin
Amanda into Tucson on the third. Can I buy you
drink while we're there?"

Bitter words came to mind that she wanted to hurl a
him, wishing she had the right to accuse him of takin
the easy way out with Mandy, giving in to Eileen be
cause she didn't want to be bothered with the chil
She bit back the words and told him, "We'll be busy.
don't plan to stay any longer than it takes to get Ri
into his apartment and check his schedules. The apar
ment is on option, and if he likes it, we'll just unloa
and I'll head back."

"I see." He waited, and when she said nothin
more, he said, "Bye, Ami," and was gone.

"Damn you." Ami touched her mouth, still throbbing in response to Jeff's kiss, drew in a sobbing breath, and turned back to her packing. By the time Rio arrived from Sandoval's, where he had spent most of the holidays, she was through packing and sorting and ready for bed. Rio was ready for a big adventure, and she wished him lots of luck, knowing how much she'd miss him.

At the school in Tucson almost everyone was still on holiday, but in the Registrar's Office, they found that all his classes had been completely scheduled and set up for him, and he was ready to start the semester on Monday of the following week. They moved his things from the truck to the small efficiency apartment, which Rio was proud of, his very first place all on his own.

"There's no need for me to stay, Rio, and I have plenty of work so I'd better get on back. If you need anything, call me."

Never demonstrative, Rio hesitated, then hugged her. "Thanks, Ami. I'll try; I really will."

She smiled. "I expect you to."

Liquid brown eyes surveyed the tall figure in front of him, a woman who had taught him to be a man when he didn't think he was ready, and he grinned. "I'll miss you."

Ami lifted her hand in a salute, turned, and ran down the walk. She could be at Wagner's before dark.

As she turned the pickup onto I-10 she was suddenly too tired to face the three-hour drive home. The holidays, plus the strain of waiting for Eileen's big moment to announce her engagement to Jeff, caught up with her. She pulled into the Best Western Motel they used after the grange dances and, as soon as she checked in, headed for the bar.

She wondered how Jeff had made out with Mandy.

She hoped she'd given him a fit; he deserved it. Poor little Mandy.

I should get absolutely skunk drunk and, even if I don't forget anything, I'll be so sick, it won't bother me, she thought. The second drink in front of her looked even better than the first, and she smiled at it, turning the pretty glass around.

"Is it a private party or can anyone join?"

Ami raised disbelieving eyes as Jeff slid into the booth across from her. She didn't speak.

"What are you drinking?"

"Piña colada."

"They'll make you sick."

"Hopefully drunk first."

Jeff looked from the drink to her. "Why?"

"Why not?"

The waitress came, and he ordered bourbon and water and another drink for her. Ami smiled at him. It was good, he already looked a little fuzzy. "You're going to aid and abet?"

"Yes. Maybe it will banish all your scruples and make it easier for me."

Turquoise eyes narrowed. "I'm not staying."

"Yes, you are. You know you can't drive after drinking three of those potent things. I'll cancel your single room and get us a double one."

She shook her head. "No." His gaze held hers, and she wet her lips, trying to look away from him but failing. The look in his eyes brought a storm of feeling into her, shaking her all the way to her toes.

The waitress came. Ami took a long drink. "Have you eaten?" Jeff asked, watching her.

"Around noon."

"Let's have sandwiches sent to the room."

"No, Jeff." She shook her head, suddenly afraid of being alone with him, knowing she was defenseless.

But he was already giving an order to the waitress.

Ami heard a room number mentioned, and he was pulling her up, leading her unprotesting through the lobby, balancing both drinks. "Come on."

She couldn't drive, but she couldn't stay with him. Her blurred thoughts made no sense even to her. Inside the room, she stood near the door as he placed the drinks on the bedside table.

"How did you get away from Mandy so soon and how did you find me?"

His tan face was grave for an instant. "I left Amanda at two." He shook his head and an uncertain look touched his eyes. "It was hard to leave her, but finding you was elementary. I followed you from the school to Rio's apartment, then here."

Ami moved to the bed farthest from him. Kicking off her boots, she sighed as she lay back. Heavy gold-tipped lashes lifted as he sat beside her. "Did you come prepared this time?"

"Yes." His whisper was against her temple.

Oh, Jeff, I love you so much. Why don't you know?

The knock was soft. "Room service."

Jeff got the sandwiches and brought them to her bed. "Here."

"I don't want any."

"Eat it anyway. Otherwise, you'll be sick." He pulled her to a sitting position and propped a pillow behind her.

They ate in silence, Jeff sitting on the bed with her. Surprisingly she didn't choke and felt better as soon as she finished. He watched as she wiped the last crumbs from her face. Turquoise eyes met dark gray ones for an instant, then she pushed the pillow away, turned on her stomach, and slept, unaware that he covered her, nor that he stood a long time looking down at her still figure before he undressed and got into the other bed.

Conscious of being in bed, fully dressed, Ami lay still. The inside of her mouth tasted like burnt woolen blankets, and the room was unfamiliar. Without moving she could see Jeff's outline in the next bed. Her head detached itself from her shoulders with a white-hot pain as she sat up and holding onto it with both hands, she padded quietly to the bathroom.

Bless you, she thought as she saw her toothbrush Jeff had brought from the other room. If only she had some aspirin now. She brushed her teeth, touched the silent light switch, and made her way back to her bed, sliding out of her clothes.

"Come here."

Startled, Ami sucked in her breath, reaching for her shirt.

"Leave it and come here." She could see he had raised himself on one elbow.

She shook her head, not sure if he could see her.

"Do you want me to come after you?"

"I can't."

"Sure, you can. Turn around, one foot in front of the other, and so on."

"Jeff, this is wrong." She stopped, unsure how to go on.

"For whom?" the quiet reasonableness in Jeff's voice confused her.

"Please." She stood, waiting, but he said nothing more.

With no will of her own, Ami moved to the side of his bed. He turned the covers back and she sat down, lifting legs that weighed a ton. He reached, pulling her farther into the bed, and gathered her against him, their naked bodies touching from head to toe.

"Don't you ever sleep in anything?" he murmured.

"No."

"I'm not complaining." She felt his lips against her hair. "You smell good." His movements unhurried, Jeff started at her head, touching her dark hair, curving his fingers over her ears, his thumb pushing her chin up so he could kiss her. "It's been a long time since New Jersey, Ami," he whispered. Parted soft lips moved as he touched them with the tip of his tongue and pulsed with the fire he roused in her.

"Kiss me the way you did the first time, Ami." His voice was quietly demanding what he wanted of her.

She made a soft sound of protest, but her mouth opened to his bruising kiss, her slender legs scissored between his. He cupped her head, keeping her mouth imprisoned, one hand coming from around her to caress her breast, staying there until the brown tip swelled and hardened for him, his hand moved downward behind her hips, forcing her even closer to him. His lips kept hers, taking the sweetness she gave as his right, his body absorbing hers, possessing her, leaving none of her heart to call her own.

"Ami, sweetheart." His breath caught against the hollow of her throat. "Love me," he demanded, giving her no choice.

She could do nothing else and she answered his demand with her heart, giving herself to him, greedily taking what would never be hers to keep. He called her name sharply and, at the hard thrust of his body, she cried out.

She knew before she opened her eyes that she was alone. How else do you explain total desolation? Turning, she saw the empty bed, not so empty as her arms and heart. She stared at the ceiling for a long time before she rolled her tired body out of bed.

In the bathroom was a note on motel stationery stuck to the mirror. "Ami: Drive carefully. Jeff." The handwriting was like Jeff. Plain and straightforward. He wasn't leading her anywhere she wasn't willing to go.

Her eyes went past the note to meet the wide-spaced eyes reflected in the mirror, and she closed them to keep from reading what was there for anyone to see. She bit hard on her lower lip, crumpled the note, and threw it in the wastebasket. Dressed, she sat on the side of the bed, thinking about Jeff, about Mandy, about Rio. Sighing, she gathered up her things, took a last look around, and closed the door.

Riding with the windows down, seeking to clear her muddled thoughts, Ami headed east on I-10, her beloved mountains ahead and to her right. It seemed forever since she left Wagner's to bring Rio to Tucson.

The sign indicating the beginning of Wagner Ranch came in sight as she topped a rise and she slowed, taking the first gravel road to her right. It ran parallel to the line of mountains, reputedly once Cochise's stronghold, and on to Camp 20. She stopped the pickup, got out, and wandered across the desert, envisioning the wagon trains of over a century ago, making their way across an endless sea of sand and mountains. She thanked heaven for those sturdy people who had left this for her.

She wished she had Remus with her. She smiled. He was the only other being who loved the desert as much as she did.

A few Black Angus cows chewed contentedly or stood in the shadow of the taller saguaro cactus. Two puffy clouds drifted toward the mountain peaks and, after observing their certain collision course, Ami walked back to the road. She could get lost out here and no one would ever find her. Somehow she was certain heartache was already there ahead of her, waiting. June was five months away, then what? Wagner's wouldn't be big enough for all of them after that. The whole world would be too small.

Her thoughts returned to the night before in spite of all her efforts not to think about what happened. If he could love her like that, then leave her without a word other than *drive carefully,* he wouldn't be apt to mind if she packed up and left. She'd better get back to the vet listings. Australia would be a good location. She didn't think Apache Junction was far enough away for her to survive. Aching with every move, she climbed into the truck and drove slowly toward camp. Carue and two other cowhands were the only ones there at that hour. Ami accepted the ever-present cup of coffee and, as she left, said, "Call in for me, Carue. I'll be out here for a day and a half, at least."

But she didn't stay. An uneasiness kept her on the move, through Camps 16 and 17, till she headed toward the ranch house on Saturday morning. She avoided Steve and Janie, taking a roan from the corral to ride into the desert east of the big house with Remus romping like a young pup beside her. She circled a several mile area, checking the cattle as she went, reaching home after dark.

Hungry, Ami glanced in the near-empty refrigerator without any luck. She shrugged. Lily's Sunday morning breakfast would make up for it. Sleep came as her head touched the pillow.

Awake early, Ami headed for the back door of the kitchen. Lily was there, and she could smell the coffee.

"Ami, I declare, you're so skinny." Lily clucked her disapproval.

"I'm starved. Fill me up." She helped herself to coffee and stood looking out the back door. "Is it going to rain, Lily? My bones ache."

"Or snow."

"Come on, Lily. I've got too much work to do for that." And too much heartache to be caged in the house. The last was only a thought.

Stuffed to Lily's satisfaction, she headed toward the corral. Charlie was nuzzling any animal that would let him and generally making a pest of himself. Swinging long legs over the gate, she went to pet him.

"Do you miss Mandy, Charlie?" Ami rubbed the

white spot over his eyes. "Me, too." Her throat ached, wondering again if she hurt more for Mandy or herself.

A shout brought her attention back. It was Janie and Steve, dressed in Sunday best on their way to church at the small mission over near Tombstone.

"Where've you been?" Steve asked.

"Earning my excellent salary."

"It's darned lonesome with you, Rio, and Mandy gone. And we haven't seen Jeff except in passing in ages." Janie was pretty in a black gabardine suit with pale pink print blouse, reflecting the color in her cheeks. "Don't forget the Valentine Dance; we don't want to miss that."

"Of course, I won't. Maybe I can scrounge up a new dress."

"Yeah, no jeans," Steve said.

Back in her cottage, Ami dug through her small store of material. In the bottom of the trunk, she found the picture of her and Tim she had tucked away—how many eons ago? She sat looking at the laughing faces—so happy, so young, so long ago. Slowly she tore the picture in half, then across again. One heartache down; one to go.

She found a piece of plain red cotton, but there was only a yard and a half. That wouldn't go far on her long frame. Inspiration came and she went to her linens, found a plain white sheet, and pulled it out. Her mind envisioned the pattern and she nodded. Gathering all the items she would need to complete her outfit, she loaded them into the truck. She could finish most of the dress in the line shacks. Satisfied with her plan, she went to work on her books, brought all the ledgers up to date and, with that out of the way, showered, slid between the fresh sheets, and heard a voice so close, she turned her head.

"Don't you ever sleep in anything?" The mind can be a dangerous, lone companion.

As time neared for the Valentine Dance Ami found herself looking forward to it. The dress turned out even better than she had hoped, considering her materials and working time. It had been a long time since she had attended either of the grange dances and Cotton-Eyed Joe and Cripple Creek would be fun if all the regular gang was there.

Darkness caught her before she reached her cottage on Friday evening. The big house was full of lights, as was Janie and Steve's place, but she didn't go near either. Somewhere in the past few days she had got a cold and her head was stuffy. She took aspirin and went to bed.

Still feeling the dragging effects of the cold on Saturday morning, she dreaded the drive alone to the dance. A call to Janie got a welcome to join them. She spent the day lying around, pampering herself with aspirin and hot lemonade.

At six Janie called to alert her that they were ready to go. "It's raining. Had you noticed?"

Ami groaned. "Maybe I shouldn't go."

"Nonsense. Do you good to get out. Besides, I haven't seen your dress. You wouldn't want all that effort to go to waste."

It wasn't Steve's truck but a sleek Mercedes that stopped by her door. Jeff's car. Ami was already running before she realzied it, and there was no turning back, although her heart was choking her. She seemed always to be at the point of no return, she thought as she slid into the front seat, where the door had opened for her.

"Greetings," Steve and Janie chorused from the back.

Her eyes met Jeff's, but a general hi was all that was expected of her. Jeff smiled at her the way he would any of his hired help and said, "The car will hold the road better in the rain."

General conversation went on around her, and Ami was glad. She didn't want to think at all, much less speculate on what the evening held in store for her.

It was almost time for a band break and, since Jeff was calling the dances, she hadn't had to be too careful. He had taken the time to tell her the dress was becoming. Ami knew it was. The white showed off her smooth tan. It had a plain sweetheart neckline with tiny appliquéd red hearts down the close-fitting bodice, and full skirt with larger red hearts around the wide circle swung just above her knees. She had touched her cheeks lightly with a tint and matched her lips with the same color. The dark cap of hair was brushed up and away from her ears, just long enough to frame her face.

Ami danced with the regulars, smilingly accepting their compliments. Her throat dry and looking for a drink, Ami skirted the crowd, digging into her handbag for aspirin. She murmured an apology as, with head down, she bumped into a solid form.

"Need some help?" Jeff asked.

On a swiftly indrawn breath, Ami looked up. "No."

"Steve wants you to join them in singing."

She shook her head. "I can't. My throat's too scratchy."

"Come on. We'll find him." Jeff took her arm. "Here. Take your aspirin with this." He handed her a glass of water, and she obeyed him, then turned with him to find Steve.

Back at the table alone with Jeff, she tried not to look at him. "Haven't seen much of you lately." His voice was teasing.

Her breath caught and she turned to see his eyes moving over her body, her slim waist accented by the tight band on her dress. When she said nothing, he said, "I thought maybe I'd pushed my luck too far."

She sat silent for another moment then, in a voice matching the lightness in his, she asked, "And if you had?"

Jeff went still, the smile fading from his face. Leaning his elbows on the table, he stared at her, eyes narrowed. "Are we in trouble?"

"We?" Her eyebrows lifted.

"I was there."

"So you were."

His voice roughened. "Answer me straight, Ami."

She surveyed him, gray eyes as serious as she had ever seen them, a questioning light in them demanding an answer. "I don't believe Eileen would look too kindly on your deserting her for your veterinarian at this late date. Let's drop it."

"The truth, Ami." The anger in his voice surprised her.

She gave in after another few seconds of silence and smiled into the angry gray eyes. "You're safe, Jeff. I told you before not to worry."

It was his turn to draw a sharp breath, and the look he sent her way was one she could only describe as disturbing. "Ami—" he began when Janie and Steve appeared.

"I know we're not supposed to talk shop, but how about those Charolais that wandered off, Ami?" Steve asked.

Jeff's head swung around at the question, but he waited for her answer. She shook her head. "They aren't in the northwest corner where I thought they were. Jasper and Scully are checking the canyons beyond that. Ed and Cecil are working the other side of Camps 17 and 18."

"How many are missing?" Jeff asked.

"At least fifty," Ami said.

His eyes narrowed. "Are they the ones you marked with clips?"

"Yes." She met his glance. "I've used clips on all I've branded."

"I'm not convinced that's an effective method," he said.

"Why?" she wanted to know.

Steve was watching him, too, but said nothing. "What's to prevent the removal of the clip and the ears healing so that rustlers could cover it or recut it in another pattern?"

"Rustlers?" Steve asked.

Jeff leaned back in his chair. "Eileen is missing about fifty head of her Charolais."

"Since when?"

"Last week."

Ami stiffened, "How are hers marked?" she asked.

"Clips in the ears as you use. Her foreman was impressed by your method and had her vet change from all brands to clips in the new shipments."

Ami's gaze went from Jeff to Steve as she recalled discussing the method with Ron Steward, Eileen's foreman on the Crooked M, and the interest he had shown. Ami didn't know he had started using the clips instead of the conventional branding. Eileen was probably unhappy at the influence she had on the man who worked for her.

"I'll get Jasper to fly over some of the lower mountain ranges next week," Steve said. "There are a lot of places they could be that we haven't been in yet."

Janie broke in. "Can we talk about something besides cows? I'm beginning to think it's the only subject Wagner people can manage."

The subject changed, but Ami's mind stayed on it and, long after she was in bed, she wondered about her cattle and the odd coincidence that Eileen, too, was missing some of the valuable stock. She sighed, thinking of Jeff's serious attention when she teased him about her being pregnant, wondering what he would have said had not Janie and Steve picked that time to return to their seats.

Chapter Ten

A week later Ami went with Janie and Steve into Tucson to the monthly grange dance. She had danced with Ben Caskey, the piano player, and was waiting for them to come back to the table when someone spoke to her.

"Ami, how's business?" It was Jim Summers.

She smiled up at him. "Hello, Jim." She motioned to the chair near her, and he sat down. She hadn't seen him since before the Christmas Ball, which he hadn't been able to attend. He was probably sixty years old, slim almost to the point of being bony, with iron-gray hair beginning to thin on top.

"Still happy at Wagner's?" Jim asked, dark brown eyes studying her.

"It's a good job, Jim."

"Not ready for a change yet?" he asked.

"What opening do you have right now? I don't think I'm qualified as a foreman."

He laughed. "I can always use another vet."

Jim didn't know how much she was tempted. When those cattle were located, maybe she'd get in touch with him, Ami thought, as he said good-bye and left her. It wasn't far away from Wagner's, but she had a feeling distance would hardly count no matter where she went.

She was quiet on the ride home, listening to Steve and Janie talking in the front. They had decided to drive back to Wagner's instead of staying over, and it was early morning when they got home.

"Jeff's home," Janie said.

Ami's heart misbehaved, but she said nothing, seeing the green Porsche belonging to Eileen also parked at the back.

"Guess our lady plans to stay the night," Steve said, his voice dry. But as they got out of his truck the door to the big ranch house opened, and they could make out two figures in the light from the house. A few minutes later the Porsche roared out of the driveway.

Ami said goodnight and went inside her house, leaning against the door in the darkness. Love Jeff, she did, but he was out of her reach; to even think about him was foolish, but what do you tell a heart that refuses to listen?

I have to leave, she decided. *The next time I see Jim Summers, I'll accept whatever job he offers me.*

The next morning she was sitting on the back steps with a cup of coffee, watching the sun make a brassy rim over the mountains to the east, when Jeff strode around the corner of the house. She had no control over the quickening of her breath. He wore jeans and a lightweight denim jacket against the chill of the late winter winds.

"Good morning," he said.

"Hello, Jeff." She stood up. "Let's go inside, and I'll get you some coffee." He nodded, following her into the kitchen.

Ami poured coffee into a heavy mug, smiling as she passed it to him. "At least sit down to enjoy it," she said, wondering at the early morning visit. Jeff was an early riser; perhaps he wanted someone to share his coffee with, and she was willing. It wasn't necessary that he know what his presence did to her.

He looked about to refuse, then sat opposite her,

pulling the mug of coffee to him. "Ami?" The questioning uncertainty in his eyes, along with something else she couldn't identify, kept her attention riveted on him. The cup of coffee must have had a lot of interesting qualities to hold his gaze so long.

Finally, he took a long breath and looked up at her. "Ami, it's time we talked." She met his look, her heart beating an abnormal amount of beats per second, but she said nothing. His mouth tightened as they sat looking at each other.

"Will you marry me?"

The question simply took Ami's breath and her body went stiff. The seconds ticked by, and the silence in the room seemed to echo through her head. Of all the things he might have asked, that question was furthest from reality to her. She stared at him, lips parted and eyes wide with shock.

He leaned forward and smiled at her, reaching across the table to pick up her hand lying beside her coffee cup. "I understand if you need time to think it over, but at least say something."

She wet her lips. "I—I—" She shook her head, but that didn't clear the jumbled thoughts zinging around inside it. "What about Eileen?" she finally managed to ask.

"She knows I planned to ask you to marry me. I told her last night."

Remembering the roar of the Porsche as it left the driveway last night, Ami could well imagine the outraged anger Eileen felt at having been told he planned to ask his veterinarian—a veterinarian!—to marry him.

Slowly she turned her hand inside his until their fingers intertwined. "You didn't announce the engagement at Christmas, and I wondered why it was never mentioned around the ranch. Was that your idea?"

He nodded. "Eileen and I have been friends all our lives, and I guess we sort of drifted toward an engagement." His fingers curved around hers. "Then you came along, and I found I wasn't ready to announce our engagement as we planned and I spent a lot of time thinking about you." He shook his head this time. "You were always ready to give Amanda attention, and when I needed you..." Jeff smiled at her as she blushed and looked away from him.

"You don't have to—" she started to say.

"No, I don't have to, but I want to, Ami." He dropped her hands and pushed his chair back from the table, moving quickly to her side, and reached for her. She stood up, and he pulled her into the circle of his arms. Her body trembled as she leaned against him, standing on tiptoe to bring her face closer to his. Head tilted back to look into his shadowed gray eyes, she watched the firm mouth come closer to hers and her lips parted against the warmth of his as he folded her to him. Love for him flowed through her, and behind closed lids she saw his face again as he demanded, "Kiss me, Ami."

He lifted his mouth just enough to whisper against her lips. "Does that mean yes?"

She nodded and pulled his head down to continue the kiss as his hands moved upward, exploring her body through the robe, curving under her small breasts, thumbs caressing the firm mounds.

She gasped as their lips parted, and he smiled down at her. "Soon?"

"Oh, yes, Jeff, yes. Soon." She rubbed her head on his chest, holding tightly around his waist. He turned her around and led her into the living room to push her down on the couch and sit beside her, holding her close, whispering, his hands stroking her shoulders and arms. Finally, he said, "Would you mind if it's a small wedding right now? If you want a big one later on, we could have two ceremonies."

She gazed at him, puzzled. "A small wedding is fine. Why do you think I need a big one?"

"Most women would," Jeff answered, smiling.

She shook her head. "Would everyone here be invited?"

He studied her face before he answered. "Not for the actual ceremony. Jasper can officiate, with Janie and Steve as witnesses."

"But I'd want Mandy and Rio to be with us," Ami protested.

He smiled. "Of course." He leaned against the back of the couch, his arm across her shoulders. "Later, we can have a reception where everyone would be invited. I'd have some mad employees and friends if I tried to get away with not having one. Perhaps Linda and Dave could be persuaded to take time off and fly out, too." He cupped her chin with his hand. "Dave called last night."

Ami sat up straight. "Is anything wrong?"

"No, but he wants us to bring Amanda back to check the grafting in her ears. She'll want you to go with her, and we can be married before we go."

She wasn't sure whether to laugh or cry. Jeff had asked her to marry him, and Mandy was doing very well, and her mind lay in total confusion. Swallowing hard, she thought of Mandy going through more tests and refused to believe that they wouldn't show that she was progressing at a good pace. But now, Mandy was hers to love freely, and Jeff—Jeff would belong to her the way he did in her dreams.

"Mandy's doing so well. I hope they find everything taking as it should," she finally managed over the uneven beat of her heart.

His reply was fervent. "I'll breathe easier when they go over her again." She sensed a hesitation in him before he went on. "Ami, perhaps you should stay near the ranch this week and not go out into the camps. How much work do you have unfinished?''

"It can wait, although I had planned to drive up that north slope above the shack at Camp 20 and look around for those Charolais. They have to be somewhere in those canyons not too far away."

His hands went to her shoulders, tightening there. "Leave it alone, Ami," he said, and she looked in surprise at the anger in his eyes. "That's the one place I don't want you to go."

"Why?" she asked.

"I asked you not to, Ami, and I want your promise."

She pulled away. "I don't understand why you want me to stay away from the camps. There's no danger there."

"If we're to be married Saturday, you'd better be doing some preparation." The anger disappeared from his eyes and he teased. "Or do you plan to be married in jeans?"

Ami was puzzled at his changed expression and, suddenly, a horrible thought occurred. He didn't know why Tim had divorced her, but she would have to tell him before she could marry him.

"I didn't know we had set such an early date," she said, unable to bring herself to volunteer the information to him right then.

"Dave wants to see Amanda as soon as possible, and I promised him we'd be there Monday. I want us to be married before we go."

She drew a sharp breath, trying to visualize belonging to Jeff after loving him so long without any idea that he returned her love. Steeling herself for his reaction to what she must confess, she reached to take his hand just as a knock sounded on the front door.

"Are you expecting someone?" Jeff asked.

She shook her head, pulling away from him to

straighten her robe and stood up to move to the door. She opened it to face Steve and Jasper. Surprised at the appearance of the friends at her door on an early Sunday morning, it was a moment before she smiled and pushed the storm door open. "Come in," she invited.

They hesitated an instant. "Is Jeff here?" Steve asked.

Warm color stung her cheeks. "Yes, he's here."

They walked past her and, uneasy for some unknown reason, she pushed the door closed and leaned against it. Jeff stood up, a questioning look on his face, but he didn't seem surprised to see the two men.

"I'll get you some coffee," Ami said and went into the kitchen. Puzzled at the visit of the three men she seldom saw all at the same time, she took mugs from the top shelf of the cabinet, rinsing them because they were never used and dust collected when things were stored anywhere in the desert. She poured the coffee, standing for a moment looking out into the bright sunlight of the late February day. Soon the weather would be in the high sixties and seventies during the day, sometimes dropping to freezing at night, but not often. Spring in the high desert was her favorite time of year.

She picked up the mugs and went toward the living room, pausing as she heard voices speaking quickly, sounding angry. Jeff was saying "I want to know who found them and why they weren't spotted a few days ago."

"They were put there as late as yesterday morning, Jeff, I'm telling you," Steve said, "because we were in there two days ago. It has to be an inside job for them to know exactly where to put them. A place we had already inspected and wouldn't likely to go back to any time soon."

"What about it, Jasper?" Jeff asked.

"No doubt about it," Jasper said. "I hate to admit it,

but the way things look now, someone could think Eileen was right, even though we know better.''

Ami's mind clicked with each bit of conversation and she walked back into the room, looking from one face to another as she handed the mugs of coffee to Steve and Jasper.

"You found the Charolais?" she asked and waited.

"Yes. In the blind canyon up from the shack at Camp 20, just across the ridge from Eileen's new property," Jeff told her.

"Eileen could be right about what?" She looked at Jasper this time.

He glanced at Jeff before he said bluntly, "She said you were responsible."

The dead silence that followed seemed to go on forever as the statement sunk in, and when she spoke, it was barely a whisper. "And you believe her?"

"No," Steve denied, "we don't. The evidence is only circumstantial, Ami, and we know it was planted to involve you."

Her lips were stiff. "What evidence?"

"The clips had been removed from the cattle and were found in the camp where you stayed last," Jeff said.

Her head came up. "You knew I'd be suspected," she said. Jeff started toward her, his hands outstretched, but before he could speak, she went on.

"What you're saying is that I masterminded the plan to take the cattle along with Eileen's, and when the search shifted to another part of the range, I'd be free to move them wherever I planned to sell them without fear of discovery until it was too late to stop me."

Jeff shook his head. "No, Ami, Steve told you that we know better than that."

Ami faced him, arms hugged around her trembling body as she asked, "Is that why you asked me to marry you?" When he hesitated, she looked at Jasper. "A husband can't be made to testify against his wife, isn't that right?''

Jasper nodded, his eyes turning to Jeff. Ami's voice grated. ''Thanks a lot. You've already decided I'm guilty.''

Jeff was in front of her, holding her arms. ''No, Ami, that isn't true and you know it. If Eileen goes to the Cattlemen's Association with charges against you, we'll have to answer them even though they're untrue.''

Turquoise eyes were wide with hurt as Ami stared into his face, remembering that he had not said he loved her, only that he couldn't stop thinking about her—thinking about his veterinarian turning out to be a cattle rustler. Her voice was dull as she said, ''I didn't rustle your cattle, Jeff, nor did I lend any assistance.'' She continued to look up at him. ''Your cattle can be identified easily from the others. The clips can be removed, but a flashlight with a simple infrared bulb can detect dye covering the ear. The same dye is sprayed on the hooves so when the cattle are shipped, the lights under the loading platform will show it, too. It's an antiseptic that helps keep insects off them.'' She turned away from him and walked to the window to stand looking out, and her voice was muffled. ''When I talked to Ron, I didn't mention the antiseptic dye because I assumed he knew about it, even though it's fairly new on the market. Maybe you should check some of the cattle that's supposed to belong to the Crooked M to see if they have dye on them.''

''Are you accusing Eileen of double-dealing?'' Jeff asked, watching her closely.

Ami swung around. ''Why not? She accused me. Does the difference in the name give her immunity? A pillar of the community against someone with a renegade Indian name like Whitelake that doesn't even belong to her.'' Hurt churned inside her. ''If you'll excuse me, I have work to do." Her eyes went again to Jeff. "The proposal wasn't necessary, Jeff, and I won't hold you to it."

Jeff looked at Steve and Jasper and nodded. The men turned and left. Jeff's arms came out to her, but she backed away, anger replacing her stunned feelings. "I'll leave as soon as I can get everything packed and send you an address when I have one, in case you decide to prosecute."

"No, Ami, you're not to leave. We're not accusing you of anything." His hands closed on her arms, pulling her to him, and he smiled down at her. "The cattle have been found, so there's no loss."

"You'll forget I'm a thief because you can recover your losses?" She shook her head, but he held her, one hand holding her head to his chest, his chin pressed to her dark head. She stayed a long time, thinking that fairy tales seldom come true in real life and her fairy-tale existence had been very short-lived.

Her hands came up, pushing him away, and she went toward her bedroom. At the door, she turned her head to look at him. "I hope Amanda will be all right." She had never called the little girl Amanda; it seemed too formal for such a tiny girl, but she'd better get used to thinking of her as a stranger. She closed the door of the bedroom behind her and stood listening, knowing that Jeff had not yet left the room.

"Ami," Jeff's quiet voice came from just beyond the door. "I know this is upsetting, but we can work it out together. We're not accusing you and surely you realize that." He waited, but she didn't answer him. "My proposal wasn't a spur-of-the-moment thing; it's permanent, and we're getting married as soon as we can." Again a moment of silence, then, "Honey?" the tenderness in that one word almost made her weaken, but she bit her lip, waiting.

Finally, she said, "It's all right, Jeff. I understand."

"I'll be back soon, Ami. Don't go out anywhere until I get back to you, okay?"

"Yes, Jeff," she told him, and she heard the outside door close as he left.

At least I didn't have to tell him why Tim divorced me, she thought and wondered why it was such a small comfort.

There was no one around to say good-bye to, and she was glad. What could she say? Janie would hear from Steve; Hammett and Lily from Janie. Ami tried to swallow the lump in her throat, but it grew larger, choking her. On the last trip to the little truck she looked toward the ranch house. The Bronco was gone, and she assumed they were checking to see if all the cattle had been recovered. Jeff would want to verify that the dye was on the cattle for identification, checking her out to see how far she'd stretch the truth.

Ami wondered for the hundreth time how all the rustling and shifting had been accomplished with the checking they had done in the past two weeks. Almost every one of Wagner's hands had, at one time, run down a trace of some kind on the missing cattle, coming up with very little in the way of evidence that would indicate what had happened to them. Inside help was needed to move so many cattle and leave nothing behind but a stray here and there. If she didn't do it, then who?

Ron Steward, Eileen's foreman, was the only person with whom she had discussed using the metal clips for cattle identification. No one had showed more than a passing interest in the method except him. She shied away from the thought that he might be involved in the missing herds, but then, she was a suspect, too. That drew her up short and she laughed aloud, a short, derisive laugh, accompanied by a shake of her head.

The boxes of books were loaded last, and the portrait

from Rio carefully placed on top. She looked around the house she had lived in for almost a year. It had been her first real home since Tim, and she refused to dwell on how much she would miss the people at Wagner's. She was a gypsy and would move her shallow roots elsewhere. Jeff could be pushed into the past the same as anyone else—if she were lucky.

One phone call was all she needed to make before her plans would be complete. She dialed long distance to Jim Summers's ranch in Apache Junction. A soft female voice inquired her business.

"This is Ami Whitelake from Wagner's Ranch. Is Mr. Summers available?"

"One moment, please."

"Hello?" The salutation was barked into the phone.

Ami identified herself, and the brusque voice changed. "Ami," he said. "Tell me you're calling about a job."

"As a matter of fact, Jim, I am looking for a job."

"Boy, do I need to hear that. Ralph Carter, my vet, broke his leg yesterday, and I'm in the middle of getting a herd ready to ship. When can you be here?" he asked.

"Wait a minute, Jim, let me tell you why I'm leaving Wagner's, then you can decide if you still want me."

"All right, Ami, tell me."

He let her talk until she faltered, and she was quiet a moment before he said, "What's wrong with Jeff, Ami? He usually has a lot more common sense than to believe that stuff." He went on slowly. "Sounds like Eileen's been using her influence to help things along."

"What do you mean?" she asked, surprise in her voice.

He laughed a little. "Well, my boys tell me she's jealous of Jeff's lady vet, and they usually carry pretty straight gossip."

She caught her breath. "Why would she be jealous of

me when they plan to marry in a few months?" But
that wasn't true anymore. Or was it? His proposal to
her was a put-up job, and he actually had no intention
of breaking with Eileen on a permanent basis. She
cringed at how she had been taken in so easily.

Jim was laughing. "Now, Ami, I don't try to figure
out lovely ladies and their peculiarities. Enough of this.
When can I expect you?"

"Do you understand what I'm accused of, Jim? A
quarter million dollars loss would upset anyone." He,
of all people, should understand the seriousness of the
charge Eileen had made.

"Wagner's loss is my gain, Ami, not the herd—you.
Let me tell you, he'd better have some hard facts to
back him or anyone else up if he comes looking for my
veterinarian with that kind of talk. Back to sensible conversation, Ami. How soon can you be here?"

"Tomorrow noon. I'd like to stop by the school and
see if I can make Rio understand what happened." It
was less than a hundred miles to Apache Junction from
Tucson, and the J&R Ranch was just north of there,
bordering the Superstition Mountains, subject of many
wild and woolly tales of disappearing prospectors hunting the rich caches of gold supposedly in the rugged
mountain ranges, some forty of them.

"That's great news. Think you can find me? You
turn left past the curve in the highway about ten miles
north of Apache Junction. There's a big white iron gate
with J&R branded into it. The house is a couple miles
inside."

"Thanks, Jim. I'll see you." She hung up and stared
at the phone, wondering if this were truly happening or
if she would wake up soon.

Locking the door behind her, something she had
never done while living there, she hung the key on the
nail beside the door and ran down the steps into the
bright moonlit night, sneaking away like a common

thief. Well, they should expect that of her. Ami opened the door of the truck to let Remus in the front seat with her and bit hard into her lip, determined not to cry.

She succeeded. As she drove through the open range country she loved and jealously considered her own, anger spread like fire inside. How could they even begin to suspect her? Jasper and Steve she had thought were very good friends, while Jeff— Well, Jeff was a different story. Perhaps she couldn't blame him, since Eileen was the accuser, a life-long friend, a respected rancher, in addition to being his fiancée, while she was only a maverick with a name like Whitelake.

The turnoff road to Camp 20 and her favorite line shack went off to her left, and her gaze followed the line of mountains standing like ghostly sentinels. Across that range was Eileen's new property, lying adjacent to the blind canyon on Wagner property where the cattle were discovered; cattle that hadn't been there for very long, according to Jasper and Steve.

Ami couldn't imagine why Eileen had bought that land. Jeff had talked about it ever since she had known him, hesitating because his property would be divided by the towering range of mountains, hard to keep an eye on unless he hired a lot more people.

The little truck skidded sideways as she slammed on her brakes and turned around in the middle of the deserted road, heading back to the turnoff to Camp 20, turning right into the familiar gravel road. She couldn't see Rio before morning, anyway, and she'd scare him to death if she went there in the middle of the night. The line shack was a good place to stop for the last time on Wagner property.

The dark outline of the small building came into sight, and she switched off her lights as the truck rolled quietly to a stop. Remus jumped out as she opened the door, walking up to the familiar building, sniffing around the steps. He whined.

Ami was reaching for a flashlight as she got out of the truck, and the whine surprised her. She stared at the closed door, wondering if the house was occupied. The clips they were using as evidence had been found there. Suppose the rustlers had come back for those clips?

"You're imagining things, Ami," she said aloud and walked up on the narrow porch, her boots making enough noise to wake anyone who might be sleeping there. The knob turned in her hand, and she let the door swing inward, holding her breath for a moment before shining the light inside. Remus trotted in, and she followed him, trusting that he would never lead her into a room full of enemies.

The kerosene lamp was where it always was, and she lit it, standing still to look around the room she had used so many times. It looked undisturbed. She shivered, realizing the temperature had dropped several degrees since she left Wagner's. A few minutes later she had a good fire going in the heater and put some water in a small pot she took from a nail on the wall.

The tea bags she left in a can were just as she had left them, and a little later she poured hot water over a bag in an old mug. She pulled the orange crate she used as a combination table and chair near the stove and went to pull the blankets from the bunk nearest the stove, shaking them to roust out any desert creatures that might be seeking refuge in them. Two tiny desert squirrels scuttled across the room and disappeared in the corner.

"Sorry," she said, spreading the blankets over the crate to warm them before she went to bed.

From where she stood, Ami couldn't see any signs of a search being made, but there was little in the cabin to disturb. Had the clips been left in plain view? How had they known to look for evidence in the shack used only by Camp 20 hands and her?

A weariness not associated with being tired filled her body. She had gone from the heights of happiness to the dungeons of despair in a few hours. It would be easy to believe none of it had ever happened.

Ami was spreading the blankets on the bunk when she heard the noise and glanced at Remus. He sat straight, short ears pointed forward, listening. The wind had changed and was coming from the north canyons, whistling around the shack. The noise she heard was a rumble, like thunder, but the night was clear.

"Sounded odd," she told the old dog. "Guess the wind is extra noisy tonight."

With the wind's icy breath, the stove wasn't putting out much heat, and she debated whether to take her clothes off to sleep or add more, finally giving in to the elements, crawling between the blankets with her clothes on. Just before she slipped into sleep, she heard Jeff's teasing voice, *"Don't you ever sleep in anything?"*

As late as it was when she finally slept, she was awake before daylight. The stove was still slightly warm from the fire she had banked not too many hours ago, and she stirred it to life with some of the dry wood stacked in the corner of the room. It didn't take long for the one cup of water she put in the small pot to boil, and she had a cup of black coffee as she refolded the blankets on the bunk, her mind going in all directions without finding an outlet. Although Jeff suspected her of the worst, he was willing to marry her to keep the trouble from being dragged through the courts, friend against friend, neighbor against neighbor. She smiled a little to herself. Just like the western stories she read when she was growing up and thought were so romantic. What was romantic about being accused of stealing your boss's cattle? And where was her rescuer on his white stallion? Still running around in his fairy tale, she guessed. Eileen would just as soon see her hung, the law of the land back in her fiction world of the wild, wild west. A thief in those days was worse than a murderer. Maybe beliefs hadn't changed that much.

Standing by the small dust-covered window, Ami finished the cup of coffee, used a precious bit of water to rinse out the cup, and placed it back on the orange crate used as table and shelf.

Daylight was beginning as she opened the door, taking one last look around before she closed it behind her. The air was cold, although the wind had dropped to only a breeze. Remus trotted around the corner of the shack and sat near her as she gazed toward the range of mountains between Wagner's and the O'Toole property Eileen had bought.

If there was any way across that peak, she was willing to bet that was how Jeff's cattle just happened to be found with some of Eileen's from her new land, Ami thought. What was she doing? Trying to say Eileen might rustle her own cattle to get even? Even with whom? With what?

"Very unlikely," Ami said aloud and walked to the truck. She started it, sitting with her eyes still on the mountains, letting the motor warm a little before she moved away from the shack. The questions continued to move through her head without answers but, nevertheless, were not to be ignored. Regardless if everyone at Wagner's thought her guilty and would stand by her anyway, she needed information for her own peace of mind. She flinched again at the realization that Jeff thought her guilty enough that he would marry her for her own protection—and his.

Straightening over the wheel of the little truck, she sighed and pulled away from the shack. A few feet from where she started, she changed from the direction of the well-traveled road heading back toward the ranch, turning instead down the trail she had been over many times, going into the foothills of the mountains.

She drove through a dry-wash creek bed where she had first seen the odd tracks and followed her own tracks a few hundred yards, stopping where she usually did before the cattle were moved for the winter. Sitting for a moment, she got out of the truck, Remus beside her, and walked across the rough terrain, through small piñon and dried sagebrush. For several moments she stood looking at the forbidding peaks, then changed her direction slightly to the north, crossing the dry-wash again as it curved into the mountains.

It had been several weeks since she had been this far into the area, and her examination of the hard soil showed no signs of the foreign marks. She bent forward a little as the ground inclined sharply and paused at the top of the crest to look over both sides. The sun was peeking over the mountains in back of her, but there was no warmth to it and she shoved her hands into her pockets to keep them warm. The line of Wagner's property went about where she was standing, but she turned back and walked on up the mountain, angling across it to get a better footing. At this elevation the scrub piñon were only large twigs, and she used them to pull herself along as her footing became more precarious. Topping another rise, she stopped, looking to her left where the canyon ran along the mountainside and disappeared from her sight.

If you could get a truck this far and head into that canyon, she thought, and let the idea drop there. She could never get her small truck to pull itself up the steep sides to get into that canyon, much less...

A rumble sounded ahead of her, and she looked up at the clear sky, frowning. Remus, sitting nearby, growled and stiffened, short ears pointed forward as he, too, listened. She watched in astonishment as a big sixteen-wheeler lumbered around the bend in the wash, inching slowly along the base of the mountain peak, close enough for her to read the huge blue letter-

ing on the side of the silver vehicle: INTERSTATE MOVING
AND HAULING.

Curious disbelief rooted her to the spot, and, suddenly, it registered. In one of the Tucson papers not
many weeks ago she had read about a gang operating
out of the northwestern states, using trucks to rustle
cattle. At the time she had shaken her head at the
ingenious means people would go to, taking chances
to get money without working for it. Her gaze rested
on the giant-size tires with tractorlike treads as she
stood transfixed by the sight she saw but scarcely believed. The truck stopped, and the doors on each side
opened to reveal two men who were looking up at her,
and she realized, too late, she was in full view of
them.

"Remus," Ami commanded sharply and turned,
running surefooted along the ridge until she was forced
to follow the incline downward, skidding and sliding as
she tried to outdistance the men she knew were following her. Her size and speed were on her side, but as she
neared her truck she saw that one of the men had cut
across another ridge and was between her and any avenue of escape. Ami made him work for his victory,
turning away from him, back toward the small piñon
trees. He made a flying tackle, and they went down
together. She came up fighting, her nails reaching for
his face. It wasn't skin she contacted, but a ski mask,
hiding any identification of the wearer.

They were both breathing hard and, suddenly, the
odor of sour sweat and tobacco was familiar. The man
holding her laughed.

"Well, well. What do we have here?" He held her
shoulders, her arms caught in back of her.

The other man came up to them. "I don't believe
it," he said. "Our little tiger. Where's your friend?"

A chill of fear shook her as she recognized Hank and
Luke, Rio's harassers from Douglas many months ago.

Remus sat in front of them, growling, showing his teeth, waiting.

"Down, Remus," she ordered, and he sat still, the growl still low in his throat.

The man standing in front of her removed his ski mask, revealing the bearded face she recalled as belonging to Hank. He grinned, showing tabacco-stained teeth.

"And what are you doing out in this deserted country, my lovely?" he asked.

Ami didn't answer him, her mind busy as things began to fall into place. All the happenings in the past several weeks began to make sense. Valuable cattle disappearing with no clues as to when or where, and everyone assuming they'd be located in the spring roundup. They wouldn't be. They had been stolen. No wonder Jasper didn't spot them from the plane; they were in a big semi, hidden from view, possibly in that blind canyon.

Luke held her in a viselike grip, and she knew better than to struggle. She kept an eye on Remus, almost reading what was going through his scarred head. If they hurt her and she made an outcry, he would attack, but she had seen the guns they carried, and she wasn't planning to tempt them to use the weapons. She shook her head, trying to wake up if it was a nightmare she was in.

"What are we gonna do with her?" Luke asked.

Hank eyed her and grinned. "We have plenty of time, since no one knows we're here." He moved toward Ami. "I suggest a little fun before we get on with the business at hand."

She cringed, realizing what was on his mind. She started talking. "We've been looking for these cattle for weeks," she said. "I didn't know you could drive a truck through here, not to the other side of that mountain."

"You just have to know how to handle a big semi, sweetie." Hank laughed. "Of course, knowing someone who owns the land and has a mind bordering on being crooked helps." He took a step nearer. "Ron mentioned Wagner's veterinarian, but he never mentioned she was a lady, a very pretty lady." He grinned into her face.

Ron, she thought. Ron Steward.

"You mean you've taken cattle from Wagner's and the Crooked M?" she asked, stalling for time.

"Well, a little here, a little there. It all adds up to a good bit of change." He was enjoying himself as he toyed with her. "Ron and Miss McKane seem to think you're overstepping your territorial rights, and they intend to put a stop to it one way or another. If you get accused of stealing your own cattle—"

"Hank, you'd better shut up," Luke told him, his arm tightening around Ami.

But he had told her more than enough. Eileen and Ron were involved. How much and how far she didn't try to guess. Jeff would never believe her, anyway, not on the say-so of two crooks.

Hank still stood in front of her, leering, his eyes going from the dark tousled hair to the tight jeans he could see beneath the jacket she wore. He reached for her. Outraged anger dictated her next move, and she suddenly kicked out, catching him in the thigh with her boot heel, and as he grunted and stumbled away from her, she went limp, sliding from Luke's surprised grasp. Ami rolled away from him, coming up to see Remus spring at Hank, who crouched a few feet away, his gun leveled at her. The shot made no sound other than a muffled thump, and she saw Remus fall. She threw herself sideways as the gun was aimed at her again, saw a flash of light, and felt the heavy shock in her side. There was no pain, but she couldn't move and lay still, waiting for whatever they planned to do.

"Damn it, Hank," Luke muttered. "We weren't supposed to use any guns. I told you to leave them in the truck. I ain't wantin' to serve no murder charge."

"We're already into it far enough for a long jail term if we're caught, so we make sure we don't get caught. Soon's Steward finds out we really took the cattle instead of just moving them like we're supposed to do, he and his boss-lady will be after us, anyway." His laugh was nasty. "Miss McKane ain't no fool and she won't stand still for a double cross, you can bet on it."

"What do we do now?" Luke asked, looking down at Ami.

"Leave her and get out of here. These cattle will keep us in beer a long time."

Their movements were blurs to Ami until she heard the truck start and move along the canyon, heading for the wash that would take them out onto the state road that intersected with Interstate 10. She lay still until the sound vanished and stillness closed in around her. Looking straight up into the clear blue sky, she guessed it was nearly noon. Jim Summers would be looking for her about now. She rolled over and grunted as she struggled to get her left arm from beneath her. It had no feeling and didn't respond to her efforts. Remus lay several feet from her, and she gazed at the still figure for a long time. Once she had given him a new lease on life, and he had tried with all he had to repay her.

If she intended to get out of this mess alive, she'd have to move and somehow get back to the truck. If she stayed here until it grew dark and much colder, she'd freeze. Ami began the struggle to make her way back to the little truck, fairly close by, but seeming miles in the distance. She looked back at Remus and saw him move, struggling to get up. Without hesitation, she turned, moving inch by painful inch toward the old dog.

Chapter Eleven

Jeff stared at the door Ami had closed behind her after giving him a look that said volumes. Indecision gnawed at him, but he finally left when she refused to answer his pleas, feeling that she needed to be alone to adjust her thinking to all that had happened in such a short time.

Outside, he turned to look back at the house, strongly tempted to go barging into her bedroom and hold her again if only to reassure her of his love. Shaking his head, he walked on to the big house, hurrying the last few steps as he heard the phone ringing. Lily turned as he went down the hallway. "It's Amanda's school, Mr. Jeff," she said, and looked worried as she handed the receiver to him.

"Yes?" Jeff asked, already apprehensive. He listened to the voice on the other end and said, "I'll be there by noon. I'd rather see her before you give her any medication." He hung up the phone and stood there. Problems never came singly. Amanda had a severe cold, and they wanted to know if they could give her medicine for it and, by his own rule, they never gave her anything without his approval.

"I'm going to see Amanda, Lily, and I'll probably be late getting back. Nothing serious, but I haven't seen her in over a week, so I'm going in."

Lily nodded, wondering what else was bothering the

boss. He was not a worrier, but something other than Amanda's cold had his attention.

On his way toward Tucson Jeff stopped by the airstrip to see Jasper, glad to see Steve's truck there, too. They came out to meet him, and he explained where he was going.

"Keep an eye on Ami and don't let her go near the camps. We still aren't sure where the rustlers are, nor if they have plans to come back for the cattle. You might make a couple of runs over that range today, Jasper, to see if anything's moving."

"I could fly you into Tucson, Jeff," Jasper offered.

He shook his head. "I'd rather you keep an eye on things here."

Jeff left them, taking an uneasy gut feeling with him, something not quite right, as though he had left out something important somewhere. When he reached the school, Amanda was fretful and feverish, and he sat with her until she went to sleep around eight thirty that night. Deciding against returning to the ranch so late, he checked into a motel and called Steve.

"Everything's quiet, Jeff. Ami hasn't left the house all day, and I've had to fight Janie to keep her away from there. Aside from the fact that I'll probably end up in a divorce court over this, I guess we can wait it out."

"I'll be home as early as I can tomorrow," Jeff promised.

He hung up the phone and dialed Ami's number. After the tenth ring, he replaced the receiver. She could be sitting outside, as he knew she loved to do, or down at the corral, walking off the worry she must be feeling. Exhausted, he went to bed to fall into a restless sleep.

Monday morning, Jeff checked on Amanda and found her in much better spirits, even though still coughing. "I'll be back Saturday and bring Ami. Would you like that?" he asked. He would have to cancel the appointment with Dave in Newark until her cold was gone.

Mandy grinned, nodding vigorously, and let him go with a big hug. Jeff's throat tightened as he left the little girl. Ami was right—she belonged at home. As soon as the rustling episode was resolved, he'd have the school locate a tutor for her, one who wouldn't mind living on an isolated ranch. Ami, he thought suddenly. Ami would be better than anyone else. What better than a combination mother and tutor? It sounded good to him and brought his thoughts back to Ami. She thought he had asked her to marry him to protect her if she was tried for rustling, and his first job was to convince her she was wrong. He had only one reason for asking her to marry him, although chances are he had gone about it in such a way that he was going to have to start over. He would have to convince her that his proposal came from his love for her; love that he had discovered many weeks ago.

It was a total shock to him to find that, after they left Newark, he was letting Ami fill his thoughts day in and day out. Even as he worried over Amanda's chances of having at least partial hearing and the fact that she would have to live away from him while attending the special school, he carried a lighthearted feeling when he saw Ami from a distance or occasionally ran into her at the grange dances.

Much to his own surprise, he balked when Eileen insisted they announce their engagement at the Christmas Ball and flinched as he remembered her accusations against Ami. They had the party, but no announcement had been made, although he knew most of his employees expected it.

Try as he would, he hadn't been able to gauge Ami's feelings for him. Even after the night in each others' arms in Newark, she had been friendly, not overly so, her turquoise eyes showing him nothing. Then, when he maneuvered her into staying with him in Tucson, he had sensed that her feelings somehow were as strong as his when she responded to him so completely. He still reeled when he thought about it. The love she gave him that night left him with a deep satisfaction, and he was biding his time before he asked her to marry him, a little sorry when she let him know she wasn't pregnant at the Valentine Dance. Mingled love and desire for the slender dark-haired girl caused him to straighten behind the wheel of the Bronco, and he pressed his foot harder on the gas pedal. She needed his assurance that he loved her and didn't believe her to be a thief, and he could give her that without any trouble at all.

The trip from Tucson had never taken so long. Not bothering to stop in the yard of the big house, Jeff drove on to Ami's and muttered an oath of disappointment when he saw the small truck was not in her yard. His stomach muscles knotted as Steve and Jasper came to meet him.

"Is Amanda all right?" Steve asked, but the expression on his face held Jeff's attention.

He nodded. "Ami?"

Jasper answered. "She's gone, Jeff. She was here when we went to bed around ten, but when we got up this morning, she was gone. She took most of her things."

He stared at them, swallowing over the uneasiness filling him. "Did she leave a note?"

Both men shook their heads. "Are you sure she took all her things? Even her books?" he asked.

"Yes. Everything."

They stood there in the bright midmorning sunlight. Jeff drew in his breath. "She'll go see Rio before she does anything else. Let's call him."

As they entered the house Jeff raged inwardly at himself for the way he handled the situation, failing to convince Ami that he believed her innocent and leaving her too soon afterward to deal with her thoughts alone.

I wouldn't much blame her if she didn't want to talk to any of us, he thought as he dialed Rio's number. He smiled as Rio answered at the other end of the line and, after pleasantries, asked, "Is Ami there, Rio?"

"No. Was she coming up here today?" he asked. "I hope so. There's some questions I need to ask her. You want her to call you if she does come by?"

Jeff thought quickly about excuses for Ami being in Tucson. "She was going for supplies, Rio, and I just thought she might stop by to see you. There was something I needed her to pick up for me and thought maybe I could catch her at your place. If she does drop by, ask her to call. She may not have time to visit you, but just in case."

"Okay, Jeff."

Jeff hung up the phone and turned, shaking his head. "Where else?"

"Jim Summers was after her to work for him," Jasper said. "He made her a great offer, I heard from some of his men." He waited, but neither of the other men commented. "I can't believe she'd go through Tucson and not stop to see Rio."

Jeff thought a moment. "If she went that way, I should have met her somewhere between here and Tucson. I stayed at the Best Western last night, the one where we usually stay, so she didn't stop there, either. Of course, we don't really know when she left here." He walked to the window. The winds from the snow-capped mountains were cold, and he thought of the cabin where Ami usually stayed, where she spent most of her time. The cold, dry air agreed with her, leaving tanned cheeks with a light tint from sun and wind, but he didn't want her there alone anymore. Nowhere alone.

He looked over his shoulder at Jasper and Steve. "I'll wait by the phone if you'll take a run over that canyon, Jasper." He grinned a little. "You'd better try to pacify Janie, Steve. All we can do is wait."

After they left him, Jeff stared out over the land he knew and loved—a vast emptiness that he knew Ami loved almost as well. He had heard her comment on the beauty around them many times in the eleven months she had been his veterinarian—and a competent one at that. It was hard to believe she had been there so long, and even harder to think of the ranch without her. It had been five months since he first made love to her in Newark, a few days after a soul-shaking kiss he had tried to ignore. It was nearly two months since they shared a night of love in Tucson. Where the hell was his mind all that time? He grimaced, remembering the look on Ami's face as he told her Eileen was planning to bring charges against her for rustling some of her cattle. He hadn't been too reassuring, only warning her they needed to hear her statement that she wasn't involved. He had never suspected her, but he hadn't said that to Ami, not in plain words. He had said— He stopped, trying to remember what he had said, but instead, remembered her soft voice, trembling as she said, "I love you, too." Had he assured her of his love? Jeff couldn't even remember and shook his head at his own ignorance. He had few occasions to mention love since he lost Myra and didn't care for the people who used the word without thinking of real emotions that should go with it. Eileen was a life-long friend, and it went without saying that he loved her, whether the all-consuming kind or not. It might have proved to be enough for an enduring marriage between them had Steve not hired a tall lady veterinarian with strange turquoise eyes.

Standing by the window, his thoughts racing like sand in the wind, he forgot Steve and Jasper. How had the cattle become mixed? How many were his and how many Crooked M stock? Ami said— What had she said? *"Has the difference in the name given her immunity?"* Eileen wouldn't deal him an underhanded blow such as rustling his cattle and some of her own to divert suspicion, he was sure.

Jeff recalled the glint in her eyes as she hurled her bomb on Friday night. "You think your veterinarian is such a treasure. I have proof that she is in with rustlers and taking stock from both of us."

"What in the world are you talking about?" he asked, not bothering to hide his disbelief.

Eileen was furious at his scoffing question. "Ron suspected Ami and went to that line shack she's always supposed to be in. There were hundreds of the clips she uses on the cattle that had been removed from my herd as well as yours." When he only stared at her, she went on. "I'm filing charges against Ami on Monday."

Eileen had the upper hand at that moment, and she knew it. Jeff had gone looking for Ami on Saturday, but she had gone into Tucson to see Rio and from there on to the grange dance. Eileen came over late Saturday night to gloat and to bargain. If he got rid of Ami, she'd drop the charges. That was when the explosion resulted as he told her he planned to marry Ami. From then on it was war between them, and his only wish was to protect the woman he'd asked to marry him.

Jeff started as the phone rang, moving toward it before the first ring was half completed. He picked up the phone to become instantly alert when he heard Jim Summers's name.

"I've been trying to call Ami, Jeff," he said. "But there's no answer at her house. Has she left to come up here?"

"Why would she be going to your place?" Jeff asked, fingers tightening around the phone.

"She finally accepted my job offer and she said she'd be here by noon today. When she didn't show, I thought maybe you'd come to your senses and talked her into staying on with you." After a moment when Jeff made no comment, he went on. "I'm prepared to offer her more money to keep her from staying with anyone who'd accuse her of stealing."

Jeff stiffened and his voice was hard with anger. "Who told you I accused her?"

"Ami. She seemed to think I ought to know what charges might be brought against her before I hired her, in case I had any doubts."

"And you didn't?"

"Never will have, Jeff, no matter who accuses her. Now, do you have any idea what time she left there?"

For a moment Jeff was tempted to hang up on him, but they had been friendly acquaintances too long to jeopardize a potential ally.

"She left here sometime during the night, Jim. She hasn't been to see Rio, and we don't know where she is." As he spoke the unease from the early morning returned. Trying not to let his fear show, he said, "To be on the safe side, I'll call Archie Denton, the sheriff in Tombstone, and have him run a check on some of the side roads. In the meantime we'll alert the camps in case she shows up there."

Jim Summers hesitated. "Do you suspect foul play?" he asked finally.

"Everything until I have her back," Jeff said.

Jim Summers grunted. "You forget, Jeff. You don't get her back."

"I haven't forgotten anything."

He heard the other man's indrawn breath. "Let me know if you hear anything, and I'll do the same."

Jeff hung up the phone and turned as Jasper and Steve came in. "Did you get through to Carue and the others?"

"Yes."

"Let's drive out to Camp 20 and go to the line shack from there."

"Why Camp 20?" Steve asked.

"It's the only one they could leave from and possibly get across that range of mountains without being seen."

"Not very likely that they could," Jasper said.

"No," Jeff admitted. "But let's check anyway." He turned to Steve. "Call Denton and tell him as much as you have to, that it's only suspicion about cattle being rustled and worry over Ami. Keep a good watch here." His smile was grim. "I imagine Janie wants to know what's going on. You may as well tell her everything, as limited as our information is." He looked at Jasper. "Let's go."

Carue's camp of hardworking cowhands was still out on the range, but the hard-bitten old trail boss came out to meet them. He looked at Jeff and Jasper and opened the door to let them walk into the cabin ahead of him.

"No word?" he asked quietly.

Jeff shook his head and gave him as many details as he could. The older man's jaw set in a hard line. "You mean to tell me you accused Ami of rustling her own stock? She's been checking for weeks, running herself ragged trying to cover seventy-five thousand acres of wilderness, and you have the nerve—" He stopped, sputtering.

Jeff listened to him then said, "We don't suspect Ami, but Eileen is bringing charges, Carue. She has more head missing than we do and the ones that have been found are on Wagner property just across from the O'Toole ranch she bought. You know when a charge like that is made by a rancher, it has to be checked out."

Carue snorted and didn't think of Jeff's feelings as

he said, "Why don't you just throttle Eileen, since she's the main source of trouble?" He looked sourly at Jeff. "I guess you assume Ami ran away?"

"No, I don't, Carue. She's either still looking to see how the cattle crossed that mountain range or—" He stopped.

Jasper spoke into the silence. "Where are a couple of your men we can take with us? We don't want to wait too long and not be able to see."

"Ed and Cecil are the closest. You can pick them up at the south end of the canyon that runs back of the Camp 20 line shack," Carue told him.

Carue walked outside with them, staring at the ground as they got into the Bronco. He looked up as Jasper started the motor. "Ami could figure she'd had enough of your accusations and just went somewhere to think it over. I wouldn't feel too friendly toward somebody who thought I'd been stealing from them. Would you?" His voice challenged his boss to answer him.

Jeff smiled a little as he agreed. "No, I probably wouldn't, Carue. But we told Ami as much as we knew and to stay put until we got some answers ourselves. We weren't trying to drive her away from Wagner's, but wanted to be sure she was protected."

"I hope you find her and aren't too late with your protection," Carue said.

Inside, Jeff cringed. Carue had put into words what he had tried to keep out of his mind. "So do I. We'll keep in touch."

At the end of the canyon they found Ed and Cecil and explained what they wanted. The two men silently unsaddled their horses, placing the equipment near a fence post and tethering the horses several yards apart. They removed rifles from their packs and carried them, barrels down, as they walked to the vehicle where Jeff and Jasper waited.

Before he climbed into the back of the Bronco, Ed asked, "Do you for one minute think Ami would be behind something like this?"

Jasper sent a long look at Jeff as he said, "No." He stopped there, figuring, rightly so, that he didn't need to say any more. The men with him had condemned Eileen before he was half through with his explanations about what had happened, and it would take a self-admission from Ami before they would believe the worst of her.

The Bronco took the hills and rough terrain easily, and they still had a good deal of daylight left when they topped the ridge above the shack. There was no sign of life from that vantage point, and Jasper drove slowly down the hill and around the building to the closed front door.

Jeff was out and moving toward it before the Bronco was fully stopped. He turned the knob slowly, letting the door swing wide before he stepped inside. He knew the men behind him had the rifles pointed at the building, just in case. He turned and motioned, and they came at a run. They stood looking around the almost bare room at the neatly folded blankets on the end of the bunk, the coffee cup turned upside down on the orange crate, and the oil lamp with the wick turned down. Jasper moved to the stove, lifting the eye to look inside and put his hand down into the ashes.

"She's been here, or someone has. The ashes aren't completely cold."

"Come on," Jeff said.

Outside again, they looked for tracks. Cecil, at the back of the shack, called. "She might have gone on down this trail. Look." He pointed to a mesquite bush that had been pushed to the side by pressure such as would come from a tire running over it. A little distance away, a small ridge of sand showed a definite tire print.

"Does that go anywhere in particular?" Jeff asked, looking to see if tracks were visible any farther from them.

"It goes into that north canyon that leads up the mountain toward the O'Toole property," Ed said. "We were in there about two weeks ago and picked up some of the strays we had been looking for. Not many. You can't go any farther that way. Turning around and going out the other side is the only way to cross over that ridge."

"Let's go," Jeff said, and they climbed into the Bronco. He pointed toward the canyon Ed had described and Jasper guided the vehicle along ridges and mounds until they came to the peak that separated Wagner's and the new Crooked M property.

Shadows were beginning to lengthen from the mountains when Jasper stopped. Ami's familiar Subaru Brat truck stood several hundred yards away from them on a slight ridge, and it took only seconds for them to pull up beside it, the men out and moving before the engine stopped.

Jeff's hand gripped the door handle of the truck and his knuckles whitened as he looked inside to see Ami crumpled on the seat with Remus on the floor, her left hand curled into the thick fur of the old dog.

The door on the opposite side opened, and Ed stared at the two still figures. 'Damn it all," he said quietly.

Jeff had opened the door he held and leaned forward to put his hand on Ami's throat. The pulse barely fluttered. He said, without turning, "Get Carue on the radio and have him contact Med-Evac out of Tucson. There isn't much time." He straightened. "Tell Carue to call Archie Denton, too, and alert all patrols state-wide."

The grimness of his voice penetrated the shock the men were feeling, and Cecil moved toward the Bronco, hoping he could raise Carue over the highest of the peaks between them and camp. Sometimes the atmosphere was too rare for them to make radio contact at this elevation.

Jasper had returned to the Bronco to pull a blanket from the back and handed it to Jeff, who spread it over Ami, letting some of it cover Remus. As he tucked the edges around her, his fingers touched the stiff shirt where blood had soaked through and dried. Carefully he unzipped her jacket and folded it back to see the dark stain beneath her left arm. He rezipped the jacket, putting her arm along the seat so that it would be covered. He touched Remus. The old dog was breathing—barely, but breathing. He couldn't see where he had been injured, but the hair on his foreleg and shoulder was matted with dark red.

After one brief glance at Ami's face, Jeff had concentrated on getting some warmth into her, but now his gaze returned to look at the dark cap of hair, full of sand. He pushed strands away from her cheek, turning her chin with his fingers. Gold-tipped dark lashes lay fanwise against the light tan of her face. The short upper lip was swollen and a reddish brown streak of blood went from the corner of her mouth over her chin.

He looked up as Cecil came back to the truck. "Carue'll get back to us as soon as he can."

Jeff nodded. "The helicopter probably won't be able to get in here after dark, Jeff," Jasper said. "We'd better try to take her back to camp."

"I told them to land in the clearing near the shack," Cecil said. "The wind's died down; they shouldn't have any problem there." He stood looking at Ami, long legs hanging partly off the seat. "How are you gonna get her out of there?"

"I won't move her. I can sit over on the side and drive the truck," Jeff said. He got in, careful to move her legs only a little, and sat on the edge of the seat.

"You follow me," he told Jasper, "in case I have trouble and have to stop."

They drove slowly back to the clearing, and Jeff looked down to see that Ami hadn't moved. Neither had Remus. Their stillness was frightening, but he turned away to step from the door of the little truck. Jasper came toward him, carrying a wide plank he had dragged from somewhere back of the cabin.

Carefully they lifted Ami from the seat of the truck onto the plank, each holding their breath as she moaned. Jeff held her so she wouldn't roll off, and they carried her inside, where Ed had relit the fire and oil lamps. Behind them, Cecil came, carrying Remus, placing him near the stove.

"Turn the lights on in the truck and the Bronco," Jeff told them. "The moon will be up enough to give them some light, but they'll need something to pinpoint the clearing."

Ed and Cecil left to figure out the angle they could aim the lights to be most effective. Jasper took one look at Jeff, sitting close to Ami, holding her hand, and turned to Remus. The old dog whimpered as Jasper straightened his bent front leg. He poured water into the small pan and put it on the stove to heat. As it simmered, he took a handkerchief from his pocket and bathed the shoulder that had been hit by the bullet.

"This is a clean wound," Jasper said. "I think he'll be all right." He was talking to hear a sound of something. He couldn't endure Ami's stillness nor Jeff's silence, wondering what was going through Jeff's mind as he sat watching Ami, unaware of anyone else in the room.

He would have been shocked at what was going through Jeff's mind. He was calmly killing the men who had done this to Ami. Jeff had never hated anyone; not even in Vietnam. Conditions, yes; people, no. Now he hated, clearly and coldly; he hated whoever was responsible. And blamed himself. He should never have left her, not even to go to Amanda. He should have taken her with him; should have made her go immediately into Tucson and marry him the first day it was possible. They could have had a big reception later at the ranch, at which everyone could have celebrated. His chance might not come again.

His hand, holding Ami's, tightened, and she moaned, turning her head restlessly. Jasper handed him a towel he found and wet it in the hot water. Jeff took it, wiping her mouth gently. The blood was dried too much to get off without force, and he stopped trying, letting the damp towel remain on her lips a moment at the time.

Jasper knelt beside them. "Her jacket is torn and full of dirt and trash." He brushed at the sleeve and turned to look at Remus. "That must be the way she got him to the truck, dragging him." Jeff stared at him with blank eyes and shook his head.

"It's hard to tell what happened," he said.

Ed came to the door. "The chopper's coming." He looked for a moment at the disquieting scene on the floor of the shack and added, "We built a fire on each side of the clearing. That should help the pilot see a little better."

Jeff nodded. "Good idea." As he spoke he heard the uneven beat of the chopper blades in the thin mountain air. "Get another blanket, Jasper, and let's make sure she stays warm."

Jasper had already moved to the bunk and was holding a blanket near the stove to warm it. He wrapped another one around Remus, who was trying to get up.

"Never mind, boy," Jasper said. "She's all right."

"If they have room, put him in there with her," Jeff said, looking up as two men entered with a stretcher between them. He stood, letting them take Ami without a word. Jasper lifted Remus and looked at the men.

"Got room for another passenger?"

The young man, looking to be in his early twenties, looked at the shaggy animal Jasper held. "I don't think we have any vets at the hospital," he said, "but we'll take him." Evidently someone had filled them in on the details of the reason for their trip, because he didn't sound surprised to find there would be an extra canine passenger.

The four men watched as the still figures were loaded into the helicopter, and as the aircraft lifted straight up from the ground, leaving a whirl of dust and sand, they turned to the fires they had started, methodically covering them to prevent any danger of spreading.

As they walked in silence to the Bronco, Jeff said, "Let's get back to the ranch and fly into Tucson."

They stopped to let Ed and Cecil off near their post, where they had picked them up many hours before. "We'll let you know whatever we find out," Jeff promised them. "I appreciate your help." He slumped against the door as Jasper headed for home.

"I don't understand, Jeff," Rio said, standing stiffly in front of him. Jasper had gone to pick him up as soon as they arrived at the hospital. The boy's eyes were dark, frightened pools as he waited for a logical explanation. That anyone would harm Ami was beyond his imagination.

Jeff tried to keep his voice even so Rio wouldn't sense the fear he felt for Ami. "We suspected some cattle had been taken and told Ami to stay away from the isolated camps, but she must have gone back there for something and ran into rustlers unexpectedly."

"But why would they shoot her?" Rio turned away and walked to the window, his shoulders hunched as if against the cold wind still whistling out of the mountains.

Jeff didn't answer. A white-coated figure came into the room, stripping a white mask from his mouth.

"I'm Dr. Barry," he said, cramming the mask in his pocket.

"Jeff Wagner, Dr. Barry. This is Rio Lawson. Miss Whitelake is his legal guardian."

The doctor grunted, but he wasted no time. "I operated to remove the bullet from her side and she's stable now. However"—here the bushy brows raised half an inch—"we have shock and pneumonia to contend with." He leaned against the wall, his eyes on Jeff. "We'll know more in about twenty-four hours. She'll be in intensive care until further notice." He straightened from the wall. "Does she have any family?"

Jeff shook his head, a cold knot choking him. He thought briefly of Tim as he faced Dr. Barry, voicing the hardest question he had ever asked. "What are her chances?"

The doctor's face was grim. "Loss of blood and shock could be fatal," he said. "She has youth and good health on her side."

Rio's swiftly indrawn breath drew Jeff's attention. The boy was deathly pale beneath the brown skin, his fists clenched at his sides.

The doctor went on. "As I said, we won't know much for a few hours. There's a coffee shop on the first floor." He started out. "Someone will call you in case of any change. Check with the nurses' station if you need anything."

Jeff glanced at the impersonal face of the standard hospital clock. It was ten thirty on Tuesday morning, and the doctor said it would be twenty-four hours before he could tell much about Ami's condition.

"Come on, Rio, let's get some coffee."

Rio's voice was muffled. "I'd rather stay here."

"They'll call us if there's any change. We need to move around."

Rio followed him, footsteps dragging. Jeff sympathized, his own heart heavy with dread of the next few hours.

It was four in the afternoon before Jeff put in a call for Steve. "Still no change. Dr. Barry was around a few minutes ago and, though he says her vital signs are stable, he's very noncommittal about her chances right now." He looked around at Rio, who leaned against the wall near the phone booth. "Rio's here, and I haven't been able to talk him into going home."

Worry edged Steve's voice. "I can't blame him, although I know he can't do any good there." He was quiet a moment. "I'd better call everybody. The guys are driving me and themselves crazy." Jeff smiled a little as he agreed and hung up.

Rio was asleep on the couch, and Jeff sat in one of the bigger chairs, his head against the back of it, when a nurse came in at six the next morning.

"Mr. Wagner, Dr. Barry is in with Miss Whitelake. She's conscious."

Rio sat up, looking from one to the other. The nurse went on. "One of you can go in for five minutes."

"You go, Jeff," Rio said.

Jeff didn't argue. He went down the long hallway and turned to the right, where the intensive care unit was. Ami's room faced the south and the blinds were open. His first thought was: She'd like the view. Her beloved mountains stood guard as far as the eye could see, the sun not yet putting in an appearance. He looked at the bed and his chest tightened. Tubes entered her body in countless places; blood dripped into one arm, clear liquid into the other. Tubes drained from her nose and mouth. The right eye was lacerated and swollen, and there were purple welts down her cheek to the cracked lips.

Jeff was glad Rio hadn't come in.

He wanted to touch her, but there didn't seem to be

anywhere to touch that wouldn't hurt. Her left hand lay palm up, and he laid his fingers across it.

"Ami?"

The purplish lid lifted, showing a hazy turquoise shadow. "Hello." It was just a whisper.

"Jeff?"

"Yes."

"I want to see Rio."

"Dr. Barry said no visitors, Ami."

"It's—it's important." The tip of her tongue touched the feverish lips. "Just one minute. I need to tell him." Her fingers closed over his hand. "Please, Jeff."

"Okay. I'll be right back."

Rio was at the window, shoulders slumped forward, staring at nothing. "Rio."

Startled, the boy straightened.

"She wants to see you."

When Rio didn't move, Jeff said impatiently, "She won't be awake long. Come on." He hesitated as the boy followed slowly. "Rio, listen. She looks bad, but she'll be all right." He pushed Rio into the room and backed away to wait outside.

I wish I could be sure she'll be all right, he thought.

A few minutes later he looked up as Rio came out of the room. Added to the shock in his face was something else. As soon as he spoke Jeff felt the anger in him. "She knows who it was."

"She knows them? How?"

Rio shook his head. "Not really. I mean, we had a run-in with them in Douglas on our way out here. Because of me."

Jeff waited, but he gave no more explanation. When Rio spoke again, he had changed subjects.

"She wants me to sketch pictures of the men and give them to you for the police."

"You mean a composite picture?"

"I can do it from memory."

"How long will it take you?"

Rio drew a deep breath. "A sketch in an hour. Probably a couple more to make it worthwhile to the police."

"By tonight?"

"Yes."

"Take a cab home and call me when you're finished."

"She went back to sleep. If she wakes up again—"

"If there's any change, I'll call you," Jeff promised.

The hours dragged on, and Ami rallied from time to time, but was never fully conscious. Every few hours Jeff was allowed in for five minutes to stand looking at her, frustration seething inside him. Her lips, cracked and dry, moved at times and once he thought she whispered his name. In memory he traced the full lower lip with his own, touching the curved upper lip, the tilted nose, and remembered the eyes with a sparkle of tears—laughing eyes as she romped with Amanda and Charlie. He looked at the slim outline under the sheets, feeling again the bare warmness of her against him, the questioning thrust of the tip of her tongue. She would hate the plain white hospital gown.

His eyes moved back to her face to find hers wide open and staring.

"Ami?" A half-smile tilted one corner of her tortured mouth, and he felt her fingers move in his hand, then they were still again and he was all alone.

Steve and Janie were in the waiting room when he went back. Steve spoke first. "We couldn't wait. Jasper flew us up. How is she?"

Jeff shook his head. "Not much change. She opened her eyes, but she hasn't said anything since she talked to Rio about the pictures."

Janie's voice was teary. "What do the doctors say?"

"Nothing really. If she can weather the shock and not get pneumonia, she'll have a fighting chance. He said twenty-four hours, and it's been almost that."

A nurse interrupted them. "Mr. Wagner, you have a call at the nurses' station."

It was Rio. "I have the drawings ready."

"I'll be right there." Jeff was on the move as soon as he hung up the phone after calling a cab. He left Steve and Janie at the hospital and picked Rio up, heading straight for the police station. The investigators, already well informed in the case, examined the sketches with deep interest, comparing them to pictures of some well-known wanted criminals.

There were two pictures of obviously the same man. "That's the one Ami said had a scar when we saw them in Douglas but had grown a beard to cover it. I couldn't get it right till I drew him without the beard, then I just covered most of the scar, except about an inch she said showed on his cheek."

The man who spoke was Sergeant Scarsdale. "Remember the teletype we got from Montana about two months ago, Cal? Without that beard, it could be the same man."

"You're right. If so, it might be part of the gang operating out of Montana and North Dakota." Excitement showed as the two men looked more closely at the sketches and the book they were checking.

"These are good, Rio. We'll do our best."

They shook hands, and Jeff took Rio back to the hospital with him. Jasper had arrived, deep concern written on his face.

"Anything at all on how bad she is?" he asked.

Jeff shook his head. "Dr. Barry said twenty-four hours, and it's been that. So far as I can tell, she's the same. No worse but no better, either." He was so tired, he couldn't remember what day it was. He hadn't slept since Sunday night, and that had been restless.

It was late as they left for the motel, all but Jeff. Jasper said, "I'll stay, Jeff. You need sleep."

He wasn't interested. "I'll sleep here. If she wakes, I want to know. Take Rio home as you go."

Between catnaps, Jeff walked the floor until morning and was standing at the window, watching the sky lighten in the east, when Dr. Barry came in.

"Ami's awake. You can see her for ten minutes."

"How is she?" He held his breath.

"Out of danger, I'd say." Dr. Barry's voice was smiling.

Ami saw blurred white that moved from her vision, then returned. She blinked, and the white became a nurse with a smile on her face, looking down at her.

"Hello, Ami. Can you hear me?"

Ami's lips were stiff and sore, but she tried to move them in answer to the question. The nurse wet a cloth and gently pressed it to her mouth. The second time, Ami felt the water cooling her parched throat. The whiteness of the nurse disappeared and another masked face appeared in her place. She closed her eyes, not wanting to think.

"Now, now. You've had enough sleep. People are waiting to see you who have been here a long time." All the time he was talking, the hands of the masked figure were busy, probing. She drew in a sharp breath as the fingers touched her ribs on the left side, sending a hot shaft of pain down her leg.

"Ah," the figure said. "Ah."

When she opened her eyes again, the masked figure was gone and in his place was Jeff. Jeff with a three-day growth of beard and bloodshot eyes. She stared at him, trying to remember what it was that bothered her. Unable to think clearly, she asked, "Remus?"

Jeff grinned, his teeth showing white against the dark beard. "He's at the nurses' station down the hall, being looked after quite well. What about you?"

Ami nodded. "I was afraid..." Her voice trailed off.

"Don't try to talk, Ami. It'll wait," Jeff said, picking up her hand to rub gently across her fingers. "If it's any consolation, we were all scared to death."

"There's something else." She frowned at her inability to recall what it was she had to tell him.

"Rio did the sketches and the police seem to think they can identify the men, possibly wanted in connection with rustling up north."

She remembered. Everything that had happened slowly came into focus and, watching Jeff, she knew she could never tell him that Eileen was part of the deal. She withdrew her hand and slid it beneath the sheet, turning away from the surprised look on Jeff's face, closing her eyes so she wouldn't give away any of what she was thinking.

His lips brushed her temple and he said, "I know you're tired. Dr. Barry said to only stay a minute. Someone will be nearby if you need anything."

Ami didn't answer as she heard him leave the room and, minutes later, she slept. When she awoke, she lay still for a moment, then reached to her left side to the bandage there, pressing it a little and flinching when it hurt. Her mouth was sore and it hurt to touch it with her tongue. She wished for water but didn't have enough energy to reach the table by her bed, wondering instead how long it had been since Hank and Luke caught her and Remus in the canyon.

The sight of the truck had been such a shock she hadn't been able to run quickly enough to escape. She still couldn't figure out how they got the huge semi into and out of the canyon when she had never seen any place wide enough for a truck to pass. The shock was greater still as she listened to Hank and Luke discuss Eileen's part in the theft, although her plan had backfired when the rustlers double-crossed her. She had merely meant to cast suspicion on Ami and then have the cattle recovered, not counting on losing the cattle and becoming a part of attempted murder. How much of the plot would Eileen explain to Jeff?

Ami turned restlessly, flexing her legs, but she

couldn't roll over on her side because of the injured ribs. Her thoughts wandered on. Had Mandy gone to Newark? She hadn't asked Jeff and he hadn't volunteered. Anyway, there was no reason for her to worry about it anymore, in spite of Jeff's proposal. She bit into her lips and moaned as they stung, and she tasted blood where her teeth cut into the tenderness of her swollen mouth. The least she could do was put his mind at ease and let him know she realized why he thought the proposal was a good idea at the time.

A smiling nurse came through the door. "Dr. Barry says you need this." She slipped a needle beneath the skin of her right arm, and Ami felt a slight sting. "You'll feel better after you sleep some more."

Ami didn't protest, too tired to argue and unwilling to try to figure out the puzzle that faced her. Reality faded, and she slipped into sleep.

Jeff called Steve. "Ami's awake and talking a little, although she doesn't remember too much that went on back there. Dr. Barry says she'll make it, barring any unforeseen complications." He breathed deeply. "Tell Jasper to come for me." He called Rio to relay the good news and told him, "She can have regular visitors starting tomorrow morning. I'm going home, but Steve and Janie will be here, and I'll be back by tomorrow afternoon."

Rio was silent for a long time before he said, "Thanks for calling me, Jeff." Jeff hung up the phone and stared at it a moment. The special bond between the young man and the woman who had befriended him was clearly evident. The loner and the orphan who had made it in spite of the odds. He thought of the old dog and wondered what had gone on to enable both of them to reach the truck, possibly saving their lives by keeping them a little warmer until they were found. How far away had they been? Why had they been left to die? If not to die, surely whoever had done the shooting wouldn't have left them alive to testify.

Ami had been too weak for him to question, but he could guess that the rustlers thought she would be left overnight and would not survive the freezing temperatures in the mountains; that, combined with the loss of blood. They were right, not counting on her rescue. He shied away from thinking they had been lucky to find them.

Jeff talked to Dr. Barry before he left the hospital. "Steve Hilton and his wife will be in this afternoon. Whatever has to be done, let them know." He managed a grin. "I'll take Remus off your hands if you think he's able to travel."

Dr. Barry laughed. "First time I've ever treated a dog, but he probably considers himself human, anyway. Yes, he's able to travel, but I daresay the nurses will miss having him around."

Jeff took a cab to the airport to wait for Jasper, holding the old dog's head on his knees all the way, lifting him carefully as he got out. He put him down beside him, and Remus promptly sat, favoring the front paw where he had been hit. They waited only a few minutes for Jasper.

"I should see Amanda while I'm here, but I'd probably frighten her to death the way I look," Jeff told Jasper. He hesitated. "I'm not sure I should tell her about Ami, but I promised her I'd be back Saturday and bring Ami with me."

"Maybe by Saturday you can take her in to see Ami," Jasper said.

Jeff looked doubtful. "If she still has a fever, Dr. Barry won't even let us in, much less a child."

Jasper nodded, concentrating on the plane. Twenty minutes later he banked for a landing on Wagner's airstrip.

Chapter Twelve

It's Friday, Ami thought, and wondered how she had arrived at that conclusion when she hardly remembered when the nightmare had started nor the length of time it lasted. All the events came back to her as she lay awake, waiting for her breakfast. At least she was out of the intensive care unit and in a normal room. A very young nurse had come to help her get to the bathroom to wash her face and brush her hair. It was filled with sand, and she was anxious to shampoo it but found she was too weak to stand alone in the shower.

"You lost a lot of blood," the nurse told her. "It will take you a few days to get your strength back."

We were lucky, Remus, she mused. *Maybe you're a cat and have nine lives and loaned me one.* Dr. Barry told her Jeff had taken Remus home with him, but the old dog was going to be fine. *We're even,* she thought, and smiled. *I saved you once, and you returned the favor.*

She tried not to think of Jeff, but he was there without any bidding. *I hope he doesn't come to see me anymore. How can I tell him Eileen was the mastermind behind the plan? I can't,* she decided, *I can't.* He would have to find out from someone other than her and decided with certainty that she couldn't marry him even if he made the offer again. It was purely self-preservation, trying to avoid a scandal, trying to avoid

Ami's prosecution by his friend, thereby preventing an unpleasant trial.

He went pretty far at that, she thought. Not many men would be so generous as to lend their good name to a suspected crook.

She looked up as her breakfast tray was placed on the table arm and moved within her reach. She wasn't hungry and, after a moment, pushed the tray away and slid down into the bed, turning carefully on her right side. The tears ran silently down her cheeks as she recalled Jeff's proposal and the happiness she held for a few minutes, thinking she would be married to the man she loved. He hadn't really lied at any time; at no time had he mentioned love. He wanted her to go to Newark for Mandy's sake; he wanted to marry her for her own protection. *Men are a puzzle,* she thought, and went to sleep.

In her dream she ran. She couldn't see who was chasing her, but she was fast losing her breath, knowing that if she stumbled, she would be caught. The path she was on ended against the side of the mountain and she turned, pressing her back into the rock, facing her pursuer. Eileen stood in front of her, laughing, blond head lifted, black Stetson swinging down her back.

"You think you have Jeff hooked, don't you?" Eileen mocked. She flicked Ami with a slim whip she carried, "But the cattle are on Wagner property, and only you could have put them all there. Only you knew about the crevice between the peaks that came after the earthquake several years ago." Her laughter echoed through the canyon. "Jeff will never marry you...never marry you...never marry you."

She awoke, trembling and wet with perspiration. Her side ached from the exertion of running. She breathed hard. *I wasn't running,* she told herself, *I was dreaming.*

Her trembling had quieted when Jeff appeared in the doorway, but her face was still damp with perspiration or tears, or both. He stood looking down at her without speaking, seeing the exhaustion in her face and the tenseness in her body.

"What's wrong?" Jeff asked, picking up her hand.

"Nothing." Her voice was totally unconvincing.

"Why are you crying?"

"I must have turned and hurt my side," she said.

He held her gaze a moment before he looked at the still-full breakfast tray. "You need to eat."

She tried to pull her hand away, but he held on. "If there's something wrong, Ami, I want to know about it. Are you thinking about what happened and worried whether the men will be caught?"

Ami didn't answer and her eyes slid away from his face. One finger beneath her chin turned her face so she'd have to look at him. "If you don't want to talk about it yet, I can understand, but the sooner you tell us all you know, the more likely it is we'll catch them. The sketches Rio drew for the police have helped a lot." He sat on the edge of the bed. "He told me you had a run-in with the rustlers sometime ago, but you never mentioned it to us."

"I didn't know they were rustlers," she said.

"What happened?"

She smoothed the white spread with her free hand. "Nothing much. They were sort of picking on Rio because they thought he was alone."

"When was that?"

"As we came through Douglas on our way out here."

"Why didn't you say anything about it?"

"I never thought about it anymore," she said truthfully.

"Do you have any idea why they happened to be in this area and picked Wagner's and Crooked M cattle to rustle?"

She stiffened. "You still think I directed them here?"

He shook his head. "I thought you might have heard them talking."

"I wasn't close to them for long," she hedged. "I was up on that last ridge before the blind canyon when they came from behind it in a big semi. I didn't even know a truck could get in there." As she spoke Ami remembered her dream and asked, "Has there ever been an earthquake through those mountains? I mean, one that was recorded?"

"As a matter of fact, a couple of years ago, one registered four point five on the Richter scale, but aside from rumblings and shakings, it didn't do any damage." He watched her. "What made you think of that?"

She shrugged. "There may be a split in the mountains where we thought there was no passageway. An earthquake could cause something like that."

Jeff continued to watch her. "I'll get some of Carue's men to check it out."

She looked up, suddenly aware of what she had said, repeating a dream, and he took her seriously. Opening her mouth to tell him it wasn't necessary, she subsided. Let him find out for himself that Eileen was involved; she couldn't be the one to tell him.

He noticed the strain beginning to show in her face and his expression changed to gentle concern. "I'll be here a while, Ami, but you'd better rest. Dr. Barry isn't going to be happy that you aren't eating."

"Don't tattle on me," she said.

Jeff raised his eyebrows. "I'll bet he gets a report from whoever picks up this tray within five minutes of its being returned to the kitchen."

He looked back at her from the door. "I'm going over to see Amanda and have lunch with her. She doesn't know you've been hurt, and I have to figure out a way to tell her so she'll agree to go with me to Newark Monday. We changed the appointment until then." She continued to look at him without answering until he smiled and left the room.

Her eyes were still on the doorway when Dr. Barry appeared. He frowned, looking down at her as he picked up her wrist. "All right, young lady, what's wrong with the food here? We have an excellent dietician who is upset because you didn't touch your breakfast." Jeff was right; someone had reported her for not finishing the meal.

Ami was tired and couldn't think of a witty reply, so she promised, "I'll eat a big lunch."

He stuck a thermometer in her mouth, still frowning. He might be angry with her, but his hands were gentle as he took the bandage loose from her ribs to examine the area where the bullet had been removed. When he finished putting on a fresh bandage, he took the thermometer and read it before shaking it and putting it on the table.

"Are you in pain?" Dr. Barry asked.

She shook her head. "When can I go home?"

"You just got here, Ami. What's your hurry?"

"I'm taking up space needed by sick people."

He smiled. "We've lots of room." He patted her hand. "As soon as you get rid of that fever, we'll talk about your going home."

Home. Her mind searched for an answer. Perhaps she could pay room and board at Jim's ranch until she was able to start her new job. She dozed fitfully, waking to doze again, and was staring at the ceiling, her main occupation lately, when Jasper came in.

"Hello, love," he said, smiling down at her. He was holding a basket of yellow roses.

She smiled back at him. "Jasper, where did you get roses like that at this time of year?"

"Picked them myself from the master's flower garden," he told her. His smile disappeared. "Jeff said you were still running a fever."

"Where did you see Jeff?" she asked, remembering that he had gone to see Mandy.

"He called home to see if I was on my way here."

She frowned. "Did you fly up?"

"Yes." He hesitated. "We got a call from the sheriff out of Kane County in Utah. They've picked up a couple of men answering the rustlers' descriptions, and we're going up this afternoon to check it out."

"Oh."

He picked up her hand. "If we can make any kind of identification, Ami, sooner or later you'll have to identify them, too."

She nodded, wondering if the crooks were loyal or if they would turn around and implicate Ron and Eileen. Jasper didn't care for Eileen; maybe she could confide in him. But he was Jeff's friend and would feel obligated to report what she told him. She pressed her lips together. If Eileen went free because she kept her mouth shut, that's the way it would have to be. She couldn't tell Jeff. Eileen had done her part to rescue a good friend, and the man she planned to marry, from the clutches of a nameless renegade. She could get out of Jeff's way so he'd need to feel no further responsibility for her.

"Do me a favor, Jasper?" she asked.

"Anything, Ami."

"Get me a phone put in here."

He squeezed her hand. "That's easy. Maybe if you call Janie, she'll stop crying and threatening to murder all of us. She's been some upset by the whole deal. Lily, too. They'll be in to see you tomorrow."

Jasper left, promising to see about the phone, and she slept. Rio was standing by her bed when she woke. Ami smiled up into worried dark eyes. "I'm okay. Honest. Dr. Barry says all I need is a little time to recuperate."

"You're looking better, at least," he said.

Ami told him what Jasper said about the rustlers. "I understand you did a fantastic job on the sketches."

Rio grinned. "It was easy once I started." The grin faded. "Ami, all I could remember about them was how cold and mean-looking they were and the thought of them shooting you for no reason." He stopped.

She touched his hand. "It's an odd coincidence that probably would never happen again in a million years. As long as we survived, we might as well try to forget it."

But she knew she never would. When Rio left, she went back to thinking. How could Eileen even pretend to love Jeff and do what she did? Love takes strange twists and curves. Tim had loved her until he found she couldn't have the children he wanted. Jeff didn't love her but would marry her to keep her out of jail. And Ami—Ami had loved unwisely, not once, but twice. Human beings had to be the weirdest creatures of all time.

Carue, Ed, and Cecil came to see her Saturday. The Howards and Trentons she knew from the grange dances came. Her room filled to overflowing with flowers, and by early afternoon she was exhausted. She looked at the telephone someone had plugged in during all the other activities. She still hesitated about calling Jim and was putting it off again when he appeared in the doorway of her room.

She smiled as he took her hand. "Must be mental telepathy."

"You were thinking about me?" Jim asked, grinning.

"As a matter of fact, I was just getting ready to call you," she said.

"Then I'll save you some money," he told her.

She took a deep breath. "Jim, can I go to your ranch from the hospital? I have no idea how long it will be before I can ride, but I don't want to go back to Wagner's. I'm willing to pay room and board."

He met her eyes and waited, but she couldn't say any more. "You know you're welcome, Ami. You're already on the payroll, so forget paying anything."

She had half-decided to tell Jim about Eileen, but changed her mind, deciding that it would be her secret and telling him about it would solve nothing. Let Eileen's conscience decide for her. "It may be awhile before I can earn a salary."

"Nonsense," he said. "Does Wagner know you don't plan to return there?"

Ami shook her head. "He and Jasper went to Utah to see some men they picked up on suspicion."

"How does Jeff feel now about your part in all this?"

"He hasn't said."

"And Eileen?"

She grimaced. "Well, she hasn't visited me, so I assume she hasn't forgiven me for whatever I've done." Her laugh was rueful.

Jim laughed out loud. "You're too pretty to be forgiven, Ami." He sobered. "When will you be getting out of here?"

"I don't know. Dr. Barry said he'd talk to me about leaving when all my fever is gone." She sighed. "Of course, I haven't seen him since early this morning. He could be avoiding me."

Jim took his leave, promising to be back on Sunday. "Your house is ready whenever you can get there, Ami. We'll take good care of you until you can make it on your own."

As tired as she was, Ami got out of bed and walked around the room, her legs shaky from nonuse. She walked for three minutes, back and forth, then sat down to catch her breath, repeating the process a couple of times. She started down the hall, moving like someone just learning to walk, when the elevator door slid back and Jeff walked toward her.

"Quite an improvement," he said, smiling down at her. "How are you?"

"Fine." She turned back to her room, and Jeff put his arm around her waist. She tried not to show any reaction to his nearness, but she trembled inside. "I thought you were in Utah."

He held her arm as she climbed on the bed. "We just got back. Jasper dropped me off." He kissed her cheek, his warm breath caressing her skin.

Her eyes questioned him as he took pictures from an envelope he carried and handed them to her. "Do any of these men look familiar?"

Her gaze still rested on his face, taking in the shadows under his eyes, tight lines around his mouth, wondering why all the worry even now. She looked down at the pictures she held, five men in the group, and studied if for a few seconds, finally pointing to one on the left and another in the middle.

"That's Hank and that's Luke," she said.

"Can you be positive?"

"Yes," she said firmly. "I'd know them anywhere and, if they were close enough, I could recognize their smell." She wrinkled her nose.

He took the pictures back. "They're the ones that were caught, Ami. However, they're also wanted in Montana and Wyoming on the same charges, and we may not see them for a while."

"What about the cattle?"

"Some of them were recovered. They told us the others are still on Eileen's property, unless they were moved by someone else."

"What do you mean?"

"That's what Hank said."

Ami frowned. "Who else would take them?"

"Eileen?" The question was soft, and her eyes widened as she looked at him. Anger and something else she couldn't determine darkened the gray of his eyes.

"Eileen?" She repeated the name as though it were unfamiliar to her.

"Did you know she was involved in taking the cattle?" Jeff asked quietly.

She sat silently watching him, wondering how much he knew. "I heard them say Eileen and Ron arranged for the cattle to be taken, but they weren't supposed to keep them, just move them to where I'd be suspected. She was double-crossed, I guess."

Jeff nodded and his voice hardened. "You could have been killed." When she said nothing, he asked, "Weren't you going to mention Eileen's part in this?"

"I wasn't sure you'd believe me," she said.

"You still think I asked you to marry me because I didn't want Eileen to bring charges against you?"

"Didn't you?"

"Ami—"

"I'm going to the J and R Ranch when I leave the hospital, Jeff. I won't be going back to Wagner's, so you don't have to make excuses for either of us." Jeff tried to interrupt, but she went on. "I never meant to come between you and Eileen; never meant to get so involved with Mandy that it would hurt her—or you." She withdrew her hands from his. "When I'm gone, you and Eileen can work it out, and you won't have to worry about my feelings."

After a long pause while he looked straight into her eyes, Jeff said, "You're right. It will be easier when you're gone."

Ami managed to control the gasp as the pain of his words ricocheted through her, and her chin went up as she met his gaze. It was what she asked for and he had given it to her without softening the blow.

He stood up. "If you want to press charges against Hank and Luke for attempted murder or against Eileen as an accomplice, Jasper can help you file the papers. Hank and Luke will probably waive extradition, and you'll have to go to Montana or Wyoming, whichever state has priority."

She nodded, waiting for him to go, but instead of leaving, he stepped closer to the bed and leaned over her, his arms going around her. He pushed her head back with his chin and lowered his mouth to hers. It was a hard, ruthless kiss, unlike any she could remember, and she struggled. In spite of herself her heart lifted to meet the urgency in his kiss, and she stopped struggling to hold on, letting him plunder with his tongue, answering his demand with fingers digging into his powerful arms.

His release was so sudden, she swayed sharply. One hand covered her mouth; the other pressed against her side as she watched him through a blur of pain.

"I'll be taking Amanda to Newark Monday, so I won't see you before you leave the hospital." His glance went from the dark cap of hair to the shapeless hospital robe that didn't quite reach her bare feet, and his eyes were the color of steel that had been frozen, just as expressionless. "Take care, Ami."

The silence in the room Jeff left was so complete, Ami realized she was holding her breath. Slowly she exhaled. She had accomplished what she wanted: convinced him she was not for him, that Eileen was his kind of people. The rich, the idle, the chosen. It hadn't taken much to convince him. Her eyes were so wide open, they hurt, and when she blinked, she found, to her surprise, there were no tears. There would be plenty of time later for tears for what she gave up today, she knew, and slid off the bed to walk around the room, pausing at the window to watch a cold-looking sun settle behind a distant ridge of mountains. She stared unseeingly until it grew dark outside and a million lights came on over the city.

Turning away, she climbed back into bed without turning on a light. It was Saturday night, she remembered. Everyone was probably at the grange dance. Two weeks ago she, too, was at a dance; just two weeks tomorrow since Jeff's proposal. Lying there in the dark, she could easily believe the past week had never happened. Hard to accept that, somehow, she and Remus had shared a near-miss with death; that Eileen was almost totally to blame; that, even so, Jeff had forgiven her and would eventually marry her as he had planned BA—before Ami.

There was a hesitant knock at the door. "Ami?" Janie called in a loud whisper.

"Oh, yes, I'm awake." She sat up and turned on the bed lamp. Janie and Lily stood just inside the door, Steve behind them.

Janie reached her first, holding her hands out. "Where can I hug you?"

"Anywhere but these ribs," Ami told her, indicating her left side. They hugged, then she was engulfed in Lily's arms, folded against the ample bosom like a child.

She whispered, "I'll bet you didn't bring me any coffee, Lily. They make the world's worst here."

"Bless your heart, child, I'll make sure you get some good coffee." She dabbed at her eyes.

"No coffee, but plenty of food," Steve said, holding up a carton. He put it on her table and bent to kiss her cheek.

"I was beginning to feel sorry for myself," Ami said. "I thought everyone was at the dance and had forgotten about me."

"Not likely," Janie said. "When will you be coming home?"

Steve met her questioning glance with a raised eyebrow. "Dr. Barry said I could leave two days after I stopped running a fever." At Steve's look, she wondered if he had been told she wasn't returning to Wagner's. Jeff kept his people informed, and she was almost sure Steve was aware of her decision.

Ami changed the subject. "How's Remus?"

Lily clucked. "Eating me out of the kitchen," she said. "I believe they left a hole in his stomach and he never gets full."

Janie showed her impatience to get in a question. "Are you going to sue Eileen for defamation of character?" Ami stared at her, stunned at the thought. "You have plenty of right, you know."

Ami looked at Lily, then at Steve, who said quietly. "She's right, Ami. That, plus being an accomplice to attempted murder."

She could get even, all right, Ami thought. But if she filed suit against Eileen, Jeff would be affected. Through Jeff, Mandy would be hurt and, eventually, all of Wagner's.

She shook her head. "No, I have no plans for that."

"But Ami—" Janie began, and Ami put her fingers on her lips.

"No, Janie. The answer is no," she said, her voice leaving no doubt she meant what she said.

Janie hesitated, glancing at Steve. "I guess I shouldn't wish hard luck on anyone, but I can't help it where she's concerned."

Ami smiled, understanding her friend. Steve patted his wife on her shoulder. "The corn fritters are still hot, Ami," he said.

"I'll have two," she said. Lily handed them to her with a napkin, and Ami sighed as she bit into the tasty bread. "You should give their dietician some cooking lessons, Lily."

As she ate, Janie talked about Mandy and the trip to Newark without daring to voice their hopes for her. "She wanted to wait for you, but Dave didn't want to put it off that long, so Jeff finally promised her you'd be home when they got back, and she stopped fussing.''

Ami withheld her comments and, when they had gone, lay back against her pillow, her mind on Janie's remark about Jeff's promise to Mandy that he would be forced to break.

She smiled grimly to herself. "I can't blame you for playing both ends against the middle, Jeff," she said aloud. "But I'll be glad when I'm no longer in the middle.''

Chapter Thirteen

Jeff stood outside the closed door of Ami's room, clenched fists rammed into his pockets. He still tasted her kiss, smelled the light cologne he liked without knowing what it was. He could feel the print of her fingers digging into his arms and saw her hand pressed against her mouth, the expression in her eyes, and wondered if he had hurt her. At the moment he didn't care, but now he remembered her hand on her side. He had forgotten the bullet wound, had forgotten everything as he took the kiss he wanted from her. He half turned, one hand out of his pocket, reaching for the door, but stopped, staring at the thick panel separating them, and moved away. He had wanted Ami with him when he took Amanda to Newark, wanted her to go as his wife, so he would have the right to make love to her the way it should be. He had the license, and Jasper could have performed the ceremony, except for the fact that Ami wanted Rio and Amanda there. Circumstances had a way of playing havoc with what he wanted lately. Without warning, he remembered Ami's nude body blending itself with his, and he lost himself for a moment to the feeling of his own body's response as he made love to her.

He let his breath out and turned away, leaving the hospital to drive to the motel, stopping by the bar for one drink before he went on to bed. Amanda would be ready to leave by ten the next morning, and they'd be home in time for a good lunch.

Stretched out on the bed, Jeff was conscious of his tiredness. Even so, he couldn't sleep. He had promised Amanda that Ami would be at Wagner's when they returned from Newark, but Ami had other ideas. The worst idea she had was that he wanted to marry her out of pity. If he could only convince her how much he loved her. His thoughts went on to Eileen. He couldn't believe what Hank and Luke implied about her involvement in the rustling of both Wagner and Crooked M cattle, but the expression on Ami's face surprised him when he mentioned that Eileen could be involved. He knew instantly that she was aware of that possibility and that, even though she believed it, she wasn't going to accuse Eileen. That hadn't bothered Eileen, who had shown no compassion when it came to showing Ami up as a rank amateur, when it came to taking what Eileen considered to be only hers. He would never have believed she would be capable of cold-bloodedly planning to accuse Ami of rustling, of planting evidence to convict her.

It was two years after Myra's death when he and Eileen sort of drifted together. He had been to a few social gatherings, always with a group, usually Janie, Steve, and Jasper. Gradually he noticed Eileen showed up a lot, always unescorted, until it became just a twosome. The outings at the grange dances became fewer, and he was either alone with Eileen or flying to some party among all her friends. They had been ready to announce their engagement even though he didn't really remember asking her to marry him, but it didn't bother him much. His one concern was Eileen's indifference to Amanda, but he thought they would be closer after their marriage.

The turning point was Ami's arrival at Wagner's. Jeff had his reservations about her when he went to El

Paso with Steve for her interview, but when Steve wanted to hire her, he had agreed.

There were many things he noticed about Ami, some of them odd to his way of thinking, at least, for a woman. She was a loner; she didn't need people around her all the time; the Mexican-American teenager who was her legal responsibility— Now, how many young women would ask for that job? And that old dog of hers would never win any prizes, except maybe for being the clumsiest-looking critter around as he loped across the desert with her.

Sometime during that period, Jeff became reluctant to think about marriage to Eileen. He thought less and less about it as he watched Ami romping with Amanda and knew she had no trouble with sign language. It wasn't until Amanda asked for Ami to go to Newark with her that he realized how close the two of them had become. He closed his eyes, seeing Ami again as he made love to her for the first time, their experimental kisses turning to a passionate sharing so strong that the memory from months ago still aroused him.

He didn't recall exactly when he admitted to himself that he loved Ami. Perhaps at the Valentine Dance, when she teased him about being pregnant, and he smiled a little as he remembered her watery eyes and pink nose, the result of a cold, and a husky voice that kept her from singing with Steve and Janie. He loved to hear her sing, but he wanted her with him on that night, wanted her to say she was going to have his baby so he would have a logical reason to ask her to marry him. Whenever the realization finally got through to him, he had told Eileen the next Saturday night before asking Ami to marry him.

He had never known Eileen could speak in such harsh tones as she used that night. "Marry her?" She stared at him in disbelief. "What about us, Jeff?" She was speechless for a moment.

He said as gently as possible, "That's why we haven't been in any hurry to marry, Eileen. We've been friends for so long, we just drifted together. It isn't that I don't love you—"

"What is it, then? You can't mean you love that—that—" She sputtered. "That nobody. A veterinarian. Why, she's—" Her eyes narrowed. "You let her put-on with sweet-talking Amanda get to you, that's what. Can't you see that's all it is? Just making up to Amanda to get to you."

"Eileen." Jeff put his hands on her shoulders. "Admit it. We've been friends all our lives and were paired together from force of habit until we thought we should get married."

Eileen wasn't to be pacified, and he heard a lot about Ami that he'd rather forget, including the rustling hints he didn't take seriously. He knew he was right, however, when he asked Ami to marry him the next day. Her complete surprise, her hesitation for only a moment, followed by her confession that she loved him, had captivated him again and he couldn't wait to claim her as his wife. He was still waiting, all because of his own ignorance. He should have yanked her up and dragged her to Jasper for a civil ceremony with a bang-up reception for the Wagner crew afterward; should never have mentioned Eileen's accusations until she was safely his; should have taken her and Amanda and gone to Newark right then.

Restless, Jeff got out of bed and walked to the window, pushing aside the draperies to look out. Even with all the lights, the mountains stood in dark silhouette against the starlit sky. Southwesterners took their spectacular scenery for granted, but not Ami. He had seen her stand absolutely still for long minutes, staring at the endless desert bordered by ragged mountain peaks, a smile of satisfaction on her face. He recalled her description of the few storms they had as wild and beauti-

ful compared to sad ones in the east. That thought
brought to mind again the first time he made love to
her, an armful of long legs and slim body curved to the
shape of his; of firm, warm lips yielding to his demands. Desire for her was alive inside him, and he
swore at himself for the way he had mishandled all his
chances.

Because of him she was almost killed, he thought.
Suddenly he made up his mind. Amanda had to go to
Newark, but when they came back, things would
change in his favor. His mouth set in a determined line.
Eileen had several things to clarify for him, and he
would take it from there.

The sun was still below the horizon Monday morning
as Jeff guided the quiet-running Mercedes around the
big house, heading southwest toward the Crooked M
ranch. His eyes followed the familiar landscape—the
landing strip on his right with the small building at the
end. Jasper's truck was parked in its usual place, and
he recalled Jasper's comment when the doctor said
Ami would recover barring any unforeseen complications.

"I can perform that ceremony before she gets
enough strength back to resist," he said and grinned.
"All's fair, you know."

Jeff had been tempted. Looking down into Ami's
scratched face, deathly pale except for the streaks, he
almost said yes, wondering if she'd forgive him later.
He'd wished a thousand times he'd given in to tempta-
tion and taken his chances on her forgiveness after she
belonged to him.

He left the road on his property, turning right
through a rock gate with the huge Crooked M logo on
the top of it, still three miles from the main house. The
sun was throwing a gold rim over the tallest mountain
peak when he pulled up beside the green Porsche. He

shook his head. The high winds this time of year would soon strip the paint off the valuable sports car, but Eileen couldn't be bothered with taking extra time to drive into the garage. Especially if she was mad, and by the looks of the skid marks, she was plenty angry when she drove in.

The doorknob turned easily under his hand, and he pushed the door inward to walk through the short entrance hall into the kitchen. He stopped short in surprise.

Eileen sat at the small table, and Ron Steward, her foreman, leaned against the refrigerator, a beer in his hand. Jeff had never known Eileen to get out of bed before sunup and had gone to the kitchen as he usually did, planning to make coffee before he woke her. She was downright unfriendly before her first cup of coffee.

When Jeff walked in, Eileen gasped, and the color rushed to her face as she threw a confused look at Ron. "Why, Jeff," she said, sounding breathless. She covered her confusion with concern. "I thought you were taking Amanda to Newark today. Is anything wrong?"

He glanced at Ron, who had straightened away from the refrigerator. "I need to talk to you, Eileen. Alone."

Ron finished the beer and put the bottle on the table. "I'll take care of that for you, Eileen," he said, nodding at Jeff as he went out.

"Problems?" Jeff asked.

Eileen laughed a little. "Not really. A couple of the boys got rowdy at the dance Saturday night, and Archie Denton locked them up. No problem." She stood up and moved toward him, hands outstretched. Jeff took them, holding her away from him. Rowdy cowboys on Saturday night weren't unusual, and he wondered why he didn't believe her statement.

He looked down at her pouting mouth, knowing she expected him to kiss her, but he didn't. Instead, he led her back to the chair and pushed her into it and sat on the edge of the table.

"The doctor says Ami will be all right," he said.

Eileen's eyes widened. "But, of course she will, Jeff. That was strictly for show anyway."

He stiffened. "What do you mean?"

She shrugged, watching to see what effect her next words would have on him. "Her partners had to make it look good so she wouldn't be blamed and whoever found her would be so busy looking after her, they wouldn't think of her rustler friends for a while." She smiled. "Rather a rough way, but effective."

He studied the confident smile, anger stirring inside him. "Where does your information come from?"

"It's common knowledge."

"I didn't know it," he told her. "Did Ron come to report on what happened?"

She looked quickly at him, then away. "I told you why Ron was here."

"And I don't believe you."

Eileen got up and leaned toward him. She was wearing a tan riding outfit that outlined her curves, a honey-beige sweater that almost matched her hair. She smelled expensive, and he thought of Ami's hair, which smelled of sunshine and the light fragrance she used.

"Jeff," Eileen said, and when he didn't move, she asked, "are you still planning to marry her after all this?" Her voice was brittle.

"All this, meaning what?"

"She hasn't explained how our herds mixed nor how they came through that canyon. It's always been blocked."

His eyes narrowed as he recalled Ami's off-the-wall question. "Do you remember the earthquake a couple of years ago?"

She looked startled. "Of course. Why?"

He decided to tell his own story. "Jasper and I went

to Utah, where they had picked up a couple of suspicious characters. Turns out they were driving the big semi Ami described with cattle from Wagner's and the Crooked M still inside." He watched closely, but her expression didn't change. "One of them volunteered that there was an opening at the end of the blind canyon where the cattle were found and that's how they passed through. Probably no one has really checked all the way to the O'Toole property since that earthquake."

"Ami must have, because she knew how to get them through there."

"Not exactly,' he said. "I believe Ron told you about it, and at the time, it seemed a good way to throw suspicion on Ami." He waited, but she didn't answer, her mouth set in a stubborn line, angry dark eyes staring at him, admitting nothing. He stood up. "I'll forgive you for the shady deal, Eileen, but if Ami had been killed—" He let the sentence drop and was rewarded when her eyes widened as she saw the danger she had put Ami in.

"I didn't mean—" she began and stopped, realizing she had admitted too much. Her chin went up. "She's not good enough for you, Jeff. I didn't want you to ruin your life tied to a nobody. She's part Indian and doesn't even know her real name."

"Then I'll give her mine if she'll have it," he said quietly, moving to the door before he turned to look at her again. "As soon as we can get to it, we'll separate the cattle and return yours."

She laughed. "How do you propose to tell how many are mine when the clips are gone and no brands on them? Another one of Ami's smart moves."

"We'll manage," he said. "Good-bye, Eileen." He closed the door behind him and ran down the steps to the Mercedes, sparing only a glance toward the corral, where he saw Ron watching him. Pulling from the well-kept yard, Jeff turned into the rising sun, knowing he had plenty of time to get to the ranch and carry out the rest of his plan before he had to get Amanda ready for their trip to Newark.

Resolutely he turned his thoughts from Eileen's betrayal. He would deal with his disappointment in her later. Right now he had some phone calls to make. At the house, he moved quickly, going by Amanda's room to see if she was still asleep. He smiled at the small figure, snuggled under the covers, only the blond hair, unbraided, visible spread over the pillow. She could sleep a little longer; their plane didn't leave Tucson till one o'clock.

The phone number of the hospital was written on a card lying near the phone. It had been used many times in the past week, and he dialed the familiar number again.

"Is Dr. Barry available?" he asked when the ring was answered. "This is Jeff Wagner."

"One moment, please."

There was a long buzz, and he heard Dr. Barry's gruff voice. Identifying himself, he asked, "Do you know how much longer you'll keep Ami?"

Dr. Barry cleared his throat. "I don't want to release her prematurely, Jeff. She's much better, but infection is still highly probable."

Jeff breathed deeply. "I understand. What I want is to ask you to keep her there till I get back from Newark. That could be as early as Wednesday or as late as Saturday."

"That can be arranged."

"Without her knowing I called?" Jeff asked.

Dr. Barry laughed. "It'll be our secret," he said and added, "I take it that I'm not to know your reasoning, besides Ami's well-being, of course."

Jeff laughed, too. "That's right, and thanks."

He called Jasper, then Steve, telling them breakfast

would be ready in thirty minutes and he wanted them to join him in the big kitchen. He stopped by to tell Lily she had five people coming for breakfast and went on to call a sleepy Amanda. He left her in Hazel's care and went to make one more phone call, this time to Jim Summers in Apache Junction.

Chapter Fourteen

Sunday passed quickly between visitors and two check-ups from Dr. Barry. "I know, I know, Ami," he said when she protested against his indefinite answer on when she could leave the hospital. "Wouldn't you rather leave permanently when you go, rather than have to come back?"

She subsided a little. "Yes, of course, but I feel good." It wasn't really true. She sneezed several times, causing a pain in her side, but she would never admit she felt more like sleeping than talking to anyone. She even dozed while Rio was with her and awakened to find him watching her with concerned dark eyes.

"Are you sure you're okay?" Rio asked.

She smiled apologetically. "Too much company maybe."

He left soon afterward, and she continued to lie there, feeling lazy. Her thoughts went to Mandy, who would be going to Newark alone with Jeff the next day. Linda had called, worried about Ami, and she had assured her she was doing great and looking forward to hearing good news about Mandy.

"I think you can be sure of it," Linda told her. "All we need to do is see that the grafts are taking from the inside out, and since she's had no pain, we feel confident everything is as it should be. However, it doesn't hurt to keep a watch for several months."

Ami wondered if Jeff had asked Eileen to go with them, almost knowing he wouldn't. Eileen didn't like to be around sick people. Mandy wasn't sick, Ami thought, smiling. There weren't many youngsters around any livelier than she. Even before Mandy could hear at all, she never considered herself sick or abnormal. It was the rest of the world that needed adjusting; and Ami conceded she was right. With nothing else to do, her thoughts wandered and she was aware that was all she did lately: lie in bed and think without solving any of her problems.

The memory of Jeff's kiss as he left her on Saturday made her want to cry, but she couldn't summon the tears she needed. He had only admitted what she had been preaching to him was right and agreed with her, so what was her problem? She turned over on her right side, noticing that it didn't pull the stitches anymore when she did so.

I'm much better, she thought. She sat up on the side of the bed and thought surely, by midweek, she could make the trip as far as Apache Junction. Jim had already told her she was looking too healthy to lie there much longer, and they were waiting for her at the J & R.

She woke early on Monday morning, wondering why she felt uneasy, and remembered it was the day for Mandy and Jeff to go to Newark. Ami didn't want to think that she should be with them and took a washcloth and towel that had been left by her bed, walking a fairly straight line into the bathroom, and bathed. She was slow, but at least she was on her own. She smiled to herself. People never thought about the small, everyday things they did until they could no longer do them automatically, then they became big things that someone else has to do for them.

She'd make a terrible patient if she had to stay in bed long, Ami knew, and along with the knowledge that she could take care of herself now, her spirits lifted. She wished for some clothing, but all she had was jeans, and she couldn't fasten a belt around her yet.

Aside from brief stops on his way down the hall, Dr. Barry avoided her as though she had the plague. When she tried to get a release date from him, he grinned and told her he needed just a little more money before he let her go. She wondered at the speculative look he gave her when she told him she was moving to Apache Junction and taking a job with Jim Summers. She hadn't meant to confide in him, but he had a way of getting information from his patients.

"It will be a few weeks before you ride another horse, Ami," Dr. Barry told her Wednesday evening as he checked the scar where stitches had just been removed. "You can drive in a week or so, but if there's any noticeable pulling, stop and call me. We don't want the cartilage under those injured ribs to get infected." He patted her arm. "Just be careful, reasonably so. I'm sure Jeff will agree with me."

It was then that she told him she wasn't returning to Wagner's, and he appeared about to say something, a frown touching his face briefly. He looked into her eyes a moment longer before he rose and gathered up his instruments.

"I don't know Jim Summers very well, but I've met him since you've been in here. He seems very concerned about you." He hesitated. "You've made lots of friends since coming to Arizona, haven't you?"

Smiling, she agreed with him. "Yes, lots of them. It was a good move for us."

"Even after the rustling?" he asked.

Ami nodded. "That was an experience I could have done without, but it's something to write home about." She looked up and grinned. "If I had a home to write."

Dr. Barry hadn't questioned her about home, but it

was obvious that he would like to have said more. He refrained from speaking, though, and that had been the last time she'd seen him. He was conspicuous by his absence.

On Thursday morning Janie brought her a pair of jeans and a red long-sleeved knit pullover. She left off the belt. She was ready; when Dr. Barry showed up, she'd tell him she wanted out of his sterile prison.

"I need a haircut," she told Janie, pushing the heavy hair off her neck. "And a good shampoo. I never did get all the sand out of my head."

"They have a beauty salon here. Want me to make an appointment for you to have it fixed?"

She turned to look at Janie. Something in her voice was different, but she couldn't decide exactly what she meant by that observation. The idea sounded pretty good, though, and she agreed. They walked together to the elevator and took it down to the basement, where a nurse's aide directed them to the shop. She made an appointment for that afternoon.

"I can't remember the last time I went to a beauty shop to have my hair fixed," she told Janie, laughing. "I feel really pampered."

After Janie left, Ami lay down a few minutes, then it was lunchtime. She dozed for a while, then at two thirty, went down to the basement to the beauty salon to keep her appointment.

"Just plain, I guess," she told the woman uncertainly after she finished trimming her thick hair. "I don't want anything fussy."

The woman nodded and proceeded to work on her. An hour later when she had finished with her, she looked at the reflection in the three-way mirror and grinned. The shining hair had been slightly curled, just enough to give it plenty of bounce, and the natural wave kept it close to her cheek. It was a great improvement.

"Looks good enough that maybe Dr. Barry will let me go home," she said, paid the woman with money Janie had left her, and went back to her room. In three minutes she was asleep.

She was eating just after five when the phone rang. It was Jim Summers. "You sound chipper, Ami," he said. "Feeling better?"

"I'm ready to leave here, Jim, as soon as I can catch Dr. Barry."

He laughed. "I know how you feel. They seem to be good at hiding, especially if you need them." He sympathized with her and, after a few minutes, said, "I won't be down tonight, Ami, since I just got in. I'm having to work for a living now that Ralph is laid up. Probably be down tomorrow sometime."

"That's okay, Jim, I understand. It takes everyone to keep up with work on a ranch."

She knew that very well. Steve told her that the school had sent two students out to help at Wagner's, and Rio had been there over the weekend to help out. The cold weather had Hammett's joints stiff, and he hadn't been doing much more than caring for the stables.

Ami sat by the window, her lights out, the city of Tucson spread out below her like a carpet of gold. It was a pretty city as cities go, but she was ready for the desert and mountains. She had never been to Apache Junction and knew only that it was a small crossroads city on U.S. 89 between Tucson and Phoenix and that the Apache Trail was the only road going up through the giant chain of the Superstition Mountains. The J & R spread lay somewhere just north of the Junction. Thinking of Jim's ranch and her new job occupied her for a few minutes, but her mind went back to Jeff and Mandy, already in Newark. She saw Jeff's eyes, anger and disappointment mixed, as he tried to reason with her about going back to Wagner's. There was no reason for her to return, back to the place she had learned to love again—someone she wasn't destined to have. Their short engagement must have set the record, with Jeff honorable to the end, still protesting they should get married.

No one had mentioned Eileen; no one had mentioned her charges against Ami nor whether they were still being considered. "I guess I should ask what's going on," she said aloud. "It must be bad if everyone avoids talking about it." She sighed and went to bed.

"Last X rays, I promise," Dr. Barry said as he turned her several different ways to see if she was completely mobile. "After we see the results of these, we'll talk about releasing you."

"About time," Ami grumbled, allowing the nurse to adjust the skimpy smock on her that was her X-ray costume. "You could have waited till I finished my breakfast."

Dr. Barry laughed. "You're the one's been rushing me."

She was back from the X-ray room in a few minutes but had lost interest in her food. Dressing in the jeans and shirt from the day before, she brushed her teeth and smoothed her hair with her fingers. It looked the same as it did when she left the beauty salon, still unruffled after she slept on it, Her watch said it was only eight thirty.

She was at the window, staring idly at Friday-morning traffic with its impatient drivers blowing horns and darting in and out of the lanes of bumper-to-bumper cars.

"Ami?"

Surprised, she turned to see Janie and Steve in the doorway. Janie walked quickly to meet her, and Ami stared. She wore a pale rose jersey dress with black suede pumps and bag to match, a fur cape slung over her arm. Behind her, Steve grinned, a wicked glint in his eyes. He was dressed in a dark blue suit, and over one arm he carried the long gown Ami had worn to the Christmas ball at Wagner's. The gold sandals dangled from his fingers.

"I thought I was well," she said, unable to keep the astonishment out of her voice. "You look like you're going to a funeral."

"Or a wedding," Steve said, spreading the dress on her unmade bed.

Ami stiffened. "Damned if I'll go to their wedding," she blurted and stopped as Jeff entered the room. Color washed into her face, but she lifted her chin and glared at him.

His hair was freshly trimmed and smoothed where usually it was rumpled. His mouth was a straight, stern line, but his eyes searched her face with a gentle look. His suit was dark gray and he wore a white shirt with maroon figures and a matching tie. He stopped a foot in front of her ramrod-straight figure.

"Janie will help you dress," Jeff said, smiling a little. He touched her hair. "It's very becoming."

Shaking her head, she stepped backward, eyes going to Janie, seeking an explanation.

Janie looked helpless and shrugged. "I was told what to do."

Her head swiveled to Jeff. "And what was that?"

"We're getting married in fifteen minutes, so don't ask questions. Go get dressed." It was an order.

"We?" She felt stupid and her questions matched her feelings.

"You, Ami; you and I," he said, pointing his fingers for emphasis. "That's what people do when they love each other—they get married."

Before she could draw her breath, Mandy and Rio came in with Jasper behind them. Mandy was wearing her Christmas dress Ami had bought for her, and Rio wore dark brown pants and a white shirt under a light brown sport coat.

Mandy walked up to her, smiling, and said, all her words plain, "I can hear you when you say I do to my daddy."

Ami stared down at her and slowly knelt, careful of her side. "No more operations?" she asked.

"No." The little girl continued to smile at her.

"Oh, Mandy," she said and gathered her into her arms, holding her until her words suddenly sunk in. "I do?" she asked and looked at Jeff as she stood up, shaking her head. "No, Jeff, I can't."

"If you want me to dress you, I will. If you want to cooperate, Janie and Amanda will help you."

Mandy giggled and caught her hand, tugging. "Come on, Ami. Hurry."

Jeff kissed her cheek and turned, motioning the others to follow him out the door.

As the door closed behind them, Ami said, "Janie, what's going on?"

Janie was all business now. "It seems Mr. Wagner has decided he needs a wife, Mandy needs a mother, and Wagner's needs a mistress. That about sums it up."

She stood still as Janie undid her jeans, pulled the shirt over her head, and held the formal gown up to slip it on her. Mandy pulled off her moccasins and reached for the gold sandals. A few minutes later Janie said, "You'll make a beautiful bride."

"Janie, I—we can't. You don't understand." Jeff didn't yet know she could never have children, and she couldn't marry him unless she told him first.

"What's there to understand? You love him, don't you?"

After a long silence, she nodded, unable to speak.

The two of them stood there until Mandy said, "It's time for us to go outside, Ami." The urgency in the low, husky voice claimed Ami's attention, and she looked down into gray eyes identical to Jeff's.

"Mandy," she began and looked up as Jeff came to the door.

"Are you ready?" he asked.

"No, Jeff, wait."

"Not any longer, Ami," he told her, gray eyes going over her slim figure, which left some room in the dress that fit so well at Christmas. He smiled. "You're beautiful, and I love you."

She was left standing alone as Jeff held the door for Mandy and Janie to go out. The door closed behind them, and Jeff turned to walk back to her. He took her cold hands, rubbing them between both of his. "Tell me, Ami, do you still love me?"

"Still?"

"You told me you loved me a few weeks ago."

"What about Eileen? What about the rustled cattle? What—?"

His mouth covered hers an instant, shutting her up effectively. "Answer my question first. It's the most important." His voice demanded but his eyes pleaded.

"I do, Jeff. Yes, I love you, but—"

Before she could finish the statement, the door opened to admit Dr. Barry. "Sorry, Jeff, but if I'm to give the bride away, I have to do it now. I'm due in surgery in half an hour."

Behind Dr. Barry came Jasper, Steve, and Janie, Mandy and Rio, and before the door could swing shut, Jim Summers came in. Jeff kissed her mouth gently before moving away to leave Dr. Barry holding her arm.

Ami didn't hear much of the words Jasper said until he said, "Who gives Ami as Jeff's bride?" and Dr. Barry released her to Jeff. She looked up at him, wondering if she was dreaming, and admitted to herself it was better than the nightmares she had been having.

He didn't smile, and she looked back at Jasper as he spoke.

"Do you, Ami, take Jeff to be your lawful wedded husband?" he asked and waited.

She stared as though hypnotized at Jasper until Jeff squeezed her hand and she transferred her gaze to him. The silence extended, and she could hear breathing around her, and still she couldn't speak.

Jeff bent his head until his lips touched her ear and he whispered softly, "Say I do, darling."

"I do," she responded automatically, her voice barely audible.

"Do you, Jeff, take Ami as your lawful wedded wife?"

Jeff's voice was firm and immediate. "I do."

There was a movement behind her, and Ami looked down as Mandy handed something to Jeff, smiling a wide smile as she did so. Jeff's hand separated her fingers and slipped a wide silver band on the third finger of her left hand. A diamond rectangle sparkled from the center of the band.

She heard the words *let no man put asunder,* followed by other sounds, but she looked straight at Jasper as he said, "I now pronounce you man and wife. You may—"

"No" she said firmly.

Jasper's head jerked upward and beside her Jeff stiffened. "No," she repeated. "If I'm his wife, then he's my husband."

Jasper's lips twitched and he inclined his head toward her. "Let me rephrase that last statement, please." He cleared his throat. "I now pronounce you husband and wife." By now, he was grinning broadly. "You may kiss your wife, Jeff."

There was movement around her, but she didn't stir until Jeff said, "Ami?"

Dark turquoise eyes met his gaze, and she tilted her

head for him to kiss her. As his mouth touched hers, warm and gentle, realization penetrated the fog she had been moving in.

"Oh," she said, and tightened her hold on him. She was married to Jeff for better or for worse.

In the confusion of congratulations, hugs and kisses, she lost track of everything except that one fact: she was married to Jeff.

Dr. Barry spoke as he hugged Ami. "My job's finished. You're in good hands now, I'm sure."

She nodded, and as he moved away, Jim Summers was in front of her. "Well, Ami, looks like my loss is Jeff's gain, and I wish the best for both of you." He turned to extend his hand to Jeff, shaking his head as their eyes met, and he grinned and moved aside as Rio came up.

Rio didn't speak but stood smiling at her. They had been the same height when they arrived at Wagner's, but now he was two inches taller, still straight and slim. He hugged Ami, holding her a long time. When he let her go, he asked, "Is Jeff my brother-in-law or my stepfather?"

She gazed in surprise at him, then turned to look up at Jeff, who had not left her since the last words of the ceremony. She blinked.

Jeff looked back at her, then at Rio. "Jasper could straighten us out, I guess, Rio. You can be either. Whatever you decide, we'll be a rather mixed family." He winked. "As long as we belong to each other, it doesn't matter, does it?'

Rio shook his head and repeated, "As long as I belong."

Mandy was standing just back of Jeff but holding on to his hand. Now she moved to look up at him. "Is Ami my mother or my sister?"

Jeff laughed. "You can choose, too, Amanda. What would you like her to be?"

"Can I have both?" she asked, and laughter swept the room.

"She's not really big enough to be two people, do you think?" Jeff asked.

Ami stooped in front of the little girl. "Friends, first, then all the others, huh?"

Mandy nodded and walked into Ami's arms. She looked over the blond head at Jeff and said, "I'm ready to go home."

He reached to help her to her feet, taking Mandy's hand as he did so. "The others are going home; you and I aren't ready to go to Wagner's just yet."

"Where?"

His eyes darkened as they went over her tall slimness standing close to him. "Somewhere you can convince me you're mine."

A few minutes later everyone was gone, leaving Ami alone in her hospital room with Jeff. He closed the door and turned to her where she still stood in the center of the room.

He smiled. "Want me to help you dress? You might not be comfortable riding in that."

She looked down at the sparkling gown she wore, then back at Jeff. "I don't have anything but jeans."

"That's fine for now. We can shop later." Reaching around her, he unzipped the dress and let it slip from her onto the floor. She wore no bra because of the tenderness in her ribs where the tight band would fit. Small, firm breasts were exposed to his view, and he brought his hands around to caress them. She stared up into half-closed gray eyes, transfixed, as she watched his mouth move closer to hers, and sighed as their lips met. His hands slid down to curve around her hips, holding her against the hardening of his thighs.

He groaned, releasing her. "Get those jeans on. I'll be outside."

She didn't move for a long moment after he left her,

then she stepped out of the gown, reached down, and picked it up to fold it. Someone had left her a big suitcase, partly filled with jeans and shirts, the pantsuit she wore on the trip to Newark with Jeff the first time with Mandy, and the old yellow terry robe. She smiled, guessing Janie was responsible.

A few minutes later, dressed in the pantsuit she chose over jeans, with a matching print blouse Janie had found somewhere, she looked around the room. She had spent almost two weeks in the white cubicle, sometimes unaware of what went on around her. Nightmares and dreams were all mixed, and there was Jeff's stubborn insistence that she marry him, his plans carried out with the precision of a battle commander, telling her he loved her. She had to believe that he meant it, because her entire being ached with love for him.

Ami caught her breath, realizing that whatever the reason, she was now his wife, too weak—or too willing—to fight his high-handed actions. Swallowing hard, she looked toward the door as a soft knock sounded and Jeff stood in the opening, smiling at her.

"I've already checked you out." He looked her over and nodded. "How do you feel?"

"Numb."

He gave her a long look and said softly, "I'll see what I can do about that." He took two steps and, without touching her with his hands, bent to kiss her cheek, turned and picked up the bag. He looked around the room and held his arm for her to take hold, leading her to the door. Down the hall past the nurses' station, where the two who had taken care of her when she was helpless stood smiling, she pulled away from him to hug them and went back to link her arm in his as they waited for the elevator. She didn't see anything as she followed Jeff out the door across the one-way street into the parking lot.

He unlocked the door of the Mercedes, helped her in, and went to put her suitcase in the trunk. Jeff slid behind the wheel and inserted the key in the ignition before he turned to look at her. "Don't look so frightened, Ami. I won't hurt you."

She looked away from him but didn't answer, never so unsure of herself as she was at that moment. Finally, as the silence went on, she said, "Who's taking care of my job if I'm off gallivanting with the boss?"

"Rio's class gets their spring break in a week, and three of the graduate students are coming with him to work. Don't worry."

"Okay," she said and meant it. Rio would see that the others did everything the way she wanted it done.

The car slowed, and she looked back at the road as they turned into the driveway of the Cameron Hotel, one of Tucson's finest, she had read. A doorman came to Jeff's side of the car, and the two of them exchanged a few words before Jeff came around to open her door and help her out.

Another tall gray-haired man opened the heavy doors leading into the lobby of the plush foyer, and Jeff guided her across the deep red carpeting to the elevator. Its door slid silently back, and they stepped into the empty car and, a moment later, stopped without seeming to have moved at all.

A few steps down the hallway Jeff's hand on her arm stopped her in front of Room 747. "Sounds like an airplane," she whispered.

Jeff looked up questioningly from the key he was fitting into the door, and she nodded toward the number above his head. He grinned as the door swung open and he went inside, reaching for her hand. It was an elegant three-room suite, consisting of a living room almost as big as the one at Wagner's and two bedrooms and two baths. They wandered through, hand in hand, without a word until they returned to the living room.

"Is this the bridal suite?" Ami asked, walking to the window to draw the draperies, looking out of glare-proof windows into the sparkling spring day.

"The nearest thing they had to it," he told her. "The man I talked to told me they don't have many requests for bridal suites these days."

She looked over her shoulder at him. "Two bedrooms?"

"I thought perhaps you might want to sleep alone for a few days."

"Why?"

"You aren't exactly in top physical condition, Ami."

She looked back out the window and knew he was right. She was already tired and hadn't been out of bed more than five hours, but a lot had happened in that time. She wondered at the preparations that had gone into the surprise wedding, where everyone but her seemed to have been informed.

"Why did you do it?" she asked finally.

"I wanted to marry you, Ami, and you're so stubborn, I decided that to do things as they should be done, I'd take a chance on your anger later." He waited. "Are you angry?"

"No, but, Jeff, there are so many things that should have been settled before we married."

He came to stand behind her, his arm encircling her. "Later," he said. "You must be tired, and I promised Dr. Barry I would take care of you, not put you back in the hospital." He turned her around to face him. "I ordered a light lunch for us, and, afterwards, you can lie down for a while and then shop, if you think it isn't too much."

She nodded and leaned against him, her hand resting on his chest. The solid thudding of his heart beneath it sent a quiet thrill through her body, and she trembled.

Jeff felt the tremor and tilted her head to look down at her. "You are tired. Come on."

As they started back toward the center of the room, there was a quiet knock. "Room service, sir."

Jeff opened the door for the man to enter, and she watched as he moved quickly and efficiently to set up their lunch. In the center of the table he placed a bottle of champagne in a silver ice bucket. He broke the seal, poured a little of the sparkling liquid into a delicate glass, and handed it to Jeff, who smelled, tasted, and returned it to him with a nod. She watched, fascinated, as the ritual went on and the man smiled, bowed, and left with a soft word to Jeff.

"Mrs. Wagner," Jeff said, indicating the chair he held for her. She stared at him and suddenly she smiled, showing the small dimple that had been missing for a long time.

"This isn't exactly what I'm accustomed to. Nothing at all like the Best Western."

"No, it isn't," he admitted, pushing her chair nearer to the table and going to the opposite side. Carefully he filled her glass to the halfway mark, set it in front of her, and filled his the same way. He straightened, lifted the glass toward her and, as she picked hers up, he touched it.

"To you, Ami; to your rapid recovery and a long, happy life."

"With you," she added, watching his eyes narrow and the gray darken. She would have given her all to know what he was thinking as he nodded and they drank.

She grimaced. "Piña coladas are better," she said and blushed, remembering the last one she had with him at the Best Western.

"Don't let the wine steward hear you say that," Jeff warned and turned his attention to serving her a portion of the cornish hens, prepared with wild rice and other condiments she didn't recognize. It was delicious, and she found her appetite had improved since yesterday, finishing every bit he gave her even though it was barely noon.

She leaned back in her chair and sighed, heavy-eyed, as she met his glance across the table. He came around to her chair, sliding it back for her to rise, and took her arm, leading her toward the bedroom off the master bathroom. At the door he kissed her cheek.

"A couple of hours of sleep is what you need right now." Not waiting for her reply, he closed the door as he left.

She undressed and, exhausted, turned back the satin coverlet on the bed, slid between ivory satin sheets, rolled over on her stomach, and went to sleep. She dreamed. She ran, trying to outdistance her pursuer, coming to the mountain where there was no way out, and she turned to face Eileen, standing with her blond head lifted, the black Stetson hanging down her back. Her laughter echoed through the blind canyon. "He'll never marry you...never marry you." Ami threw up her hands and cried out as Eileen flicked her with the riding whip she carried.

"Ami, Ami." The voice penetrated her dream, and she opened her eyes to see Jeff sitting on the side of her bed, holding her arms as she fought with her dream. She drew a shuddering breath, and he gathered her to him, holding her until she stopped shaking.

"What's wrong?" The concern in Jeff's voice brought her back to realization, and she looked down at her body only half-covered by the satin sheets. She gulped and tried to pull away, but he held on to her for a moment longer, then slowly let her lie back on the pillows. His glance went over her exposed breasts, lingering on the purple scar just below the left one, before he pulled the sheet up to cover them.

"What were you dreaming of?" he asked.

Ami frowned, unable to recall what she had been running from. "It's a dream I've had before, but I can't remember what it was." She shivered. "I don't want to remember."

He kissed her cheek. "You will, in time, then you'll stop having the dream. Does it have anything to do with your run-in with Hank and Luke?"

"I think so."

Jeff nodded. "It's natural that it will bother you, but let's try to forget them." He stood up. "You slept about two hours. Do you feel up to shopping?"

"Yes." She smiled up at him. "Our room clerk will probably be glad to see something besides jeans in such a fancy place."

He laughed. "We'll help him if you're game." From the door he blew her a kiss and went out.

Dressed in regular jeans with a pale yellow sweater over a loose-fitting shirt, she joined him a few minutes later. As they left the building the doorman brought the car to the curb, and Jeff helped her in before he went around to the driver's side, where the doorman stood ready to close the door as Jeff slid behind the wheel.

The line shack for Camp 20 was never like this, she thought, and resolutely turned her thoughts away from Wagner's to keep her mind on shopping for a trousseau. Three hours later they piled boxes into the car and went back to the Cameron. They walked sedately across the plush lobby, took the elevator to the seventh floor, and entered the suite they had been in such a short time.

Ami dropped into a chair. "Do we have to give up this place after that shopping spree?"

She watched him through half-closed eyes as he looked down at her. "Why would we do that?"

"Didn't we spend my whole month's salary just now?"

Jeff's expression was grave. "We didn't spend any of *your* money, Ami. We spent *ours*."

"Oh." Her eyes flew open. She continued to watch him as he knelt by her, long tanned fingers holding her chin as he bent to place his mouth on hers. It started as a gentle caress that lit fires in both of them, and her lips parted, giving him access to the warm moistness inside her mouth. The length of her body was alive as he proceeded to explore with the tip of his tongue, teasing along the ridge of her teeth. She put her hands on his shoulders and sat up in the chair, responding to the urgency in his kiss. His breath came quickly as he released her lips to move over her throat to the throbbing pulse at the base where the bone curved to make a hollow. His mouth rested there until he raised his head to look down at her and stood up as a knock sounded at the door. They both stared toward the sound until he said, "Must be the results of our toil," and went to answer the knock.

Still shaken by the kiss, she barely saw the young man bring in the boxes they had purchased. When he had gone, Jeff said, "Come on and let's look." He sounded normal as though he hadn't just wrenched her heart from its mooring as he had done many times before.

He's my husband, she thought. *He's supposed to affect me that way.*

Jeff opened boxes and took out garments, placing them neatly on the bed for her to see. She shook her head. "Where will I ever wear all of that?" she asked.

"It's only five outfits, Ami," he said, picking up a pale green dress. "Try this."

She took it from him and, with an effort, refrained from looking at the price tag. It was cotton gauze with a demure Peter Pan collar, the bodice smocked in darker green and stitched onto a wide band attached to a skirt of tiny unpressed pleats.

"Do these shoes match that?" Jeff asked, holding up dark green suede pumps.

"Yes." She continued to look at him, holding the dress in front of her.

"Do you want me to leave?" he asked.

She swallowed hard but shook her head, spreading the dress on the bed, standing with her back to him as she pulled off the shirt and sweater. Kicking off her slippers, she pushed the jeans over her hips and reached for the dress, hesitating.

"I need a slip," she told him.

He handed it to her, and, a moment later, she slipped the dress over her head, turning to let him zip it for her. She sat on the edge of the bed as he put the pumps on her narrow feet.

As she stood up he moved back and smiled. "Yes." He reached to smooth her hair. "We have reservations for the dinner theater at seven thirty. That is, if you feel up to it."

"We don't even have to leave the hotel? What's playing?"

"Same Time Next Year," he said. "I'd better get changed, too. Won't be a minute." He turned and left her, and she walked into the bathroom to look at herself in the new clothing.

"Funny, you don't look like a bride," she told the pale reflection in the mirror. She wrinkled her nose. "You haven't been treated like one, either." The dress was becoming. The thick smocking and blouse effect from the gathers hid the fact that she was braless, and the long full sleeves would be warm enough without worrying about a jacket, since they weren't going outside the hotel.

Her eyes returned to her reflection. The scars from the scratches on her face were covered by well-matched makeup, which hid the shadows beneath her eyes.

There was a tint of color to her cheeks, probably still from Jeff's kiss. Going back into the bedroom, she pulled the heavy drapes to look out over the city where lights were beginning to come on. Tall palms in the courtyard seven stories below her swayed gently in the spring breeze. The door opened behind her, and Jeff came toward her with his hands outstretched. He was handsome in the gray suit he had worn for the wedding ceremony. She felt a moment of pity for Eileen that was gone the next instant as Jeff kissed her cheek and turned her around to lead her back into the living room.

"We've time for a glass of champagne they were nice enough to keep chilled for us," he said, indicating the silver bucket filled with ice, where the half-finished bottle of sparkling liquid still rested.

Jeff's hands drew her attention. They were tanned strong hands with long fingers that she had seen gently dress Mandy; hands that on her body were demanding, yet tender, that could force her attention or let her go, sometimes when she wasn't quite ready to be let go.

"Ami?" he said, handing her the glass. Her eyes went back to his face to find him watching her with a slight smile, his eyes questioning. "If you don't feel up to going to the theater, we can cancel," he said. "I just thought—"

He was putting off the inevitable confrontation over who sleeps with whom as long as he could, she surmised before she answered him. "I feel fine, and I'd like to see the play. I haven't been to one since college."

Jeff was standing in front of her and smiled as he touched her glass with his and they drank. He surveyed her slim figure and said, "The color of the dress is perfect for you." He continued to look down at her. "Amanda is right; you do have funny-colored eyes." She laughed with him.

"Tell me what Linda and Dave said about her. I haven't had a chance to ask—or was too wrapped up in what was happening to think about it."

Jeff put his glass down beside hers and nodded. "They're absolutely elated about everything and plan to write her up in the journal they publish semiannually, and they'll make sure we get a copy."

Ami stared at him, feeling emotions that were all mixed up with love and gratefulness for Mandy; and love alone for Jeff. She said slowly, "A year can make a vast difference in the outlook of things, can't it?"

"Yes," he said and stepped closer to her before he stopped, shaking his head. "We'd better go if we plan to eat before the show starts."

At that moment she would have liked to have canceled the show and walked into his arms, but he was all attention as he opened the door to let her walk out ahead of him, and they were quiet going down in the elevator and following the maître d' to their reserved table.

The look of money was everywhere as Ami glanced around at the other diners, smiling as her gaze encountered Jeff, who was watching her. As he gave their order a soft blue spotlight moved around the room to settle on a lovely dark-haired woman standing at the edge of the stage. The beginning of the band playing was hardly noticeable, subdued to blend with the woman's voice as she sang a torch song, sending chills along Ami's spine.

As the music sounds faded away Ami sighed and sat back in her chair, looking up to meet Jeff's gray eyes. She smiled. "She's very good."

"Yes, she is," he agreed. "Which reminds me of the message I'd forgotten to give you from the grange clubs waiting for you to come back. They miss you."

Their dinners arrived, and conversation wasn't necessary as they ate. Tender lobster with just the right amount of melted butter sauce claimed her complete attention. She looked up at Jeff. "Beats C rations all to pieces."

"No more C rations for you until Lily puts some weight on you," he said. "That's an order, Ami."

She met his glance, and his eyes darkened as the look held. The moment was interrupted by the waiter returning with coffee, and they finished the meal in silence.

She shook her head when he asked if she'd like a drink, and they turned to the stage as the lights were lowered and the opening scene began. The players were excellent in their parts, and she wondered how two people with simple settings could hold the attention of all the diners. They had to be good.

After a brief interlude when the action scenery changed, the next scene showed the woman enter the motel room where her partner was waiting. She was very much pregnant, causing the man to gaze at her in astonishment.

Ami, too, stared at the awkward, bulging figure the woman presented and her hands tightened in her lap against her flat stomach. Envy of the girl in the play rose inside her and she looked away. It had been a long time since she allowed herself any self-indulgence in thinking about a child of her own. She was Jeff's wife; she could share Mandy and Rio. That was enough for her, but what about her new husband? She turned her head to meet his look.

Jeff smiled and leaned toward her to whisper, "Are you getting tired?"

She smiled back at him, made a negative movement of her head, and looked back at the stage. When the lights came on, she rose as Jeff moved her chair back and followed him out of the dining room theater to the hallway into the elevator. They held hands going down the hallway, and he didn't release her hand as he inserted the key into the lock and opened the door. A soft light had been left on, and she gazed around at the luxurious furnishings in the suite they had occupied for

about twelve hours. It would be a wedding day to remember, whether for the conventional reasons or not.

Jeff tugged at her hand, turning her to face him.
"You'd better get some rest. Did Dr. Barry give you
anything to take?"

"Yes."

Leading her to the bedroom, he let go of her hands.
"Turn around and I'll unzip you."

Ami did as she as told, and Jeff kissed the back of
her neck. "I'll see you in the morning," he said, and
she heard the door close behind him. Closing her mind
to her roving thoughts, she got water from the bathroom to swallow the small green capsule Dr. Barry gave
her to take as needed, turned out the lights, and slipped
between the sheets. There was no sound from the
other rooms. She stretched her long legs until her side
pulled a little, then she lay still.

Sleep wouldn't come and, restless, she turned, waiting for the little pill to take effect. The connecting door
to Jeff's bedroom was only a blur in the dim room, but
her eyes stayed on the faint outline until, without
thought, she slid her feet over the edge of the bed and
walked across to turn the knob. The door opened quietly, and she stood just inside Jeff's room until her eyes
became accustomed to the dimness and she could
make out his outline on the bed.

He sat up quickly. "Are you all right?"

"Yes." She moved slowly to his side. "May I sleep
with you?"

Without a word he moved over to let her get into the
bed with him. She lay on her back, her head turned
slightly to look at him, still propped on his elbow to
watch her.

"I thought you had something to take to help you
sleep."

"I'm not very sleepy yet."

He lay back on his pillow and reached for her hand.

"Try to go to sleep, Ami. It's been a long day for you."

Her fingers tightened around his. "We're married, Jeff. Why can't you tell me you love me?"

"If we're married, you should know I love you." One hand, resting below the injured ribs, slid around her, his fingers massaging her spine.

"Tell me."

"I love you, Ami. I would never have married you otherwise. If I sometimes neglect to state that fact, always remember it's true. I've loved you for a long time, but I thought you knew without my saying so." He drew her close. "Go to sleep."

Her naked body in close contact with his had a will of its own and moved gently against him. His breath caught and he pulled away from her.

"Ami, honey, you'd better—"

Her mouth reached his, cutting off the protest, and she gasped as he responded. She was clasped tightly to him and she felt the groan go through him, his lips going from hers to her throat.

"You're making it awfully hard for me to take care of you, sweetheart," he whispered.

She pulled his face up to her pillow. "Jeff." There was no space between them now and she fitted herself into his arms. "Take care of me," she told him softly. "Love me."

He caught his breath at the demand in her voice and slowly began to kiss her, their bodies blending together as he let his fingers soothe the tenseness from her. She sighed as he released her mouth and turned her on her back, moving his hands from the slightly raised skin where the scar was, down over her hipbones to the long thighs. His kisses started at her waist, drifting over the flatness of her belly to follow his hands. She murmured satisfied sounds as his lips and fingers caressed and stroked her with tenderness that brought an unbelievable emotion cascading through her body. Her fingers lay lightly on his head as he touched her, tightening to hold him closer.

"Jeff," she whispered. "Oh." A long ecstatic shiver shook her body.

He lay back on the pillow, pulling her into his arms, his breath coming harshly from deep within his chest. She moved on top of him, keeping her legs close together down the hardness of his body.

He bit into his lip. "Honey," he sighed. It took only a moment of sensuous manipulation of their bodies, her mouth moving over his, whispering words only for him, until he gave in and his convulsive response shook them both.

"Are you convinced?" she asked.

"Of what?"

"That I'm yours?"

He laughed softly, his mouth against her hair. "Yes."

Close in each other arms, they slept.

Chapter Fifteen

It was bright in the room when Ami awakened, and she lay there, trying to sort out what had happened. She was Mrs. Jeff Wagner, a fact she no longer doubted as she recalled her wedding night. Having to make the first move to get Jeff to make love to her didn't bother her; at least he didn't refuse.

Turning to look at the pillow still showing the shape of Jeff's head, she smiled, remembering his arms around her, his vibrant voice telling her he loved her. With Jeff's love to back her up, she could face anything, even Eileen's accusations. She pushed the ugly thoughts away and slid out of bed, wondering where her husband was, glancing at her watch to see that it was almost ten o'clock.

Moving to the window to push the drapes aside to look out upon a sunny world, her gaze rested on the mountains and she smiled, turning after a moment to make her way to the bathroom. The reflection of her naked body was the way it had always been except for the purplish-blue flesh surrounding the small scar where Dr. Barry had removed the bullet from Hank's gun.

"You almost had it, my girl," she said aloud and thought about Remus protecting her, possibly taking the bullet that would have been fatal to her. They were both rather beat up, a little the worse for wear, but they'd make it. She went to shower.

Wrapped in a big terry towel, she went to look at some of the clothing purchased the day before. Choosing an off-white pantsuit with tan flecks through the linen material and a beige-striped long-sleeved blouse, gathered from a front yoke, she decided it would camouflage her braless figure. Absently her fingers smoothed over the ridge of the scar on her ribs, only a little tender now.

In answer to a light knock on the door she called, "Come in."

Jeff opened the door and stood looking at her, and she realized she was anything but dressed. Dark gray eyes went over her tall figure clothed only in a towel. He asked softly, "Did you sleep well?"

He's my husband, she thought, gazing at the tall man just inside the door. Her lips parted as she continued to look at him. Without answering his question, she went to stand in front of him and lifted her hands to place them on his shoulders, standing on tiptoe to bring her face nearer to his. He bent slightly to place his mouth over hers, sending a thrill racing through her.

When he lifted his head to smile down at her, she said, "Looks like I overslept."

Jeff grinned. "I was beginning to think we could order lunch instead of breakfast. I'm starved."

"I'll only be a minute," she promised as he turned to leave her.

Jeff was standing at the window, where he had drawn the draperies, and as she went into the room he turned to watch her walk to join him. The striped blouse was tucked into the pants, which fit smoothly over her hips, and she carried the matching jacket over her arm.

He nodded approvingly, and they went downstairs to join the many others of the hotel clientele enjoying a late breakfast. A giant pendulum clock silently proclaimed that it was eleven thirty as they finished eating.

He looked across at her as she sipped a last cup of coffee. "Let's check out and take a ride up through the country. Have you ever been through the Superstition Mountains?"

Startled, she replied, "No. I was planning to look them over...." She let her voice drop.

He waited, but she didn't add anything. "You mean when you went to work for Jim Summers you thought you'd have plenty of time?"

"Yes."

Jeff leaned toward her. "Since you won't be working for him, suppose we tour the area. Do you feel up to it?"

She blushed suddenly, remembering the night in Jeff's arms. "I feel good." But she added, "I'm not tired now and the food here is not exactly like what I've been served the past couple of weeks."

He laughed. "Decidedly not." His mouth curved with tenderness as he stood up to move her chair back, and she felt her doubts dissolve.

Back in their room, they packed, leaving most of her purchases in the boxes. Jeff called to have their luggage picked up and the car brought around front, and they went down to check out. Jeff's conversation with the man at the desk was low, and she found herself wondering if he was being congratulated on his marriage. Aside from the new softness about him as he took care of getting their things together, he hadn't mentioned their wedding night, and she was curious to know if he compared her boyishly straight body to Eileen's luscious curves.

"Ready?" Jeff asked at her elbow.

Ami nodded and walked with him outside, slipping into the car seat as the doorman held the car door open for her. She concentrated on the city scenery as Jeff drove through early Saturday afternoon traffic, heading almost directly into the sun, turning north as they left the interstate just outside of Tucson, taking U.S. 89. Highway signs indicated Apache Junction was eighty miles away. The landscape was her favorite; desert surrounded by mountains; mountains giving way to desert. there was no smoke or pollution from city industry, the only blot on the view an occasional mine opening.

At Apache Junction Jeff drove slowly. "When we head north, there's very little in the way of civilization. A few ranches, Jim Summers's among them. It's strictly for scenery and searchers for the Lost Dutchman's cache of gold."

"Wonder if that's a fairy tale, too?"

"Fairy tale?" he echoed.

Ami felt the blush rise in her cheeks and kept her face turned away from him. She had been thinking that love was a fairy tale, highly improbable, and they were entering country that was filled with legends and tall stories originating in the fertile imaginations of generations long gone.

"It's unlikely that all the stories are true, isn't it?"

He laughed. "I believe them, Ami," he said. "It makes for fascinating listening, not nearly as dull as some history is."

"I suppose so," she agreed, watching the spindly cactus and piñon trees that reached to the edge of the Lost Dutchman, only one of the many peaks of the Superstition Mountain chain. She could well believe that lots of gold as well as people had been lost in the vast wilderness when their only means of transportation was walking or an old mule or burro and, when extremely lucky, a good horse. Neither of them spoke as they passed the heavy gate with the J & R Ranch sign on top of it.

They began to climb at a sharp angle, turning around curves that met them coming the opposite way. She held her breath, looking down over the side of the mountain into a blue-green lake hundreds of feet below them.

"That body of water comes from Stewart Mountain Dam," Jeff said. "There's plenty of water up through here; it just happens to be hard to reach." He pointed through a range of tall peaks to a narrow road twisting out of sight. "This is the Apache Trail, which ends at Roosevelt Dam."

A sudden sharp turn in the road brought them into an area resembling a movie set. On the right was a motel, rustic logs squatting by the side of the road. Nearby was a sign proclaiming TORTILLA FLATS: POPULATION 6.

"Six people?" she asked in astonishment.

Jeff grinned as he pulled into a parking place near the motel. "That may include the dogs."

They sat a moment looking at the blue-green scenery that dominated the wide place in the road. Fifty feet past the motel was a café with a sign that said: WELCOME, RESTAURANT AND POST OFFICE, TORTILLA FLATS. A few yards farther up the narrow street was the zoo. At least there were two monkeys, according to the sign.

Jeff got out and came around to open Ami's door, holding her arm to help her step up on the bricked sidewalk. They walked around to the side where a door stood open to the late afternoon sun.

"May I help you?" a voice asked from the dim interior.

"Yes, we have reservations. Mr. and Mrs. Jeff Wagner," He turned to look back at her where she had stopped just inside the door and held out his hand.

"Sign here, Mr. Wagner," the older woman said, indicating the registry book on the counter. She smiled at Ami. "Where you folks from?" she asked without bothering to look at what Jeff had written.

"Southeastern Arizona, near Tombstone," Jeff told her.

The woman nodded. "I'm Mrs. Sandstrom. Just let me know if you need anything."

Jeff thanked her and led Ami through another door, looking at the number on the key he held. They walked down the hall to the last room, and Jeff stopped, looking down at her. "Okay?"

Ami nodded, and Jeff pushed open the heavy wooden door to reveal a big airy room, two wide windows looking out over green terrain running into the side of the mountain that reached into an incredibly blue sky. Two queen-size beds dominated the furnishings in the room.

"More like the Best Western," Jeff said, smiling at her.

Yes, she thought, even to having two beds.

"I'll get our luggage," he said and disappeared through the door.

She walked over and sat on the edge of the bed farthest from the windows, feeling tired. Or lazy. The thin air at this elevation might be a reason, or the events of the past two days could be catching up with her. She stretched out across the bed, staring at the heavy beamed ceiling. When Jeff came in, she didn't sit up but turned her head to smile at him.

He came to stand looking down at her. "As soon as we unpack, you can take a nap."

"That's all I've done lately," she protested. "I want to see the sights."

He laughed. "I think you saw them all but, okay, we can go see the two monkeys in the zoo." He placed their luggage on the racks in the area by the bathroom and came back, taking her hand to pull her up. "Let's go sight-seeing."

Outside, they walked past the restaurant and Post Office to the wired area that took in the zoo. The medium-size monkeys swung across the bars to stand regarding the strange two-legged creatures who looked

curiously back at them. In the corner were two big
cages holding multicolored parrots, one of whom carried on a one-way conversation of "Halt. Who goes
there?" and "They went that-a-way."

"The population listed must not include the zoo,"
she said, turning to take his arm as they retraced their
footsteps back to the motel. The sun was dropping rapidly behind the lofty mountain the historical marker
named the Mazatzal Peak. The air had become chilly.

Inside the room Jeff turned her into his arms, bending to place his mouth over hers, holding her tightly for
a moment. "Go lie down for a while."

"Where are you going?" Ami asked, curious as any
wife whose husband would leave her alone in a strange
motel so soon after marrying her, wanting him to stay
with her.

"I saw some good-looking horses down below us in a
corral. You need your own."

"I do?" she asked, surprised.

"You'll be back to riding in no time, Ami. You don't
expect to sit around the ranch and do nothing, do
you?" He smiled back at her from the door. "I won't
be long. Rest," he instructed and closed the door behind him.

Slowly she undressed, hung up the neat suit she removed, and turned back the covers on the bed she had
chosen, lying down to close her eyes wearily. Jeff said
he loved her, but was it just assurance he thought she
needed to get through what might prove to be a nasty
time if Eileen really brought rustling charges against
her? In the past few hours he had shown his feelings
only a little, and that was after she initiated their love-
making. Sighing, she slept.

Jeff stopped to look across the line of trees that
marched straight up the side of the mountains. The
sweater he wore felt good in the air, where the tem-

perature had dropped over ten degrees since their arrival. His thoughts went to the woman in the room he had
just left. Ami was puzzled at his actions; she wasn't
sure why he had married her, and he wasn't sure if he
had convinced her the way he wished he could. He
smiled. There was a lifetime ahead to show his deep
love for her and he meant to use it all. After confessing
to loving him, she fought against marrying him after
she found out about Eileen's charges, but that was settled as far as he was concerned. Eileen's conscience was
her own to come to terms with, and the rustlers had
been caught, the cattle returned.

According to Jasper and Steve, all Wagner cattle had
been easy to identify, using the method Ami had described, that of turning a spotlight on them as they
were corraled, cutting out the ones that showed no sign
of the dye solution. There were less than fifty of Eileen's among the nearly one hundred and fifty in the
herd. Ron Steward had signed a paper releasing Wagner's of any further responsibility for the cattle. Jeff
grinned to himself, wondering how much persuasion
Jasper and Steve used to get his signature. One look at
Jasper when he was angry, which wasn't often, was
enough to convince most people that they should follow the right course. Steve was not one to be crossed,
either, as he recalled, thinking of a run-in with enemy
ground forces once in Vietnam.

His thoughts returned to Ami as he strolled down
the steep hillside toward the corral he had seen from the
highway. He leaned on the cedar fence and watched the
half dozen horses grazing. Ami rode any of the horses
in the corral when she needed one, but he wanted
something special for her. One, in particular, interested
him as he watched the playful nudgings of the younger
animals. A dark gray filly, perhaps a year old, with a
white blaze down her face, stood with head lifted toward the mountains. The sleek neck was strong and she

assumed a proud stance that kept his attention, somehow reminding him of Ami, a no-nonsense independent carriage much in evidence.

"Pretty, ain't she?"

Jeff turned to see a grizzled old-timer, gnarled hands hitched into faded, worn jeans. He nodded. "She's a beauty. Who does she belong to?"

The old man laughed. "Since I'm about all there is here," he said, "guess she's mine."

"Is she for sale?"

The old man looked at him with interest. "Well, now," he said, "anybody interested in Gray Lady would have to have a bit of money."

"How big a bit?"

The old man thought a moment, spit a well-aimed stream of tobacco juice into a weed patch. "I been known to bargain."

Jeff looked back at the horse, the strong neck now arched as she bent to resume grazing. He studied the lines of her back and hind legs and turned to grin at the old man.

"Let's talk."

Ami opened her eyes to stare at the same log beams she had been looking at when sleep overtook her. She turned her head as the door to the room opened quietly and Jeff came in.

She stretched and smiled at him. "Did you find the horses?"

He nodded, his eyes going over the outline of her body beneath the covers. He sat down on the edge of the bed as Ami moved over to give him room, and touched her cheek, pushing the thick hair away from her face, and bent to kiss her. His lips, warm and light on hers, parted to allow his teeth to graze her chin as he nuzzled against her. He raised his head, half-closed eyes taking in her sleep-flushed face and whispered, "Ami."

Desire for him enveloped her, and she wished for words to express her feelings for him, feelings that made her tremble. Her hands went to his face, cupping it, pulling him down to her. Lips parted, the tip of her tongue entered his mouth for an instant and was withdrawn as he drew a sharp breath.

Jeff started to pull away, then groaned, bringing her up into his arms, holding her close. He pushed her back on the pillow and slowly bent to her, taking her lips and caressing them with his own, letting the tip of his tongue intrude inside her mouth, withdrawing it to trail kisses over her chin to her throat, down into the cleft between the small, firm mounds. He lay beside her on top of the covers, his arm across her.

"Take off your clothes," she said suddenly.

His arm tightened and he laughed softly. "Brazen." But he did as he was told, turning the covers back to get into bed beside her.

"I want you, Ami," he said and held her without talking for a long time. He stirred. "I came so close to losing you and I can't bear having anything hurt you." He caressed the length of her body, one hand returning to explore the scar on her side. "Does it hurt?"

"No."

"Isn't it sore?"

"Tender, a little."

His hand moved from the scar across her flat stomach, up over the small breasts. "Did Dr. Barry give you any special dos and dont's?"

"He told me not to drive the truck or ride a horse for a while."

"What about sex?" Jeff's question was against her mouth. "I mean my having you completely?"

"It wasn't mentioned." Ami moved her body closer to him, her arm across his shoulder.

"Will you stop me if I hurt you?"

"No." Her lips parted against his.

"Sweetheart." Jeff held her away, but she pulled him back to her, pushing her thigh between his legs, her hand behind his head to keep his mouth on hers. Her back arched and there was no way he could withstand the pulsing desire filling them both, and he took her slowly, holding back until she cried out and he let go as the sweetness drained them both.

"Are you all right?" he asked.

"Yes," she whispered. "Jeff?"

"Hmmm?"

"I'm not numb anymore." Ami put her head back on the pillow to look at him. "Kiss me again."

He shook his head. "If I do—"

He kissed her as her hands inventoried his body from the thick chest hair across the tautness of his stomach, drifting downward slowly. He groaned without releasing her mouth, murmuring against her lips, and his hands moved down to fit behind her hips, pulling her up until he nestled inside her thighs. With gentle strokes he took possession of her, looking into wide-open turquoise depths. He whispered, "I love you, darling," as they floated in a never-never world.

Holding tightly, she cherished the sound of those words. With her face still against his throat, she said, "Jeff, we have to talk."

"All right," he agreed.

She waited, but he didn't say any more. "There's something I have to tell you, something I should have told you before you married me." She waited again. "Jeff?"

He continued to hold her close. "Does it have anything to do with your not being able to have children?"

Her body jerked and she moved her head swiftly back, eyes almost black as she stared at him in the room, which was growing dark. "How—how did you know?"

"While you were unconscious, you talked quite a bit," he told her. "Is it so important to you to be able to have a baby?"

Ami stared at him. "I always thought so." She bit her lip. "That's why Tim divorced me."

"I can't believe a man would give you up for that reason. Didn't you think about adoption?"

"Tim didn't want someone else's children; he wanted his own flesh and blood."

His long fingers caressed her cheek. "I understand that it hurts not to be able to have your own baby, Ami, but we have Amanda and Rio, and if you want more, I'm sure we can adopt a couple." His voice was quietly reassuring as he went on. "The fact that you can't get pregnant doesn't alter my feelings for you, if you're concerned about that." She lay still in his arms, their hearts beating in unison. Her heart was filled to the bursting point with love for the man who held her, overflowing when he declared his love for her.

"You really don't mind?" she asked after a long time.

"It won't matter to me as soon as you accept it, Ami."

"I love you, Jeff."

He gathered her to him for long moments, their bodies as close as they could get to each other. Slowly his hand moved over the small mound of her breast, his thumb gently massaging the brown tip until it swelled. He raised himself up on his elbow and pushed her over on her back, lowering his face until he could close his mouth over her throbbing breast. Her breathing became more rapid as he trailed a row of kisses across her to the other tip waiting for him. Their bodies moved together in a slow, sensuous rhythm, and as she fitted herself to him, he came back to kiss her, his tongue thrusting inside her mouth, demanding her complete surrender. She gave it gladly, feeling liquid fire singing through her veins, gasping as their bodies met fiercely, then were still.

As they drew near Wagner's, Ami tensed, wondering what awaited her as the new mistress of the ranch. A big hand closed over hers and she turned to look at Jeff. He had told her the rustling episode was finished as far as she was concerned, and any further negotiations or investigations would be handled by Jasper.

"Nervous?" he asked, and she nodded. He smiled but said no more. He drove past the airstrip and, a few moments later, turned into the lane leading to the big house. She stared as they pulled into the yard. Strung between the two big cottonwoods was a banner with bright red letters that read: WELCOME HOME, AMI AND JEFF.

"We're home, darling," Jeff said softly beside her.

Her eyes left the banner to swing toward him. "I believe in fairy tales," she said and leaned over for his kiss.

Chapter Sixteen

She stood behind the shack at Camp 20, where the drama of a few months ago had taken place and, even now, seemed somewhat unreal. Filling in where she was needed as veterinarian on the huge ranch, Ami didn't spend much time in the line camps anymore, leaving most of the work up to the graduate students from the college who needed on-the-job training as veterinarians. In a few years Rio would take over full-time, but in the meantime she and Hammett shared a lot of the duties around the home corral and less of the ones requiring extended stays from the big house. Jeff frowned on her being away from him even a few days.

She smiled, thinking of her husband, who had long since convinced her that even though he wasn't much on voicing his love for her, he certainly could show her in other ways. A soft whinny called her attention to the beautiful horse a few feet from her, the young filly Jeff had bargained for from the old mountain man in Tortilla Flats when they were on their honeymoon. The strong neck arched as she lifted her head into the wind blowing from the southeast, and Ami turned as she heard the sound of a motor.

It was Jeff in the Bronco. He came up to her, smiling. "Okay, lady, time to return to the home corral. You've been gone too long."

She laughed, walking into his arms. "One night.

What are you going to do when you go to that auction in Abilene?''

"Take you with me," he said, kissing her uplifted mouth.

She shook her head. "Mandy has a checkup coming."

"Mandy can do without her checkup easier than I can do without you." His arm tightened around her. "We'll take her in earlier and be back before the auction."

Ami leaned closer to his hard body. "Jeff, does it ever occur to you how much we have to be thankful for?"

"Every day," he said, turning to lead her toward the shack.

Ami matched her steps to his, musing briefly on the recent past events: Eileen's and Ron's confession to their part in the fake rustling that turned out to be real; the sizzling editorial in the *Tombstone Gazette,* condemning them; the extended legal entanglements worked out between Jasper and the state. It had ruined the friendship between the Wagners and McKanes, bringing a tight look of disappointment to Jeff when the subject came up. Jeff tried to take some of the blame for what happened on himself, but Ami didn't agree with that at all; however, she made no comment, recognizing the torment he went through because of the situation.

I won all the way around, she thought, smiling up at Jeff as he pushed the door to the shack open. Jeff was hers as well as the spunky little Mandy, who would be starting to attend a regular school in the fall. Mandy accepted Ami as naturally as though she had expected this to happen, never showing any jealousy of Ami's relationship with Jeff. As soon as Rio established the fact that he belonged in the family, his affection embraced Jeff and Mandy fully.

The interior of the shack was almost dark, but Jeff made no attempt to light the oil lamp. He pulled Ami close, brushing his lips over her face, lingering at her ear to whisper, "I miss you so much, Ami." He moved to her mouth, making soft kisses across it, and moaned.

He drew her with him to the bunk and they lay down, close together of necessity, on the narrow bed.

"I hate to be impatient, but it's been a long time," Jeff whispered.

"Mmmm," she acknowledged, searching for and finding his mouth as their hands busied themselves discarding clothing. His quickening breath matched hers as their bodies came together, the roughness of his hairy chest against her small breasts creating a fiery tumult through them.

For a moment his fingers touched the nearly-forgotten scar beneath her ribs, going downward to her waist, over her hip to separate her thighs.

"Ami, oh, Ami." He murmured her name over and over as he claimed the body eagerly surrendering to his desires. Love for each other swept them away, wiping out the world and its problems.

"I love you." The words came simultaneously from them, and Ami knew her fairy tale was no longer a tale, but true in every sense of the word.

LAVYRLE SPENCER
SWEET MEMORIES

a special woman... a special love... a special story

Sweet Memories is the poignant tale of Theresa Brubaker and Brian Scanlon, separated by Brian's Air Force officer training, but united in spirit by their burning love.

Alone and unsure, Theresa decides on a traumatic surgical operation that proves devastating for both her and Brian, a proud sensitive man whose feelings of betrayal run deep. Through the tears and pain, Theresa emerges from her inhibitions a passionate, self-confident woman ready to express her love.

The Complete Pokémon Pocket Guide
Volume 1

POKÉMON DIAMOND PEARL ZEN CHARA DAIZUKAN Vol. 1
All rights reserved.
Original Japanese edition published by SHOGAKUKAN in 2007.
English translation rights in the United States of America and Canada
arranged with SHOGAKUKAN.

Original Japanese Edition
Text & Composition / Jun SAKATA
With the Cooperation of / Shogakukan-Shueisha Productions
Illustrations / Mitsuo KIMURA, OLM
Design / Tariji SASAKI

VIZ Media Edition
Translation/Kaori Inoue
Interior Design/Courtney Utt, Bustah Brown Design Inc., Hidemi Sahara
Cover Design/Hitomi Yokoyama Ross
Editor/Leyla Aker
Senior Editorial Director/Elizabeth Kawasaki

The stories, characters and incidents mentioned in this publication are entirely fictional.

Printed in Korea

Published by VIZ Media, LLC
P.O. Box 77010
San Francisco, CA 94107

10 9 8 7 6 5 4 3 2
First printing, January 2017
Second printing, August 2022

viz.com

PARENTAL ADVISORY
THE COMPLETE POKÉMON POCKET
GUIDE is rated A and is suitable for
readers of all ages.
ratings.viz.com

How to Use This Book

Everything you need to know about
Pokémon can be found here in this
comprehensive two-volume guide.

This is volume 1 of 2!

The Pokémon in this book are presented
in their National Pokédex order. This
volume contains numbers 001 to 245,
Bulbasaur to Suicune. Volume 2 contains
numbers 246 to 491, Larvitar to Darkrai.

If you would like to look up a Pokémon
by name, there is an alphabetical index
at the end of both volumes.

BULBASAUR

Pokémon Data

Seed Pokémon

TYPE	Grass
	Poison
ABILITIES	Overgrow
	. . .
HEIGHT	2′04″
WEIGHT	15.2 lbs

National Pokédex No.
001

Description

As Bulbasaur grows, the plant bulb on its back grows too. When it's very young it draws nutrients from the bulb.

Special Moves

Leech Seed, Vine Whip, Poison Powder

EVO LUT ION

Bulbasaur → Ivysaur → Venusaur

IVYSAUR

Pokémon Data

Seed Pokémon

TYPE	Grass
	Poison
ABILITIES	Overgrow
	. . .
HEIGHT	3´03˝
WEIGHT	28.7 lbs

1-
49

100-
149

150-
199

200-
249

250-
299

300-
349

350-
399

400-
449

450-
491

Description

A sweet smell fills the air when the bud on Ivysaur's back begins to open. But if the bud gets too big, Ivysaur has trouble walking.

Special Moves

Razor Leaf, Sweet Scent, Take Down

National Pokédex No.
002

EVO
LUT
ION

Bulbasaur → **Ivysaur** → **Venusaur**

VENUSAUR

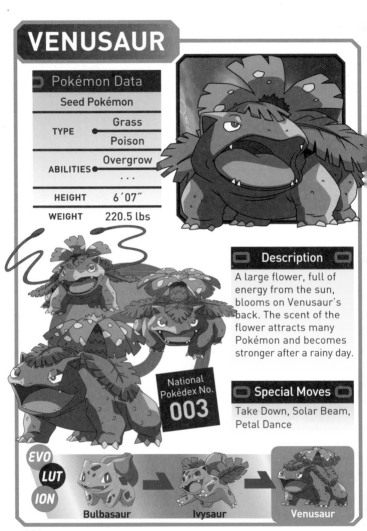

Pokémon Data

Seed Pokémon	
TYPE	Grass
	Poison
ABILITIES	Overgrow
	. . .
HEIGHT	6´07"
WEIGHT	220.5 lbs

Description

A large flower, full of energy from the sun, blooms on Venusaur's back. The scent of the flower attracts many Pokémon and becomes stronger after a rainy day.

National Pokédex No.
003

Special Moves

Take Down, Solar Beam, Petal Dance

EVO LUT ION

Bulbasaur → Ivysaur → Venusaur

CHARMANDER

Pokémon Data

Lizard Pokémon

TYPE	Fire ...
ABILITIES	Blaze ...
HEIGHT	2'00"
WEIGHT	18.7 lbs

National Pokédex No.
004

Description

The fire on the tip of Charmander's tail burns from the moment it is born and doesn't go out until its life comes to an end. The flame burns more brightly when it is happy and energetic.

Special Moves

Smokescreen, Growl, Scratch, Ember

EVO LUT ION

Charmander → Charmeleon → Charizard

1-49
50-99
100-149
150-199
200-249
250-299
300-349
350-399
400-449
450-491

CHARMELEON

Pokémon Data

Flame Pokémon

TYPE	Fire
	. . .
ABILITIES	Blaze
	. . .
HEIGHT	3´07˝
WEIGHT	41.9 lbs

National Pokédex No.
005

Description

Because of its flame, the temperature of the air around Charmeleon is higher by several degrees.

Special Moves

Fire Fang, Slash, Flamethrower

EVO LUT ION

Charmander → Charmeleon → Charizard

CHARIZARD

Pokémon Data

Flame Pokémon

TYPE	Fire
	Flying
ABILITIES	Blaze
	. . .
HEIGHT	5'07"
WEIGHT	199.5 lbs

National Pokédex No. **006**

Description

Charizard can fly almost a mile straight up into the sky and spew scorching flames from its mouth. The more battles it experiences, the hotter its flames become.

Special Moves

Fire Spin, Heat Wave, Flare Blitz

49

50-
99

100-
149

150-
199

200-
249

250-
299

300-
349

350-
399

400-
449

450-
491

EVO LUT ION

Charmander   Charmeleon

Charizard

SQUIRTLE

Pokémon Data

Tiny Turtle Pokémon

TYPE	Water . . .
ABILITIES	Torrent . . .
HEIGHT	1´08˝
WEIGHT	19.8 lbs

Description

Squirtle's shell hardens right after it's born. It protects itself by hiding in its shell. Then, at the right moment, it will counterattack with blasts of water.

National Pokédex No.
007

Special Moves

Withdraw, Water Gun, Bite

EVO LUT ION

Squirtle → Wartortle → Blastoise

WARTORTLE

Pokémon Data

Turtle Pokémon

TYPE	Water
	...
ABILITIES	Torrent
	...
HEIGHT	3'03"
WEIGHT	49.6 lbs

National Pokédex No.
008

Description

Wartortle lives for a very long time, so its fluffy tail is popular as a symbol for longevity. By moving its ears to adjust its direction, it is able to swim faster underwater.

Special Moves

Rapid Spin, Protect, Water Pulse

EVO
LUT
ION

Squirtle Wartortle Blastoise

1-49
50-99
100-149
150-199
200-249
250-299
300-349
350-399
400-449
450-491

BLASTOISE

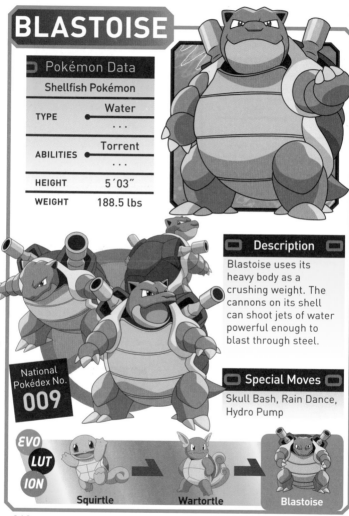

Pokémon Data

Shellfish Pokémon

TYPE	Water ...
ABILITIES	Torrent ...
HEIGHT	5'03"
WEIGHT	188.5 lbs

Description

Blastoise uses its heavy body as a crushing weight. The cannons on its shell can shoot jets of water powerful enough to blast through steel.

National Pokédex No.
009

Special Moves

Skull Bash, Rain Dance, Hydro Pump

EVO LUT ION

Squirtle → Wartortle → Blastoise

CATERPIE

1-49
50-99
100-149
150-199
200-249
250-299
300-349
350-399
400-449
450-491

Pokémon Data

Worm Pokémon

TYPE	Bug
	...
ABILITIES	Shield Dust
	...
HEIGHT	1'00"
WEIGHT	6.4 lbs

National Pokédex No.
010

Description

Because its feet are actually suction cups Caterpie can easily navigate slopes and walls. The stink that emanates from its red horn can repel its enemies.

Special Moves

Tackle, String Shot

EVO LUT ION

Caterpie → Metapod → Butterfree

METAPOD

Pokémon Data

Cocoon Pokémon	
TYPE	Bug
	...
ABILITIES	Shed Skin
	...
HEIGHT	2´04"
WEIGHT	21.8 lbs

National Pokédex No.

011

Description

Metapod waits inside its hard shell to Evolve. Although its shell is as hard as steel, its innards are very soft. If Metapod sustains a hard blow, they might get injured.

Special Moves

Harden

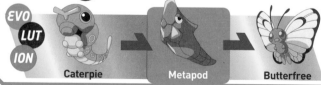

EVO LUT ION

Caterpie → Metapod → Butterfree

BUTTERFREE

Pokémon Data

Butterfly Pokémon

TYPE	Bug
	Flying
ABILITIES	Compound Eyes
	...
HEIGHT	3´07˝
WEIGHT	70.5 lbs

National Pokédex No.
012

Description

Because its wings are covered with a fine, water-repellent dust, it can fly even on rainy days. Butterfree loves flower nectar and can locate fields of flowers just by smell.

Special Moves

Gust, Psybeam, Silver Wind, Bug Buzz

EVO LUT ION

Caterpie → Metapod → Butterfree

1-49
50-99
100-149
150-199
200-249
250-299
300-349
350-399
400-449
450-491

WEEDLE

Pokémon Data

Hairy Bug Pokémon

TYPE	Bug
	Poison
ABILITIES	Shield Dust
	. . .
HEIGHT	1′00″
WEIGHT	7.1 lbs

Description

Weedle lives in forests and grasslands. Every day it eats its body weight in leaves. When attacked, it defends itself using the small poisonous needle atop its head.

National Pokédex No.
013

Special Moves

Poison Sting, String Shot

EVO LUT ION

Weedle → Kakuna → Beedrill

KAKUNA

Pokémon Data

Cocoon Pokémon

TYPE	Bug
	Poison
ABILITIES	Shed Skin
	...
HEIGHT	2´00″
WEIGHT	22.0 lbs

1-49

50-99

100-149

150-199

200-249

250-299

300-349

350-399

400-449

450-491

Description

Unable to move on its own, Kakuna avoids predators by hiding under leaves and in between branches, where it patiently waits to Evolve.

National Pokédex No.
014

Special Moves

Harden

EVO LUT ION

Weedle

Kakuna

Beedrill

BEEDRILL

Pokémon Data

Poison Bee Pokémon

TYPE	Bug
	Poison
ABILITIES	Swarm
	. . .
HEIGHT	3´03˝
WEIGHT	65.0 lbs

National Pokédex No.
015

Description

Beedrill attacks by darting in with great speed, jabbing its opponents with the poisonous needles on its forelimbs and tail, and then quickly flying away.

Special Moves

Twineedle, Pin Missile, Poison Jab

EVO LUT ION

Weedle → Kakuna → Beedrill

PIDGEY

Pokémon Data

Tiny Bird Pokémon

TYPE	Normal
	Flying
ABILITIES	Keen Eye
	Tangled Feet
HEIGHT	1´00˝
WEIGHT	4.0 lbs

National Pokédex No.
016

Description

Pidgey lives in forests and grassy thickets, where it hunts small bugs, and tends to shy away from fighting. Although timid, it will defend itself bravely if threatened.

Special Moves

Gust, Quick Attack, Whirlwind

1–49
50–99
100–149
150–199
200–249
250–299
300–349
350–399
400–449
450–491

EVO LUT ION

Pidgey

Pidgeotto

Pidgeot

PIDGEOTTO

Pokémon Data

Bird Pokémon	
TYPE	Normal
	Flying
ABILITIES	Keen Eye
	Tangled Feet
HEIGHT	3'07"
WEIGHT	66.1 lbs

National Pokédex No. **017**

Description

Pidgeotto constantly patrols its large territory and will attack any enemies that enter it. Its strong claws enable it to fly long distances while carrying its food.

Special Moves

Wing Attack, Tailwind, Mirror Move, Air Slash

EVO LUT ION

Pidgey → Pidgeotto → Pidgeot

PIDGEOT

Pokémon Data

Bird Pokémon

TYPE	Normal
	Flying
ABILITIES	Keen Eye
	Tangled Feet
HEIGHT	4'11"
WEIGHT	87.1 lbs

National Pokédex No.
018

Description

Pidgeot intimidates its opponents by spreading its beautiful wings out wide. With one hard flap, it can create a gust of wind strong enough to snap a large tree.

Special Moves

Whirlwind, Feather Dance, Roost, Mirror Move

1-49

50-99

100-149

150-199

200-249

250-299

300-349

350-399

400-449

450-491

EVO LUT ION

Pidgey → Pidgeotto → Pidgeot

RATTATA

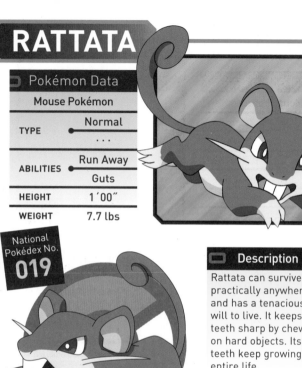

Pokémon Data

Mouse Pokémon

TYPE	Normal
	. . .
ABILITIES	Run Away
	Guts
HEIGHT	1′00″
WEIGHT	7.7 lbs

National Pokédex No.
019

Description

Rattata can survive practically anywhere and has a tenacious will to live. It keeps its teeth sharp by chewing on hard objects. Its teeth keep growing its entire life.

Special Moves

Bite, Hyper Fang, Sucker Punch

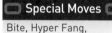

EVO LUT ION

Rattata → Raticate

RATICATE

1-49
50-99
100-149
150-199
200-249
250-299
300-349
350-399
400-449
450-491

Pokémon Data

Mouse Pokémon

TYPE	Normal
	. . .
ABILITIES	Run Away
	Guts
HEIGHT	2´04˝
WEIGHT	40.8 lbs

National
Pokédex No.
020

Description

Raticate wears down its ever-growing fangs by chewing on hard objects. Its whiskers help it maintain its balance and its back feet are webbed, which enables it to swim.

Special Moves

Crunch, Super Fang, Hyper Fang

EVO
LUT
ION

Rattata   Raticate

SPEAROW

Pokémon Data

Tiny Bird Pokémon

TYPE	Normal
	Flying
ABILITIES	Keen Eye
	. . .
HEIGHT	1´00˝
WEIGHT	4.4 lbs

National Pokédex No.
021

Description

Spearow must always beat its short wings furiously in order to fly. Nevertheless, it constantly flies about, patrolling its territory.

Special Moves

Fury Attack, Pursuit, Peck, Aerial Ace, Mirror Move

EVO LUT ION

Spearow   Fearow

FEAROW

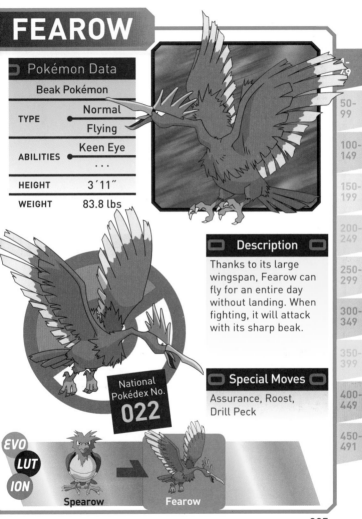

Pokémon Data

Beak Pokémon

TYPE	Normal
	Flying
ABILITIES	Keen Eye
	...
HEIGHT	3´11″
WEIGHT	83.8 lbs

Description

Thanks to its large wingspan, Fearow can fly for an entire day without landing. When fighting, it will attack with its sharp beak.

Special Moves

Assurance, Roost, Drill Peck

National Pokédex No.
022

EVO
LUT
ION

Spearow → Fearow

1–
49

50–
99

100–
149

150–
199

200–
249

250–
299

300–
349

350–
399

400–
449

450–
491

EKANS

Pokémon Data

Snake Pokémon

TYPE	Poison
	. . .
ABILITIES	Intimidate
	Shed Skin
HEIGHT	6´07˝
WEIGHT	15.2 lbs

National Pokédex No.
023

Description

Ekans attacks from behind by hiding its presence while advancing on its prey. It can sense if there is danger in the area by tasting the air with flicks of its tongue.

Special Moves

Bite, Glare, Acid

EVO LUT ION

Ekans → Arbok

ARBOK

1-49
50-99
100-149
150-199
200-249
250-299
300-349
350-399
400-449
450-491

Pokémon Data

Cobra Pokémon

TYPE	Poison
	. . .
ABILITIES	Intimidate
	Shed Skin
HEIGHT	11'06"
WEIGHT	143.3 lbs

National Pokédex No.
024

Description

Arbok frightens its foes with the scary, face-like pattern on its body. While its opponent is paralyzed with fright, Arbok coils around it and squeezes.

Special Moves

Crunch, Mud Bomb, Gunk Shot

EVO LUT ION

Ekans → Arbok

027

PIKACHU

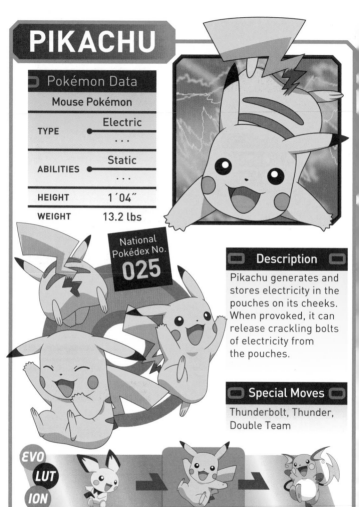

Pokémon Data

Mouse Pokémon

TYPE	Electric . . .
ABILITIES	Static . . .
HEIGHT	1´04˝
WEIGHT	13.2 lbs

National
Pokédex No.
025

Description

Pikachu generates and stores electricity in the pouches on its cheeks. When provoked, it can release crackling bolts of electricity from the pouches.

Special Moves

Thunderbolt, Thunder, Double Team

EVO LUT ION

Pichu ➔ Pikachu ➔ Raichu

RAICHU

Pokémon Data

Mouse Pokémon

TYPE	Electric
	. . .
ABILITIES	Static
	. . .
HEIGHT	2'07"
WEIGHT	66.1 lbs

National Pokédex No.

026

Description

Raichu often uses Thunderbolt in battle. If too much power builds up in its body, it sticks its tail into the ground and discharges some of the electricity.

Special Moves

Quick Attack, Thunderbolt, Thunder Shock

EVO LUT ION

Pichu → Pikachu → Raichu

1- 9

100- 149

150- 199

200- 249

250- 299

300- 349

350- 399

400- 449

450- 491

SANDSHREW

Pokémon Data

Mouse Pokémon	
TYPE	Ground ...
ABILITIES	Sand Veil ...
HEIGHT	2´00˝
WEIGHT	26.5 lbs

National Pokédex No.
027

Description

Even in areas that have very little rainfall, Sandshrew's body can absorb enough water to survive just fine. It can repel any kind of attack when it protects itself by rolling up into a ball.

Special Moves

Sand Attack, Rapid Spin, Fury Swipes

EVO LUT ION

Sandshrew

Sandslash

SANDSLASH

1–49

50–99

100–149

150–199

200–249

250–299

300–349

350–399

400–449

450–491

Pokémon Data

Mouse Pokémon

TYPE	Ground
	. . .
ABILITIES	Sand Veil
	. . .
HEIGHT	3´03˝
WEIGHT	65.0 lbs

National Pokédex No.
028

Description

Sandslash attacks its opponent by rolling up into a ball and body slamming them. It then slashes the stunned enemy with its claws. It can inflict great damage with its spikes.

Special Moves

Rollout, Crush Claw, Sand Tomb

EVO LUT ION

Sandshrew → Sandslash

031

NIDORAN♀

Pokémon Data

Poison Pin Pokémon

TYPE	Poison . . .
ABILITIES	Poison Point Rivalry
HEIGHT	1´04˝
WEIGHT	15.4 lbs

National
Pokédex No.
029

Description

Although Nidoran is
physically small in size,
its poison is still
extremely powerful.

Special Moves

Double Kick, Poison
Sting, Fury Swipes

EVO LUT ION

Nidoran → Nidorina → Nidoqueen

NIDORINA

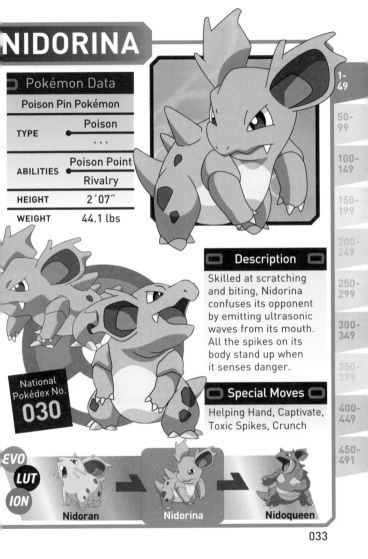

1-49
50-99
100-149
150-199
200-249
250-299
300-349
350-399
400-449
450-491

Pokémon Data

Poison Pin Pokémon

TYPE	Poison
	. . .
ABILITIES	Poison Point
	Rivalry
HEIGHT	2'07"
WEIGHT	44.1 lbs

Description

Skilled at scratching and biting, Nidorina confuses its opponent by emitting ultrasonic waves from its mouth. All the spikes on its body stand up when it senses danger.

Special Moves

Helping Hand, Captivate, Toxic Spikes, Crunch

National Pokédex No.
030

EVO LUT ION

Nidoran → Nidorina → Nidoqueen

NIDOQUEEN

Pokémon Data

Drill Pokémon

TYPE	Poison
	Ground
ABILITIES	Poison Point
	Rivalry
HEIGHT	4′03″
WEIGHT	132.3 lbs

National Pokédex No.
031

Description

Nidoqueen's entire body is covered with armor-like scales. These scales stand up when it's provoked. It will lay its life on the line to protect its offspring.

Special Moves

Body Slam, Earth Power, Superpower

EVO LUT ION

Nidoran → Nidorina → Nidoqueen

034

NIDORAN♂

Pokémon Data

Poison Pin Pokémon

TYPE	Poison
	. . .
ABILITIES	Poison Point
	Rivalry
HEIGHT	1´08˝
WEIGHT	19.8 lbs

1-49
50-99
100-149
150-199
200-249
250-299
300-349
350-399
400-449
450-491

Description

The bigger the horn on Nidoran's head, the stronger its poison. It surveys its surroundings by sound, sticking its ears up and flicking them around to catch far-away noises.

National Pokédex No.
032

Special Moves

Focus Energy, Double Kick, Poison Sting

EVO LUT ION

Nidoran → Nidorino → Nidoking

NIDORINO

Pokémon Data

Poison Pin Pokémon

TYPE	Poison
	...
ABILITIES	Poison Point
	Rivalry
HEIGHT	2′11″
WEIGHT	43.0 lbs

National Pokédex No.
033

Description

An advanced-stage Nidorino's horn is strong enough to pierce diamonds. The horn releases poison after it stabs an opponent.

Special Moves

Helping Hand, Flatter, Poison Jab, Horn Drill

EVO LUT ION

Nidoran ➡ Nidorino ➡ Nidoking

NIDOKING

Pokémon Data

Drill Pokémon	
TYPE	Poison
	Ground
ABILITIES	Poison Point
	Rivalry
HEIGHT	4′07″
WEIGHT	136.7 lbs

National Pokédex No.
034

Description

Nidoking has rock-hard skin, long claws, and a poisonous horn. One strike from its thick tail has enough power to snap a transmission tower in two.

Special Moves

Thrash, Earth Power, Megahorn

EVO LUT ION

 Nidoran → Nidorino → Nidoking

1-49

150-199

200-249

250-299

300-349

350-399

400-449

450-491

037

CLEFAIRY

Pokémon Data

Fairy Pokémon	
TYPE	Normal
	Fairy
ABILITIES	Cute Charm
	Magic Guard
HEIGHT	2´00˝
WEIGHT	16.5 lbs

National Pokédex No.
035

Description

Clefairy lives deep in quiet forests, so it is extremely hard to find. It floats by collecting moonlight on the wings on its back. It is a very popular Pokémon because of its cuteness.

Special Moves

Metronome, Moonlight, Meteor Mash

EVO LUT ION

Cleffa → Clefairy → Clefable

CLEFABLE

Pokémon Data

Fairy Pokémon

TYPE	Normal
	Fairy
ABILITIES	Cute Charm
	Magic Guard
HEIGHT	4´03″
WEIGHT	88.2 lbs

National Pokédex No.
036

Description

Clefable is rarely seen by humans. It plays on remote lakes during nights of a full moon. Its hearing is so sharp that it can hear a pin drop over half a mile away.

Special Moves

Sing, Double Slap, Metronome

EVO LUT ION

Cleffa → Clefairy → Clefable

1-49
50-99
100-149
150-199
200-249
250-299
300-349
350-399
400-449
450-491

VULPIX

Pokémon Data

Fox Pokémon	
TYPE	Fire . . .
ABILITIES	Flash Fire . . .
HEIGHT	2′00″
WEIGHT	21.8 lbs

National
Pokédex No.
037

Description

When Vulpix is born, it has just one tail. If it is taken very good care of, its tail separates into six new ones. It regulates its body temperature by occasionally releasing some heat.

Special Moves

Will-O-Wisp, Fire Spin, Tail Whip, Roar

EVO LUT ION

Vulpix   Ninetales

NINETALES

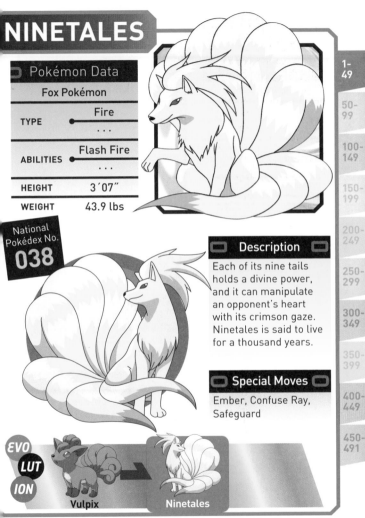

Pokémon Data

Fox Pokémon

TYPE	Fire
	. . .
ABILITIES	Flash Fire
	. . .
HEIGHT	3´07˝
WEIGHT	43.9 lbs

National Pokédex No.
038

Description

Each of its nine tails holds a divine power, and it can manipulate an opponent's heart with its crimson gaze. Ninetales is said to live for a thousand years.

Special Moves

Ember, Confuse Ray, Safeguard

EVO LUT ION

Vulpix ➝ Ninetales

1–49
50–99
100–149
150–199
200–249
250–299
300–349
350–399
400–449
450–491

JIGGLYPUFF

Pokémon Data

Balloon Pokémon

TYPE	Normal
	Fairy
ABILITIES	Cute Charm
	Competitive
HEIGHT	1´08˝
WEIGHT	12.1 lbs

National Pokédex No.
039

Description

Jigglypuff lures its opponents close with its big eyes, then puts them to sleep with its lullabies. It sings at the perfect pitch to put each particular opponent to sleep.

Special Moves

Pound, Sing, Defense Curl, Hyper Voice

EVOLUTION

Igglybuff → Jigglypuff → Wigglytuff

WIGGLYTUFF

Pokémon Data

Balloon Pokémon

TYPE	Normal
	Fairy
ABILITIES	Cute Charm
	Competitive
HEIGHT	3′03″
WEIGHT	26.5 lbs

National Pokédex No.
040

Description

Wigglytuff can expand to an enormous size by sucking in air. Its air-filled body can float about gently on the breeze. Its fine fur is soft to the touch.

Special Moves

Sing, Defense Curl, Double Slap

EVO LUT ION

Igglybuff ➤ Jigglypuff ➤ Wigglytuff

1-49
50-99
100-149
150-199
200-249
250-299
300-349
350-399
400-449
450-491

ZUBAT

Pokémon Data

Bat Pokémon

TYPE	Poison
	Flying
ABILITIES	Inner Focus
	...
HEIGHT	2´07″
WEIGHT	16.5 lbs

National Pokédex No.
041

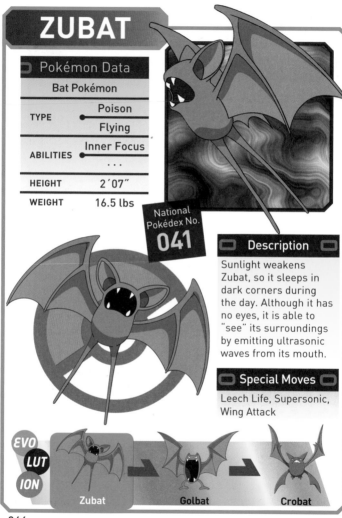

Description

Sunlight weakens Zubat, so it sleeps in dark corners during the day. Although it has no eyes, it is able to "see" its surroundings by emitting ultrasonic waves from its mouth.

Special Moves

Leech Life, Supersonic, Wing Attack

EVO LUT ION

Zubat → Golbat → Crobat

GOLBAT

1-
49

50-
99

100-
149

150-
199

200-
249

250-
299

300-
349

350-
399

400-
449

450-
491

Pokémon Data

Bat Pokémon

TYPE	Poison
	Flying
ABILITIES	Inner Focus
	. . .
HEIGHT	5′03″
WEIGHT	121.3 lbs

Description

Golbat flies around in the dead of night and on moonless nights. It loves the blood of both humans and Pokémon. Once it begins to suck with its four fangs, it will not stop.

National Pokédex No.
042

Special Moves

Mean Look, Poison Fang

EVO LUT ION

Zubat ➤ Golbat ➤ Crobat

045

ODDISH

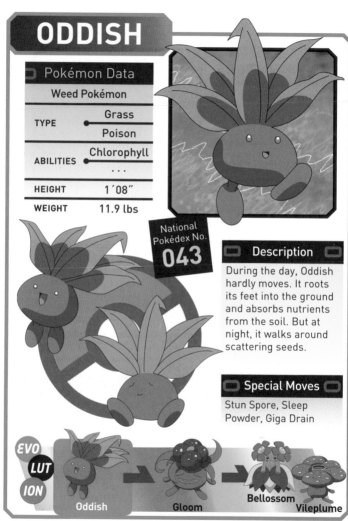

Pokémon Data

Weed Pokémon	
TYPE	Grass
	Poison
ABILITIES	Chlorophyll
	. . .
HEIGHT	1´08˝
WEIGHT	11.9 lbs

National Pokédex No.
043

Description

During the day, Oddish hardly moves. It roots its feet into the ground and absorbs nutrients from the soil. But at night, it walks around scattering seeds.

Special Moves

Stun Spore, Sleep Powder, Giga Drain

EVO LUT ION

Oddish → Gloom → Bellossom / Vileplume

GLOOM

Pokémon Data

Weed Pokémon

TYPE	Grass
	Poison
ABILITIES	Chlorophyll
	...
HEIGHT	2'07"
WEIGHT	19.0 lbs

National Pokédex No.
044

Description

The liquid that drools from its mouth is so smelly it can make opponents gag. Gloom also emits a foul odor from the flower on top of its head.

Special Moves

Lucky Chant, Natural Gift, Giga Drain

EVO LUT ION

Oddish → Gloom → Bellossom / Vileplume

9
50-99
100-149
150-199
200-249
250-299
300-349
350-399
400-449
450-491

VILEPLUME

Pokémon Data

Flower Pokémon

TYPE	Grass
	Poison
ABILITIES	Chlorophyll
	. . .
HEIGHT	3´11˝
WEIGHT	41.0 lbs

National Pokédex No.
045

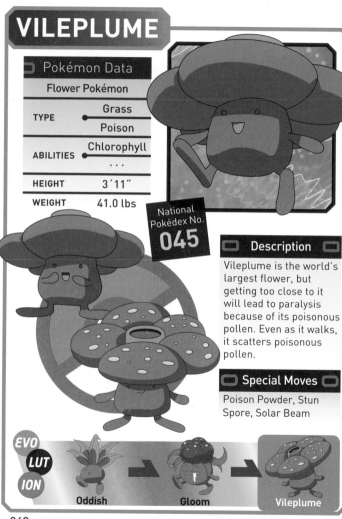

Description

Vileplume is the world's largest flower, but getting too close to it will lead to paralysis because of its poisonous pollen. Even as it walks, it scatters poisonous pollen.

Special Moves

Poison Powder, Stun Spore, Solar Beam

EVO LUT ION

Oddish ▸ Gloom ▸ Vileplume

PARAS

1-
49

50-
99

00-
49

150-
199

200-
249

250-
299

300-
349

350-
399

400-
449

450-
491

Pokémon Data

Mushroom Pokémon	
TYPE	Bug
	Grass
ABILITIES	Effect Spore
	Dry Skin
HEIGHT	1´00″
WEIGHT	11.9 lbs

National
Pokédex No.
046

Description

Paras digs down deep
to feed off tree roots.
Mushrooms named
"tōchūkasō" grow on
its back.

Special Moves

Leech Life, Stun Spore,
Slash

EVO
LUT
ION

Paras   Parasect

PARASECT

Pokémon Data

Mushroom Pokémon

TYPE	Bug
	Grass
ABILITIES	Effect Spore
	Dry Skin
HEIGHT	3´03″
WEIGHT	65.0 lbs

National
Pokédex No.
047

Description

Parasect seeks out damp places to live. The mushroom on its back, now larger than Parasect's own body, controls its mind and scatters poison spores wherever Parasect walks.

Special Moves

Stun Spore, Giga Drain, X-Scissor

EVO LUT ION

Paras   Parasect

VENONAT

1-
49

50-
99

100-
149

150-
199

200-
249

250-
299

300-
349

350-
399

400-
449

450-
491

Pokémon Data

Insect Pokémon

TYPE	Bug
	Poison
ABILITIES	Compound Eyes
	Tinted Lens
HEIGHT	3′03″
WEIGHT	66.1 lbs

National Pokédex No.
048

Description

Venonat gather around sources of light when night falls. Its two big eyes are actually composed of many small eyes. It can move around in the dark by using a kind of radar.

Special Moves

Confusion, Poison Powder, Signal Beam

EVO LUT ION

Venonat

Venomoth

VENOMOTH

Pokémon Data

Poison Moth Pokémon

TYPE	Bug
	Poison
ABILITIES	Shield Dust
	Tinted Lens
HEIGHT	4'11"
WEIGHT	27.6 lbs

National Pokédex No.
049

Description

Venomoth scatters toxic powder from its wings as it flies. Poison seeps into the body when the powder makes contact with the target's skin.

Special Moves

Psychic, Poison Powder, Gust, Stun Spore

EVO
LUT
ION

Venonat → Venomoth

DIGLETT

Pokémon Data

Mole Pokémon

TYPE	Ground
	. . .
ABILITIES	Sand Veil
	Arena Trap
HEIGHT	0´08"
WEIGHT	1.8 lbs

1-49

50-99

100-149

150-199

200-249

250-299

300-349

350-399

400-449

450-491

National Pokédex No.
050

Description

Diglett lives under the ground, feeding on the roots of plants, and only occasionally pokes its head above ground. Since it lives within the darkness underground, sunlight weakens it.

Special Moves

Magnitude, Sucker Punch, Dig

EVO
LUT
ION

Diglett

Dugtrio

DUGTRIO

Pokémon Data

Mole Pokémon

TYPE	Ground
	. . .
ABILITIES	Sand Veil
	Arena Trap
HEIGHT	2′04″
WEIGHT	73.4 lbs

National Pokédex No.
051

Description

Dugtrio have great teamwork. No matter how hard the ground is, by working together they can dig more than fifty miles down into the earth.

Special Moves

Sand Tomb, Mud Bomb, Earthquake, Fissure

EVO LUT ION

Diglett → Dugtrio

MEOWTH

Pokémon Data

Scratch Cat Pokémon

TYPE	Normal
	. . .
ABILITIES	Pickup
	Technician
HEIGHT	1′04″
WEIGHT	9.3 lbs

Description

Meowth is active at night and sleeps all day. It loves round and shiny things, so as it goes about its business at night it will pick up dropped coins.

Special Moves

Fury Swipes, Feint Attack, Pay Day

National Pokédex No.
052

EVO
LUT
ION

Meowth → Persian

1–49
50–99
100–149
150–199
200–249
250–299
300–349
350–399
400–449
450–491

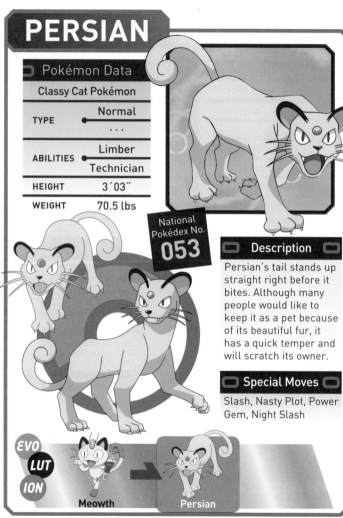

PERSIAN

Pokémon Data

Classy Cat Pokémon

TYPE	Normal . . .
ABILITIES	Limber Technician
HEIGHT	3´03˝
WEIGHT	70.5 lbs

National Pokédex No.
053

Description

Persian's tail stands up straight right before it bites. Although many people would like to keep it as a pet because of its beautiful fur, it has a quick temper and will scratch its owner.

Special Moves

Slash, Nasty Plot, Power Gem, Night Slash

EVO LUT ION

Meowth → Persian

PSYDUCK

Pokémon Data

Duck Pokémon

TYPE	Water
	. . .
ABILITIES	Damp
	Cloud Nine
HEIGHT	2′07″
WEIGHT	43.2 lbs

National
Pokédex No.
054

Description

When Psyduck's headache gets bad, it's able to use mysterious psychic powers. But while doing so, it enters a trance-like state, so it doesn't remember anything afterwards.

Special Moves

Water Gun, Disable, Confusion

EVO
LUT
ION

Psyduck   Golduck

1-
49
50-
99
100-
149
150-
199
200-
249
250-
299
300-
349
350-
399
400-
449
450-
491

GOLDUCK

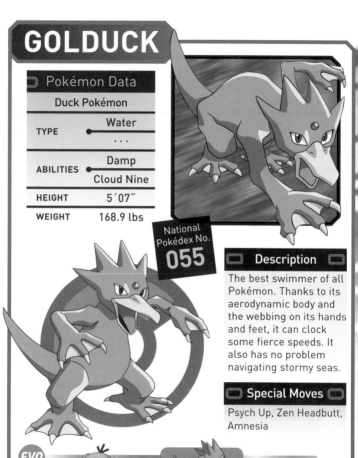

Pokémon Data

Duck Pokémon

TYPE	Water
	. . .
ABILITIES	Damp
	Cloud Nine
HEIGHT	5′07″
WEIGHT	168.9 lbs

National Pokédex No.
055

Description

The best swimmer of all Pokémon. Thanks to its aerodynamic body and the webbing on its hands and feet, it can clock some fierce speeds. It also has no problem navigating stormy seas.

Special Moves

Psych Up, Zen Headbutt, Amnesia

EVOLUTION

Psyduck → Golduck

MANKEY

Pokémon Data

Pig Monkey Pokémon

TYPE	Fighting
	...
ABILITIES	Vital Spirit
	Anger Point
HEIGHT	1´08″
WEIGHT	61.7 lbs

National Pokédex No.
056

Description

Mankey live in trees. If even just one member of the troop gets angry—and even the smallest thing causes them to get angry—they'll all start fighting.

Special Moves

Karate Chop, Seismic Toss, Thrash

EVOLUTION

Mankey → Primeape

50-99
100-149
150-199
200-249
250-299
300-349
350-399
400-449
450-491

PRIMEAPE

Pokémon Data

Pig Monkey Pokémon

TYPE	Fighting . . .
ABILITIES	Vital Spirit
	Anger Point
HEIGHT	3´03˝
WEIGHT	70.5 lbs

National Pokédex No.
057

Description

For some reason, Primeape is always angry. Even just making eye contact will infuriate it. It will pursue anything that runs away from it. And if it loses, it gets even madder.

Special Moves

Rage, Cross Chop, Thrash

EVO LUT ION

Mankey → Primeape

GROWLITHE

1-
49

50-
99

100-
149

150-
199

200-
249

250-
299

300-
349

350-
399

400-
449

450-
491

Pokémon Data

Puppy Pokémon

TYPE	Fire
	...
ABILITIES	Intimidate
	Flash Fire
HEIGHT	2'04"
WEIGHT	41.9 lbs

National
Pokédex No.
058

Description

Growlithe is very
protective of its territory
and will growl and snap
if it feels threatened. It's
very obedient to its
Trainer; it won't take
even a single step
unless ordered.

Special Moves

Ember, Roar, Flame
Wheel, Take Down

EVO LUT ION

Growlithe

Arcanine

ARCANINE

Pokémon Data

Legendary Pokémon

TYPE	Fire
	...
ABILITIES	Intimidate
	Flash Fire
HEIGHT	6′03″
WEIGHT	341.7 lbs

National Pokédex No.
059

Description

With its luxurious mane and proud bearing, Arcanine has enjoyed a devoted following among humans since ancient times. It can run at incredible speeds.

Special Moves

Fire Fang, Odor Sleuth, Extreme Speed

EVO LUT ION

Growlithe → Arcanine

POLIWAG

Pokémon Data

Tadpole Pokémon

TYPE	Water
	. . .
ABILITIES	Water Absorb
	Damp
HEIGHT	2′00″
WEIGHT	27.3 lbs

National Pokédex No.
060

Description

Because Poliwag has just grown its feet, it can't walk very well. The spiral pattern on its belly is actually part of its intestines, which are visible through its thin skin.

Special Moves

Hypnosis, Water Gun, Rain Dance

1-49
50-99
100-149
150-199
200-249
250-299
300-349
350-399
400-449
450-491

EVO
LUT
ION

Poliwag

Poliwhirl

Politoed   Poliwrath

POLIWHIRL

Pokémon Data

Tadpole Pokémon

TYPE	Water
	. . .
ABILITIES	Water Absorb
	Damp
HEIGHT	3′03″
WEIGHT	44.1 lbs

National
Pokédex No.
061

Description

Poliwhirl can live both on land and in water. While on land, it keeps its body moist with a slimy film. Staring at the spiral pattern on its belly can cause one to become drowsy.

Special Moves

Body Slam, Belly Drum, Wake-Up Slap

EVO
LUT
ION

Poliwag → Poliwhirl → Politoed Poliwrath

POLIWRATH

Pokémon Data

Tadpole Pokémon

TYPE	Water
	Fighting
ABILITIES	Water Absorb
	Damp
HEIGHT	4'03"
WEIGHT	119.0 lbs

National Pokédex No.
062

Description

Poliwrath is very good at swimming and can use many different strokes. It's very strong and muscular, so it can swim across wide oceans without rest.

Special Moves

Submission, Dynamic Punch, Mind Reader

1-49

50-99

100-149

150-199

200-249

250-299

300-349

350-399

400-449

450-491

EVO LUT ION

Poliwag

Poliwhirl

Poliwrath

ABRA

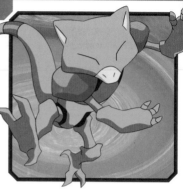

Pokémon Data

Psi Pokémon	
TYPE	Psychic . . .
ABILITIES	Synchronize Inner Focus
HEIGHT	2′11″
WEIGHT	43.0 lbs

National Pokédex No.

063

Description

Abra is unable to use its psychic powers unless it gets at least eighteen hours of sleep a day. When it senses the presence of an enemy it escapes by teleporting.

Special Moves

Teleport

EVO LUT ION

 Abra

 Kadabra

 Alakazam

KADABRA

1-49

50-99

100-149

150-199

200-249

250-299

300-349

350-399

400-449

450-491

Pokémon Data

Psi Pokémon

TYPE	Psychic
	. . .
ABILITIES	Synchronize
	Inner Focus
HEIGHT	4′03″
WEIGHT	124.6 lbs

National Pokédex No.
064

Description

Whenever Kadabra uses its psychic powers, it unleashes a surge of powerful alpha waves. The spoon in its hand is said to strengthen the power of the alpha waves.

Special Moves

Psybeam, Reflect, Psycho Cut

EVO LUT ION

Abra → Kadabra → Alakazam

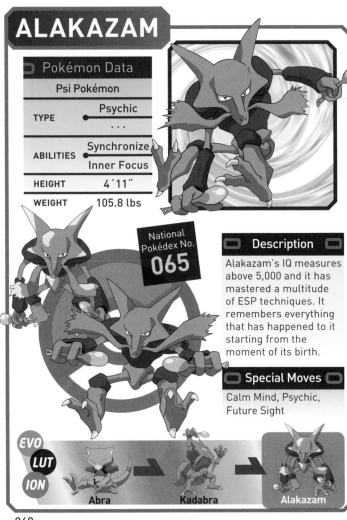

ALAKAZAM

Pokémon Data

Psi Pokémon

TYPE	Psychic ...
ABILITIES	Synchronize Inner Focus
HEIGHT	4'11"
WEIGHT	105.8 lbs

National Pokédex No.
065

Description

Alakazam's IQ measures above 5,000 and it has mastered a multitude of ESP techniques. It remembers everything that has happened to it starting from the moment of its birth.

Special Moves

Calm Mind, Psychic, Future Sight

EVO LUT ION

Abra → Kadabra → Alakazam

MACHOP

Pokémon Data

Superpower Pokémon

TYPE	Fighting
	. . .
ABILITIES	Guts
	No Guard
HEIGHT	2´07˝
WEIGHT	43.0 lbs

National Pokédex No.
066

Description

Machop works out by lifting Graveler. Some Machop travel the world in order to hone their fighting skills.

Special Moves

Focus Energy, Karate Chop, Foresight

1-49

50-99

100-149

150-199

200-249

250-299

300-349

350-399

400-449

450-491

EVO LUT ION

Machop → Machoke → Machamp

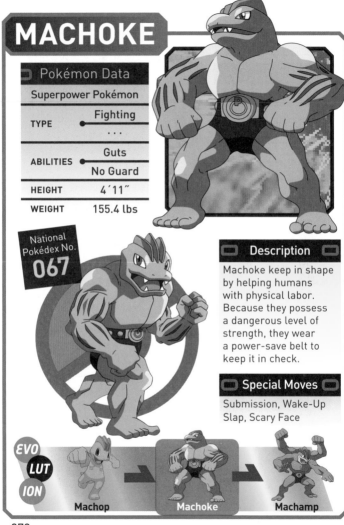

MACHOKE

Pokémon Data

Superpower Pokémon

TYPE	Fighting
	. . .
ABILITIES	Guts
	No Guard
HEIGHT	4'11"
WEIGHT	155.4 lbs

National Pokédex No.
067

Description

Machoke keep in shape by helping humans with physical labor. Because they possess a dangerous level of strength, they wear a power-save belt to keep it in check.

Special Moves

Submission, Wake-Up Slap, Scary Face

EVO LUT ION

Machop ▶ Machoke ▶ Machamp

MACHAMP

Pokémon Data

Superpower Pokémon

TYPE	Fighting
	. . .
ABILITIES	Guts
	No Guard
HEIGHT	5′03″
WEIGHT	286.6 lbs

National Pokédex No.
068

Description

Using the combined power of its four arms, Machamp can throw its opponent all the way to the horizon. It has mastered a variety of fighting techniques, and it's blindingly fast.

Special Moves

Vital Throw, Submission, Cross Chop

1-
49

50-
99

100-
149

150-
199

200-
249

250-
299

300-
349

350-
399

400-
449

450-
491

**EVO
LUT
ION**

 Machop

 Machoke

 Machamp

071

BELLSPROUT

Pokémon Data

Flower Pokémon

TYPE	Grass
	Poison
ABILITIES	Chlorophyll
	. . .
HEIGHT	2´04˝
WEIGHT	8.8 lbs

National Pokédex No. **069**

Description

Bellsprout loves damp places where it can suck up water from the ground through its foot roots. It captures opponents by snaring them with its vines.

Special Moves

Poison Powder, Sleep Powder, Stun Spore, Vine Whip

EVOLUTION

Bellsprout → Weepinbell → Victreebel

WEEPINBELL

Pokémon Data

Flycatcher Pokémon

TYPE	Grass
	Poison
ABILITIES	Chlorophyll
	. . .
HEIGHT	3'03"
WEIGHT	14.1 lbs

National Pokédex No.
070

Description

Weepinbell captures prey that wander near it by dusting them with Poison Powder. It can shoot out razor-sharp leaves, and it can spit an acid-like liquid from its mouth.

Special Moves

Odor Sleuth, Mud-Slap, Powder Snow, Endure

EVOLUTION

Bellsprout ▶ Weepinbell ▶ Victreebel

1-49
50-99
100-149
150-199
200-249
250-299
300-349
350-399
400-449
450-491

VICTREEBEL

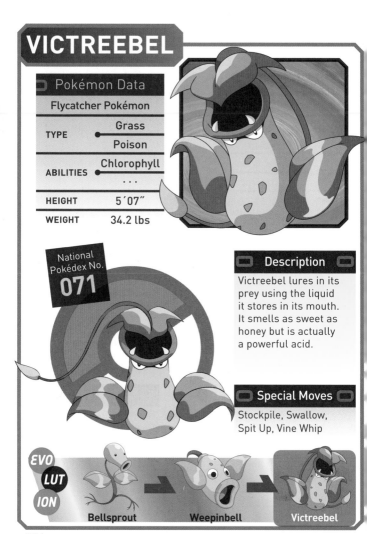

Pokémon Data

Flycatcher Pokémon

TYPE	Grass
	Poison
ABILITIES	Chlorophyll
	. . .
HEIGHT	5'07"
WEIGHT	34.2 lbs

National Pokédex No.
071

Description

Victreebel lures in its prey using the liquid it stores in its mouth. It smells as sweet as honey but is actually a powerful acid.

Special Moves

Stockpile, Swallow, Spit Up, Vine Whip

EVO LUT ION

Bellsprout ➤ Weepinbell ➤ Victreebel

TENTACOOL

Pokémon Data

Jellyfish Pokémon	
TYPE	Water
	Poison
ABILITIES	Clear Body
	Liquid Ooze
HEIGHT	2′11″
WEIGHT	100.3 lbs

National Pokédex No.
072

1-49
50-99
100-149
150-199
200-249
250-299
300-349
350-399
400-449
450-491

Description

Because Tentacool's body is made mostly of water it will shrivel up if it's taken out of the ocean. It can emit mysterious energy beams from its crystalline eyes.

Special Moves

Poison Sting, Acid, Toxic Spikes, Bubble Beam

EVO LUT ION

Tentacool

Tentacruel

TENTACRUEL

Pokémon Data

Jellyfish Pokémon

TYPE	Water
	Poison
ABILITIES	Clear Body
	Liquid Ooze
HEIGHT	5'03"
WEIGHT	121.3 lbs

National Pokédex No. **073**

Description

It captures its prey using its extendable tentacles and then weakens it with poison. When it senses danger it transmits the information to its mates by using the red orbs on its head.

Special Moves

Poison Jab, Hydro Pump, Barrier

EVO LUT ION

Tentacool → Tentacruel

GEODUDE

Pokémon Data

Rock Pokémon

TYPE	Rock
	Ground
ABILITIES	Rock Head
	Sturdy
HEIGHT	1′04″
WEIGHT	44.1 lbs

National Pokédex No.
074

1-49
50-99
100-149
150-199
200-249
250-299
300-349
350-399
400-449
450-491

Description

It rolls along slopes in search of food. When it sleeps, it buries half its body in the ground. The older it gets, the more its edges are worn away, making its body round and smooth.

Special Moves

Defense Curl, Mud Sport, Rollout, Self-Destruct

EVO LUT ION

Geodude

Graveler

Golem

GRAVELER

Pokémon Data

Rock Pokémon	
TYPE	Rock
	Ground
ABILITIES	Rock Head
	Sturdy
HEIGHT	3´03˝
WEIGHT	231.5 lbs

National Pokédex No.

075

Description

Graveler grows by eating a ton of rocks a day. It especially loves rocks with moss on them. It eats rocks as it climbs hills; once it reaches the top, it rolls down to the bottom again.

Special Moves

Magnitude, Rollout, Double-Edge

EVO LUT ION

Geodude ➤ Graveler ➤ Golem

GOLEM

Pokémon Data

Megaton Pokémon

TYPE	Rock
	Ground
ABILITIES	Rock Head
	Sturdy
HEIGHT	4'07"
WEIGHT	661.4 lbs

National Pokédex No.

076

Description

Golem shed their shells once a year. The shells are so hard that even dynamite won't scratch them. Sometimes Golem come tumbling down mountains after earthquakes.

Special Moves

Magnitude, Rollout, Double-Edge

1-49

50-99

100-149

150-199

200-249

250-299

300-349

350-399

400-449

450-491

EVOLUTION

Geodude   Graveler   Golem

PONYTA

Pokémon Data

Fire Horse Pokémon

TYPE	Fire ...
ABILITIES	Run Away Flash Fire
HEIGHT	3′03″
WEIGHT	66.1 lbs

National Pokédex No.
077

Description

Ponyta's legs are extremely strong: it can trample under its hooves anything that gets in its way. Within an hour of being born, its tail and mane of flames grow out.

Special Moves

Ember, Stomp, Fire Spin, Take Down

EVO LUT ION

Ponyta → Rapidash

RAPIDASH

Pokémon Data

Fire Horse Pokémon

TYPE	Fire
	. . .
ABILITIES	Run Away
	Flash Fire
HEIGHT	5´07″
WEIGHT	209.4 lbs

National Pokédex No.
078

Description

Rapidash's mane forms a roaring blaze as it runs. In a mere ten steps, it can achieve maximum speed. When it sees something that moves fast, it will want to race against it.

Special Moves

Fire Blast, Fury Attack, Flare Blitz

50-99
00-9
150-199
200-249
250-299
300-349
350-399
400-449
450-491

EVO LUT ION

Ponyta

Rapidash

SLOWPOKE

Pokémon Data

Dopey Pokémon	
TYPE	Water
	Psychic
ABILITIES	Oblivious
	Own Tempo
HEIGHT	3′11″
WEIGHT	79.4 lbs

National Pokédex No.
079

Description

Although it moves very slowly, Slowpoke is skilled at fishing using its tail. Since it's oblivious to almost everything, it doesn't feel any pain, even when its tail is bitten.

Special Moves

Curse, Confusion, Water Gun, Yawn

EVO LUT ION

Slowpoke

Slowbro

Slowking

SLOWBRO

Pokémon Data

Hermit Crab Pokémon	
TYPE	Water
	Psychic
ABILITIES	Oblivious
	Own Tempo
HEIGHT	5′03″
WEIGHT	173.1 lbs

National Pokédex No.

080

Description

Slowbro Evolved from a Slowpoke when it was bitten by a Shellder while searching for food. Whenever the Shellder bites down hard on its tail, Slowbro becomes inspired.

Special Moves

Amnesia, Psychic, Psych Up

1-49
50-99
100-149
150-199
200-249
250-299
300-349
350-399
400-449
450-491

EVO LUT ION

Slowpoke   Slowbro   Slowking

MAGNEMITE

Pokémon Data

Magnet Pokémon

TYPE	Electric
	Steel
ABILITIES	Magnet Pull
	Sturdy
HEIGHT	1´00˝
WEIGHT	13.2 lbs

National Pokédex No. **081**

Description

Magnemite attaches itself to power lines to feed off electricity. It moves by emitting electromagnetic waves from its side units. If its internal charge runs too low, it can no longer fly.

Special Moves

Thunder Wave, Spark, Magnet Bomb

EVOLUTION

Magnemite → Magneton → Magnezone

MAGNETON

Pokémon Data

Magnet Pokémon	
TYPE	Electric
	Steel
ABILITIES	Magnet Pull
	Sturdy
HEIGHT	3′03″
WEIGHT	132.3 lbs

National Pokédex No. **082**

Description

Magneton is made up of three Magnemite stuck together. It can create a powerful magnetic force field and discharge a voltage high enough to cause most machinery to malfunction.

Special Moves

Discharge, Mirror Shot, Magnet Bomb

EVO LUT ION

 Magnemite

 Magneton

 Magnezone

1-49
50-99
100-149
150-199
200-249
250-299
300-349
350-399
400-449
450-491

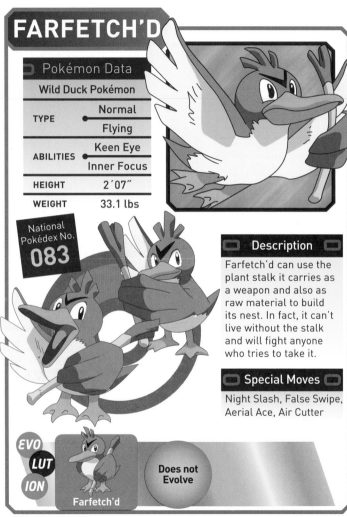

FARFETCH'D

Pokémon Data

Wild Duck Pokémon

TYPE	Normal
	Flying
ABILITIES	Keen Eye
	Inner Focus
HEIGHT	2′07″
WEIGHT	33.1 lbs

National Pokédex No.
083

Description

Farfetch'd can use the plant stalk it carries as a weapon and also as raw material to build its nest. In fact, it can't live without the stalk and will fight anyone who tries to take it.

Special Moves

Night Slash, False Swipe, Aerial Ace, Air Cutter

EVO LUT ION

Farfetch'd

Does not Evolve

086

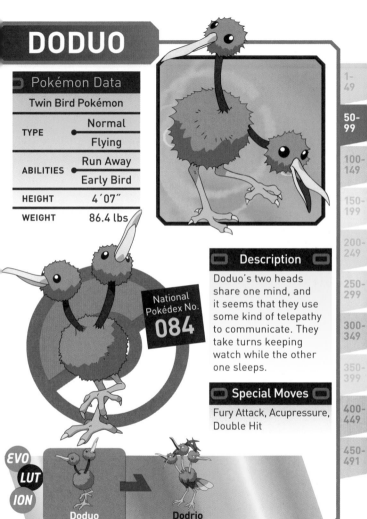

DODUO

Pokémon Data

Twin Bird Pokémon

TYPE	Normal
	Flying
ABILITIES	Run Away
	Early Bird
HEIGHT	4′07″
WEIGHT	86.4 lbs

National Pokédex No.
084

Description

Doduo's two heads share one mind, and it seems that they use some kind of telepathy to communicate. They take turns keeping watch while the other one sleeps.

Special Moves

Fury Attack, Acupressure, Double Hit

EVO LUT ION

Doduo → Dodrio

1-49
50-99
100-149
150-199
200-249
250-299
300-349
350-399
400-449
450-491

DODRIO

Pokémon Data

Triple Bird Pokémon

TYPE	Normal
	Flying
ABILITIES	Run Away
	Early Bird
HEIGHT	5'11"
WEIGHT	187.8 lbs

National Pokédex No.
085

Description

When Doduo Evolves, one of its heads splits into two, creating a total of three heads. Dodrio has three hearts and three set of lungs in one body. It can run for great distances.

Special Moves

Uproar, Tri Attack, Drill Peck

EVO LUT ION

Doduo → Dodrio

SEEL

Pokémon Data

Sea Lion Pokémon

TYPE	Water
	. . .
ABILITIES	Thick Fat
	Hydration
HEIGHT	3´07˝
WEIGHT	198.4 lbs

National Pokédex No.
086

Description

Seel lives on icebergs. The horn on its head is extremely hard and it uses this to break the ice as it swims. Its thick skin and white fur keep it comfortable in cold temperatures.

Special Moves

Icy Wind, Aurora Beam, Brine

49

50–
99

100–
149

150–
199

200–
249

250–
299

300–
349

350–
399

400–
449

450–
491

EVO LUT ION

Seel

Dewgong

DEWGONG

Pokémon Data

Sea Lion Pokémon

TYPE	Water
	Ice
ABILITIES	Thick Fat
	Hydration
HEIGHT	5´07˝
WEIGHT	264.6 lbs

National Pokédex No. **087**

Description

Dewgong stores up heat in its body and becomes more active the colder it gets. Because the fur on its entire body is pure white, it is camouflaged well from enemies in the snow.

Special Moves

Dive, Aqua Tail, Safeguard

EVO LUT ION

Seel

Dewgong

GRIMER

1–
49

50–
99

100–
149

150–
199

200–
249

250–
299

300–
349

350–
399

400–
449

450–
491

Pokémon Data

Sludge Pokémon

TYPE	Poison
	...
ABILITIES	Stench
	Sticky Hold
HEIGHT	2′11″
WEIGHT	66.1 lbs

National
Pokédex No.
088

Description

Grimer was born when sludge in a dirty stream was exposed to lunar x-rays. It leaks bacteria-laden ooze from every pore on its body and can pass through even the narrowest of openings.

Special Moves

Poison Gas, Minimize, Sludge

EVO
LUT
ION

Grimer   Muk

MUK

Pokémon Data

Sludge Pokémon

TYPE	Poison
	. . .
ABILITIES	Stench
	Sticky Hold
HEIGHT	3´11″
WEIGHT	66.1 lbs

National Pokédex No.
089

Description

Muk loves to eat filthy things. A deadly, poisonous and horribly noxious fluid oozes from its body The fluid is so powerful that it kills plants and trees on contact.

Special Moves

Sludge Bomb, Gunk Shot, Acid Armor

EVO LUT ION

Grimer

Muk

SHELLDER

Pokémon Data

Bivalve Pokémon

TYPE	Water
	. . .
ABILITIES	Shell Armor
	Skill Link
HEIGHT	1′00″
WEIGHT	8.8 lbs

1-
49

50-
99

100-
149

150-
199

200-
249

250-
299

300-
349

350-
399

400-
449

450-
491

National
Pokédex No.
090

Description

Shellder swims by rapidly opening and closing its two shells, which are harder than diamonds. Its large tongue is always sticking out.

Special Moves

Icicle Spear, Protect, Clamp

EVO
LUT
ION

Shellder

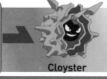

Cloyster

093

CLOYSTER

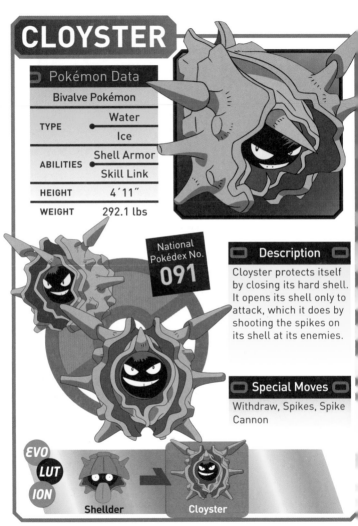

Pokémon Data

Bivalve Pokémon

TYPE	Water
	Ice
ABILITIES	Shell Armor
	Skill Link
HEIGHT	4′11″
WEIGHT	292.1 lbs

National Pokédex No.
091

Description

Cloyster protects itself by closing its hard shell. It opens its shell only to attack, which it does by shooting the spikes on its shell at its enemies.

Special Moves

Withdraw, Spikes, Spike Cannon

EVO LUT ION

Shellder → Cloyster

GASTLY

1–49
50–99
100–149
150–199
200–249
250–299
300–349
350–399
400–449
450–491

Pokémon Data

Gas Pokémon

TYPE	Ghost
	Poison
ABILITIES	Levitate
	...
HEIGHT	4'03"
WEIGHT	0.2 lbs

National Pokédex No.
092

Description

Because Gastly's body is composed mostly of poisonous gases, it gets blown away whenever there's a strong wind. It knocks its opponents out by enveloping them with gas.

Special Moves

Lick, Spite, Curse, Night Shade

EVOLUTION

Gastly → Haunter → Gengar

095

HAUNTER

Pokémon Data

Gas Pokémon

TYPE	Ghost
	Poison
ABILITIES	Levitate
	...
HEIGHT	5'03"
WEIGHT	0.2 lbs

National Pokédex No.
093

Description

Haunter can move through any substance. It hides in dark shadows and watches and waits. It absorbs life force by licking its prey with its gaseous tongue.

Special Moves

Payback, Destiny Bond, Shadow Punch

EVOLUTION

Gastly

Haunter

Gengar

GENGAR

Pokémon Data

Shadow Pokémon

TYPE	Ghost
	Poison
ABILITIES	Levitate
	...
HEIGHT	4´11"
WEIGHT	89.3 lbs

National Pokédex No.
094

Description

Gengar lurks in dark corners. On the nights of a full moon, when your shadow moves on its own and starts laughing, Gengar is most likely behind it.

Special Moves

Dream Eater, Dark Pulse, Destiny Bond, Nightmare

EVO
LUT
ION

Gastly   Haunter   Gengar

1-
49

50-
99

100-
149

150-
199

200-
249

250-
299

300-
349

350-
399

400-
449

450-
491

ONIX

Pokémon Data

Rock Snake Pokémon

TYPE	Rock
	Ground
ABILITIES	Rock Head
	Sturdy
HEIGHT	28´10˝
WEIGHT	463.0 lbs

National Pokédex No. **095**

Description

Onix lives underground. As it grows, its body gradually becomes darker and harder, until it's tough as diamonds. It can move as fast as fifty miles per hour.

Special Moves

Bind, Rock Throw, Rock Tomb

EVOLUTION

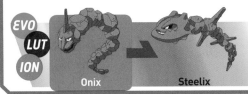

Onix → Steelix

DROWZEE

Pokémon Data

Hypnosis Pokémon

TYPE	Psychic
	...
ABILITIES	Insomnia
	Forewarn
HEIGHT	3´03˝
WEIGHT	71.4 lbs

1–
49

50–
99

100–
149

150–
199

200–
249

250–
299

300–
349

350–
399

400–
449

450–
491

Description

Drowzee eats human dreams. If it eats too many nightmares, though, it can get a stomachache. It uses its nose to sniff out what a person is dreaming.

National Pokédex No.
096

Special Moves

Hypnosis, Confusion, Psybeam

EVO LUT ION

Drowzee   Hypno

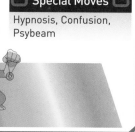

HYPNO

Pokémon Data

Hypnosis Pokémon

TYPE	Psychic . . .
ABILITIES	Insomnia Forewarn
HEIGHT	5′03″
WEIGHT	166.7 lbs

National
Pokédex No.
097

Description

Hypno carries around a pendulum. By swinging the pendulum back and forth in front of an opponent's eyes, it can make that opponent fall asleep in just three seconds.

Special Moves

Psych Up, Psychic, Future Sight

EVO LUT ION

Drowzee → Hypno

KRABBY

Pokémon Data

River Crab Pokémon

TYPE	Water
	. . .
ABILITIES	Hyper Cutter
	Shell Armor
HEIGHT	1´04˝
WEIGHT	14.3 lbs

1-
49

50-
99

100-
149

150-
199

200-
249

250-
299

300-
349

350-
399

400-
449

450-
491

National Pokédex No.
098

Description

Krabby uses its claws to keep its balance as it scuttles along. Even if it loses a claw during battle, it can quickly grow a new one.

Special Moves

Harden, Bubble Beam, Metal Claw

EVO LUT ION

Krabby   Kingler

KINGLER

Pokémon Data

Pincer Pokémon

TYPE	Water . . .
ABILITIES	Hyper Cutter Shell Armor
HEIGHT	4′03″
WEIGHT	132.3 lbs

National Pokédex No. **099**

Description

Its enormous scissor claw can exert force equivalent to 10,000 horsepower. But because the claw is so heavy, Kingler has a hard time being accurate with it.

Special Moves

Guillotine, Brine, Crabhammer

EVO LUT ION   Krabby → Kingler

102

VOLTORB

1–49
50–99
100–149
150–199
200–249
250–299
300–349
350–399
400–449
450–491

Pokémon Data

Ball Pokémon

TYPE	Electric
	. . .
ABILITIES	Soundproof
	Static
HEIGHT	1'08"
WEIGHT	22.9 lbs

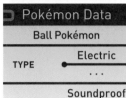

National Pokédex No.
100

Description

Voltorb are thought to be created when Poké Balls are exposed to very strong electrical fields. Touching one accidentally might result in an electric shock.

Special Moves

Spark, Charge Beam, Self-Destruct

EVO LUT ION

Voltorb

Electrode

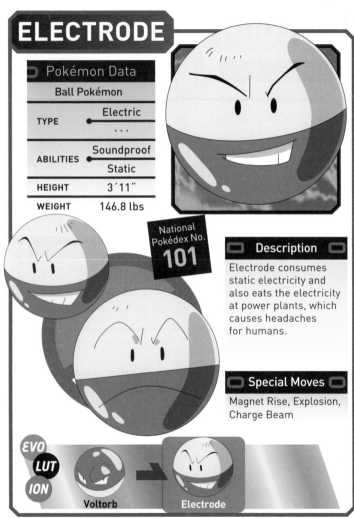

ELECTRODE

Pokémon Data

Ball Pokémon

TYPE	Electric
	. . .
ABILITIES	Soundproof
	Static
HEIGHT	3'11"
WEIGHT	146.8 lbs

National Pokédex No.
101

Description

Electrode consumes static electricity and also eats the electricity at power plants, which causes headaches for humans.

Special Moves

Magnet Rise, Explosion, Charge Beam

EVOLUTION

Voltorb → Electrode

104

EXEGGCUTE

Pokémon Data

Egg Pokémon

TYPE	Grass
	Psychic
ABILITIES	Chlorophyll
	. . .
HEIGHT	1´04˝
WEIGHT	5.5 lbs

National Pokédex No.
102

1-49
50-99
100-149
150-199
200-249
250-299
300-349
350-399
400-449
450-491

Description

Although they look like eggs, Exeggcute are actually more like plant seeds. They can communicate with others of their kind by telepathy.

Special Moves

Barrage, Reflect, Bullet Seed

EVO LUT ION

Exeggcute

Exeggutor

EXEGGUTOR

Pokémon Data

Coconut Pokémon

TYPE	
	Grass
	Psychic

ABILITIES	
	Chlorophyll
	. . .

HEIGHT	6′07″
WEIGHT	264.6 lbs

National Pokédex No.
103

Description

Exeggutor is sometimes called "The Walking Jungle." If one of the matured heads gets too heavy and falls off, it's said that it becomes an Exeggcute.

Special Moves

Stomp, Egg Bomb, Wood Hammer

EVO LUT ION

Exeggcute → Exeggutor

CUBONE

Pokémon Data

Lonely Pokémon

TYPE	Ground ...
ABILITIES	Rock Head Lightning Rod
HEIGHT	1´04"
WEIGHT	14.3 lbs

National
Pokédex No.
104

Description

Sometimes Cubone cries, remembering its mother. When it does so, the skull it wears on its head rattles. The marks on the skull are stains from its tears.

Special Moves

Bone Club, Headbutt, Focus Energy, Rage

EVO LUT ION

Cubone

Marowak

1-49
50-99
100-149
150-199
200-249
250-299
300-349
350-399
400-449
450-491

MAROWAK

Pokémon Data

Bone Keeper Pokémon

TYPE	Ground
	. . .
ABILITIES	Rock Head
	Lightning Rod
HEIGHT	3′03″
WEIGHT	99.2 lbs

National
Pokédex No.
105

Description

Marowak holds a bone from the moment it's born and can use it like a boomerang. It continues to use bones as weapons as it grows, and its personality becomes fiercer.

Special Moves

Bonemerang, Thrash, Bone Rush

EVO LUT ION

Cubone → Marowak

HITMONLEE

Pokémon Data

Kicking Pokémon

TYPE	Fighting
	. . .
ABILITIES	Limber
	Reckless
HEIGHT	4′11″
WEIGHT	109.8 lbs

National Pokédex No.
106

49
50-
99
100-
149
150-
199
200-
249
250-
299
300-
349
350-
399
400-
449
450-
491

Description

Hitmonlee's legs can stretch to twice their original length, so it can kick an opponent who is far away. Most first-time fighters against Hitmonlee are surprised by its range.

Special Moves

Focus Energy, High Jump Kick, Mega Kick

EVO LUT ION

Tyrogue → Hitmonlee

109

HITMONCHAN

Pokémon Data

Punching Pokémon

TYPE	Fighting
	. . .
ABILITIES	Keen Eye
	Iron Fist
HEIGHT	4'07"
WEIGHT	110.7 lbs

National Pokédex No.

107

Description

Hitmonchan's corkscrew punches are strong enough to destroy concrete. It might seem like it's standing still, but it's actually throwing punches too fast to be seen with the naked eye.

Special Moves

Vacuum Wave, Sky Uppercut, Counter

EVO LUT ION

Tyrogue

Hitmonchan

LICKITUNG

Pokémon Data

Licking Pokémon

TYPE	Normal . . .
ABILITIES	Own Tempo Oblivious
HEIGHT	3´11˝
WEIGHT	144.4 lbs

National Pokédex No.
108

Description

Its tongue can extend twice as long as Lickitung is tall. The tongue is as dexterous as a hand and its slimy saliva can make anything stick to it.

Special Moves

Lick, Stomp, Wrap

EVO LUT ION

Lickitung

Lickilicky

1-49

50-99

100-149

150-199

200-249

250-299

300-349

350-399

400-449

450-491

111

KOFFING

Pokémon Data

Poison Gas Pokémon

TYPE	Poison
	. . .
ABILITIES	Levitate
	. . .
HEIGHT	2´00˝
WEIGHT	2.2 lbs

National Pokédex No.
109

Description

Koffing floats because its body is filled with a gas that's lighter than air. This gas is a combination of the vapors from fermenting trash and Koffing's own poisonous fumes.

Special Moves

Smokescreen, Smog, Self-Destruct, Sludge

EVO LUT ION

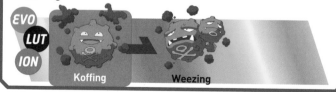

Koffing → Weezing

WEEZING

Pokémon Data

Poison Gas Pokémon

TYPE	Poison
	. . .
ABILITIES	Levitate
	. . .
HEIGHT	3´11˝
WEIGHT	20.9 lbs

Description

Weezing likes to feed on the gases emitted by decomposing trash. It infests dirty houses and raids the trash in the middle of the night.

National Pokédex No.
110

Special Moves

Explosion, Sludge Bomb, Memento

1- 49
50- 99
100- 149
150- 199
200- 249
250- 299
300- 349
350- 399
400- 449
450- 491

EVO LUT ION

Koffing → Weezing

RHYHORN

Pokémon Data

Spikes Pokémon

TYPE	Ground
	Rock
ABILITIES	Lightning Rod
	Rock Head
HEIGHT	3′03″
WEIGHT	253.5 lbs

National Pokédex No.
111

Description

Rhyhorn's hide is so tough that even steel is no match for it. But Rhyhorn is also so dimwitted that sometimes it forgets its target even as it is charging.

Special Moves

Stomp, Fury Attack, Rock Blast

EVO LUT ION

Rhyhorn   Rhydon   Rhyperior

RHYDON

Pokémon Data

Drill Pokémon

TYPE	Ground
	Rock
ABILITIES	Lightning Rod
	Rock Head
HEIGHT	6´03″
WEIGHT	264.6 lbs

National Pokédex No.
112

Description

Rhydon's brain grew in size after it Evolved. It can crush diamonds with its horn and can smash buildings with its tail. It can also dig tunnels by using its horn as a drill.

Special Moves

Charge, Horn Drill, Stone Edge

1-49
50-99
100-149
150-199
200-249
250-299
300-349
350-399
400-449
450-491

EVO LUT ION

Rhyhorn → Rhydon → Rhyperior

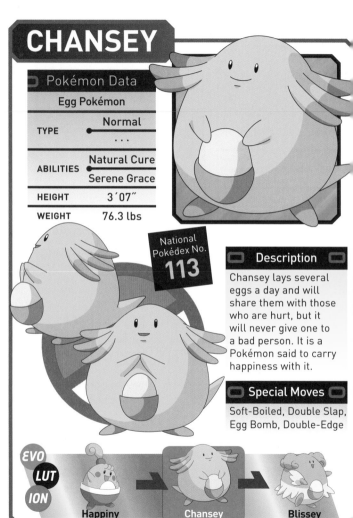

CHANSEY

Pokémon Data

Egg Pokémon

TYPE	Normal
	...
ABILITIES	Natural Cure
	Serene Grace
HEIGHT	3′07″
WEIGHT	76.3 lbs

National Pokédex No.
113

Description

Chansey lays several eggs a day and will share them with those who are hurt, but it will never give one to a bad person. It is a Pokémon said to carry happiness with it.

Special Moves

Soft-Boiled, Double Slap, Egg Bomb, Double-Edge

EVO LUT ION

Happiny → Chansey → Blissey

TANGELA

Pokémon Data

	Vine Pokémon
TYPE	Grass · · ·
ABILITIES	Chlorophyll
	Leaf Guard
HEIGHT	3´03˝
WEIGHT	77.2 lbs

National Pokédex No.
114

Description

Tangela's true form is unknown since it is covered in a mass of tangled blue vines. The vines undulate like seaweed as it walks.

Special Moves

Vine Whip, Bind, Mega Drain

EVO LUT ION

Tangela → Tangrowth

1-49
50-99
100-149
150-199
200-249
250-299
300-349
350-399
400-449
450-491

KANGASKHAN

Pokémon Data

Parent Pokémon	
TYPE	Normal . . .
ABILITIES	Early Bird Scrappy
HEIGHT	7´03˝
WEIGHT	176.4 lbs

National Pokédex No.
115

Description

Kangaskhan raises its offspring in its belly pouch. After about three years, the young Kangaskhan strikes out on its own.

Special Moves

Mega Punch, Endure, Double Hit

EVOLUTION

Kangaskhan

Does not Evolve

HORSEA

1–
49

50–
99

100–
149

150–
199

200–
249

250–
299

300–
349

350–
399

400–
449

450–
491

Pokémon Data

Dragon Pokémon

TYPE	Water
	. . .
ABILITIES	Swift Swim
	Sniper
HEIGHT	1´04˝
WEIGHT	17.6 lbs

Description

Horsea makes its nest among coral colonies, where it feeds on algae and tiny sea creatures. If the current gets too strong, it will anchor itself by wrapping its tail around the coral.

Special Moves

Water Gun, Bubble Beam, Focus Energy

National Pokédex No.
116

EVO
LUT
ION

Horsea

Seadra

Kingdra

SEADRA

Pokémon Data

Dragon Pokémon	
TYPE	Water
	. . .
ABILITIES	Poison Point
	Sniper
HEIGHT	3′11″
WEIGHT	55.1 lbs

Description

Seadra protects itself using its poisonous spikes. It weakens its prey by whirling its tail to create a whirlpool, and then it swallows its prey whole.

National Pokédex No. **117**

Special Moves

Twister, Hydro Pump, Dragon Dance

EVO LUT ION

Horsea   Seadra   Kingdra

GOLDEEN

1-49
50-99
100-149
150-199
200-249
250-299
300-349
350-399
400-449
450-491

Pokémon Data

Goldfish Pokémon

TYPE	Water . . .
ABILITIES	Swift Swim Water Veil
HEIGHT	2′00″
WEIGHT	33.1 lbs

National
Pokédex No.
118

Description

Goldeen is known as the "Queen of the Water" because of its beauty. If it's ever placed in an aquarium, it will use its horn to break the glass and escape.

Special Moves

Water Sport, Horn Attack, Water Pulse

EVO LUT ION

Goldeen   Seaking

121

SEAKING

Pokémon Data

Goldfish Pokémon

TYPE	Water
	. . .
ABILITIES	Swift Swim
	Water Veil
HEIGHT	4´03″
WEIGHT	86.0 lbs

Description

Seaking creates a nest for its eggs by using its horn to dig into the river bottom. Until the eggs hatch, it keeps watch around the nest and will protect the eggs with its life.

National Pokédex No.
119

Special Moves

Waterfall, Agility, Megahorn

EVO LUT ION

Goldeen → Seaking

STARYU

Pokémon Data

Star Shape Pokémon

TYPE	Water
	. . .
ABILITIES	Illuminate
	Natural Cure
HEIGHT	2´07″
WEIGHT	76.1 lbs

National Pokédex No.
120

Description

Staryu's central red core blinks off and on during the night; it seems to be communicating with the stars. As long as it retains its core, it can regenerate body parts that have been torn off.

Special Moves

Swift, Recover, Rapid Spin, Bubble Beam

1-49
50-99
100-149
150-199
200-249
250-299
300-349
350-399
400-449
450-491

EVO LUT ION

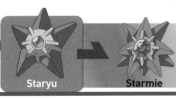

Staryu → Starmie

STARMIE

Pokémon Data

Mysterious Pokémon

TYPE	Water
	Psychic
ABILITIES	Illuminate
	Natural Cure
HEIGHT	3′07″
WEIGHT	176.4 lbs

National Pokédex No.
121

Description

The center of Starmie's body is composed of a gem-like, shimmering, rainbow-colored core. It transmits electronic signals from its core into the night sky.

Special Moves

Recover, Confuse Ray

EVO LUT ION

Staryu → Starmie

MR. MIME

Pokémon Data

Barrier Pokémon

TYPE	Psychic
	...
ABILITIES	Soundproof
	Filter
HEIGHT	4'03"
WEIGHT	120.1 lbs

1-49
50-99
100-149
150-199
200-249
250-299
300-349
350-399
400-449
450-491

Description

Mr. Mime can create solid walls using wave pulses emitted from its fingertips. These walls can deflect even violent attacks. Interrupting its miming will elicit a Double Slap.

National Pokédex No.
122

Special Moves

Light Screen, Barrier, Trick, Psychic

EVO LUT ION

Mime Jr. → Mr. Mime

SCYTHER

Pokémon Data

Mantis Pokémon

TYPE	Bug
	Flying
ABILITIES	Swarm
	Technician
HEIGHT	4'11"
WEIGHT	123.5 lbs

Description

It is extremely difficult to defend against an attack by Scyther if it uses both its arms. Its movements are so fast that it seems as if there are several Scyther at once.

Special Moves

Wing Attack, Fury Cutter, Razor Wind

National Pokédex No.
123

EVO
LUT
ION

Scyther → Scizor

JYNX

Pokémon Data

Human Shape Pokémon

TYPE	Ice
	Psychic
ABILITIES	Oblivious
	Forewarn
HEIGHT	4'07"
WEIGHT	89.5 lbs

National Pokédex No.
124

Description

Jynx's vocalizations are very similar to human speech, but the meaning behind them is unknown. Watching the rhythmic way Jynx walks might trigger a sudden urge to dance.

Special Moves

Avalanche, Blizzard, Lovely Kiss

49
50-99
100-149
150-199
200-249
250-299
300-349
350-399
400-449
450-491

EVO LUT ION

Smoochum

Jynx

127

ELECTABUZZ

Pokémon Data

Electric Pokémon

TYPE	Electric . . .
ABILITIES	Static . . .
HEIGHT	3´07″
WEIGHT	66.1 lbs

National Pokédex No.
125

Description

Electabuzz frequently turns up at large power plants. It loves to eat strong electric currents and can suck up all a plant´s power.

Special Moves

Swift, Thunder Punch, Discharge

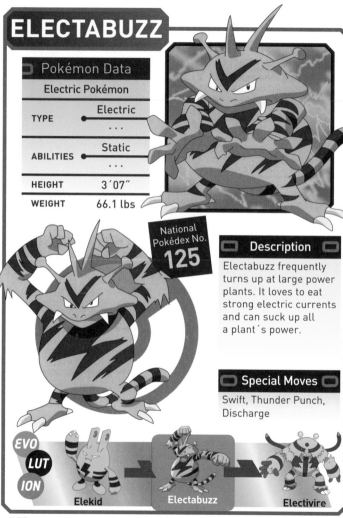

EVO LUT ION

Elekid Electabuzz Electivire

MAGMAR

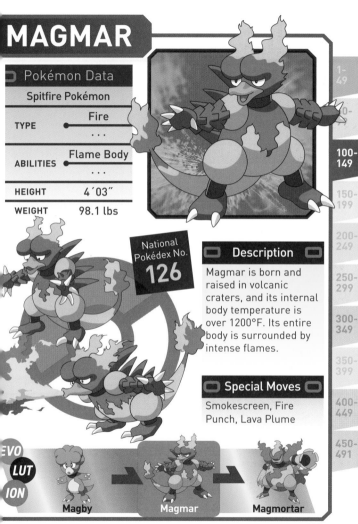

Pokémon Data

Spitfire Pokémon

TYPE	Fire
	...
ABILITIES	Flame Body
	...
HEIGHT	4´03˝
WEIGHT	98.1 lbs

National Pokédex No. **126**

Description

Magmar is born and raised in volcanic craters, and its internal body temperature is over 1200°F. Its entire body is surrounded by intense flames.

Special Moves

Smokescreen, Fire Punch, Lava Plume

EVO LUT ION

Magby → Magmar → Magmortar

1-49
50-
100-149
150-199
200-249
250-299
300-349
350-399
400-449
450-491

PINSIR

Pokémon Data

Stag Beetle Pokémon	
TYPE	Bug
	...
ABILITIES	Hyper Cutter
	Mold Breaker
HEIGHT	4′11″
WEIGHT	121.3 lbs

National Pokédex No.
127

Description

Pinsir's horns are covered with spikes that dig deep into flesh and enable it to pin down its prey. It's sensitive to temperature and its movements slow down in the cold.

Special Moves

Seismic Toss, Bind, Guillotine

EVOLUTION

Pinsir

Does not Evolve

TAUROS

1-49
50-99
100-149
150-199
200-249
250-299
300-349
350-399
400-449
450-491

Pokémon Data

Wild Bull Pokémon

TYPE	Normal
	. . .
ABILITIES	Intimidate
	Anger Point
HEIGHT	4′07″
WEIGHT	194.9 lbs

National Pokédex No.
128

Description

Once Tauros zeroes in on its opponent, it charges forward in a straight line of attack, whipping itself on with its three tails. It has a tough and spirited personality.

Special Moves

Rage, Horn Attack, Tackle, Thrash

EVOLUTION

Tauros — Does not Evolve

131

MAGIKARP

Pokémon Data

Fish Pokémon

TYPE	Water
	. . .
ABILITIES	Swift Swim
	. . .
HEIGHT	2′11″
WEIGHT	22.0 lbs

National
Pokédex No.
129

Description

For some reason,
Magikarp is always
leaping and splashing
about. It's rumored
to be the world's
weakest Pokémon but
was said to be more
powerful eons ago.

Special Moves

Splash, Tackle, Flail

EVO LUT ION

Magikarp → Gyarados

GYARADOS

1-
49

50-
99

100-
149

150-
199

200-
249

250-
299

300-
349

350-
399

400-
449

450-
491

Pokémon Data

Atrocious Pokémon

TYPE	Water
	Flying
ABILITIES	Intimidate
	...
HEIGHT	21´04″
WEIGHT	518.1 lbs

National
Pokédex No.
130

Description

After it Evolves from Magikarp, Gyarados's personality turns aggressive. Once it begins to go on a rampage, it will not calm down until its rage has run its course.

Special Moves

Thrash, Hydro Pump, Hyper Beam

EVO
LUT
ION

Magikarp → Gyarados

133

LAPRAS

Pokémon Data

Transport Pokémon

TYPE	Water
	Ice
ABILITIES	Water Absorb
	Shell Armor
HEIGHT	8′02″
WEIGHT	485.0 lbs

National Pokédex No. **131**

Description

Lapras was overhunted in the past, so it is now rarely seen. It loves to travel the seas carrying humans or Pokémon on its back. It can understand human speech.

Special Moves

Water Pulse, Brine, Sheer Cold

EVO LUT ION

Lapras

Does not Evolve

DITTO

Pokémon Data

Transform Pokémon

TYPE	Normal
	...
ABILITIES	Limber
	...
HEIGHT	1′00″
WEIGHT	8.8 lbs

National Pokédex No.
132

Description

Ditto has the power to instantly copy another being's cellular structure and transform itself into an exact replica. However, it has a hard time doing this from memory.

Special Moves

Transform

EVO LUT ION

Ditto

Does not Evolve

1-49
50-99
100-149
150-199
200-249
250-299
300-349
350-399
400-449
450-491

EEVEE

Pokémon Data

Evolution Pokémon	
TYPE	Normal . . .
ABILITIES	Run Away Adaptability
HEIGHT	1´00˝
WEIGHT	14.3 lbs

National Pokédex No.
133

Description

A Pokémon with unstable genes, it adapts to extreme environments by transforming its appearance and powers. Evee is a highly unusual Pokémon.

Special Moves

Growl, Quick Attack, Bite

EVO LUT ION

Eevee → Jolteon, Vaporeon, Flareon, Espeon, Umbreon, Leafeon, Glaceon

VAPOREON

Pokémon Data

Bubble Jet Pokémon

TYPE	Water
	. . .

ABILITIES	Water Absorb
	. . .

HEIGHT	3´03˝
WEIGHT	63.9 lbs

1-49

50-99

100-149

150-199

200-249

250-299

300-349

350-399

400-449

450-491

Description

The Evolved form of an Eevee, Vaporeon lives underwater. Vaporeon can become invisible after entering water. It has a scaly tail like a fish's.

National Pokédex No.
134

Special Moves

Aqua Ring, Haze, Hydro Pump

EVOLUTION

Eevee ➡ Vaporeon

JOLTEON

Pokémon Data

Lightning Pokémon

TYPE	Electric
	. . .
ABILITIES	Volt Absorb
	. . .
HEIGHT	2´07˝
WEIGHT	54.0 lbs

National Pokédex No.

135

Description

Jolteon can absorb the negative ions in the air and then blast bolts of electricity of up to 10,000 volts. Its fur stands on end when it is angry or startled.

Special Moves

Thunder Fang, Thunder Wave, Thunder

EVOLUTION

Eevee → Jolteon

FLAREON

Pokémon Data

Flame Pokémon

TYPE	Fire
	. . .
ABILITIES	Flash Fire
	. . .
HEIGHT	2´11˝
WEIGHT	55.1 lbs

National Pokédex No.

136

Description

Flareon has a fire chamber within its body. After taking a deep breath, it can blast out flames of 1700°F. Its internal temperature can rise to 900°F during battle.

Special Moves

Fire Fang, Smog, Fire Blast

EVO LUT ION

Eevee → Flareon

1-49
50-99
100-149
150-199
200-249
250-299
300-349
350-399
400-449
450-491

PORYGON

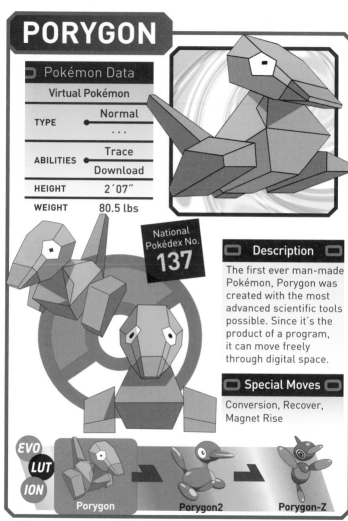

Pokémon Data

Virtual Pokémon

TYPE	Normal
	. . .
ABILITIES	Trace
	Download
HEIGHT	2´07″
WEIGHT	80.5 lbs

National Pokédex No.
137

Description

The first ever man-made Pokémon, Porygon was created with the most advanced scientific tools possible. Since it's the product of a program, it can move freely through digital space.

Special Moves

Conversion, Recover, Magnet Rise

EVO LUT ION

Porygon   Porygon2   Porygon-Z

OMANYTE

1-
49

50-
99

100-
149

150-
199

200-
249

250-
299

300-
349

350-
399

400-
449

450-
491

Pokémon Data

Spiral Pokémon

TYPE	Rock
	Water
ABILITIES	Swift Swim
	Shell Armor
HEIGHT	1´04″
WEIGHT	16.5 lbs

National
Pokédex No.
138

Description

An aquatic Pokémon
that lived in prehistoric
times, Omanyte was
resurrected by scientists
from a fossil of its
helical shell. It swims by
wriggling its ten legs.

Special Moves

Protect, Ancient Power,
Bite

EVO
LUT
ION

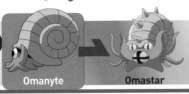

Omanyte → Omastar

OMASTAR

Pokémon Data

Spiral Pokémon

TYPE	Rock
	Water
ABILITIES	Swift Swim
	Shell Armor
HEIGHT	3´03˝
WEIGHT	77.2 lbs

National
Pokédex No.
139

Description

Omastar was believed to have gone extinct because the shell on its back became too large, preventing it from being able to capture prey. It has a sharp beak and dextrous tentacles.

Special Moves

Tickle, Rock Blast, Hydro Pump

EVO LUT ION

Omanyte → Omastar

KABUTO

1-49
50-99
100-149
150-199
200-249
250-299
300-349
350-399
400-449
450-491

Pokémon Data

Shellfish Pokémon

TYPE	Rock
	Water

ABILITIES	Swift Swim
	Battle Armor

HEIGHT	1´08˝
WEIGHT	25.4 lbs

National Pokédex No.
140

Description

Kabuto lived on sandy beaches 300 million years ago. It was resurrected from a fossil discovered in an area of land that had been the floor of an ancient ocean.

Special Moves

Harden, Absorb, Aqua Jet

EVO LUT ION

Kabuto   **Kabutops**

143

KABUTOPS

Pokémon Data

Shellfish Pokémon	
TYPE	Rock
	Water
ABILITIES	Swift Swim
	Battle Armor
HEIGHT	4´03˝
WEIGHT	89.3 lbs

National Pokédex No.
141

Description

It captures its prey with its sharp claws and is able to move swiftly both through water and over land. It's thought that Kabutops Evolved to live on land because its prey began to do so.

Special Moves

Slash, Ancient Power, Night Slash

EVO LUT ION

Kabuto

Kabutops

AERODACTYL

Pokémon Data

Fossil Pokémon

TYPE	Rock
	Flying
ABILITIES	Rock Head
	Pressure
HEIGHT	5′11″
WEIGHT	130.1 lbs

National Pokédex No.

142

Description

Scientists re-created Aerodactyl from genetic material trapped in amber. It has teeth like saws and screeches loudly as it soars through the sky.

Special Moves

Wing Attack, Crunch, Rock Slide

EVOLUTION

Aerodactyl

Does not Evolve

1-
50-99
100-149
150-199
200-249
250-299
300-349
350-399
400-449
450-491

SNORLAX

Pokémon Data

Sleeping Pokémon

| TYPE | Normal |
| | . . . |

| ABILITIES | Immunity |
| | Thick Fat |

| HEIGHT | 6´11˝ |
| WEIGHT | 1014.1 lbs |

National Pokédex No.
143

Description

Except for when it's sleeping, Snorlax is eating. It consumes over 800 pounds of food a day. Not surprisingly, it just keeps getting fatter.

Special Moves

Yawn, Rest, Sleep Talk, Giga Impact

EVO LUT ION

Munchlax → Snorlax

ARTICUNO

Pokémon Data

Freeze Pokémon

TYPE	Ice
	Flying
ABILITIES	Pressure
	. . .
HEIGHT	5′07″
WEIGHT	122.1 lbs

1-49
50-99
100-149
150-199
200-249
250-299
300-349
350-399
400-449
450-491

National Pokédex No. **144**

Description

Articuno creates blizzards by freezing water particles in the air. One of the three Legendary Bird Pokémon of the Kanto region.

Special Moves

Blizzard, Sheer Cold, Ice Beam, Tailwind

EVOLUTION

Articuno — Does not Evolve

ZAPDOS

Pokémon Data

Electric Pokémon

TYPE	Electric
	Flying
ABILITIES	Pressure
	. . .
HEIGHT	5´03˝
WEIGHT	116.0 lbs

National Pokédex No. **145**

Description

One of the three Legendary Bird Pokémon of the Kanto region, Zapdos can control thunder and is said to live within thunderclouds.

Special Moves

Discharge, Drill Peck, Thunder

EVOLUTION

Zapdos — Does not Evolve

148

MOLTRES

Pokémon Data

Flame Pokémon

TYPE	Fire
	Flying
ABILITIES	Pressure
	. . .
HEIGHT	6´07˝
WEIGHT	132.3 lbs

1-49

50-99

100-149

150-199

200-249

250-299

300-349

350-399

400-449

450-491

National Pokédex No.
146

Description

One of the three Legendary Bird Pokémon of the Kanto region, Moltres has bright orange plumage that flames up beautifully every time it flaps its wings.

Special Moves

Flamethrower, Heat Wave, Sky Attack

**EVO
LUT
ION**

Moltres

Does not Evolve

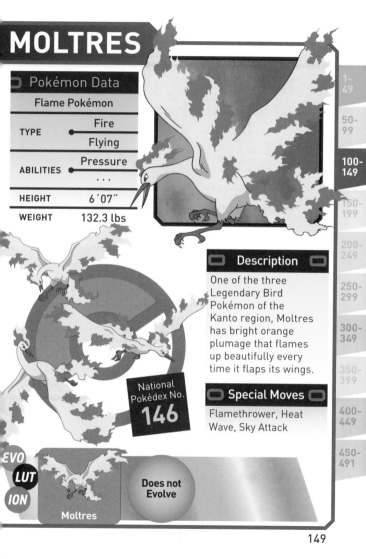

DRATINI

Pokémon Data

Dragon Pokémon

TYPE	Dragon . . .
ABILITIES	Shed Skin . . .
HEIGHT	5′11″
WEIGHT	7.3 lbs

National Pokédex No.
147

Description

Because it's so rare, for a long time it wasn't considered to be a real Pokémon. Dratini grows in stages, shedding its skin each time.

Special Moves

Wrap, Dragon Rage, Slam, Twister

EVOLUTION

Dratini → Dragonair → Dragonite

DRAGONAIR

Pokémon Data

Dragon Pokémon

TYPE	Dragon
	...
ABILITIES	Shed Skin
	...
HEIGHT	13´01″
WEIGHT	36.4 lbs

1–
49

50–
99

100–
149

150–
199

200–
249

250–
299

300–
349

350–
399

400–
449

450–
491

National
Pokédex No.
148

Description

Dragonair lives in lakes and oceans. Weather changes can be predicted by the auras that surround its body. Although it does not have wings, it can fly.

Special Moves

Twister, Aqua Tail, Dragon Rush

EVO LUT ION

Dratini   Dragonair   Dragonite

DRAGONITE

Pokémon Data

Dragon Pokémon	
TYPE	Dragon
	Flying
ABILITIES	Inner Focus
	. . .
HEIGHT	7´03˝
WEIGHT	463.0 lbs

National Pokédex No.
149

Description

Dragonite live far out in the ocean and have been seen by very few humans. They will help the crews of shipwrecked boats by guiding them back to land.

Special Moves

Wing Attack, Outrage, Hyper Beam

EVO LUT ION

Dratini → Dragonair → Dragonite

MEWTWO

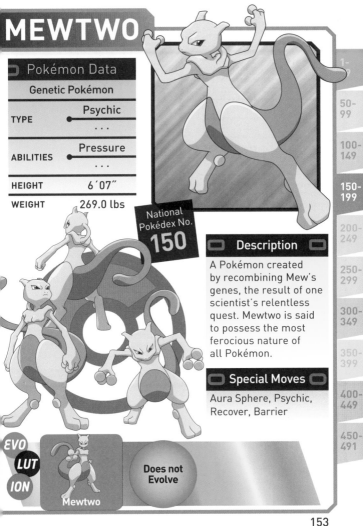

Pokémon Data

Genetic Pokémon

TYPE	Psychic
	...
ABILITIES	Pressure
	...
HEIGHT	6´07″
WEIGHT	269.0 lbs

National Pokédex No.
150

Description

A Pokémon created by recombining Mew's genes, the result of one scientist's relentless quest. Mewtwo is said to possess the most ferocious nature of all Pokémon.

Special Moves

Aura Sphere, Psychic, Recover, Barrier

EVO LUT ION

Mewtwo — Does not Evolve

1-
50-99
100-149
150-199
200-249
250-299
300-349
350-399
400-449
450-491

MEW

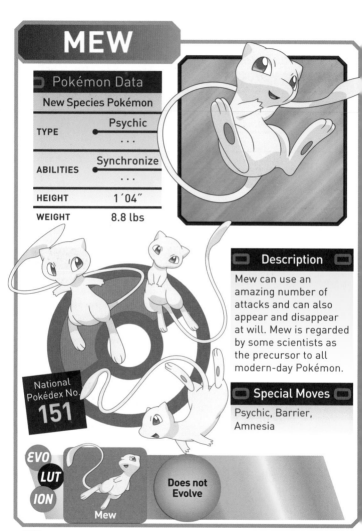

Pokémon Data

New Species Pokémon

TYPE	Psychic . . .
ABILITIES	Synchronize . . .
HEIGHT	1´04″
WEIGHT	8.8 lbs

National Pokédex No.
151

Description

Mew can use an amazing number of attacks and can also appear and disappear at will. Mew is regarded by some scientists as the precursor to all modern-day Pokémon.

Special Moves

Psychic, Barrier, Amnesia

EVO LUT ION

Mew — Does not Evolve

CHIKORITA

1-49
50-99
100-149
150-199
200-249
250-299
300-349
350-399
400-449
450-491

Pokémon Data

Leaf Pokémon

TYPE	Grass
	. . .
ABILITIES	Overgrow
	. . .
HEIGHT	2´11˝
WEIGHT	14.1 lbs

National Pokédex No.
152

Description

Chikorita is very mild-mannered and loves to bask in the sun. It can read the humidity and temperature of the surrounding area using the sweet-smelling leaf on its head.

Special Moves

Razor Leaf, Synthesis, Poison Powder

EVO LUT ION

Chikorita

Bayleef

Meganium

BAYLEEF

Pokémon Data

Leaf Pokémon

TYPE	Grass
	...
ABILITIES	Overgrow
	...
HEIGHT	3´11˝
WEIGHT	34.8 lbs

National
Pokédex No.
153

Description

The buds around Bayleef's neck have a very sharp, distinctive scent that energizes those who smell it, so much so that they may even get aggressive.

Special Moves

Magical Leaf, Sweet Scent, Body Slam

EVO LUT ION

Chikorita ▶ **Bayleef** ▶ Meganium

MEGANIUM

Pokémon Data

Herb Pokémon	
TYPE	Grass . . .
ABILITIES	Overgrow . . .
HEIGHT	5′11″
WEIGHT	221.6 lbs

National Pokédex No.
154

Description

Meganium's breath can bring dead grasses and flowers back to life. The scent from the petals around its neck has the power to calm an aggressive heart.

Special Moves

Petal Dance, Body Slam, Aromatherapy, Solar Beam

1-49

50-99

100-149

150-199

200-249

250-299

300-349

350-399

400-449

450-491

EVO
LUT
ION

 Chikorita → **Bayleef** → **Meganium**

CYNDAQUIL

Pokémon Data

Fire Mouse Pokémon

TYPE	Fire
	. . .
ABILITIES	Blaze
	. . .
HEIGHT	1´08˝
WEIGHT	17.4 lbs

National Pokédex No.
155

Description

Cyndaquil is timid in nature, but when it's angered or surprised flames burst out of its back. It uses the flames as a defense mechanism.

Special Moves

Smokescreen, Ember, Quick Attack

EVO LUT ION

Cyndaquil　　　Quilava　　　Typhlosion

QUILAVA

Pokémon Data

Volcano Pokémon

TYPE	Fire
	. . .
ABILITIES	Blaze
	. . .
HEIGHT	2´11˝
WEIGHT	41.9 lbs

National Pokédex No.
156

Description

Quilava uses the heat of its flames to intimidate opponents; the intensity of the flames increases in battle. The fur on its body is flame retardant.

Special Moves

Flame Wheel, Lava Plume, Flamethrower

1-49
50-99
100-149
150-199
200-249
250-299
300-349
350-399
400-449
450-491

EVOLUTION

Cyndaquil → Quilava → Typhlosion

TYPHLOSION

Pokémon Data

Volcano Pokémon

TYPE	Fire
	. . .
ABILITIES	Blaze
	. . .
HEIGHT	5´07˝
WEIGHT	175.3 lbs

National Pokédex No.

157

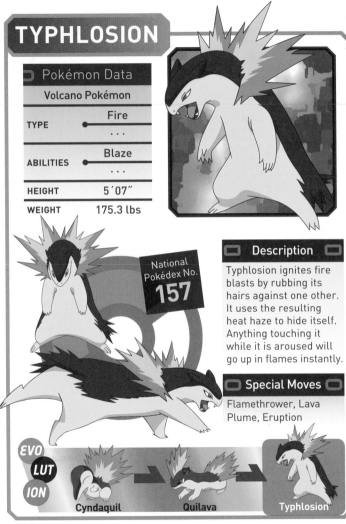

Description

Typhlosion ignites fire blasts by rubbing its hairs against one other. It uses the resulting heat haze to hide itself. Anything touching it while it is aroused will go up in flames instantly.

Special Moves

Flamethrower, Lava Plume, Eruption

EVO LUT ION

Cyndaquil → Quilava → Typhlosion

TOTODILE

Pokémon Data

Big Jaw Pokémon

TYPE	Water ...
ABILITIES	Torrent ...
HEIGHT	2´00˝
WEIGHT	20.9 lbs

National Pokédex No.
158

Description

Although it is small physically, Totodile can crush anything in its highly developed jaws. It instinctively bites anything that moves. Even its Trainer must be careful.

Special Moves

Water Gun, Bite, Thrash

1–49
50–99
100–149
150–199
200–249
250–299
300–349
350–399
400–449
450–491

EVO
LUT
ION

Totodile

Croconaw

Feraligatr

CROCONAW

Pokémon Data

Big Jaw Pokémon	
TYPE	Water . . .
ABILITIES	Torrent . . .
HEIGHT	3´07˝
WEIGHT	55.1 lbs

Description

Once Croconaw bites something and latches on with its big mouth, it does not let go until its teeth fall out. These teeth grow back quickly and it always has all forty-eight ready.

Special Moves

Rage, Crunch, Slash, Screech

EVO LUT ION

Totodile

Croconaw

Feraligatr

162

FERALIGATR

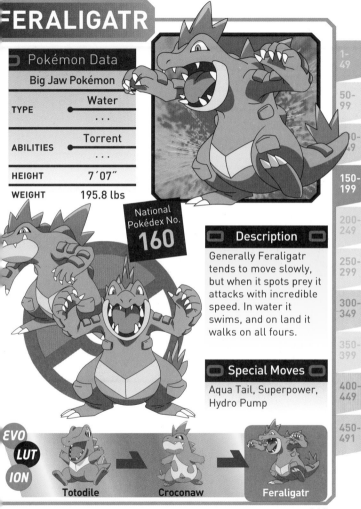

Pokémon Data

Big Jaw Pokémon

TYPE	Water ...
ABILITIES	Torrent ...
HEIGHT	7'07"
WEIGHT	195.8 lbs

National Pokédex No.
160

Description

Generally Feraligatr tends to move slowly, but when it spots prey it attacks with incredible speed. In water it swims, and on land it walks on all fours.

Special Moves

Aqua Tail, Superpower, Hydro Pump

EVO LUT ION

Totodile → Croconaw → Feraligatr

1-49
50-99
100-149
150-199
200-249
250-299
300-349
350-399
400-449
450-491

SENTRET

Pokémon Data

Scout Pokémon

TYPE	Normal
	. . .
ABILITIES	Run Away
	Keen Eye
HEIGHT	2′07″
WEIGHT	13.2 lbs

National
Pokédex No.
161

Description

Sentret is nervous by nature and always alert. It keeps watch far and wide by constantly stretching up on the tip of its tail. When it spots an enemy, it warns its companions.

Special Moves

Fury Swipes, Helping Hand, Slam

EVO LUT ION

   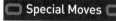

Sentret   Furret

FURRET

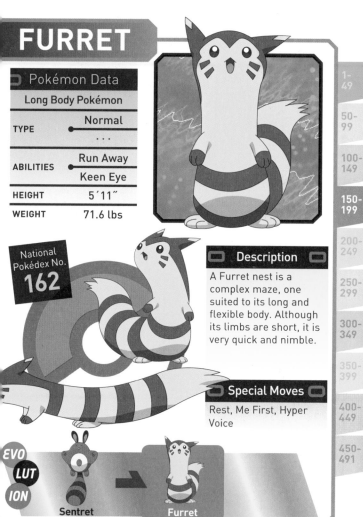

Pokémon Data

Long Body Pokémon

TYPE	Normal
	. . .
ABILITIES	Run Away
	Keen Eye
HEIGHT	5´11″
WEIGHT	71.6 lbs

National Pokédex No.
162

Description

A Furret nest is a complex maze, one suited to its long and flexible body. Although its limbs are short, it is very quick and nimble.

Special Moves

Rest, Me First, Hyper Voice

EVO LUT ION

Sentret → Furret

1-49
50-99
100-149
150-199
200-249
250-299
300-349
350-399
400-449
450-491

HOOTHOOT

Pokémon Data

Owl Pokémon

TYPE	Normal
	Flying
ABILITIES	Insomnia
	Keen Eye
HEIGHT	2´04″
WEIGHT	46.7 lbs

National Pokédex No.
163

Description

Hoothoot's internal rhythm is extremely accurate, and it calls out at the same time every day. It always stands on one foot; it changes feet so quickly no one can see it.

Special Moves

Hypnosis, Peck, Growl

EVO LUT ION

Hoothoot → Noctowl

NOCTOWL

Pokémon Data

Owl Pokémon	
TYPE	Normal
	Flying
ABILITIES	Insomnia
	Keen Eye
HEIGHT	5′03″
WEIGHT	89.9 lbs

National Pokédex No.
164

Description

If there's even the faintest amount of light, Noctowl can still see. When pondering difficult topics, it increases the effectiveness of its brain by turning its head upside down.

Special Moves

Foresight, Air Slash, Zen Headbutt, Hypnosis

EVO
LUT
ION

Hoothoot → Noctowl

1-
49

50-
99

100-
149

150-
199

200-
249

250-
299

300-
349

350-
399

400-
449

450-
491

LEDYBA

Pokémon Data

Five Star Pokémon

TYPE	Bug
	Flying
ABILITIES	Swarm
	Early Bird
HEIGHT	3′03″
WEIGHT	23.8 lbs

National Pokédex No. **165**

Description

Ledyba always group together; being alone makes them stricken with doubt and unable to move. When it gets cold, they huddle together for warmth.

Special Moves

Tackle, Supersonic, Comet Punch

EVO LUT ION

Ledyba → Ledian

LEDIAN

Pokémon Data

Five Star Pokémon

TYPE	Bug
	Flying
ABILITIES	Swarm
	Early Bird
HEIGHT	4′07″
WEIGHT	78.5 lbs

1-49

50-99

100-149

150-199

200-249

250-299

300-349

350-399

400-449

450-491

National Pokédex No.
166

Description

Ledian uses starlight as energy. On star-lit nights, it flies about scattering shimmering powder. The patterns on its back change depending on the stars in the night sky.

Special Moves

Tackle, Mach Punch, Bug Buzz

EVO LUT ION

Ledyba

Ledian

SPINARAK

Pokémon Data

String Spit Pokémon	
TYPE	Bug
	Poison
ABILITIES	Swarm
	Insomnia
HEIGHT	1´08˝
WEIGHT	18.7 lbs

National Pokédex No.
167

Description

Spinarak creates traps by spinning webs of fine but sturdy silk. It waits, motionless within its nest, until prey becomes entangled in its web.

Special Moves

String Shot, Leech Life, Night Shade

EVO
LUT
ION

Spinarak

Ariados

170

ARIADOS

1–49
50–99
100–149
150–199
200–249
250–299
300–349
350–399
400–449
450–491

Pokémon Data

Long Leg Pokémon	
TYPE	Bug
	Poison
ABILITIES	Swarm
	Insomnia
HEIGHT	3′07″
WEIGHT	73.9 lbs

National Pokédex No.
168

Description

Initially, Ariados allows its prey to escape, but it leaves a silk thread attached so it can follow later and capture its prey's companions as well.

Special Moves

Spider Web, Pin Missile, Poison Jab

EVO
LUT
ION

Spinarak

Ariados

171

CROBAT

Pokémon Data

Bat Pokémon

TYPE	Poison
	Flying
ABILITIES	Inner Focus
	. . .
HEIGHT	5´11″
WEIGHT	165.3 lbs

Description

Using its four wings, Crobat is able to fly faster and more quietly than it could before it Evolved. It rests by hanging upside-down from branches using its back wings.

Special Moves

Cross Poison, Astonish, Haze

National Pokédex No.
169

EVO LUT ION

Zubat → Golbat → Crobat

CHINCHOU

1–49
50–99
100–149
150–199
200–249
250–299
300–349
350–399
400–449
450–491

Pokémon Data

Angler Pokémon

TYPE	Water
	Electric
ABILITIES	Volt Absorb
	Illuminate
HEIGHT	1´08˝
WEIGHT	26.5 lbs

National Pokédex No.
170

Description

Chinchou can run an extremely powerful electric current between its antennae. It shocks its prey by sending positive and negative bolts through the tips of its antennae.

Special Moves

Thunder Wave, Spark, Water Gun

EVO
LUT
ION

Chinchou   Lanturn

173

LANTURN

Pokémon Data

Light Pokémon

TYPE	Water
	Electric
ABILITIES	Volt Absorb
	Illuminate
HEIGHT	3'11"
WEIGHT	49.6 lbs

National Pokédex No.
171

Description

Lanturn blinds its prey by shining a very bright light in their eyes, then swallows them whole while they are stunned. Because of the strength of its light, it's called the "Deep-Sea Star."

Special Moves

Bubble Beam, Discharge, Hydro Pump

EVO LUT ION

Chinchou → Lanturn

PICHU

Pokémon Data

Tiny Mouse Pokémon

TYPE	Electric
	...
ABILITIES	Static
	...
HEIGHT	1´00˝
WEIGHT	4.4 lbs

National Pokédex No.
172

Description

The electricity pouches on its cheeks are still quite small. Although it cannot store a lot of electricity yet, it plays with its friends by shooting sparks from the tip of its tail.

Special Moves

Thunder Shock, Tail Whip, Thunder Wave

EVO LUT ION

Pichu → Pikachu → Raichu

1-49
50-99
100-149
150-199
200-249
250-299
300-349
350-399
400-449
450-491

CLEFFA

Pokémon Data

Star Shape Pokémon

TYPE	Normal
	. . .
ABILITIES	Cute Charm
	Magic Guard
HEIGHT	1´00˝
WEIGHT	6.6 lbs

National Pokédex No.
173

Description

Cleffa are shaped like stars and gather on nights when there are lots of shooting stars. Because of this, it's said that they came to Earth on shooting stars.

Special Moves

Charm, Sweet Kiss, Encore

EVOLUTION

Cleffa → Clefairy → Clefable

IGGLYBUFF

Pokémon Data

Balloon Pokémon

TYPE	Normal
	. . .
ABILITIES	Cute Charm
	. . .
HEIGHT	1´00˝
WEIGHT	2.2 lbs

1-
49

50-
99

100-
149

**150-
199**

200-
249

250-
299

300-
349

350-
399

400-
449

450-
491

National
Pokédex No.
174

Description

Igglybuff's elastic body feels very nice to the touch. Once it starts bouncing it's quite hard to stop it. It can damage its throat if it keeps singing for a long time.

Special Moves

Defense Curl, Sing, Sweet Kiss

EVO LUT ION

Igglybuff

➤

Jigglypuff

➤

Wigglytuff

TOGEPI

Pokémon Data

Spike Ball Pokémon

TYPE	Normal . . .
ABILITIES	Hustle Serene Grace
HEIGHT	1′00″
WEIGHT	3.3 lbs

National Pokédex No.
175

Description

Togepi's shell is said to be stuffed to the brim with happiness, which it shares with kind-hearted people. Getting a sleeping Togepi to stand up also brings one happiness.

Special Moves

Metronome, Sweet Kiss, Yawn

EVO LUT ION

Togepi → Togetic → Togekiss

TOGETIC

1–
49

50–
99

100–
149

150–
199

200–
249

250–
299

300–
349

350–
399

400–
449

450–
491

Pokémon Data

Happiness Pokémon

TYPE	Normal
	Flying
ABILITIES	Hustle
	Serene Grace
HEIGHT	2′00″
WEIGHT	7.1 lbs

Description

Togetic appears before kind-hearted people and sprinkles them with a glowing down known as "Joy Dust." It loses energy if it does not stay close to kind people.

Special Moves

Wish, Follow Me, Last Resort

National Pokédex No.
176

EVO
LUT
ION

Togepi

Togetic

Togekiss

NATU

Pokémon Data

Tiny Bird Pokémon

TYPE	Psychic
	Flying
ABILITIES	Synchronize
	Early Bird
HEIGHT	0´08˝
WEIGHT	4.4 lbs

National Pokédex No.
177

Description

Since its wings have not fully grown yet, Natu cannot fly. Instead, it uses its jumping skills to move around. It eats cacti, skillfully picking its way around the buds and spines.

Special Moves

Teleport, Lucky Chant, Confuse Ray

EVOLUTION

Natu → Xatu

180

XATU

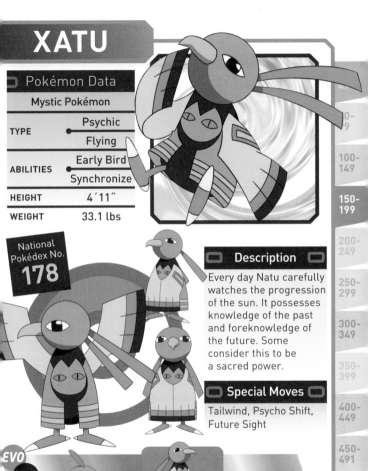

Pokémon Data

Mystic Pokémon

TYPE	Psychic
	Flying
ABILITIES	Early Bird
	Synchronize
HEIGHT	4´11˝
WEIGHT	33.1 lbs

National Pokédex No.
178

Description

Every day Natu carefully watches the progression of the sun. It possesses knowledge of the past and foreknowledge of the future. Some consider this to be a sacred power.

Special Moves

Tailwind, Psycho Shift, Future Sight

EVO LUT ION

Natu → Xatu

27
0-
9
100-
149
150-
199
200-
249
250-
299
300-
349
350-
399
400-
449
450-
491

MAREEP

Pokémon Data

Wool Pokémon

TYPE	Electric . . .
ABILITIES	Static . . .
HEIGHT	2´00˝
WEIGHT	17.2 lbs

National Pokédex No.
179

Description

Static electricity is created when Mareep's wool is rubbed, and when this electricity builds up, its wool doubles in size. Anyone who touches it then will get an electric shock.

Special Moves

Growl, Thunder Shock, Thunder Wave

EVO LUT ION

 Mareep → Flaaffy → Ampharos

FLAAFFY

Pokémon Data

Wool Pokémon

TYPE	Electric
	...
ABILITIES	Static
	...
HEIGHT	2´07"
WEIGHT	29.3 lbs

National Pokédex No.
180

1-49
50-99
100-149
150-199
200-249
250-299
300-349
350-399
400-449
450-491

Description

Electricity tends to build up in its wool, and when it's fully charged the ball on the tip of its tail glows. Because of its rubbery skin, Flaaffy itself is protected from electric shocks.

Special Moves

Cotton Spore, Charge, Discharge, Thunder

EVOLUTION

Mareep ▶ Flaaffy ▶ Ampharos

183

AMPHAROS

Pokémon Data

Light Pokémon

TYPE	Electric
	. . .
ABILITIES	Static
	. . .
HEIGHT	4'07"
WEIGHT	135.6 lbs

National Pokédex No. **181**

Description

The tip of Ampharos's tail glows with a light strong enough to be seen a long distance away. Long ago, people used this light as a beacon to transmit messages to one another.

Special Moves

Light Screen, Power Gem, Thunder

EVO LUT ION

Mareep   Flaaffy   Ampharos

Pokémon Data

Flower Pokémon

TYPE	Grass
	. . .
ABILITIES	Chlorophyll
	. . .
HEIGHT	1´04"
WEIGHT	12.8 lbs

National Pokédex No.
182

Description

When the rainy season ends, Bellossom dances while basking in the warm rays of the sun. The stinkier it was as Gloom, the more beautiful it will be as Bellossum.

Special Moves

Sweet Scent, Sunny Day, Leaf Storm

EVO LUT ION

Oddish → Gloom → Bellossom

1-49
50-99
100-149
150-199
200-249
250-299
300-349
350-399
400-449
450-491

185

MARILL

Pokémon Data

Aqua Mouse Pokémon

TYPE	Water
	. . .
ABILITIES	Thick Fat
	Huge Power
HEIGHT	1´04"
WEIGHT	18.7 lbs

Description

The ball at the tip of its tail is filled with an oil lighter than water. It uses the ball as a float when it dives down to feed on its favorite water grasses on riverbeds.

National Pokédex No.
183

Special Moves

Bubble Beam, Water Gun, Defense Curl, Rollout

EVOLUTION

Azurill → Marill → Azumarill

AZUMARILL

Pokémon Data

Aqua Rabbit Pokémon

TYPE	Water
	...
ABILITIES	Thick Fat
	Huge Power
HEIGHT	2´07˝
WEIGHT	62.8 lbs

National Pokédex No.
184

Description

Azumarill lives in rivers and lakes. It uses its long ears to pick up the sounds of its prey. When it's in the water, it rolls up its ears so water doesn't get in them.

Special Moves

Aqua Ring, Rain Dance, Hydro Pump

EVOLUTION

Azurill → Marill → Azumarill

1-49
50-99
100-149
150-199
200-249
250-299
300-349
350-399
400-449
450-491

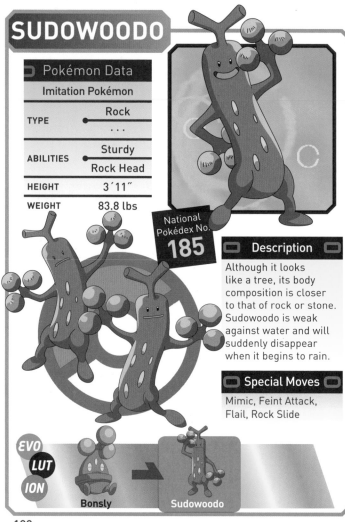

SUDOWOODO

Pokémon Data

Imitation Pokémon

TYPE	Rock
	...
ABILITIES	Sturdy
	Rock Head
HEIGHT	3′11″
WEIGHT	83.8 lbs

National Pokédex No.

185

Description

Although it looks like a tree, its body composition is closer to that of rock or stone. Sudowoodo is weak against water and will suddenly disappear when it begins to rain.

Special Moves

Mimic, Feint Attack, Flail, Rock Slide

EVO LUT ION

Bonsly → Sudowoodo

188

POLITOED

Pokémon Data

Frog Pokémon

TYPE	Water
	. . .
ABILITIES	Water Absorb
	Damp
HEIGHT	3´07″
WEIGHT	74.7 lbs

1–49

50–99

100–149

150–199

200–249

250–299

300–349

350–399

400–449

450–491

Description

Politoed calls together Poliwag and Poliwhirl to form a group with itself as the leader. When more than three Politoed assemble, they begin to sing in a chorus.

National Pokédex No.
186

Special Moves

Bounce, Swagger, Bubble Beam

EVO LUT ION

Poliwag

Poliwhirl

Politoed

189

HOPPIP

Pokémon Data

Cottonweed Pokémon

TYPE	Grass
	Flying
ABILITIES	Chlorophyll
	Leaf Guard
HEIGHT	1´04″
WEIGHT	1.1 lbs

National Pokédex No.
187

Description

Because Hoppip is so light, it frequently gets carried off by a breeze. It is said that when Hoppip congregate on the hills and fields, spring is just around the corner.

Special Moves

Splash, Tackle, Stun Spore, Poison Powder

EVOLUTION

Hoppip → Skiploom → Jumpluff

SKIPLOOM

Pokémon Data

Cottonweed Pokémon

TYPE	Grass
	Flying
ABILITIES	Chlorophyll
	Leaf Guard
HEIGHT	2′00″
WEIGHT	2.2 lbs

National Pokédex No.
188

Description

The flower on the top of Skiploom's head blooms when the temperature rises and closes as it goes down. It floats about in the sky so that it can absorb the sun's rays.

Special Moves

Sleep Powder, Bullet Seed, Mega Drain

EVOLUTION

Hoppip

Skiploom

Jumpluff

1-49
50-99
100-149
150-199
200-249
250-299
300-349
350-399
400-449
450-491

JUMPLUFF

Pokémon Data

Cottonweed Pokémon

TYPE	Grass
	Flying
ABILITIES	Chlorophyll
	Leaf Guard
HEIGHT	2′07″
WEIGHT	6.6 lbs

National Pokédex No.
189

Description

Jumpluff scatters cotton spores about as it is buffeted by the winds. They have been known to circle the world by being blown along by the seasonal winds.

Special Moves

Cotton Spore, Worry Seed, Giga Drain

EVOLUTION

Hoppip ▶ Skiploom ▶ Jumpluff

AIPOM

Pokémon Data

Long Tail Pokémon

TYPE	Normal
	. . .
ABILITIES	Run Away
	Pickup
HEIGHT	2´07″
WEIGHT	25.4 lbs

National Pokédex No.
190

Description

Aipom has a tail that is actually more dextrous than its hands, which is very useful when it needs to hang upside-down or when it needs to get food.

Special Moves

Tail Whip, Fury Swipes, Tickle

EVOLUTION

Aipom ➤ Ambipom

1–49
50–99
100–149
150–199
200–249
250–299
300–349
350–399
400–449
450–491

SUNKERN

Pokémon Data

Seed Pokémon

TYPE	Grass
	. . .
ABILITIES	Chlorophyll
	Solar Power
HEIGHT	1´00″
WEIGHT	4.0 lbs

Description

Sunkern survives on the morning dew that forms on its leaves. A cold summer generally points to a bumper crop the following year.

Special Moves

Ingrain, Leech Seed, Razor Leaf

National Pokédex No. **191**

EVO LUT ION

 Sunkern → Sunflora

SUNFLORA

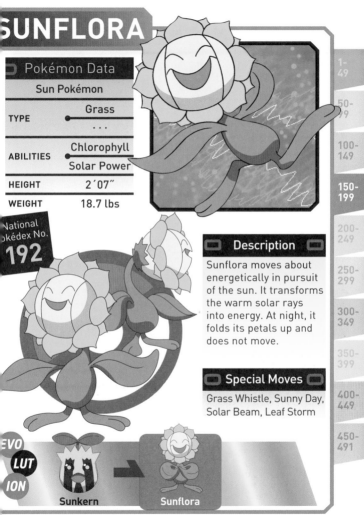

Pokémon Data

Sun Pokémon

TYPE	Grass
	. . .
ABILITIES	Chlorophyll
	Solar Power
HEIGHT	2´07˝
WEIGHT	18.7 lbs

National Pokédex No.
192

Description

Sunflora moves about energetically in pursuit of the sun. It transforms the warm solar rays into energy. At night, it folds its petals up and does not move.

Special Moves

Grass Whistle, Sunny Day, Solar Beam, Leaf Storm

EVO LUT ION

Sunkern → Sunflora

1-49
50-99
100-149
150-199
200-249
250-299
300-349
350-399
400-449
450-491

YANMA

Pokémon Data

Clear Wing Pokémon

TYPE	Bug
	Flying
ABILITIES	Speed Boost
	Compound Eyes
HEIGHT	3´11˝
WEIGHT	83.8 lbs

National Pokédex No.
193

Description

Thanks to its big eyes and 360° vision, Yanma can see everything in its vicinity and even catch prey that's behind it. The beating of its wings can cause shock waves.

Special Moves

Sonic Boom, Detect, Supersonic, U-turn

EVOLUTION

Yanma   Yanmega

WOOPER

Pokémon Data

Water Fish Pokémon

TYPE	Water
	Ground
ABILITIES	Damp
	Water Absorb
HEIGHT	1′04″
WEIGHT	18.7 lbs

National Pokédex No. **194**

Description

Wooper lives in cold waters. When it walks on land, it covers its body with a poisonous protective film. When it sleeps, it half-buries its body in mud.

Special Moves

Water Gun, Mud Sport, Mud Shot

1-49
50-99
100-149
150-199
200-249
250-299
300-349
350-399
400-449
450-491

EVO LUT ION

Wooper → Quagsire

QUAGSIRE

Pokémon Data

Water Fish Pokémon

TYPE	Water
	Ground
ABILITIES	Damp
	Water Absorb
HEIGHT	4′07″
WEIGHT	165.3 lbs

National Pokédex No.

195

Description

Quagsire lounges on river bottoms, waiting for prey. It's so easy-going that even if it bumps its head against rocks or boat bottoms while swimming, it doesn't mind.

Special Moves

Amnesia, Muddy Water, Earthquake, Yawn

EVO LUT ION

Wooper → Quagsire

ESPEON

Pokémon Data

	Sun Pokémon
TYPE	Psychic
	...
ABILITIES	Synchronize
	...
HEIGHT	2′11″
WEIGHT	58.4 lbs

National Pokédex No.
196

Description

Espeon's body is covered in very fine fur. As air currents pass through its fur, it's able to sense things like changes in the weather or an opponent's next move.

Special Moves

Future Sight, Psych Up, Morning Sun

EVO LUT ION

Eevee   Espeon

50-99

100-149

150-199

200-249

250-299

300-349

350-399

400-449

450-491

UMBREON

Pokémon Data

Moonlight Pokémon

TYPE	Dark
	. . .
ABILITIES	Synchronize
	. . .
HEIGHT	3′03″
WEIGHT	59.5 lbs

National Pokédex No.
197

Description

An Umbreon is an Eevee transformed by the light of the moon. The ring patterns on its body glow when night falls. It secretes a poisonous sweat when it needs to defend itself.

Special Moves

Feint Attack, Assurance, Moonlight

EVO LUT ION

Eevee

Umbreon

MURKROW

Pokémon Data

Darkness Pokémon

TYPE	Dark
	Flying
ABILITIES	Insomnia
	Super Luck
HEIGHT	1´08˝
WEIGHT	4.6 lbs

National Pokédex No.
198

Description

It's said that seeing a Murkrow at night will bring bad luck. They lure travelers onto mountain roads leading deep into the woods and get them utterly lost.

Special Moves

Astonish, Pursuit, Wing Attack, Sucker Punch

EVO LUT ION

Murkrow → Honchkrow

1-49
50-99
100-149
150-199
200-249
250-299
300-349
350-399
400-449
450-491

SLOWKING

Pokémon Data

Royal Pokémon

TYPE	Water
	Psychic
ABILITIES	Oblivious
	Own Tempo
HEIGHT	6´07"
WEIGHT	175.3 lbs

National Pokédex No.
199

Description

Being bitten by Shellder made Slowking smarter, due to the way Shellder's poison reacted with its brain. It has such an easy-going personality that it never gets stressed.

Special Moves

Psychic, Water Pulse, Zen Headbutt, Swagger

EVO LUT ION

Slowpoke → Slowking

MISDREAVUS

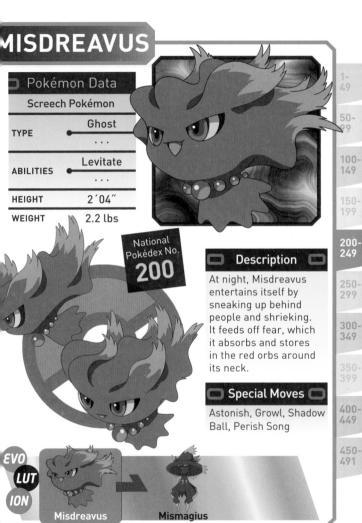

Pokémon Data

Screech Pokémon

TYPE	Ghost
	...
ABILITIES	Levitate
	...
HEIGHT	2'04"
WEIGHT	2.2 lbs

National Pokédex No.
200

1–
49

50–
99

100–
149

150–
199

200–
249

250–
299

300–
349

350–
399

400–
449

450–
491

Description

At night, Misdreavus entertains itself by sneaking up behind people and shrieking. It feeds off fear, which it absorbs and stores in the red orbs around its neck.

Special Moves

Astonish, Growl, Shadow Ball, Perish Song

EVO LUT ION

Misdreavus → Mismagius

UNOWN

Pokémon Data

Symbol Pokémon

TYPE	Psychic
	...
ABILITIES	Levitate
	...
HEIGHT	1´08˝
WEIGHT	11.0 lbs

National Pokédex No.
201

Description

Unown are usually found stuck to walls. They look like ancient glyphs, and their forms are said to have some hidden meaning. They are able to communicate telepathically.

Special Moves

Hidden Power

EVO LUT ION

Unown → Does not Evolve

WOBBUFFET

Pokémon Data

Patient Pokémon	
TYPE	Psychic . . .
ABILITIES	Shadow Tag . . .
HEIGHT	4'03"
WEIGHT	62.8 lbs

National Pokédex No.
202

1–49
50–99
100–149
150–199
200–249
250–299
300–349
350–399
400–449
450–491

Description

A stoic Pokémon that stays calm through practically anything—except when its tail is attacked. When two or more Wobbuffet gather, they play by testing each other's endurance.

Special Moves

Counter, Mirror Coat, Safeguard

EVOLUTION

Wynaut → Wobbuffet

205

GIRAFARIG

Pokémon Data

Long Neck Pokémon

TYPE	Normal
	Psychic
ABILITIES	Inner Focus
	Early Bird
HEIGHT	4'11"
WEIGHT	91.5 lbs

National Pokédex No.
203

Description

The head of Girafarig's tail is able to attack by reacting to smells and sounds. Since the tail head does not need any sleep, it is constantly on the lookout.

Special Moves

Stomp, Double Hit, Psychic

EVO
LUT
ION

Girafarig

Does not Evolve

PINECO

Pokémon Data

Bagworm Pokémon

TYPE	Bug
	...
ABILITIES	Sturdy
	...
HEIGHT	2′00″
WEIGHT	15.9 lbs

1-
49

50-
99

100-
149

150-
199

200-
249

250-
299

300-
349

350-
399

400-
449

450-
491

National Pokédex No.
204

Description

Pineco makes its shell thicker by layering it with tree bark. As it dangles from trees, waiting for prey, it's occasionally pecked at by birds who mistake it for a pinecone.

Special Moves

Self-Destruct, Rapid Spin, Natural Gift

EVO LUT ION

Pineco

Forretress

207

FORRETRESS

Pokémon Data

Bagworm Pokémon

TYPE	Bug
	Steel
ABILITIES	Sturdy
	. . .
HEIGHT	3´11˝
WEIGHT	277.3 lbs

National Pokédex No.

205

Description

Forretress hangs from tree branches, protected by a steel armor shell. It can counterattack by scattering shards of its outer shell. What's inside the shell is a mystery.

Special Moves

Explosion, Iron Defense, Gyro Ball

EVO LUT ION

Pineco

→

Forretress

DUNSPARCE

Pokémon Data

Land Snake Pokémon

TYPE	Normal
	. . .
ABILITIES	Serene Grace
	Run Away
HEIGHT	4′11″
WEIGHT	30.9 lbs

National
Pokédex No.
206

Description

Dunsparce digs a long,
maze-like nest with its
tail. If detected, it will
escape by burrowing
backwards. It can fly
just a little.

Special Moves

Glare, Pursuit, Dig, Flail

EVO
LUT
ION

**Does not
Evolve**

Dunsparce

GLIGAR

Pokémon Data

Fly Scorpion Pokémon	
TYPE	Ground
	Flying
ABILITIES	Hyper Cutter
	Sand Veil
HEIGHT	3'07"
WEIGHT	142.9 lbs

Description

Gligar is usually found hanging onto the sides of cliffs; when its prey approaches, it swoops down and attacks. It latches onto the face of its prey and jabs with its poison stinger.

Special Moves

Poison Sting, Fury Cutter, Feint Attack

National Pokédex No.
207

EVO
LUT
ION

Gligar   Gliscor

STEELIX

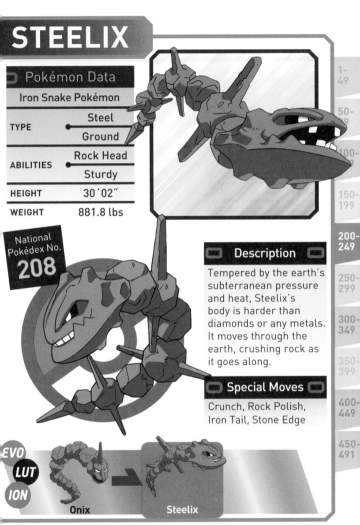

Pokémon Data

Iron Snake Pokémon

TYPE	Steel
	Ground
ABILITIES	Rock Head
	Sturdy
HEIGHT	30′02″
WEIGHT	881.8 lbs

National Pokédex No.
208

1–49
50–99
100–149
150–199
200–249
250–299
300–349
350–399
400–449
450–491

Description

Tempered by the earth's subterranean pressure and heat, Steelix's body is harder than diamonds or any metals. It moves through the earth, crushing rock as it goes along.

Special Moves

Crunch, Rock Polish, Iron Tail, Stone Edge

EVO LUT ION

Onix → Steelix

SNUBBULL

Pokémon Data

Fairy Pokémon

TYPE	Normal
	. . .
ABILITIES	Intimidate
	Run Away
HEIGHT	2´00˝
WEIGHT	17.2 lbs

National Pokédex No.

209

Description

Snubbull's face is so scary that small Pokémon run away in fright, but it is actually a very kind-hearted Pokémon. Very popular with women because it's devoted and loyal.

Special Moves

Tackle, Scary Face, Bite, Roar

EVO LUT ION

Snubbull

Granbull

GRANBULL

Pokémon Data

Fairy Pokémon

TYPE	Normal
	. . .
ABILITIES	Intimidate
	Quick Feet
HEIGHT	4′07″
WEIGHT	107.4 lbs

National Pokédex No.
210

Description

Despite Granbull's fierce appearance, it is actually quite timid. But once it is angered, it will attack with its huge fangs.

Special Moves

Roar, Rage, Take Down, Crunch

EVO LUT ION

Snubbull → Granbull

1-49
50-99
100-149
150-199
200-249
250-299
300-349
350-399
400-449
450-491

QWILFISH

Pokémon Data

Balloon Pokémon

TYPE	Water
	Poison
ABILITIES	Poison Point
	Swift Swim
HEIGHT	1´08˝
WEIGHT	8.6 lbs

National Pokédex No.
211

Description

It can shoot out the poisoned spines on its body in any direction, but in order to do so it must suck in water to puff up its body. But this makes it hard for Qwilfish to swim.

Special Moves

Water Gun, Pin Missile, Poison Jab

EVO LUT ION

Qwilfish

Does not Evolve

SCIZOR

Pokémon Data

Pincer Pokémon

TYPE	Bug
	Steel
ABILITIES	Swarm
	Technician
HEIGHT	5'11"
WEIGHT	260.1 lbs

National Pokédex No.
212

1–
49

50–
99

100–
149

150–
199

**200–
249**

250–
299

300–
349

350–
399

400–
449

450–
491

Description

Scizor intimidates its opponents with its claws; thanks to its eerie eye patterns, they make it look like it has three heads. Its body is as hard as steel.

Special Moves

Swords Dance, Razor Wind, X-Scissor

EVO LUT ION

Scyther → Scizor

SHUCKLE

Pokémon Data

Mold Pokémon	
TYPE	Bug
	Rock
ABILITIES	Sturdy
	Gluttony
HEIGHT	2′00″
WEIGHT	45.2 lbs

National Pokédex No.
213

Description

Shuckle hides under rocks to avoid its enemies. It collects Berries and stores them in its shell, where they ferment into a delicious liquid.

Special Moves

Bide, Safeguard, Wrap, Gastro Acid

EVO LUT ION

Shuckle → Does not Evolve

HERACROSS

1-
50-
99
100-
149
150-
199
200-
249
250-
299
300-
349
350-
399
400-
449
450-
491

Pokémon Data

Single Horn Pokémon

TYPE	Bug
	Fighting
ABILITIES	Swarm
	Guts
HEIGHT	4'11"
WEIGHT	119.0 lbs

National Pokédex No.
214

Description

Heracross lives in forests, where it feeds off tree sap. Its limbs are very powerful. Rooting its claws in the ground, it can throw its opponents far away with a toss of its horn.

Special Moves

Night Slash, Close Combat, Megahorn

EVO
LUT
ION

Heracross

Does not Evolve

217

SNEASEL

Pokémon Data

Sharp Claw Pokémon

TYPE	Dark
	Ice
ABILITIES	Inner Focus
	Keen Eye
HEIGHT	2´11″
WEIGHT	61.7 lbs

Description

Sneasel keeps its claws hidden, extruding them suddenly to slash at an enemy's weak point. It will not stop attacking until its opponent is too weak to move.

National Pokédex No.
215

Special Moves

Fury Swipes, Icy Wind, Taunt, Feint Attack

EVOLUTION

Sneasel → Weavile

TEDDIURSA

Pokémon Data

Little Bear Pokémon

TYPE	Normal
	. . .
ABILITIES	Pickup
	Quick Feet
HEIGHT	2´00˝
WEIGHT	19.4 lbs

Description

Teddiursa is constantly licking its paws, which have been soaked in sweet honey. When it finds some honey, the crescent pattern on its forehead glows.

Special Moves

Fury Swipes, Feint Attack, Charm

National Pokédex No.
216

EVO LUT ION

Teddiursa → Ursaring

1-49
50-99
100-149
150-199
200-249
250-299
300-349
350-399
400-449
450-491

URSARING

Pokémon Data

Hibernator Pokémon

TYPE	Normal
	...
ABILITIES	Guts
	Quick Feet
HEIGHT	5′11″
WEIGHT	277.3 lbs

National Pokédex No.
217

Description

Ursaring can sniff out food buried deep underground. It leaves claw marks on the trees within its territory that bear the most delicious nuts and fruits.

Special Moves

Scary Face, Hammer Arm, Thrash

EVO LUT ION

Teddiursa → Ursaring

SLUGMA

Pokémon Data

Lava Pokémon

TYPE	Fire
	...
ABILITIES	Magma Armor
	Flame Body
HEIGHT	2´04″
WEIGHT	77.2 lbs

National Pokédex No. **218**

1-
49

50-
99

100-
149

150-
199

200-
249

250-
299

300-
349

350-
399

400-
449

450-
491

Description

Slugma's body is made of lava; instead of blood, extremely hot magma runs through its veins. It can't stop moving, or its body will cool off and harden.

Special Moves

Smog, Lava Plume, Ember

EVO LUT ION

Slugma

Magcargo

MAGCARGO

Pokémon Data

Lava Pokémon	
TYPE	Fire
	Rock
ABILITIES	Magma Armor
	Flame Body
HEIGHT	2´07˝
WEIGHT	121.3 lbs

Description

Magcargo's shell is created by magma that has cooled and hardened. High-temperature flames burst out from between cracks in the shell.

National Pokédex No.
219

Special Moves

Rock Slide, Body Slam, Flamethrower

EVO LUT ION

Slugma → Magcargo

SWINUB

Pokémon Data

Pig Pokémon	
TYPE	Ice
	Ground
ABILITIES	Oblivious
	Snow Cloak
HEIGHT	1´04˝
WEIGHT	14.3 lbs

1-
49

50-
99

100-
149

150-
199

200-
249

250-
299

300-
349

350-
399

400-
449

450-
491

National
Pokédex No.
220

Description

Swinub loves the mushrooms that grow under dead grass. It will search for them with its nose to the ground, tracking their scent. It also can find hot springs.

Special Moves

Odor Sleuth, Powder Snow, Mud-Slap, Endure

EVO LUT ION

Swinub

Piloswine

Mamoswine

PILOSWINE

Pokémon Data

Swine Pokémon	
TYPE	Ice
	Ground
ABILITIES	Oblivious
	Snow Cloak
HEIGHT	3'07"
WEIGHT	123.0 lbs

National Pokédex No.
221

Description

Although it can't see well because of the long hair that hangs down over its eyes, Piloswine perceives its surroundings using its sensitive nose. It is also very sensitive to sound.

Special Moves

Powder Snow, Ice Fang, Take Down, Earthquake

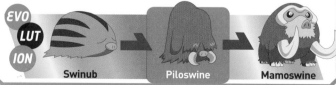

EVO LUT ION

Swinub → Piloswine → Mamoswine

CORSOLA

Pokémon Data

Coral Pokémon

TYPE	Water
	Rock
ABILITIES	Hustle
	Natural Cure
HEIGHT	2´00″
WEIGHT	11.0 lbs

National
Pokédex No.
222

1–
49

50–
99

100–
149

150–
199

200–
249

250–
299

300–
349

350–
399

400–
449

450–
491

Description

Many Corsola live in
the warm, clean waters
of the southern seas.
They cannot survive
in polluted waters.
If one of its spikes is
broken off, it can be
regrown overnight.

Special Moves

Harden, Rock Blast,
Spike Cannon

EVO
LUT
ION

Corsola

**Does not
Evolve**

225

REMORAID

Pokémon Data

Jet Pokémon	
TYPE	Water
	. . .
ABILITIES	Hustle
	Sniper
HEIGHT	2´00″
WEIGHT	26.5 lbs

National Pokédex No. **223**

Description

Remoraid shoots down prey by squirting jets of water from its mouth. Its aim is very accurate. It attaches itself to Mantine, feeding off of the larger Pokémon's scraps.

Special Moves

Water Gun, Lock-On, Aurora Beam

EVO LUT ION

Remoraid → Octillery

226

OCTILLERY

1–
49

50–
99

100–
149

150–
199

200–
249

250–
299

300–
349

350–
399

400–
449

450–
491

Pokémon Data

Jet Pokémon	
TYPE	Water
	...
ABILITIES	Suction Cups
	Sniper
HEIGHT	2′11″
WEIGHT	62.8 lbs

National Pokédex No.
224

Description

Octillery constructs its nest by digging under rocks and in holes on the sea floor. It confuses its foes by emitting a cloud of murky ink, and catches its prey by snaring it with its arms.

Special Moves

Octazooka, Wring Out, Ice Beam

EVO
LUT
ION

Remoraid   Octillery

DELIBIRD

Pokémon Data

Delivery Pokémon

TYPE	Ice
	Flying
ABILITIES	Vital Spirit
	Hustle
HEIGHT	2′11″
WEIGHT	35.3 lbs

National Pokédex No.

225

Description

Delibird builds its nest on sharp cliffs. It wraps food in its tail, then brings the food to its chicks waiting at the nest. It also shares its food with anyone who's lost in the mountains.

Special Moves

Present

EVOLUTION

Delibird — Does not Evolve

MANTINE

Pokémon Data

Kite Pokémon

TYPE	Water
	Flying
ABILITIES	Swift Swim
	Water Absorb
HEIGHT	6'11"
WEIGHT	485.0 lbs

National Pokédex No.
226

Description

Even with Remoraid stuck to it, Mantine easily and swiftly roams the oceans. By building up enough speed, it can jump up out of the waves.

Special Moves

Bounce, Water Pulse, Hydro Pump

EVO LUT ION

Mantyke

Mantine

1-49
50-99
100-149
150-199
200-249
250-299
300-349
350-399
400-449
450-491

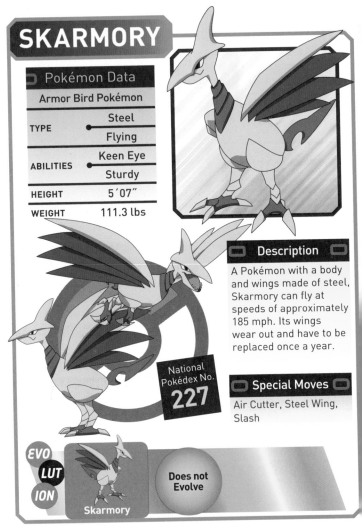

SKARMORY

Pokémon Data

Armor Bird Pokémon

TYPE	Steel
	Flying
ABILITIES	Keen Eye
	Sturdy
HEIGHT	5′07″
WEIGHT	111.3 lbs

Description

A Pokémon with a body and wings made of steel, Skarmory can fly at speeds of approximately 185 mph. Its wings wear out and have to be replaced once a year.

National Pokédex No.
227

Special Moves

Air Cutter, Steel Wing, Slash

EVO LUT ION

Skarmory

Does not Evolve

230

HOUNDOUR

Pokémon Data

Dark Pokémon

TYPE	Dark
	Fire
ABILITIES	Early Bird
	Flash Fire
HEIGHT	2′00″
WEIGHT	23.8 lbs

National Pokédex No.
228

Description

Houndour communicate with their pack mates using a wide variety of calls, the meaning of which only they can understand. They take down prey by using a tag-team approach.

Special Moves

Howl, Bite, Fire Fang

1–49
50–99
100–149
150–199
200–249
250–299
300–349
350–399
400–449
450–491

EVO LUT ION

Houndour

Houndoom

231

HOUNDOOM

Pokémon Data

Dark Pokémon

TYPE	Dark
	Fire
ABILITIES	Early Bird
	Flash Fire
HEIGHT	4'07"
WEIGHT	77.2 lbs

National Pokédex No.

229

Description

After hearing one of Houndoom's eerie howls, most Pokémon get scared and run away. A burn caused by the flames breathed out by Houndoom will almost never heal.

Special Moves

Fire Fang, Crunch, Flamethrower

EVO
LUT
ION

Houndour → Houndoom

KINGDRA

1-
49

50-

100-
149

150-
199

200-
249

250-
299

300-
349

350-
399

400-
449

450-
491

Pokémon Data

Dragon Pokémon

TYPE	Water
	Dragon
ABILITIES	Swift Swim
	Sniper
HEIGHT	5′11″
WEIGHT	335.1 lbs

National
Pokédex No.

230

Description

Kingdra lives in caves at the bottom of the ocean. Whenever a typhoon comes up it awakens and goes in search of food. When it moves it creates a gigantic whirlpool.

Special Moves

Agility, Dragon Pulse, Brine

EVO
LUT
ION

Horsea

Seadra

Kingdra

PHANPY

Pokémon Data

Long Nose Pokémon

TYPE	Ground
	. . .
ABILITIES	Pickup
	. . .
HEIGHT	1´08˝
WEIGHT	73.9 lbs

National Pokédex No.
231

Description

Phanpy live in holes dug next to riverbanks. They splash each other with water using their long snouts. Although Phanpy is small it can carry a full-grown human.

Special Moves

Defense Curl, Tackle, Slam

EVO LUT ION

Phanpy → Donphan

DONPHAN

Pokémon Data

Armor Pokémon

TYPE	Ground
	...
ABILITIES	Sturdy
	...
HEIGHT	3´07"
WEIGHT	264.6 lbs

National Pokédex No.

232

Description

Donphan attacks by rolling up its body and charging straight into its enemy. It puts its strength to good use by helping to remove rockslides that have blocked mountain roads.

Special Moves

Fury Attack, Earthquake, Horn Attack, Rollout

EVO LUT ION

Phanpy → Donphan

1-49
50-99
100-149
150-199
200-249
250-299
300-349
350-399
400-449
450-491

235

PORYGON2

Pokémon Data

Virtual Pokémon

TYPE	Normal
	. . .
ABILITIES	Trace
	Download
HEIGHT	2'00"
WEIGHT	71.6 lbs

National Pokédex No.
233

Description

An improvement on the original Porygon, Porygon2 was created for experimental space travel use. Occasionally it acts outside of its programming.

Special Moves

Signal Beam, Recycle, Conversion 2

EVO LUT ION

Porygon → Porygon2 → Porygon-Z

STANTLER

1-
49

50-
99

100-
149

150-
199

200-
249

250-
299

300-
349

350-
399

400-
449

450-
491

Pokémon Data

Big Horn Pokémon

TYPE	Normal
	...
ABILITIES	Intimidate
	Frisk
HEIGHT	4'07"
WEIGHT	157.0 lbs

National
Pokédex No.
234

Description

Staring at its antlers causes the senses to go haywire. This is because the antlers' curvature subtly changes the airflow around them, creating what seems to be a warping of space.

Special Moves

Stomp, Take Down, Zen Headbutt

EVO LUT ION

Stantler

Does not
Evolve

237

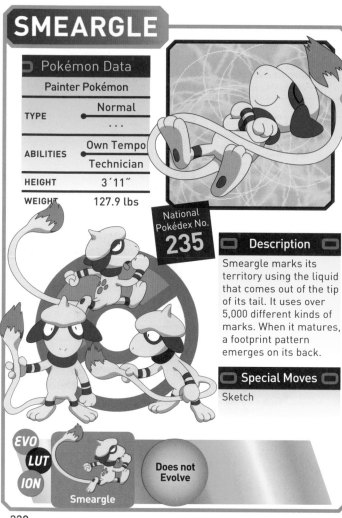

SMEARGLE

Pokémon Data

Painter Pokémon

TYPE	Normal
	. . .
ABILITIES	Own Tempo
	Technician
HEIGHT	3′11″
WEIGHT	127.9 lbs

National Pokédex No.
235

Description

Smeargle marks its territory using the liquid that comes out of the tip of its tail. It uses over 5,000 different kinds of marks. When it matures, a footprint pattern emerges on its back.

Special Moves

Sketch

EVO LUT ION

Smeargle

Does not Evolve

238

TYROGUE

1-49
50-99
100-149
150-199
200-249
250-299
300-349
350-399
400-449
450-491

Pokémon Data

Scuffle Pokémon

TYPE	Fighting
	. . .
ABILITIES	Guts
	Steadfast
HEIGHT	2′04″
WEIGHT	46.3 lbs

National Pokédex No.

236

Description

Known for being quick to start a fight, Tyrogue likes to fight against opponents larger than itself, and so is constantly covered with cuts and bruises.

Special Moves

Tackle, Helping Hand, Fake Out

EVO LUT ION

Tyrogue

Hitmonchan   Hitmontop   Hitmonlee

239

HITMONTOP

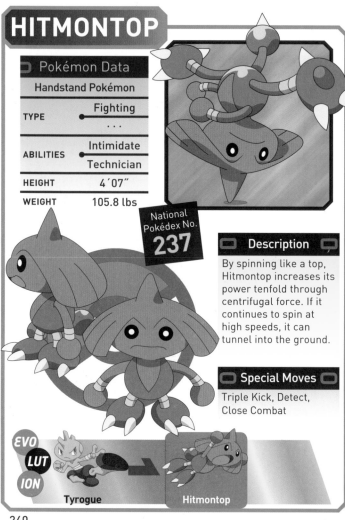

Pokémon Data

Handstand Pokémon

TYPE	Fighting
	...
ABILITIES	Intimidate
	Technician
HEIGHT	4'07"
WEIGHT	105.8 lbs

National Pokédex No.

237

Description

By spinning like a top, Hitmontop increases its power tenfold through centrifugal force. If it continues to spin at high speeds, it can tunnel into the ground.

Special Moves

Triple Kick, Detect, Close Combat

EVO LUT ION

Tyrogue → Hitmontop

SMOOCHUM

Pokémon Data

Kiss Pokémon

TYPE	Ice
	Psychic
ABILITIES	Oblivious
	Forewarn
HEIGHT	1′04″
WEIGHT	13.2 lbs

National Pokédex No.
238

1- 49
50- 99
100- 149
150- 199
200- 249
250- 299
300- 349
350- 399
400- 449
450- 491

Description

Smoochum determines the nature of things by first touching them with its very sensitive lips. It constantly bobs its head back and forth in a kissing motion.

Special Moves

Sweet Kiss, Powder Snow, Confusion

EVO LUT ION

Smoochum → Jynx

ELEKID

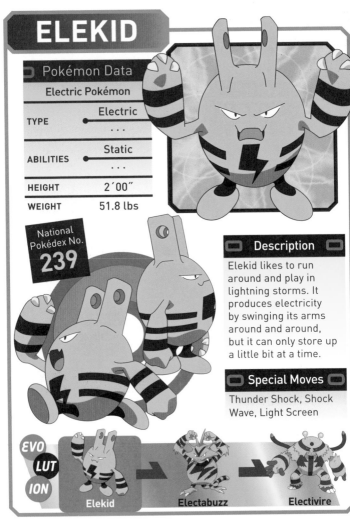

Pokémon Data

Electric Pokémon

TYPE	Electric
	. . .
ABILITIES	Static
	. . .
HEIGHT	2′00″
WEIGHT	51.8 lbs

National Pokédex No.
239

Description

Elekid likes to run around and play in lightning storms. It produces electricity by swinging its arms around and around, but it can only store up a little bit at a time.

Special Moves

Thunder Shock, Shock Wave, Light Screen

EVOLUTION

Elekid → Electabuzz → Electivire

MAGBY

Pokémon Data

Live Coal Pokémon

TYPE	Fire
	. . .
ABILITIES	Flame Body
	. . .
HEIGHT	2′04″
WEIGHT	47.2 lbs

1-
49

50-
99

100-
149

150-
199

200-
249

250-
299

300-
349

350-
399

400-
449

450-
491

National
Pokédex No.
240

Description

As Magby breathes, fire embers spill from its mouth and nose. When it's happy and energetic, it emits yellow flames. Its internal temperature is over 1,200°F.

Special Moves

Ember, Smokescreen, Smog

EVO LUT ION

Magby

Magmar

Magmortar

MILTANK

Pokémon Data

Milk Cow Pokémon

TYPE	Normal . . .
ABILITIES	Thick Fat Scrappy
HEIGHT	3′11″
WEIGHT	166.4 lbs

National Pokédex No.
241

Description

Miltank's nutrient-rich milk makes children strong and helps sick patients to get better.

Special Moves

Body Slam, Heal Bell, Rollout, Milk Drink

EVO LUT ION

Miltank

Does not Evolve

BLISSEY

Pokémon Data

Happiness Pokémon

TYPE	Normal
	. . .
ABILITIES	Natural Cure
	Serene Grace
HEIGHT	4´11″
WEIGHT	103.2 lbs

National Pokédex No.
242

Description

Blissey is a Pokémon that brings happiness. It nurses weakened Pokémon until they are better. It has a very gentle personality.

Special Moves

Sing, Egg Bomb, Healing Wish

EVOLUTION

Happiny ▶ Chansey ▶ Blissey

1-49
50-
?0-149
150-199
200-249
250-299
300-349
350-399
400-449
450-491

RAIKOU

Pokémon Data

Thunder Pokémon

TYPE	Electric
	. . .
ABILITIES	Pressure
	. . .
HEIGHT	6´03˝
WEIGHT	392.4 lbs

National Pokédex No.
243

Description

Raikou is said to have come down to earth with the thunder. It can shoot out thunderbolts from the rain clouds on its back.

Special Moves

Crunch, Thunder Fang, Thunder, Discharge

EVO LUT ION

Raikou

Does not Evolve

ENTEI

Pokémon Data

Volcano Pokémon

TYPE	Fire
	. . .
ABILITIES	Pressure
	. . .
HEIGHT	6′11″
WEIGHT	436.5 lbs

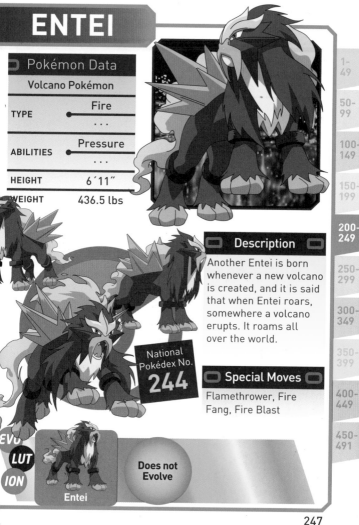

Description

Another Entei is born whenever a new volcano is created, and it is said that when Entei roars, somewhere a volcano erupts. It roams all over the world.

National Pokédex No.

244

Special Moves

Flamethrower, Fire Fang, Fire Blast

EVO LUT ION

Entei

Does not Evolve

1-49
50-99
100-149
150-199
200-249
250-299
300-349
350-399
400-449
450-491

SUICUNE

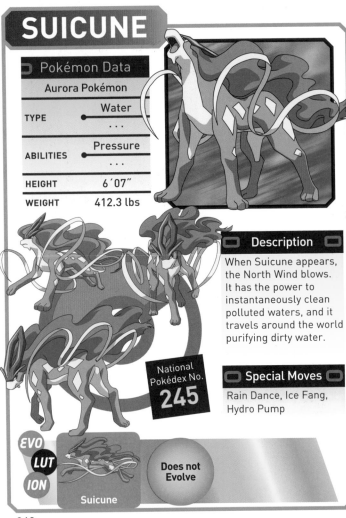

Pokémon Data

Aurora Pokémon

TYPE	Water
	. . .
ABILITIES	Pressure
	. . .
HEIGHT	6'07"
WEIGHT	412.3 lbs

Description

When Suicune appears, the North Wind blows. It has the power to instantaneously clean polluted waters, and it travels around the world purifying dirty water.

National Pokédex No.
245

Special Moves

Rain Dance, Ice Fang, Hydro Pump

EVO
LUT
ION

Suicune — Does not Evolve

Michelle

Carolyn E. Phillips

A Division of GL Publications
Ventura, CA U.S.A.

The foreign language publishing of all Regal books is under the direction of GLINT. GLINT provides financial and technical help for the adaptation, translation and publishing of books for millions of people worldwide. For more information write: GLINT, P.O. Box 6688, Ventura, California 93006.

Mass Edition, 1982
Third Printing, 1982

Published by Regal Books
A Division of GL Publications
Ventura, California 93006
Printed in U.S.A.

Library of Congress Catalog Card No. 80-52202
ISBN 0-8307-0810-3

Contents

Dedication

This book is
lovingly dedicated
to the memory of

Sheli Lois Hansen
October 13, 1974 to
September 26,1979
Her contagious enjoyment
of all God's creations and
unwavering acceptance of life
as it unfolded
make her short five years
an unquenchable inspiration
to those of us who love her
so very, very much.
Time will never
take her from us.

Preface

When I told Wayne Newton I was writing a book about Michelle Price he raised his eyebrows and said slowly, "You've undertaken a monumental task." Nearly a year later the book is complete and I've learned that *monumental* was an understatement. Trying to capture Michelle's spark and enthusiasm has been an incredible challenge, the sweetest challenge of my writing career thus far.

At twelve years old, Michelle can be found walking gracefully down a flight of stairs or zipping down the banister. She can talk your arm off or sit quietly, an attentive listener. But she is always ready to love you.

Love overflows the Price household and those who know them know their love. Dick and Laura have an ability to gently draw others out, without revealing their own hardships. Many people they meet have no idea of the magnitude of trials this family has shared. Dick and Laura are busy loving others, supporting someone who may be hurting.

The story you are about to read is one of love in growth. Friends and professionals, communities and clergy were sacrificially supportive to the Prices in their times of need. Much has been left unsaid because no book could contain it all. Some of the characters you'll meet are combinations of several people, patched together to give the story a readable flow. But this is the true story of Michelle—the portrait of a victor.

Author's Acknowledgments

Thanks to the many people whose cooperation and support have made this book possible.

First and foremost my heartfelt thanks to Michelle and her delightful family—now, treasured friends. You opened your hearts and hurts to me, pushing back into painful memories to share your story. Your active, day-by-day faith walk has been an example to me over and over again.

To my husband, Chip, and our children, Rob and Cara, for your countless silent trips past my closed door. I couldn't have done it without you.

To my parents for the setting—a writer's dream—for more than your fair share of moral support, and for all the free food.

To Robert VanKampen for your personal endorsement of the manuscript.

To Terri Hansen for tons of typing.

To Linda Kurz for introducing me to the Prices and for the finest friendship on wheels.

To the many people who were so generous with their time and observations about Michelle and her family, especially Dr. Robert Rosen of the City of Hope and Mr. Wayne Newton.

Special thanks to my dear friend Cheri Hansen whose sensitive reading and rereading of the manuscript inspired compassion and empathy in this writer's heart. For the pain it caused you, Cheri, my continued respect and gratitude.

And to our miraculous Lord for the marvelous way He weaves the tapestries of our lives together for His perfect purpose.

The Family's Acknowledgments

We want to publicly thank our older daughter, Kim, for the supportive part she played in helping care for Rick and Michelle. She selflessly carried more than her share of the load, hurting deeply with us, encouraging us when we needed it and giving of herself with no concern for the cost. Thank you, Kim, for being you. We're crazy about you!

We both want to thank our parents for the consistent Christian example their lives have always been to us. We are very proud to be a part of a fine Christian heritage. Our gratitude encompasses *every member* of the family. You've *each* added so much to our lives.

To modern "medicine men and women" who trust their knowledge *and* their hearts. Dr. Glick, we'll never be able to thank you enough for suspecting more than medicine could prove and following your feelings that November morning.

To Riverside Thrift and Loan a special thanks for reasons only you will fully understand.

To NHSRA, Winter Park and Hal O'Leary our warmest thanks and deepest gratitude for opening a new world to Michelle.

To the City of Hope, the Sportsmen's Club and Bill Hughes for caring so deeply, for giving from the heart.

To Wayne for giving of yourself, for being a friend, for loving our daughter.

To Dellene for helping make a dream come true.

There are many other people who have become a part of our lives and have given so much to us—*prayer,* love and support. It would be virtually impossible to name names here. Experiencing the outpouring of love so sincerely and warmly expressed has sustained us in difficult times and demonstrated our Lord's command to love one another. The only way we'll ever be able to thank you for *your* love is to reach out to others as you have to us.

We must express our appreciation to Carolyn Phillips for the many hours of effort, joy and tears that you have expended in reliving our story with us. In writing this book you have cried when we cried, laughed when we laughed and caught the spirit of our lives on paper. Even more important to us are the prayers you offered in our behalf—before we'd met, before there was "a book."

1
Needing a Miracle

"Death has to be waiting at the end of the ride before you truly see the earth, and feel your heart, and love the world."
—Jean Anouilh, *The Lark*

Dr. Abrams's stylish wooden heels clicked on the brown tile floor as she walked briskly into the crowded waiting room. "I've seen the biopsy reports on Michelle," she said, singling out a man and woman sitting stiffly upright on a chrome-legged couch.

Dick Price pulled himself up to his full six-foot two-inch height and looked down at the small-framed woman in charge of his daughter's case here at Children's Hospital.

Dr. Abrams slipped her hands into the starched white pockets of her lab coat and said, "She's got bone cancer. We'll have to take the leg right away."

Dick gulped in air, struggling to get a deep breath. He felt as if he'd been hit in the stomach as he sank back onto the couch. His dazed mind was buzzing, trying to comprehend what he'd just heard, "Michelle has cancer."

Laura sat motionless beside her husband Dick, stunned and silent. Her heart pounded in her ears and time ground to a halt around her. She felt like an observer, watching a play unfolding one scene at a time.

She shut her eyes against the words Doctor Abrams spoke, then forced them open again, afraid of the darkness that enveloped her. "You can't mean that," she said shaking her head, denying the cancer. "You can't take her leg. She's only eight years old!" Her voice sounded strange to her, as if it came from someone else. Tears blurred her vision as she searched the doctor's face for a glimmer of hope she knew was not there.

In the chair beside her, Michelle's 17-year-old sister, Kim, buried her head in both hands and cried deep, soul-wracking sobs. Laura reached out touching Kim's arm. She felt sick and empty, helpless to comfort her daughter.

"What she's got," the doctor continued in a clinical tone of voice, "is *osteogenic sarcoma*, a very fast, very deadly kind of bone cancer. You have to understand, her chances of beating this are extremely slim, less than four percent."

"You mean, only four in a hundred live with—?"

She interrupted Dick, "*Less* than four in a hundred, actually. I want you to be realistic about this from the beginning. The type of cancer your daughter has is extremely difficult to deal with."

People sitting around the waiting room grew uneasy. Some idly turned pages in tattered magazines. Others nervously glanced toward Dick and Laura, then quickly looked away again, embarrassed—like children peeking at forbidden things, afraid of being caught in the act.

"I'm going up to talk to Michelle," the doctor reported, moving quickly into the hallway. "I'll let you know about the surgery time—"

"Wait a minute," Dick said, springing to his feet and following her from the room, "we're not sure that's what we're going to do yet."

"There's no time to waste!" she replied, agitated. *He's too concerned, too cautious and only a layman. There isn't time for that now,* she thought to herself.

"There's no room for a mistake in something like this either." Dick answered looking directly into her eyes. He could feel her resistance but he was standing his ground. "We want another opinion."

"That's up to you," she said curtly, her expression cold. "Let me know."

Turning smartly on her heel she walked away without looking back.

They stood staring blankly after her, lost in their thoughts, unaware of clacking typewriters and the nasal buzzing of the busy hospital switchboard just beyond them in the lobby. Submerged in helplessness and fear, they watched as Dr. Abrams disappeared around the corner.

Dick suddenly felt much older than his 40 some years. The pain and tension of the past few days were taking their toll much too fast; he looked older, worn and tired.

Laura, her face suddenly pale, reached for Dick's hand. A week ago their lives had been so normal. Kim was involved in senior pep squad finals; Rick, the oldest, was working hard at his new job at the gas station. And Michelle was adjusting well to the routine of a third grader.

When Michelle complained about her right leg hurting, Laura thought it seemed a little swollen and warm to the touch. But she was sure it was nothing serious. She called the family doctor expecting the problem to be shin splints or a need for corrective shoes at most. But something in the doctor's "I don't like it," made her blood run cold. Even at that she never dreamed it might be this bad—*never*—cancer!

Dr. Abrams is a good doctor, a specialist, Laura thought as she struggled to stay composed. *Our doctor recommended her so highly.* She quickly reviewed the past few days. *Everything's happened so fast! A biopsy two days ago and now—now she says Michelle's going to lose her leg? A bad dream, that's what it is, a nightmare!* Fear and frustration mounted. She walked a few steps away from Dick. What she wanted to do was run as far and as fast as she could. Yet she knew she had to stay.

Kim leaned against the thick plaster wall outside the waiting room. "How can she be so hard?" she asked angrily. Her voice cracked as tears pressed against her throat. "How could *anybody* do what she just did?" Like a sudden summer shower, tears ran down her face.

Laura walked quickly to Kim's side and put both arms around the trembling girl. "I guess she's just doing her job, honey," she said not really convinced herself.

"Then why do I feel like she hit me?" Kim cried. "That woman's like a tank!"

"I don't like her methods either," Dick spoke hotly, "but we can't change her. What we can do is find someone else to work with."

"Do you think she might be right?" Laura asked. She reached for Dick's arm, suddenly very weak.

"I don't know what to think," he pondered running his fingers through his slightly graying hair. "I'm sure she's a good doctor. Everyone we've talked to seems to think so highly of her. And we *know* it's a good hospital." Thoughtfully he reviewed the facts and weighed his anxieties—he didn't feel confident in Dr. Abrams. "I still think we need to talk to somebody else," he said, the decision made.

"I wouldn't want her operating on me," Kim added, her eyes flashing anger. Usually good-natured, Kim was fiercely protective of her family, especially Michelle.

The three of them walked toward the elevator. As Laura reached out to press the button, Dick caught her hand and pulled her into his arms, then reached around Kim and drew her close to them both. They stood holding tightly to each other, tears washing over the pain that pierced them so deeply.

"Oh, Dick," Laura cried as she clung to him, "I'd give anything if it could be me instead!"

"I know," he comforted, straining for control as tears flowed down his face. "We'd all trade if we could."

"Why Shelly, Daddy?" Kim asked. "Why?"

"Oh, God!" Dick sobbed holding his family close to him, "We need you now like we've never needed you before. Please, make us strong—"

He whispered hoarsely, "Somehow God's going to get us through this."

They struggled for composure as they walked back to the elevator, then waited while a group stepped off. Three women talking in low voices walked toward the door. Behind them followed a teenage girl. Her eyes were red-rimmed and she tightly clutched a stuffed turtle. An older couple, arm in arm, completed the group.

Laura found herself wondering whether these people were there to see children as ill as Michelle. Her heart pounded so loudly in her chest she was afraid they could hear it. Did they know what it was to face the threat of losing a child? Did they share the same burden, know the same fluttering of fear in their stomachs? Did their heads throb like hers?

"I don't think I'll go with you right now," Kim said breaking into Laura's train of thought. "I'm not ready to see Shelly yet." Her eyes swam with tears. "I think I'll take a walk." The love ties between Kim and the little sister she'd helped to raise ran deep.

"Are you alright, Kim?" Laura asked, gently touching her arm.

"Yeah," Kim responded nodding weakly, "I'm OK. I just need some time to think, that's all. I want to be by myself for awhile."

She quickly kissed her mom and dad. *How they must hurt,* she thought looking into their tear-stained faces. She turned slowly and walked through the big double doors feeling sick at her stomach with grief.

Inside the elevator Dick pushed "2" and the big metal doors bumped slightly as they slid shut.

"Are you OK?" he asked slipping an arm around his wife. He usually felt warm and content holding Laura. Right now all he felt was fear and helplessness. He couldn't ease Laura's pain. He looked down at her, brushing a tear from her cheek. He pulled her closer.

"I'm OK," she said sighing deeply. She wrapped her arm around his waist and laid her head on his shoulder. With her free hand she gently patted his tummy, a family tradition. Michelle's round, smiling face flashed through her mind and another tear slid down her cheek.

God, please, Dick prayed silently as the elevator slowed to a stop at their floor, *make us strong.* He drew in a deep breath, bracing himself. The doors parted with a weary groan and they stepped into the hall just a few feet away from Michelle's room.

A familiar laugh greeted them and they turned to see Michelle rolling toward them in a wheelchair. Her feet stuck straight out in front of her in bright yellow fuzzy slippers. She was flapping like a grounded bird, pushing the chair as fast as she could. Her dark eyes were wide and full of fun; sandy curls bounced around her pink cheeks and wide, infectious grin. She leaned into a quick turn at the end of the hall, her yellow robe adding a touch of spring to a colorless day.

Close behind came Kathy Graham, a widely grinning child in pigtails. Kathy was wheelchair competition for this race and also a patient on this floor. Her blue gingham nightgown dusted the large steel wheels of her chair, revealing long white casts on both legs as she rolled past Dick and Laura, hot on Michelle's tail.

"I'm gonna beat you!" Shelly called over her shoulder.

"You had a head start," Kathy protested giggling, pushing as fast as she could.

Dick and Laura, hand in hand, smiled in spite of heavy hearts.

"Alright you two!" Joy Sutera, the green-eyed Italian nurse, called out as she headed for the girls, her face stern and reproving. But it wasn't hard for Dick and Laura to spot the fun in her large warm eyes. As she passed them she flashed a quick grin, never missing a beat in her pursuit of the racers.

"This race track is closed for the day," she called continuing after the girls. "You nearly flattened your parents at the elevator."

"Aw, Joy," the girls chorused. "Just one more race?—from here to the nurse's station?"

"No!" She was smiling, but the girls knew it was time to quit. "You settle down now. It's almost time for your lunch."

She picked her way between the wheelchairs and started back down the hall. Michelle swung around like an old pro and rolled closely after Joy.

"Can I help with the lunch trays when they come? Can I?" she asked looking up at the pretty dark-haired nurse.

"I don't think so," Joy stalled. "You're supposed to be a guest here." She playfully grabbed Michelle by the chin and looked her square in the eyes, their foreheads touching. "If they find out you're the one who does all the work they might decide they don't need me and I'll be out of a job."

"Hey, Price," Dick said latching onto the wheelchair. "Joy has work to do. Let's go see what we can find in the playroom." He whirled her chair around and they headed down the hall, giving Joy a quick "hope she hasn't worn you out" glance. Joy smiled back at them as she continued toward the nurse's station.

"How come you call me 'Price,' Daddy?" Michelle asked, temporarily resigning herself to adult supremacy. Grabbing the arms of the chair she lifted herself up off the seat as they rolled toward the playroom door.

"Oh, I don't know," he teased, letting the chair free-roll a few feet and tucking Laura's hand under his arm, "it just fits you sometimes."

"I like it," she said dropping herself back onto the seat with a thud.

"What'll we play today?" she asked absently looking over the assortment of toys and games scattered just inside the door. A clutter of colorful boxes, books and toys lay before them.

To Laura and Dick Michelle looked delicate, almost fragile in her soft green nightie and yellow robe. Shelly seriously studied the array of treasures stretching across the room, measuring their worth. The hope of victory in a rousing game of "Candyland" or checkers was written in her eyes.

Dick and Laura's choice would be not to play games, especially now, but Michelle needed a diversion, something to fill some time. She could not guess how ill she was. She didn't know how their hearts ached.

Time, Dick thought watching Michelle carefully unfold a checkerboard. *How much time do we have left with Shelly?* He opened his big hand and scooped up several checker pieces scattered on the play table.

"I'll be red," he said.

Back in the nurse's station, Joy commented to another nurse, "Michelle's a cute kid."

The other nurse looked up briefly from a patient's chart she was writing in and smiled at Joy. "She can sure be a pest though," she replied. "Sometimes I'd like to ignore her, but she won't be ignored."

Joy reached across the counter and picked up a clipboard. She started recording blood pressures and temperatures from a slip of paper she'd taken on her rounds earlier. "She just decides you're her friend, so you *have to* want her around."

"Yeah," the young woman responded closing the metal chart and replacing it in the rack beside her. "Michelle never wonders whether she's welcome."

"Most of the time she's right," Joy added as she finished her list. "I like having her around."

She reached into a white wire basket for the small stack of lab reports just delivered. Leafing through them she stopped at a pink slip from pathology. Michelle's name was on top.

In large, handwritten letters was the word "POSITIVE." Her eyes widened as she took in the next two words, *"Osteogenic sarcoma."*

Numb, she dropped the reports back into the basket and clutched at the chair beside her, lowering herself to the seat. *Cancer!* she thought. *She's really got cancer.* She blinked several times trying to clear her thoughts. *I knew it! Every time I care about a patient it's some awful disease.* She tightened her jaw and clenched her fist, digging her fingernails into the palm of her hand.

She could not believe the flood of emotion crowding in on her. Anger, so much anger. "Why, God?" she called out. The sound of the anger in her voice made her conscious of the others in the nurse's station around her. Her cheeks flushed with rage and embarrassment. *Why Michelle?* she thought. Questions shot through her mind. *How can you let this happen to me over and over again?*

She quickly got up and started into the utility kitchen. Tears stung her throat and she wanted out of the mainstream of activity. She had to be alone.

This is stupid! she scolded herself, shoving a stack of supplies to the back of a counter and knocking them over. *I'm a nurse. Sickness and death aren't supposed to bother me like this. It's part of my job.*

She walked nervously to the door then back again. She thought about the surgeries, the chemotherapy. . . . *They're so sick with chemotherapy, so deathly sick*—She thought about the pain, the risks that lay ahead of this small, smiling child, the little girl she thought was so special.

Shaking her head as if to deny the truth she'd learned, she cried out loud, "I can't watch her go through it!" She clenched her teeth, "I just can't!"

She wiped her nose and her tear-filled eyes as she thought about Michelle, only there four days. But there were few other kids she'd taken a liking to quite so fast. Michelle's warmth and maturity would be a credit to someone many times her age. Her sense of humor kept her own troubles in perspective and helped the other children—and adults—to take themselves a little less seriously. She was exceptional, with the spirit of a champion.

It isn't fair Michelle has to go through this! Joy thought as she slammed her fist on the counter. *With so many self-centered freeloaders in this world, why Michelle?*

She paced the small kitchen like a caged animal. Then carefully, with deepening resolve, she forced her emotions into a protective sheath of indifference. *I'm not going to get wrapped up in her, that's all. I won't let it bother me this time.* She stopped pacing and shoved both hands into her uniform pockets, *I just can't take it.*

She stared up at the big black and white face of the clock on the wall. It was nearly three o'clock, time to go home. Grabbing the pins that secured her cap she angrily pulled it off her head and jammed it into the plastic bag in her locker. Snapping her sweater off the hook and flinging it over her shoulders she walked briskly down the corridor, past the nurse's station.

"I've gotta go," she muttered without slowing down, "something's come up." She pushed open the stairwell door and walked out.

During the 7:00 A.M. briefing the next morning Joy was relieved to learn that it had been arranged for Michelle to transfer to the City of Hope in Duarte, another California hospital specializing in catastrophic diseases. *Good,* she thought, her new resolve still intact. *At least I won't have to watch her go through it. I'm glad the surgery won't be done here.*

A little later, Joy stood before a wall of shelves preparing for her morning routine when a student nurse interrupted her thoughts.

"Joy, I was just in Michelle Price's room and they're packing her things."

Pulling a small stack of bed sheets from one of the shelves Joy said, without turning around, "She's being transferred to the City of Hope today."

"I know," the young woman in the blue uniform continued. "But she's really upset over the move."

Joy wrapped both arms around the stack of linen she held and turned to face the young nurse. Dispassionately she asked, "What's wrong?"

"It's you."

"Me? I haven't even been in there this morning. How could I have upset her?" she said defensively.

"You won't be at the City of Hope when she gets there," the girl went on. "She doesn't want to leave you, Joy."

Joy fixed her eyes on the student nurse feeling like she'd been struck. Waves of compassion, a need to "be there" swept through her. All her defenses weren't enough to keep one small child out of her heart. She handed the stack of linen to the student nurse and walked down the hall toward Michelle's room.

"I hear somebody's been getting tears on my clean sheets in here," she said putting a hand on Michelle's shoulder.

Michelle was lying face down across the bed, but hearing Joy, she turned and threw herself into the nurse's arms. "I don't want to go," she sobbed onto Joy's crisp uniform. "If you won't be there I don't want to go."

Joy held tightly to the little girl heaving great sobs in her arms, and weighed her feelings. She knew there was pain ahead of her if she let herself love this child. She lightly stroked Michelle's back, and tears filled her eyes as she made her decision. "I'll be there, honey," she said. She was opening herself to more hurt than she cared to have, but she knew now it was a risk she wanted to take. "I won't be your nurse but I'll always be your friend. You couldn't keep me away."

"Will you come and see me?" Michelle asked, squatting on her knees on the bed. Never taking her eyes off Joy she rubbed the tears away with the back of one small hand.

"My day off is Sunday," Joy said. "Could I come see you then?"

"Oh, Joy," Michelle grinned, hugging her around the waist, "I can't wait till Sunday."

2
No Hiding Place

Laura sat dozing in a chair, every now and then pulling her head upright as she nodded forward. There'd been so little time for things like sleep in the past week. You simply took it where you could.

With a jerk she startled herself, then sighed wearily as the feelings of fright subsided. The sleep hadn't refreshed her. Groggy and disoriented, she stared through weary eyes at the small bouquet of dainty yellow roses Jim and Linda brought for Michelle yesterday. The miniature buds were easing open in their fluted milk-glass bowl. She could smell their perfume across the room.

Slowly she came out of the fog. She remembered now—Michelle's room, City of Hope. *It must be Thursday . . . or is it Friday?* It slowly swirled back.

It is Friday, she thought. *Yesterday was Thanksgiving Day. It was so strange celebrating a family holiday like Thanksgiving in the hospital.*

She thought about the dinner they'd shared in the play yard. The staff worked so hard to make it nice. Special trims on the trays, little cardboard turkeys and cherub-like Pilgrims smiling up beside the cranberry sauce.

Thanksgiving, she mused. *Sometimes it's hard to be thankful.*

"In everything give thanks. . . ." She'd quoted that verse so glibly before. Now she wondered. "*Everything,* Lord?" she whispered looking at Shelly asleep in the hospital bed. "How can I thank you for this?"

She rested her head against the back of the chair and thought about yesterday. The whole family, even Laura's mother from the east, sitting around the yellow metal picnic table. Kim, her long brown hair shining in the sun, kept Michelle entertained with sisterly teasing and silly jokes.

Michelle looked so pretty in her fancy new blue dress with the ruffled neck and sleeves. She was in good spirits, sneaking the treats from everyone's tray when they weren't looking.

And Rick, broad shouldered and tan—the picture of health in his blue plaid sport shirt—carrying Michelle from place to place, patiently pushing her on the big tire swing.

And then there was Dick, gentle Dick, so open about his feelings, so deeply reflective, so unafraid of vulnerability.

"We might be closer to the real meaning of thankfulness now than we've ever been," Dick had said, thinking out loud.

"What do you mean, Dad?" Rick asked, stopping beside Dick to let Michelle debark from a piggyback ride.

Dick picked up his fork and pushed a couple of green beans around the plate into his mashed potatoes. "Well," he answered thoughtfully, "my Christianity really didn't have much meaning before that awful accident of yours."

"What'd my accident have to do with your faith?" Rick asked, sitting down on the bench with his back against the table.

Dick heaved a sigh packed with deep emotion. He propped his fork on the edge of his plate and looked beyond the fence across the grounds. "Seeing you all cut up and bleeding after the truck hit you on the freeway—" His face flushed and his throat felt tight as all the feelings of that night rushed through him again.

"Oh, Rick," he went on, "you were so bad, the doctors and nurses running around trying to help, trying to save your life. There was nothing they could do."

"But I made it," Rick added.

"Yeah," Dick said raising his eyebrows, "only because God gave you back to us. I couldn't do anything to help you, no one could." He leaned forward, his elbows on the table, his voice quieter, intimate as though sharing a secret.

"Rick," he said looking steadily into his son's eyes, "I *saw* God at work in you." He put his hand on Rick's shoulder. "The doctors said you were going to *die*. They admitted it. There was *nothing* they could do. God healed you, son, and He let me see Him at work. I'll *never* be the same. Never. For the first time in my life I saw what it meant to really trust God."

That's so hard to do, Laura thought letting yesterday's memory slip away. She walked to Michelle's bed and slid her fingers around the cold, steel railing, gripping it tightly. Shelly lay sleeping on her stomach, a pale blue blanket drawn across her. Laura reached out and lightly touched the little legs. She shook her head, tears slowly filling her eyes.

"Oh, Lord," she cried quietly, "there isn't any hope. They all agree with Dr. Abrams—they want to take part of her leg or they say she'll die. Please, God, don't let her die."

Limp, she dropped to her knees beside the bed and wept hot, stinging tears. "Oh, Lord," she cried. She rested her forehead against the backs of both hands as she gripped the rail with her fingers. "I know I should trust you, give Shelly to you completely," she paused, trembling as she drew a breath. "But I don't *want to!*" A cry burst from her, the bed shaking with her sobs. Helplessness engulfed her and hopelessness loomed so close. She wanted to strike out and make someone, something stop pulling Michelle from her. She wanted to *do* something to keep her, to force death far away from them. She longed to return to familiar routines—school, work, dirty dishes, each other.

For several minutes she knelt beside Michelle, nauseated and uncomfortably warm, too weak, too drained to get up. She ran her hand under the hair resting on her neck, now wet with perspiration.

Slowly she stood to her feet. "I can't do anything to stop this, Lord" she cried. Shelly stirred and Laura put her hand over her mouth to muffle her sobs. "I can't fight it anymore either," she whispered.

Moving to the chair she sat down and rested both hands on its cool chrome arms, closing her eyes and tipping her head back as if waiting for a downpour of strength.

I can't hold onto Shelly even if I try, she thought. *It's as though I've already lost her. I have no control. There's nothing I can do,*

Lord. You're the only one who can help. She's all yours.

Quietly, the early dawn erased the surrounding darkness. Pale light filtered through the skylight overhead. Shadows lightened and disappeared as warm sunlight slowly streamed into the room.

Deep inside her an assurance came, almost like a voice, "I love her, Laura, more than you do."

Laura's heart was pounding, pulsing in her back against the chair. Her options were clear. She could turn Shelly over to God and trust Him to do what was best, or she could keep fighting Him . . . just as long as she liked.

"I can't fight anymore," she said softly. As a calming peace flowed through her she rested her head against the back of the chair and whispered, "Lord, you can have her back—even to death."

Scraps of a Bible verse she once knew pushed into her mind. *He who began a good work . . . will complete it. . . .*

She couldn't remember the rest but it didn't really matter. She looked at Shelly and turned the words over again in her mind, *He who began a good work will complete it. . . .*

"This isn't something He can't finish," she whispered. "He loves Shelly, even more than I do."

The battlefield within her fell quiet. "No more fighting, Lord."

Peace and refreshment swept over her. She closed her eyes and sighed deeply. For the first time in days she felt rested, able to breathe again. The tenseness slowly left her body as she lay quietly in the warmth of a new and unexplainable sense of security.

The bright sheaths of sunlight soon woke Michelle. She rolled onto her back and slowly blinked her eyes, adjusting to the brightness.

"Well," Laura teased from her chair. "You *are* going to wake up today. I thought you might sleep till tomorrow."

"I might," Michelle said stretching like a cat in a patch of hot summer sun.

"Mommy," she said sitting upright, suddenly wide awake, "can we go home today?"

"Not for awhile yet," Laura answered evenly.

"But I miss my *frieennds*," Michelle said dramatically emphasizing the last word. Then remembering the puppy Rick said was waiting for her at home she added, "And I'll bet Lady thinks I ran away."

"I'll bet you're right," Laura said moving to the bed and sitting down. "I'll bet they all miss you too."

Michelle snuggled up to Laura and hugged her around the waist, "I love you, Mommy," she said enthusiastically.

"And I love you too, honey," Laura responded. Her voice was light for Michelle's sake, but the words sank deep within her.

Over the familiar sounds of breakfast trays clattering in the hall, Michelle heard Kim and Rick coming in the door. Soon the room was filled with chatter, with everyone warmly involved.

By choice, Dick was not part of the broadening realm of absentee fathers. He'd promised himself he never would be. The uniqueness and importance of all three kids to him and Laura was one of the threads in their strong family ties.

They were a tight unit. Nobody in the family was too busy to take the time when somebody needed encouragement, support or someone to share with. They'd all taken turns staying with Michelle since her illness began. They knew the same supportive love would be there for any one of them if they ever needed it.

"Hey, Michelle," Kim said, "hurry up and get dressed. It's neat outside. Let's go."

Before long Michelle, dressed in a red T-shirt and blue jeans, plopped into the wheelchair and rolled toward the door, grinning at her father. Looking every bit the swashbuckling musketeer, Dick opened it with a flourish and bow. Everybody laughed, and it felt good.

In the hall, antiseptic hospital odors met them, underscoring the reality of what lay ahead. Laura reached for Dick's hand. In the world they created with love and each other, cancer seemed very far away. Walking through these halls they realized it was not far enough away.

As Rick pushed her along the hall Michelle looked into a room where a young boy walked slowly toward the door.

"Hi," she called smiling broadly at him.

He leaned up against the end of the bed, pulled his blue terry cloth robe tighter around him and looked at her without changing his expression or returning her greeting.

She looked back as they passed the door, puzzlement replacing her fading smile.

In a room on the other side of the hall a little preschooler wiggled expertly, protesting the face-washing his mother patiently persisted with. With a "weary-but-loving-it" expression, the mother glanced up as they wheeled by and spoke volumes with her look.

As they turned the corner a young girl near Michelle's age sat on her bed in her room, tugging at an unruly T-shirt, rumpled and clinging to her head.

"See, Michelle," Kim teased, "other people get stuck in their T-shirts too."

The child forced her head through and emerged, free, blonde hair flying in all directions.

"Hi," Michelle grinned, trying again.

The little girl smiled shyly from her bed and dropped her eyes. She was still trying to sort out how to get her arms in her shirt sleeves as Michelle and her family turned the corner and moved through the lobby.

Outside the hospital doors, the rich russet-and-brown painted trees contrasted with deep green spruce and firs on this mild November day.

"Let's play hide-and-seek!" Michelle said.

"How're you going to do that in here?" Rick asked patting the arm of the wheelchair. "Did you forget you have to stay in this thing?"

"You can push me. I'll tell you where," she improvised. "Come on, Kim. You be it. We can all hide in the roses."

"Oh, Michelle," Laura argued, "if we—"

"Come on, Mommy, it's fun!"

Before Laura had a chance to finish her sentence Kim had covered her eyes and was counting, "One . . . two . . . three . . ."

Michelle directed Rick in a hoarse whisper. "Over there, Rick. Over there!"

Laura and Dick looked at each other and shrugged. They didn't feel like playing games but Michelle did. Maybe one round.

Dick felt foolish sneaking around the garden all crouched down. He watched Laura inching between the tall rosebushes hunched over so "it" couldn't find her.

"If I look like that" he thought, "I hope nobody we know comes by." He glanced over his shoulder as he crept along a path and there was Michelle, ducked down in the wheelchair, completely involved in the game. She looked like a small commander of an important secret mission. Her expression made his feeling foolish worthwhile. What looked like a silly child's game to anyone else was really love-in-action to this family.

Michelle seemed to sense the seriousness of her illness, though no one had said anything to her. They kept her waiting, secretly hoping the doctors would change their diagnosis. Maybe they were wrong. But Michelle asked questions—like the one earlier in the week, "You used to be a policeman, didn't you, Daddy?"

"I sure was," he answered.

"They take care of us and protect us, don't they?"

"Policemen?" he asked.

"Uh-huh," she said.

"They sure do."

"And you didn't let the doctors take Rick's leg when it was hurt, did you?" she went on intently watching his face.

Dick looked at her, afraid of what she was thinking.

"You'll take care of me too, huh!" she said confidently.

How could he let her down like this? His stomach churned. He wasn't going to be able to do what she trusted him to do so easily. God knew he tried. Oh, how he tried! He'd done his best. But now he knew his best wasn't good enough to save her leg. The surgery was set for Monday.

All week she had lapsed into short, deep silences—time spent thinking things through—and quickly followed with bursts of activity. Her family recognized her attempt to bury thoughts that surfaced to disturb her. Hide-and-seek was one way she could keep things off balance.

After Kim "found" everybody, Dick and Laura settled on the grass while the kids played on.

"It doesn't seem real," Dick said. "She sure doesn't *look* sick." After a long pause he added, "It's all so crazy."

They sat in silence for a time, alone in private thoughts.

"We've got to tell her, Laurie."

"I know we do," she said watching the kids bobbing through the rainbow of rose blossoms. "I know."

"What day is it?" Dick asked. It's hard to keep track of time.

"Saturday," Laura said breaking off a piece of clover.

"That doesn't leave much time," he said almost to himself.

"What if there's nothing wrong with her?" Laura said. Dick looked startled. "I mean, you said yourself she doesn't look sick. What if . . ." she searched for words, ". . . what if she's been healed? There are so many people praying for her, it's possible, you know."

She looked for Dick's reaction. He was listening, not sure what he thought.

"Maybe," she continued, "we could have them do another biopsy before they—" she paused still unable to say the words.

"We could, I suppose," Dick responded finally. *Another biopsy.* He thought for a minute running his fingers back and forth across his forehead. "But God won't let her lose her leg if she's not supposed to. I mean, something will stop the surgery. A power failure maybe; all the lights will go out."

The thought of doctors and nurses feeling their way around surgery in the dark amused Laura. "They can't operate in the dark," she said wryly. She thought a minute, and added, "Maybe lightning will strike their instruments and they'll be too hot to handle."

They looked at each other and smiled at their fantasy.

"Dick, we're terrible!" Laura said in mock rebuttal. "Poor doctors. I don't wish them any harm."

"Yeah," he mused, "but it'd be worth just about anything if Shelly could keep her leg."

He took Laura's hand. "Honey," he continued, "we're going to have to see this thing through no matter how much we hate it. And we've got to tell Shelly—today."

"I know," she said soberly. "She needs some time to get used to the idea, and there isn't much time left."

She put her head on Dick's shoulder and wrapped one arm around him. Hot tears spilled onto his shirt. "We've got to tell her. But where do we start?"

"I've gone over and over it in my head. I rehearsed different ways with Kim last night. I still don't know what to say."

"Oh, Dick, how can we tell her she'll never run again?"

"It's the hardest thing we've ever had to do, Laurie." He pulled her close and leaned back against the weathered old tree. Tears rolled down his cheeks and disappeared in his beard. "Our only other choice is to tell her she's going to die."

3
Rose Garden Promises

Later that afternoon Dick walked over to the bed where Michelle sat on top of the blankets with her legs straight out in front of her. Kim sat cross-legged on the floor, leaning against the wall. They laughed over a private joke and Shelly grabbed her rabbit, flinging it at her sister. Kim ducked in exaggerated fear.

"Lousy shot," she teased Shelly.

"Honey," Dick said sitting on the bed close to Michelle. "The results are back from all the tests and we want to tell you what the doctors found."

Kim tightened her grip on the floppy stuffed rabbit and stared at the floor. She knew Shelly had to be told but it hurt so much to think of her little sister's pain and loss.

Shelly looked at Dick, studying his face carefully. Then she flopped back against the pillow. She missed the mischief in his eyes and the almost-smile he usually wore when he spoke to her. Twisting a ribbon on the front of her shirt she said, "I want you to tell me, Daddy. Nobody else."

Shelly's request caught Dick off guard. Everything was shared in their family. It was always that way with them. Did she know what he was going to say? Could she possibly sense the seriousness of her illness?

"I have to have Mommy with me, honey," he stammered.

"OK," she said still not looking at him, "but just you and Mommy. Just you."

Dick nodded his head and closed his big hand around both of hers. "OK. It'll be just us."

Ten minutes later, walking out into the sunlight with Laura and Michelle, Dick began to realize how frightened he was. His breathing was fast and shallow, his mouth was dry. He leaned forward pushing Shelly's chair down the walk to the rose garden. That's where she wanted to go, by the waterfall.

He began perspiring in the warm sun. It was an effort just to raise his feet off the ground. *What will I say, Lord?* he thought as they walked through the winding paths. *I can't tell her. I can't.*

He looked away to keep Laura from seeing the tears he couldn't hold back. But she was lost in her own thoughts, feeling the heaviness of the burden they were shouldering together. Tears blurred her own vision fusing the reds and yellows and pinks of the roses around them.

Maybe we should have let the doctors tell her, she thought. *How's she going to take it? Oh, Lord, give us the right words. Prepare her. Somehow help her understand.* She reached for Dick's arm and moved closer to him, lacing her fingers together and pressing his arm against him. She'd never noticed how long these paths were before. It felt like miles right now.

"I hear it, Daddy," Michelle said; "it's over there under those trees." As she turned toward the waterfall the sun warmed her face. Her eyes were large and serious. For the first time since she'd found this place she did not seem happy to be here.

As they walked the last few steps to the shaded waterfall, Laura looked up. The sky was blue and the wind was pushing big billowy clouds around. *How can the world still look so much the same? Shelly's losing a leg . . .* She looked at Michelle sitting stiffly in the wheelchair in front of her, . . . *maybe even her life.*

An evergreen canopy shaded the falls and a cool mist filtered down on them, mingling with the heady perfume of the roses.

Dick set the brake on the wheelchair and sat down next to the falls on a short stone bench. Laura took Michelle on her lap and they settled in the wheelchair beside him.

"Honey," he said, trying to find the right words. Pausing, he drew a deep breath, fighting to get enough air. He looked into Michelle's eyes; her face tipped up slightly as she watched his expression intently. She sensed something was very wrong. He knew she did.

"The doctors have studied all the tests they made on your leg," he began, "and they've found out why it's been hurting you so much. There's a tumor in the bone." Michelle's eyes searched her father's as he continued, "There isn't any medicine that can make it better."

"That's why we've taken you to the very best hospitals," Laura said, "and to so many good doctors. We want you to have the best chance you can to get better."

Dick took his daughter's small hand in his. "The only way they can treat a disease like the one you have is to remove the bad bone."

A puzzled look came across her face, "Can they take the bone out and leave my leg?"

"No, honey," Dick said. He wasn't able to say more. His voice broke and he hoped Michelle hadn't noticed.

She caught her breath as though suddenly seized with stabbing pain. "Oh, Daddy," she cried, tears filling her eyes, "I won't be able to dance anymore if I don't have my leg!" The thought gripped her. "I don't *want* to be a *cripple!*"

Wrenching her hand away from her father's, she covered her face, burying herself in Laura's arms. Her small shoulders shook as she wept, the sobs coming from deep inside.

Dick leaned forward, his head in his hands. Tears squeezed between his trembling fingers. "Oh, God," he cried, "I feel so helpless!"

Weeping, sharing a grief they'd never dreamed possible, Laura and Michelle rocked slowly back and forth in the wheelchair, crying softly together. Laura stroked Shelly's soft hair, closing her eyes and pulling her daughter closer to her.

A few long moments passed. Shelly stopped crying and took a deep breath. She pulled away from Laura, straightening up and rubbing the tears from her cheeks.

She looked at her mother's tear-streaked face and a new sadness filled her dark eyes. She reached up taking her mother's face in her two small hands.

"I'm gonna be OK, Mommy," she said soothingly. "Don't cry anymore." Michelle's tenderness made Laura's tears flow faster.

Michelle patted her mother's face and reassured her, "I was scared when Daddy told me, but Jesus made me feel safe inside. I'm gonna be alright. You'll see." She circled Laura's neck with one short arm and they held each other tightly without a word.

"I hate to interrupt," a young nurse said quietly. They looked up at her, their faces wet with crying. She shifted her attention to the pink rosebud she held in her fingers. "I'm sorry to have to break in on you." she went on, "but Michelle is scheduled for x-ray now."

"It's alright," Laura said reaching into her purse for a Kleenex.

"We were having a talk about Shelly's operation," Dick said taking off his glasses and wiping his face.

"I know," the nurse said. She stooped down next to the wheel-chair and held the rose out to Shelly. "I picked this for you."

Michelle took the flower and, with her head down, softly said, "Thank you." The nurse kissed Michelle lightly on the forehead and walked back down the path toward the children's wing.

They collected themselves a little, then started pushing slowly back along the garden path to x-ray.

"Daddy," Shelly asked, turning the rosebud slowly around in her fingers, "why would God let this happen to me?"

Dick and Laura looked at each other, tears welling up in their eyes. *Why indeed. Oh, God, I wish we knew.*

"Honey," he said slowly, "we don't have any idea why this happens to anybody." They pushed on in silence, the muffled sound of rubber tires rolling on cement.

"Maybe I know," Michelle said as they entered the building. "If they don't have any medicine to fix this kind of sickness yet, maybe they can study my leg and find some. Then they can help other kids when they get sick." She glanced up at Laura walking beside her. Michelle looked contented, satisfied. It was answer enough for her.

Dick raised his eyebrows and looked at Laura. She just shook her head in amazement. Love and pride flavored their sorrow.

As they approached the elevator Laura stepped ahead of them and pushed the button.

"Watch this!" Michelle said secretively. The elevator settled on their level. At the perfect moment she dramatically snapped her fingers and commanded the doors, "Open!" They yielded obedi-ently to her magical command.

Dick and Laura thought they saw a little bit of "magic" in the way she was dealing with her loss too.

As they rounded the corner to x-ray a dark-haired, bearded young man wearing a lab coat stepped into the corridor. His badge tapped against the pens in his pocket as he walked toward them.

"Hi, Ron," Michelle chirped.

"Hi, Michelle," he called back. "How are you today?"

"I'm fine. What are you doin'?"

"I'm taking some x-rays in here. You want to help me develop them? I'll be through in a minute." He winked and pushed his way through the swinging door into the treatment room.

"She's going to be here a little while," another technician told Laura. "If you'd like to do something else we'll bring her back to the room when she's finished."

"Thanks," Laura said. "She loves to follow Ron around. But don't let her give him a bad time."

"We won't," the girl said smiling. "She's a big help."

Michelle grinned broadly and scooted a little higher in the chair.

Walking through the underground tunnel from x-ray to the children's wing, Dick and Laura silently pondered the events of the last few minutes. It seemed like a lifetime.

"She sure took it well," Dick said thinking out loud. He wanted to forget all of it, but couldn't. He had to talk, to share the heaviness he felt.

"If I hadn't heard her say what she did about not wanting to be a cripple, I'd wonder if she'd even heard us." Laura thought back, amazed at Michelle's strength and maturity.

"Well, honey," Dick said slipping his arm around her, "we've been praying. Maybe God's answering our prayers by helping her accept all this."

"It's funny, isn't it?" Laura asked looking up at Dick as they walked on through the tunnel. "Her faith has always been so strong. I mean, God's been a working part of her life ever since she was little."

"Do you remember that time she was talking about Jesus coming back?" He smiled thinking about his little five-year-old talking about the second coming of Christ.

"When she told us we should be going to church?" Laura asked.

"Yeah," Dick answered. "What was it she said?"

"Oh, something like, 'One of these days Jesus is coming back and we're gonna be embarrassed 'cause we won't know what to say to Him.'"

Dick remembered. "That's right. She thought we needed to know more about the Bible stories so we would have something to talk to Him about when He comes back."

Laura thought for a minute then added, "Funny part is she was right."

"It didn't take us long to get active in a good church and start maturing in our faith after that," Dick added, a faint smile playing around his mouth.

"Dick," Laura said soberly, "can you imagine going through these last six months without Christ?"

"We'd never have made it, Laurie," he said quietly, "never."

Stepping off the elevator in the children's wing Dick and Laura met Dr. Rosen on his way to his office. He was a thin man, quiet in speech and manner, always warm and pleasant to adults and children alike.

"Have you had a chance to talk to Shelly yet?" he asked, matching the pace of his steps to theirs.

"Yes," Dick responded, "just a few minutes ago—in the rose garden."

Dr. Rosen stopped and turned to face the Prices. "How did she seem to take the news?" he asked looking intently into their faces.

"Very well," Laura said with some enthusiasm. He looked doubtful. "Really, extremely well," she added.

"She's her old self again," Dick said. "When we took her to x-ray just now she was snapping the doors open and pestering Ron like always."

"Are you sure she *understood* what you told her?" the doctor asked in a steady voice. He tipped his head slightly and narrowed his eyes adding, "It's very important that she really understands what's happening Monday if we want her to accept and adjust well to the amputation."

"She said she doesn't want to be a cripple," Laura recounted, "and she was upset about not being able to dance anymore." She was slightly unsure herself now in the face of the doctor's questions.

"She even asked us why God would allow this to happen," Dick offered. "She decided for herself, that it might be so you could study her leg and find a medicine to help other children so they wouldn't lose their legs."

"Well," the doctor straightened his narrow bow tie with one hand, "it does sound as if she heard you. But her carefree attitude concerns me some. I don't think she really understands what's happening. I'd like to talk with her too, maybe to answer questions she might have. I'd really like to get a feel of her understanding."

"Sure," Dick responded, "we'd appreciate that."

"Fine then," the doctor said resuming his stride toward his office, "this afternoon, about two? In the conference room." He pointed in the direction of the room he meant and nodded at them as he rounded the corner.

At two o'clock several people began to gather around the chrome-legged conference table in the tiny room. Bright yellow bookshelves lining the wall behind the door were the only color to the otherwise all white room.

Michelle, in a perky yellow dress, sat with her hands in her lap. Her sassy rabbit, tucked snugly into the corner of her chair, peeked out beside her. Dick and Laura sat at the table next to Michelle and Kim settled into the chair on her other side.

Rick still found it uncomfortable sitting for very long, so he chose to stand behind Michelle. As they waited for things to get under way he impatiently shifted his weight from one foot to the other. Everything in him wanted to run as far and as fast as he could, but something constrained him and kept him in the room.

On the other side of the table Dr. Lee sat nodding in agreement to a comment from Dr. Jackson. Dr. Rosen took the empty seat beside Dr. Jackson and laid Michelle's hospital chart on the table. He pulled a pen from his pocket and wrote something in the corner of a small yellow tablet. Laura smiled to herself wondering if the doctor was writing down the final link in a cure the medical world was waiting for, or if he was reminding himself to get a loaf of bread on the way home.

She liked the doctors they'd met here. Dr. Jackson was a thin, attractive woman in her late thirties. Her dark complexion accented large brown eyes and an easy smile. She was friendly and open with people.

Dr. Lee, about the same age as Dr. Jackson, was very efficient in manner and dress. Her sleek shoulder-length hair was pulled back from her face and secured with tiny combs. She was thorough, one who questioned rapidly, and listened intently when others spoke.

Then there was Dr. Rosen. From the first day at the City of Hope Michelle loved him. He was a gentle man with a well-trimmed moustache that moved emphatically as he spoke. Michelle especially liked his warm hands, just a part of his overall warm ways.

Dr. Rosen rolled his pen in his fingers as he said, "Michelle, we know you talked with your parents this morning. Dr. Lee, Dr. Jackson and I wondered if you have any questions you'd like to ask us about your operation."

"Well, yeah," she said reaching for Kim's hand. "I do have one." She looked down at her leg briefly, twisted her foot around slowly. "Is it true I'm going to lose my *whole* leg?"

Dr. Rosen looked at Dick and Laura with an expression of shock. They were just as surprised as he was.

"Where did you get that idea, Shelly?" the doctor asked gently.

"I heard them talking in x-ray. Somebody said my name. They said I was the girl who was going to lose her leg."

Dr. Rosen shot a quick glance at Dick. "No, it's not true, Michelle." The doctor looked at the child across from him and marveled at her strength. She sat quietly listening to his explanation, nodding occasionally, or making a face when she didn't understand something he said. She gave no sign of fear, no anger over the impending loss of a limb, she was not emotional. She held tightly to her sister's hand and accepted information that reduced grown men to tears,

"We want to be sure we get all of that diseased tumor so it can't cause any more trouble. So we'll probably go a couple of inches above your knee. But you'll have a nice long stump so you can use an artificial leg later on. We call that a prosthesis."

"Will you sew the pros . . ."

"Prosthesis," Dr. Jackson prompted.

". . . the prosthesis on my little leg?"

"No," Dr. Lee answered, "your 'little leg' will have to heal first before you can get a prosthesis. Then we'll fit you with one just right for you. It will strap on in a special way and you can use it like a new leg. But you can take it off when you want to."

"Will I be able to wiggle the toes on my new leg like real ones? I like my toes."

Dr. Jackson smiled slightly, "It will have toes but they won't wiggle, Shelly."

Michelle was candid and uninhibited, asking questions for several minutes. The doctors spoke patiently and were thorough in their answers to her.

Finally Dr. Rosen asked, "Is there anything else we need to talk about, Shelly?"

"I was wondering," she began. Then pausing briefly she touched her hand to her hair. "Am I going to lose my hair?"

The room was silent as the adults tried to collect their thoughts. No one had mentioned chemotherapy and no one in the room knew where she might have gotten the idea. It was too soon to get involved in the subject, though. She had enough to accept already. "We'll talk about that later, OK, Michelle?" Dr. Jackson asked gently.

Dr. Lee clicked the point back into her pen. "We've talked about so many things today I'd think you need some time to think about what you've heard."

Dr. Rosen closed the chart in front of him and put the pen back into his breast pocket with several others. "Michelle," he said, "if you think of other questions, I want you to ask me or one of the other doctors. We care very much about what happens to you."

Emptying out of the tiny conference room everyone filed into the hall. As Rick steered Michelle toward the play yard, Dr. Jackson caught Laura's arm. "Mrs. Price," she said quietly, her eyes darker and very wide, "that is a very special little girl. I'll never forget her."

She looked intently at Laura, then self-consciously drew her hand back and pushed it into her lab coat pocket. Turning, she walked briskly down the hall past the others.

4
Before

Dick sat up slowly and swung his feet to the floor one at a time. He leaned forward resting his elbows on his knees, and rolled his head slowly from side to side trying to work the stiffness out of his neck. He rubbed the back of his neck and his shoulder. His whole body ached. It had been a long night. The makeshift bed in Michelle's room had seemed to get shorter and narrower as the night wore on.

He looked sleepily at his watch. Laura and the two older kids were due back soon. He hoped Laura had been able to get some rest. She was looking so tired.

Absentmindedly he rolled the stem of his watch between his thumb and forefinger as he looked over at Shelly. He thought about his family—Laura, with her easy smile and willing attitude. She'd put up with a lot from him in the 20 plus years they'd been married. How many unannounced relatives and needy friends had he brought home that she'd fed and housed without complaint? How many good laughs they'd shared. There would be no way to count.

And there wasn't any way to count the tears they'd shed together either—over the two babies they'd lost, the hard times they'd faced, the tragic deaths of parents, the house fire, Rick's accident . . .

Rick—handsome, strong, eager. Finally pulling a lot of the straggling ends of his life together, leaving behind the adolescent he'd been to become the man he now was. He'd been through a lot.

Dick smiled at his own choice of words, *been through a lot?* If God hadn't intervened, Rick would be *dead*.

That horrible accident. A shudder ran through Dick thinking about it. Rick on his motorcycle, speeding down the freeway. The truck. Every wheel on the left side of the diesel passing across his body. Nineteen thousand pounds of weight on each of the five axles. Dick shook the thought from his head. He couldn't think about his son lying helpless in the road, the crushing weight of that enormous truck. . . .

I'll never forget it. The scene in the emergency room flashed through his mind again.

Rick lay so still on the big hospital cart. There must have been 10 doctors and nurses working in the flurry of action around him; some in white uniforms, some wearing surgical greens, their conversation static and muffled as they scurried around the room feverishly trying to stay ahead of death. They didn't say much but their faces betrayed them, showing how bad off Rick really was.

"Will he live?" It startled Dick to hear himself say the words.

"I wish I could say what you want to hear, Mr. Price," the young red-headed doctor said, stepping out of the activity, away from the table where Rick lay motionless. "He's strong. Awfully strong. The incredible, extensive injuries, the blood he's lost; it's hard to believe he's still alive, let alone conscious."

"That's a good sign, then?" Dick asked hopefully. "His being conscious, I mean?"

"I don't know." The doctor took Dick's elbow and led him to an x-ray viewer mounted on the pale green wall behind them.

"These are some of his x-rays. You can see for yourself, his pelvis is fractured." Taking the black and white x-ray off the monitor he chose two smaller ones from the large pile of films on the table in front of them. Jamming them quickly into the clamps at the top of the viewer, he pointed to the negative on the left. "Here's a view of his left leg, the femur's broken in several places." The doctor turned away from the x-rays to face Dick.

"Mr. Price," he continued slowly, "I can run my hand all the way down the bone inside the muscle of his thigh. I'm afraid he's going to lose that leg." He paused watching Dick closely.

"From what we've been able to see here in the emergency room, all his internal organs are floating." He went on, "The urethra is completely severed, and his bladder is burst. There are deep abrasions on his lower back with openings from inside the body cavity clear through his back. The muscle and tissue on his left buttock have been ground away . . . just gone."

The young man's voice became gentler. "We won't know until we get him into surgery just how extensive his injuries really are, and what we've missed here in our preliminary examination. We'll try our best to save him, but," he paused again and looked at the floor, "it doesn't look good."

"You're not even giving me any hope," Dick said pleadingly.

"It's a pretty hopeless situation." The doctor's voice was compassionate and there was a slight tremor in the hand he put on Dick's shoulder. "He's lost so much blood, Mr. Price. He may not even be able to take the stress of surgery."

Tears welled up in Dick's eyes as he sought strength to sort out what he was hearing, to make decisions that needed to be made for his son. He looked across the room where Rick lay. A pile of ragged, blood-soaked clothes cluttered the floor where they'd been cut off him and dropped out of the way. Rick's boots were under the gurney where he lay fighting for his life.

"I want to talk to him," Dick said moving toward the center of activity. "I want to see my son."

As he and the doctor approached the side of the table a nurse glanced up and stepped back, opening a space where Dick could stand beside the boy.

He looked down into the face of his only son, and swallowed hard. Rick's face was terribly puffy, his eyes nearly swollen shut. He lay naked under strong overhead lights, lacerations, abrasions, gaping wounds covering most of his body. The team worked around Dick preparing Rick for surgery, trying to stop some of the endless bleeding.

Dick drew a deep breath, obviously shaken by what he saw. Someone slipped a supportive arm around him and Dick suddenly noticed how strangely weak his legs felt. He hoped his expression wouldn't let Rick know how little hope there seemed to be, or how hard it was for Dick to look at the ravages of the accident.

Rick opened his eyes and looked at his father standing beside him. "Dad," he said, venturing a weak smile, "some girl in a car forced me into the other lane. I couldn't do anything to stop . . ."

"I know," Dick answered, nodding as he gently touched Rick's shoulder avoiding the abrasions that nearly covered him. "Don't worry about that now. You just get well."

Rick reached toward his father with one hand, but the effort was too great. He let the hand fall limply back onto the sheet and closed his eyes.

Fear gripped Dick like a cold hand. The doctor beside him, wearing surgical greens, reached over Rick, quickly checking his eyes and listening for a pulse. He flashed a quick look at Dick and both men relaxed a little. Rick was still alive.

"Mr. Price," someone said behind him, "we need your signature on these consent papers for surgery."

Dick turned to face a small green-eyed clerk holding a clipboard. They took a few steps away from the others.

"The permission will cover," she continued clinically, reading from the form in her hand, "repairs of internal injuries, closing of lacerations, and amputation of the left leg at the hip."

Dick grabbed the papers from her hand and turned them around so he could read them. "Amputation?" he repeated astonished. "I'm not giving permission to amputate! Not now."

"But, Mr. Price—" the woman persisted.

Overhearing the conversation one of the doctors stepped over to them. "Maybe I can help," he broke in. "I'm Dr. Dixon, Mr. Price. We need your signature to do what has to be done to keep your son alive. Until we get in there we won't know just how extensive the injuries are, and—"

"I understand all that," Dick said forcing a calm tone. "I'll be right here if you need permission for something else." He looked intently at the dark-complexioned man beside him. *These men are all so young,* he thought. *I hope they know what they're doing.*

"But time is of the essence, Mr. Price," Dr. Dixon continued pressing for the signature.

"Then we're wasting time right now," Dick said. He tightened then relaxed the muscles in his jaw, training his eyes on the doctor's. "Look," Dick said in explanation, "from what you've said we're practically working with . . ." the words stuck in his throat, ". . . with a dead man," it came out in a hoarse whisper. "Am I right?"

Crumpling the surgical mask hanging at his neck the doctor lowered his eyes to the floor and slowly nodded his head, "That's right."

"If you don't take the leg right now will it make a difference whether he lives?" Dick asked.

"No, Mr. Price," the young man answered hesitantly, "it won't."

"Then do what you have to do to save him," Dick said, tears stinging his throat. "If he's going to . . ." he swallowed hard, "going to die, let's leave him a whole man."

He could hold back the tears no longer. The young man in green put his hand on Dick's shoulder as Dick stood weeping in his helplessness. They agreed that the important thing was keeping Rick alive. The operative permits were changed and the amputation postponed.

Dick left the emergency room treatment area to find his family. Laura and Kim were sitting in the waiting room, their faces drawn and filled with signs of worry. He watched them search his face for some sign of what was happening as he walked slowly toward them. He opened his arms and Laura and Kim walked inside, close to him. For a moment or two they simply wept.

"Oh, Lord," Dick prayed aloud, "Rick's so bad. You're the only one who can even keep him alive. Help him make it through surgery. . . ." Mid-sentence he stopped praying. Putting his hands onto Kim and Laura's shoulders he gently moved them away from him, where he could see their faces.

"I don't know why I'm saying this exactly," he said, his forehead furrowed, "but for some reason . . ." he paused, "I'm sure Rick's going to be OK. In fact," he emphasized, "he's going to be 100 percent restored." He thought about what he'd just said and what the doctors had been telling him. "Somehow I know he's going to be alright. I have such a peace about it."

The peacefulness spread between them with a special measure of hope as they hugged each other and prepared to wait as long as it took.

Before leaving for the hospital Laura had taken two minutes to call a couple of close Christian friends to ask their prayers for Rick. They, in turn, had set prayer chains of several hundred people praying for God's best in all of this. And before long, friends made their way into the waiting room to wait with them, to comfort in any way possible, just to be there.

Eleven hours later Rick was wheeled into the Intensive Care Unit. His left leg was in traction, a steel pin inserted through his lower leg under the shin bone with cords and pulleys attached to the pin holding his leg high. Tubes,–IVs–ran from everywhere, some carrying glucose and badly needed fluids, others replacing the precious blood he'd lost; still others—catheters—ineffectively carrying off the waste. The urologist told them that Rick's bladder was in such bad shape that to expect catheters to help was like hoping to catch the waterflow from an inverted glass with a single straw in the center of it.

BUT HE WAS ALIVE!

Hours crept by like days as machines beeped rhythmically, pulsing out a copy of Rick's steady heartbeat. Soft, noiseless steps of nurses, moving around the room, carrying out functions to keep death at bay, faded into the dimly lit, too quiet ICU. The stale smell of urine leaking from Rick's broken body forced its way into Dick and Laura's consciousness and, in that moment, it seemed that death stood beside them, its chilling breath blowing across the backs of their necks. A darkness hung in every corner of the room almost like smoke. It was hard to believe that just outside those curtained windows life was being lived by others as though there was no death.

Laura moved to the window next to Rick's bed and pushed back the heavy drapes. Dawn was breaking slowly, the gray sky taking on a soft rosy warmth. It was a new day, the day after Mother's Day, 1976, one she'd never forget.

Later that morning Dick and Laura sat propped against each other in the hallway outside ICU; Kim was sleeping, curled up on the floor at their feet. It had been 72 hours since Rick was brought in. His condition was still unstable, his blood pressure dangerously low and unsteady. There had been no sleep for either Dick or Laura, and Kim had gotten very little, mostly on the floor of the waiting room. Rick's life was still in the balance and none of them could bring themselves to be anywhere else.

Good friends were still praying and a steady stream of visitors had come by to check on Rick and them. From what people said there had to be hundreds of people praying for them. God would answer.

"Mr. Price," the nurse said beside them. They opened their eyes with a start and immediately stood to their feet. It was news about Rick. There had been some kind of change. The excitement in her voice was obvious as the gray-haired woman smiled widely and said, "His vital signs just stabilized. He's going to pull through!"

Dick and Laura hugged each other, with tears of joy and relief streaming down their faces, and the nurse helped Kim to her feet with a self-conscious hug. Their prayers were being answered. Rick *was* going to make it! And to make sure he got well as soon as possible the doctors ordered a couple of pints of whole blood for him. He needed the red cells to speed the healing.

Soon after the blood was started, Dick was sitting outside ICU waiting to see Rick while Laura phoned some of their faithful friends to let them know about the good things taking place, when a different nurse called Dick inside. "I'm sorry, Mr. Price, but it suddenly looks very bad," she said in urgent tones.

He glanced over at Rick's bed. Half a dozen hospital personnel and doctors were working rapidly over Rick, dragging equipment into his cubicle. Confusion.

"What's happened?" Dick asked, his eyes wide with concern and amazement. "Everthing was fine. What happened?"

"The whole blood," she said shaking her head. "He's had a bad reaction to the whole blood he was given."

Dick walked quickly to the foot of Rick's bed and could not believe what he saw. Rick was lying perfectly still, his face red, his eyes closed, his hands and feet red and swollen to twice their normal size. He could feel the heat of Rick's raging fever rising from the bed as he stood there.

The nurses and doctors moved in and out of the space around Rick's bed administering emergency treatment to get the burning fever under control, to reverse the circumstances. Dick saw fear in their eyes as they soaked and changed cold compresses to lay on his head and chest. Without a word Dick moved to Rick's side and took the boy's swollen red hand between his own. Kneeling there beside the bed, in the confusion of tubes and equipment and people moving in and out, he said simply, "God, whatever went wrong with the blood, reverse it and give Rick a comfortable night's sleep."

Before he stood to his feet he felt the fever leave Rick's hand, moving out of it and up the boy's arm. *How funny,* he thought, standing beside Rick and lightly touching his forehead, *I was praying for him just as the fever broke.* He pushed the hair off Rick's forehead and discovered Rick's skin was cool and dry. "I thought a person perspired when a fever broke," he said almost to himself.

"They do," the doctor beside him answered.

"But. . :" Dick said still puzzled, "feel his head. He's cool and dry. Look at his hands," he said picking Rick's hand up off the sheet. "The swelling's gone."

"You're right," the doctor agreed in astonishment as he moved to the foot of the bed to check Rick's feet. "There's absolutely no sign of fever. He was burning up 15 seconds ago. I can't figure that."

"I was praying . . ." Dick paused as the truth began to sink in. "God healed him, just like I asked Him to. God healed my boy." He felt a mixture of awe and excitement rushing through him like a rapid river. God had done *exactly* what he'd asked Him to. He wanted to turn handsprings. "God, you've done what I asked. You took the fever from him. His body is cool. The fever is gone!"

He pushed aside the privacy curtain hanging around Rick's bed and walked, nearly ran out of ICU. Kim sat waiting on the bench outside the door.

"Go sit with Rick," he said not slowing his pace or explaining. Kim quickly turned to go into the room, looking back at her father as he disappeared down the hall.

"Kim," Rick said as she approached the bed, "I think Dad just prayed for me." He seemed a little disoriented. "Something's happening inside me. I feel . . . different, kinda warm and . . . different."

Down the hall, Dick pushed the button for the elevator. *What's taking so long?* He swung around and pushed open the door behind him to the stairwell. Bounding down the stairs two at a time, his excitement grew with every step. "God, it's you!" he said. It echoed off the walls in the stairwell. "You answered my prayer. You're here. You're really here!"

Outside, he paced back and forth in front of the hospital, laughing and crying, half expecting to be dragged off and locked up because of his joy. The only other time he remembered feeling like this was when he was four years old and gave his life to Christ: All the way home he kept feeling like he couldn't touch the sidewalk.

And now Dick thought over what had just happened. There was no doubt about it, the fever was gone. God did just what he'd asked. "I could ask you for *anything* right now, Lord, and you'd do it. I know it!" A picture of the emergency room doctor popped into his mind just then. Rick was lying on the table and the doctor was running his hand "all the way down the bone inside the muscle of his thigh," while Dick stood beside them praying that God would heal Rick's leg. Suddenly in his mind, he saw Rick's leg healed, so rapidly, in fact, that the doctor's hand was still inside the thigh, permanently! Dick laughed out loud at the ludicrous thought of Rick wearing the doctor the rest of his life.

As the strange, somewhat comical scene faded in his mind he was filled with an intense feeling of responsibility. It didn't lessen his joy but opened instead a new focus to him.

"I think Rick needs to see your power, Lord," he concluded. "I love him, and there's nothing I want more than for him to be well and whole, but I want him to know your love and your purpose in this for him." He stood with his hands in his pockets, looking up at the windows of ICU. "I *know* you're here, and I know you're going to heal him, complete and whole. Just take us through this one day at a time, Lord. Let us all see your power, feel your presence. And let Rick know how much you love him."

Dick turned toward the hospital again, satisfied and content with an assurance that brought complete peace in the middle of pain. He'd been with God. God had never been more real to Dick Price.

They all spent that night at home; the last three had been spent in the hospital. When they got back to the hospital the following morning they met Rick's urologist in the hall outside ICU.

"Have you heard the good news?" the doctor asked them, lighting his pipe and looking over his hands at them.

"You mean about Rick's fever?" Laura asked smiling.

"No," he said pocketing his lighter and blowing a puff of smoke out the side of his mouth. "I mean about the catheters working."

Dick and Laura looked at each other, a mixture of "I-knew-it-all-along" and "I-don't-believe-it" written on their faces.

"*Your prayer* . . ." Laura said putting both hands to her face and looking at Dick.

"That's exactly what I prayed for," Dick said almost to himself, remembering what he'd said the day before when he'd asked for God's healing.

"Well, I don't know about that," the doctor continued, "but I came up here this morning to find you and tell you I was taking Rick back to surgery to do some more bladder repair. In light of this happening last night, though, I'm going to wait another 48 hours. If those catheters aren't working right we're going to have to divert that urine flow through his bowel. Without that little sphincter muscle there's really no choice. He'll never control his bladder again without it and we have no substitutes. But we'll see. Forty-eight hours."

Raising his hand in a salute and shaking his head as he walked to the elevator, the doctor left them standing in the hall, the aroma of his pipe tobacco lingering in the air.

Laura hugged Dick tightly. "Isn't it funny," she said, "how we take things for granted until something goes wrong? We haven't been this interested in Rick's bladder since he was potty trained."

All that day and the next the nurses had to change Rick's bed every hour because of the severe leakage of urine he was experiencing through the wound in his back. His bladder wasn't functioning at all and time was running out.

The urologist was scheduled to check on Rick and decide about the surgery within a couple of hours when one of the nurses checked the plastic bags hanging from Rick's bed and discovered the one designated to catch urine was filling. For no apparent reason Rick's nonfunctioning bladder began to operate within minutes of the doctor's deadline. Rick never did have that surgery, yet his bladder functioned normally from that day.

Three weeks after his accident Rick was moved from ICU to a surgical floor where he continued making rapid progress. It was hard for him to accept his limitations as he began feeling better. "Let me get up and sit in a chair," he insisted. "It's silly for you to change my bed with me in it."

Forcing him to stay put, the nurses told him, "You *can't* get out of bed. You're a very sick man, Mr. Price."

"Look," he persisted, "I've had wrecks on my bike before. I'm a fast healer."

"You were run over by a semi-truck," one young nurse finally explained.

Rick smiled wryly, looking at her out of the corner of his eye, "*Nobody* gets run over by a semi and *lives*."

Slowly, as he healed and began to do more for himself, he also began to understand what a miracle it was that he was still alive. As he began to realize how badly he'd been hurt, he saw the miracle God had done in him.

Quietly, Dick reflected on miracle after miracle surrounding Rick: by rights, he should have died on the freeway; instead he was conscious, even able to remember his phone number; he lived through the ordeal of an 11-hour surgery; he'd received 139 pints of blood without ever becoming jaundiced; his ravaged bladder now functioned normally in spite of the fact doctors never found the tiny, irreplaceable muscle needed to control retention; with additional surgery, a 10-inch stainless steel pin in his femur and several skin grafts, he was walking and running on the leg doctors wanted to amputate.

Dick remembered how his own life had changed through Rick's experience. His faith, kind of a "decoration" before, was now vital to him, a part of everything he did.

He stood to his feet and walked slowly to Michelle's bed. She slept, the little girl who brought them so much joy, always singing and telling elaborate, fanciful stories.

Sighing deeply, his shoulders rounded as if bearing a heavy load. "Dear God," he whispered leaning heavily against the railing of the bed, "where does it stop?"

5
And Then There Was One

The sun was warm and a crisp autumn breeze teased leaves off overhanging limbs. It was Sunday, the day before surgery.

"Hurry up, Rick," Michelle complained impatiently. "I want to see the bears."

"OK! OK!" he shot back. "Keep your shirt on. I'm going as fast as I can. You don't want me to run people down, do you?"

"Well . . ." she mockingly weighed the possibility.

"There they are, Shelly," Kim said pointing down one of the tree-lined zoo trails. "There's a big black one in the pond."

"Where, Kim?" she asked craning her neck to see beyond the crowd. "I can't see."

People milled around in front of the exhibit watching the show-off bears doing their tricks for peanuts. Rick finally found a spot beside the guardrail and pushed Michelle's chair in beside it. She grabbed the rail and pulled herself up out of the wheelchair high enough to see the animals in the pit.

"I like it better when I can do my own walking," she said a little irritated. "I can find little places to squeeze into, and I'm faster than you are." She glanced over her shoulder to Rick, flashing an impish expression.

He ruffled her hair and said, "Look at that fat little bear in the corner. He looks just like you."

They moved onto the next exhibit where brown bears were lying in a heap, soaking up the sun. Michelle watched them as they sprawled lazily around the water hole. Two little cubs in the corner cuffed playfully and tumbled together around the sleeping adults.

"I wonder why God let this happen to a rowdy kid like me," she asked indirectly, "instead of some little girl who likes to sit still a lot and read books?"

Before anyone could say anything, a woman standing next to Michelle backed away from the railing, talking to someone, and bumped into the wheelchair.

"Oh, excuse me," she said smiling as she turned to see who she'd walked into. When she saw the short-haired little girl smiling up at her her expression changed, and the smile was replaced with a troubled look.

"I . . . I'm sorry," she said backing off. "I didn't see you there. I'm really sorry," and she disappeared uncomfortably into the crowd.

"She looked like something was wrong," Kim said.

"She sure did," Dick agreed. "Maybe the bears reminded her of somebody she doesn't like."

They pulled Michelle away from the railing and pushed on to the other exhibits. Before long they were collecting reactions to Michelle and her wheelchair. Some people glanced at her dispassionately, then turned to stare after she'd passed. Others coming toward them went out of their way to make enough room for her. Children looked, often asking questions when they didn't understand. Their parents appeared embarrassed and uncomfortable, stammering apologies, sometimes to Dick and Laura, not as often to Michelle.

When someone did ask what happened, Michelle tried to explain about the tumor. But it was clumsy and uncomfortable for her and the person asking. By the end of the morning she had a selection of answers ready. "I hurt my leg," was all that needed to be said, especially to the children. Those who wanted to know more she referred to Dick or Laura.

But the day was beautiful. Autumn smells mingled with the crisp breezes and everywhere they went they laughed. There was a real feeling of closeness and harmony. Laura's mother was with them, and it meant so much to Michelle to have her grandma along.

After the zoo they stopped for an old-fashioned picnic in the park.

They spread their blanket on top of crackly brown and yellow maple leaves dotting the ground all around them, and they took funny pictures of Rick and Michelle and Kim doing "hear no evil, see no evil, speak no evil."

Lying on her back on the blanket with Dick and Laura, Michelle looked up through the skinny fall fingers of the trees over their heads. She said quietly, "I like today. It's been fun." She watched the clouds move silently across the blue sky then rolled onto her stomach with both hands under her chin. "I like being us, Daddy, and *not* being at the hospital."

"Hey, Price," Dick said sitting cross-legged beside her, "is there anything we haven't done today that you think we should have?"

She thought for a minute, then said, "I sure had a good time, but . . ." she scooted herself into his lap and circled his neck with both arms, "there is one thing. We re-e-e-ally need to go to Farrell's."

Farrell's—where bells ring and ragtime music plays, and waiters and waitresses sing "Happy Birthday" over sirens announcing huge portions of ice cream being served to people with insatiable ice cream appetites. It's a noisy, raucous place that Michelle loves dearly.

Dick and Laura hoped for a little quietness, even solitude, on the afternoon before Michelle's surgery. At Farrell's, both were out of the question.

"You sure that's where you want to go?" Dick asked hoping she'd reconsider.

"That's it," she said putting her nose against his and opening her eyes wide. "Can we, Daddy? Huh?"

Dick grinned melting under her warmth and wilyness. "OK with you, honey?" he asked Laura.

"I guess so," she answered, "if that's really where Shelly wants to go." They took a family vote and Farrell's won by a landslide.

With great fanfare and an honest joy they packed up Michelle and what was left of the picnic and headed for Farrell's. Before long Dick and Laura walked into the restaurant trailed by members of their chattering family crew. The noise level inside was just as they remembered—deafening. From somewhere in the middle of the din a rickey-tick player piano played bravely on unnoticed.

They settled around a table near the center of the room and Michelle turned her thoughts to enjoying herself completely. She clapped and sang along with the music, taking in all the sights. With every bell and siren she loved it more—talking and laughing, eating ice cream and drinking in life.

Most of the people around them were also talking and laughing together. But here and there others seemed lost in their own worlds in the middle of all the confusion. Laura watched one young couple sitting in the corner as they ate their ice cream like mechanical people, hardly speaking to each other between bites. She looked back at her family—happy, animated faces and a genuine caring for each other. Different ages, different personalities drawn together by a common bond—love. No one in the room would guess that in a few short hours this animated little girl across from her would lose her leg. There wasn't a sign from her.

Laura saw a kind of dignity in Michelle she'd never noticed before. At eight years old, still a small child, she trusted Jesus enough to simply *accept* the loss of her leg and give Him the worry. She was honestly enjoying herself the night before surgery!

The ice cream was soon gone, but the glow in Michelle's eyes lingered for a long time. They dropped Laura's mother off at her home and continued along the darkened freeway toward the City of Hope. Kim was teaching Michelle a new song with help from their dad and Rick. And Laura listened, smiling to herself. She was proud of her nutsy children, proud of Dick, and glad to be part of these warm people who loved each other enough to set aside their own pain to help one who hurt more.

Riding along the freeway she looked out at the lights of homes lining the area all around them. *They look like diamonds on black velvet,* she thought. *I wonder if they're really as lovely and beautiful up close as they are from here. Some of those peaceful-looking homes must be falling apart inside, full of hurting people crying because somebody they love has died, or torn apart by divorce. . . . There must be abused, mistreated children in some of them and men or women hiding, afraid of alcoholic partners, maybe even fearing for their lives. Crime . . . drugs . . . hatred . . . loneliness. . . .*

Oh, Lord, she prayed as they sped toward the hospital, *what a pretense we all put up. Nobody in that restaurant could have guessed we hurt the way we do right now.* The silly song the family was singing broke into her thoughts again. The lustiest voice of all was Michelle's.

Tears rolled down Laura's face, hidden in the darkness. *Father, keep my pain in perspective. I want to hear the cries of those around me who hurt so much. Give me peace, and comfort so I can comfort others. Don't let me get so wrapped up in my own pain that I miss theirs. We need each other to get through this. And we need you.*

Laura's thoughts were interrupted when Dick turned the car through the entrance to the City of Hope. Apprehension rode with them, an unwanted passenger—a feeling one gets at the top of a high roller-coaster just before plunging to the bottom. A feeling with many faces and no single name.

The well-lit hospital ahead of them underscored the reality they'd pushed into the background all day. Everyone's secret wish was to wake up and find it had all been a nightmare; but to them reality *was* the nightmare.

Dick steered the car into a parking place near the children's wing, turned off the engine and pulled the keys slowly from the ignition. For a moment they sat in the darkened car, each with his own thoughts, no one wanting to step back inside the world of what was coming.

"I'm scared," Michelle said timidly. She sat rigidly staring into the darkness outside the car. Kim put both arms around her kid sister and held her tightly. She seemed so small.

"Oh, honey," Laura said touching Michelle's hand, "we understand how frightening this must be for you." The words sounded hollow to her as she spoke them. No one knew how frightened Michelle felt. No one could know except Michelle.

Finally with resolute determination Dick tightened his grip on the keys in his hand and opened the door wide. "It's been a great day," he said, his voice too cheerful, "but we gotta get back. C'mon, you guys."

Michelle sat on her bed with both feet straight out in front of her. She stared blankly at her dinner tray on the side table stretched in front of her. Running the tip of her spoon around the outside of the plate, she announced flatly, "I don't like peas."

"You don't have to eat them if you don't want to," Laura said absently, recrossing her legs and sighing quietly as she leaned back in the chair. She reached for one of the many cards standing on the night table and reread it. Michelle wrinkled her nose in distaste as she looked back at the pile of gray-green peas on her plate. She scooped three peas onto her spoon and looked at them closely. Then she turned the spoon around and flipped them into the air.

"I don't like peas," she said again scooping up a half-dozen more and flipping them off the spoon in like fashion. Finally realizing what was going on, Laura jumped up and sprung at the mischievous culprit.

"Mich-elle!" Laura was gifted at packing entire sermons into single words. The spoon clattered onto the thick crockery plate and terror filled Shelly's eyes. She grabbed her throat dramatically as Laura descended on her. Michelle's startled look, added to the electric tension everyone was under, broke everybody up. Laughter filled the room warming the apprehensive chill that hung silently around them.

"Sounds like things are going well in here," the tall man said widening his tiny mouth into a smile. "I'm Dr. Moor." He walked toward Dick extending his hand, "I'll be doing the surgery on Michelle in the morning."

"Shelly," Dick said standing beside her and putting his hands on her shoulders, "this is Dr. Moor. He's going to do your operation."

"Do you know Dr. Rosen?" she asked reaching up and circling one of Dick's fingers with her small fist.

Dr. Moor smiled again, "I know him very well. In fact, he's the one who called me up and asked if I'd come be your surgeon because he likes you so much. So we're going to be sure everything goes well tomorrow for you, Michelle."

They talked for awhile and discussed the procedures. Dr. Moor was at City of Hope on a fellowship and would be working with Dr. Ralph Byron through the entire surgery. His attitude was warm and friendly and Michelle liked him immediately.

After Dr. Moor left, Kim helped Michelle wash up and wiggle into a new pink nightgown with short puffed sleeves. She crawled up on the bed, grabbed Rabbit around the middle and settled back against the pillows. Her feet stuck out below the hem of her gown and she stared down at them wiggling her toes, smiling to herself.

"Can you do this, Kimmy?" she asked spreading all 10 toes apart. She opened her eyes and mouth wide with concentration.

"I'm just not that talented," Kim said settling into one of the rocking chairs. She looked at her sister's small foot briefly, then quickly looked away, forcing the thoughts out of her mind.

"I can do it," Michelle said as she spread wide her little pink toes and wiggled them slowly, watching as they moved back and forth. Her smile faded as she looked at her feet and in one quick motion she pulled the covers up over her legs and curled up on her side.

Dick and Laura looked painfully at each other. As Laura stood to go to Michelle, the door opened and in walked Joy Sutera, their friend from Children's Hospital.

"Anybody home?" she greeted, a smile lighting her face.

Michelle sprang to a sitting position at the sound of her favorite nurse's voice and squealed, "Oh, my old gray elephant! You remembered, you remembered to come!"

She held her arms up and Joy matched her enthusiastic embrace. Michelle clung tightly to Joy's neck as they rocked slowly from side to side enjoying the closeness.

Sitting down on the bed beside Michelle, Joy put her arm around the little girl and they leaned back against the pillows.

"They'll probably chase me out of here for sitting on the bed," Joy laughed, "but it'll be worth it, huh, Michelle?"

"I won't let them chase you out without me." She said snuggling into Joy's shoulder, hugging her again. "I'm so glad you came."

"We couldn't have asked for better medicine," Dick added sincerely.

"Or better timing," Laura said, sitting on the edge of the bed across from Joy and patting Joy's hand affectionately. "We're all glad you came, Joy."

"Well," Joy asked taking a quick look around the room, "how are they treating you, Michelle?"

"OK," she said sitting up, "but I still wish you were my nurse. I can't even race a wheelchair in the halls. They won't let me."

"Imagine that," Joy commented, her smile broadening.

Michelle pulled the covers back and turned around facing Joy, sitting cross-legged. Holding the hem of her nightgown out, she asked, "How do you like my new nightie?"

"It's very pretty! What's it say on the front?" She read, " 'Now I lay me down to sleep, I pray Thee, Lord, my soul to keep.' "

"He will too, Joy," Michelle said, nodding with emphasis.

"You're right, honey," Joy agreed. "When He makes a promise He keeps it, and He promised to stay with us always, didn't He"

"Even in the operating room tomorrow," Michelle said thoughtfully. "I won't have to be all by myself."

Other visitors came and went for a couple of hours that evening and there were numerous phone calls they all took turns answering. The evening slipped by quickly.

Finally Joy said, "It's time for me to go now, Michelle, but I'll be back real soon."

"Don't go, Joy," Michelle cried gripping Joy's hand tightly. "I want you to stay here."

"I'd love to, Michelle, but I can't," Joy answered softly. "But I'll tell you what I can do."

Michelle lowered her eyes in disappointment.

"I can pray for you, honey," Joy continued, "and I'll be doing just that. Everything is going to go exactly the way Jesus wants it tomorrow. And I'll be here with you in my heart, even though I have to be at work."

"I love you, Joy," Michelle said with tears in her eyes.

Joy held the little girl close, rocking slightly, burying her nose in Michelle's hair she said softly, "And I love you too, my little friend."

Good-byes were said around and as Joy approached the door Laura picked up her sweater. "Where are you going?" Joy asked.

"We're walking you to your car," Laura responded, "and it's cold outside."

"You don't have to walk me anywhere," Joy protested. "I'm a big girl. I'll be OK, honest."

"Now," Dick said, "you just listen to your 'mother' and you'll be fine."

Laura teased maternally, "Where's your sweater, young lady?"

"In the car."

"Well, it's not doing much good out there," Laura said in mock reprimand as she slipped her arm around Joy.

Each time Joy visited with the Price family they were becoming more and more a part of her, like adopted parents, and she loved it.

The three of them stood in the parking lot beside Joy's car and talked for several minutes. Dick stood behind Laura with his arms around her most of the time.

"You two are hard to believe," Joy said finally, opening her car door and rolling the window down a couple of inches. "Here we are enjoying each other's company, talking about *my* life. You're supposed to be telling me about *your* problems." Dick and Laura smiled a little self-consciously. "A nurse learns quickly," Joy continued. "Most people in your situation don't want to listen, they want to talk about their fears, about their pain."

She took their hands in her own, "I want you to know something. I've been a Christian a long time, and I've seen Christians under pressure in the hospital. Christ makes a difference in some of their lives, in others there's not much to see. But what He's doing in your lives and in Michelle's is incredible. He's using you in ways you'll probably never know. I came out here hoping to encourage you. I want you to know, I'm the one who's been encouraged."

They shared a warm hug and Dick squeezed Joy's hand tightly adding, "You're family with us, Joy. You're a special friend."

Very early the following morning a nurse walked softly into Michelle's room. Dick and Laura sat in two rocking chairs near her bed. Kim and Rick sat together on the window seat talking quietly.

"It's time for your medication, Michelle," the nurse said waking her.

Shelly, drowsy from medication she'd been given the night before, mumbled, "OK," and obediently rolled over for the shot.

As the nurse finished giving the injection, a man in green surgical clothes, his mask hanging loosely around his neck, walked through the door.

"Hi, Michelle, remember me? I'm Dr. Fisher, the anesthetist." Bending slightly over Michelle he said, "How are you feeling this morning?"

She sleepily opened her eyes and looked into his. They were black and clear and shaded by bushy eyebrows that nearly grew together. "I'm OK," she said to the man. "How are you doing?"

He smiled warmly and began to explain what he would be doing to make her sleep. "Do you understand what we're going to do then, Michelle?" he asked his sleepy patient.

"Uh-huh," she responded, her eyes closed again.

"Do you have any questions, honey?" he double-checked.

"Uh-huh," she said lifting heavy lids and looking right into his eyes, "Do I *have* to do this?"

He drew a slow, deep breath. "I wish I could say you didn't have to," he said taking her hand, "but if we don't get rid of that bad tumor in your leg you'll just get sicker and sicker, and finally you'll have to stay in bed all the time. That would be awful wouldn't it, Michelle?"

She looked steadily into his eyes thinking about what he'd said. "I guess it would," she answered finally, "but I don't want to be a cripple." Tears filled her eyes and her chin quivered slightly.

"After you heal from the operation," the doctor reassured her, "we're going to help you find a new leg that will work almost as good as the old one. I don't think you'll be a cripple. You aren't the kind of person who stops trying, and *quitting* is what cripples people. Shelly." He left, nodding to Dick and Laura as he walked through the door. Michelle looked at the closed door for a long time, then shut her eyes.

Before long a nurse and orderly rolled a gurney into the room, up beside the bed. "Time to go for a ride, Michelle," the nurse said. "Can you scoot over here on this table for me?"

They helped her onto the gurney, removed her nightgown and tossed it on the bed. The nurse opened a clean white sheet and draped it over Michelle's naked body. Laura thought how very small her daughter looked lying on the table.

The young orderly in surgical greens raised the sides of the gurney. "You can walk with us over to the other wing if you'd like to," he told the family. "I'm sure she'd like some company," he added maneuvering the gurney out the door and down the hall.

Michelle made groggy attempts at conversation in the elevator but had a hard time keeping her eyes open. They walked silently through the underground passage from the children's wing to the adult wing where surgery was. The big rubber wheels of the gurney made a whirring sound as they drew closer to the end of the underground hallway. Michelle held Kim's hand tightly as she watched the blurred lights slip past overhead. Dick kept a firm grip on Laura's arm.

"You need pictures on your walls," Michelle said loudly. "It's too dark in here."

"That's a great suggestion," her driver said. "We'll have to do something about that."

Approaching the end of the passage he stopped the gurney,

turned to the family and said, "I'm sorry, this is as far as you can go."

"We won't be very far away, honey," Dick said bending over her. "You keep being a great kid. Hear, Price?"

She smiled sleepily at him.

"Don't forget, Shelly," Laura said, "you're not alone in there. Jesus is right beside you." Her voice broke as she quickly kissed Michelle and stepped away from the gurney.

Rick and Kim did their best to send her off with a funny line and a smile, but as the gurney pulled up the corridor Rick doubled up his fist and smashed it into the wall, crying, "Why? Why! It isn't fair!" As the fury inside him began to subside he moved into the comfort of his father's arm. They turned slowly and began the long walk back through the tunnel to the room where they would wait.

Laura looked back down the corridor one last time. She saw the gurney rounding a corner, carrying a very small girl with two legs.

6
Life After Loss

Dick stood at the window of the waiting room looking across the road to the entrance of the building where Michelle was. Through the blinds he could see the fountain in the approach, its three figures—a mother, father and small child—their arms lifted high above them in a joyous expression of family love. Water sprayed around them, splashing into the crystal pool beneath, the mist settling gently on blooming rose bushes and other flowering plants all around.

He looked blankly at the fountain, unable to share its joyful feeling. Finally, he focused on the building where Michelle lay, still and sleeping by this time, under bright lights in an operating room. He knew she was in good hands, the best. But part of his daughter was dying even now as he stood thinking of her, and he was helpless to stop it.

And yet at the same time it was for living that the dying must be done. Without the death of this part of her, she would not live.

What a grim paradox, he thought to himself blinking back hot tears. The bronze statue family caught his attention fully. *There's got to be good time ahead somewhere,* he thought, trying to feel some measure of hope. Tears pushed into his eyes, *Oh, God, there's just got to be.*

From across the room Laura could see dark clouds forming beyond the window where Dick stood. The gray November sky was drab and dismal. She focused just inside the window studying her husband's outline against the gray sky. He looked so worn and tired. His shoulders drooped slightly and he sighed heavily, and often. Her feelings matched the mood she sensed from him.

I feel about as blah as the day looks, she thought sadly. She drew a slow, expansive breath and tried to loosen the tension in her neck and shoulders a little. She realized she'd been "tight" almost constantly since this whole thing began. How long was it now? Two weeks? Only two weeks?

It seemed impossible that just two short weeks ago they'd been leading rather normal lives. No hospitals, now that Rick was well again. No tests or cancer. None of this pain for Shelly. *How can one little girl take all this, Lord?* she wondered. *Maybe Rick's right. It shouldn't have been Michelle.* She thought about what she'd just said, and Who she'd said it to. *I don't mean to tell you how to run things, but. . . .* The hot tears started down her pale cheeks. *She's just a baby, Lord. Her whole life ahead of her. One leg! Oh, Lord, I wish it could have been me instead.*

The tenseness in her shoulders tightened into knots and her head began to throb as she brushed her tears away quickly. "Kim," she said softly.

Kim looked up from a dog-eared *Ladies' Home Journal.*

"Would you rub my neck for me?" she asked hopefully. "I'm really stiff. . . ."

"Sure," Kim said, setting the magazine on the end table beside her and walking behind Laura's chair.

"I can wait if you're reading," Laura added.

"I've just about got that article memorized—maybe even the whole magazine," she responded beginning to move her fingers up and down along Laura's tight muscles. Slowly she began to relax under Kim's touch.

"I think hospitals should keep only new magazines for people," Kim chatted absently. "I read that one when Rick was in the hospital, and it was two months old then."

Dick caught Kim's remark and smiled slightly as he moved to the couch beside Rick. He leaned back against the light green wall and welcomed the coolness. "Things are sure different than they were with you, son."

"Different?" Rick responded a little puzzled.

"Well," Dick said sighing heavily, sorting through his thoughts, "to begin with, we weren't given any choice in whether we would give you up. When we got to the hospital you were already 'gone.' We had to trust God to give you *back* to us."

"And with Michelle," Rick said following Dick's comparison, "we've gotta give her up and she doesn't even look sick."

"Yeah," Kim added. "It's almost like we did it to her ourselves."

Ken and Nancy Millett entered the room breaking the tedious waiting. "You don't know how good it is to see you," Laura said sharing a hearty hug with Nancy.

Dick stood up and wrapped both arms around his friend, "Ken, Nancy, thanks for coming."

"Dick," Nancy said slipping her arm under his and squeezing his hand, "we couldn't have stayed home. You know that."

"I've gotta admit," Ken added, settling onto the couch next to Rick, "we'd prefer being with you at a ball game or over dinner someplace. We're just sorry it has to be for this."

"We know," Laura said. "We'd give anything to change it. But in spite of everything, God's peace is so real to us. Especially to Michelle."

"You know, I was just thinking," Dick said furrowing his brow slightly, "a few years ago Shelly told me something I'd almost forgotten. It makes sense now."

"What'd she say?" Ken asked.

"She said, 'Daddy, something very serious is going to happen to me someday. I know Jesus has something important for me to do.' " For a long time no one spoke.

Laura glanced at the orange enamel wall clock for what seemed the hundredth time that morning. The hands weren't moving fast enough. What was taking so long in there? Where was that doctor, telling them that everything was over, that everything was going to be fine? She watched the gray sky grow darker until rain wept onto the roses outside the window.

They talked easily with Ken and Nancy. It meant so much to have friends sharing their hopes and fears. Sharing some of the things Michelle had said and her attitude of acceptance made the whole thing a little easier. Dick and Laura, without a doubt, were concerned about Michelle's circumstances but they believed and acted on God's promises of provision. Through the whole morning they experienced a deep and continuous peace, almost the same as what they had known when Rick was so ill. There was sadness but an unexplainable peace ran underneath everything. Visitors found themselves bouyed up by the faith they saw upholding this family in their time of need.

Several hours passed before Dr. Moor, the surgeon, pushed the door to the waiting room open and walked in. He still wore his greens but had pulled a white lab coat over them and stood with his hands stuffed in the pockets. A surgical mask hung limply around his neck.

"She's in recovery and she's doing well," he began.

"She's alright?" Laura questioned anxious to hear the words.

"She's just fine," Dr. Moor said reassuringly. "She's a little trouper, that one." He shook his head reflecting on Michelle's cooperative attitude from the beginning.

"The surgery went well," he continued. "We removed the leg four to five inches above the knee joint, just as we planned, and there didn't appear to be any sign of tumor spread. It looks like we got it all but we'll have the lab follow through on that. We'll know more in a day or two."

"How soon can we see her?" Kim asked taking Laura's hand and holding it tightly.

The doctor spoke as he drew the door open again, "You could go back to her room anytime. She'll be there within the hour."

"Doctor," Dick said walking toward the surgeon, "thank you, for everything."

"I'm sure we did the right thing," Dr. Moor responded. "I'd have done the same if she were my daughter." He paused, then added, "I'll be back later to check on her," and he was gone.

"Thank you, Lord," Laura sighed, "she made it! I just hope they got it all."

"Dr. Moor seemed to think they did," Kim reassured. "I don't think we ought to even worry about it."

"Let's not worry about anything now," Rick added. "We've all worried enough today to give it up for good."

"I can't believe how much better I feel just knowing Shelly's OK," Kim said as they made their way slowly through the halls to room

146. "But it's going to be so hard to see her . . . without . . ." She groped for better words, but there were none, "without her leg." Tears quickly filled her eyes.

"Kimmy, you're going to do fine," Dick comforted. "We'll just all have to lean heavy on the Lord for what's ahead of us. You'll make it."

"We're all going to make it!" Laura added softly, putting her arm around Kim.

Waiting in Michelle's room Kim looked around. The ceiling was very high with a large skylight over the bed. She guessed that was because it was an inside room, with the only window looking directly into the nurse's station. Room 146 was one of the rooms where very ill patients and those requiring close observation were assigned, and Shelly would be here for several days.

The oatmeal-colored floor tiles echoed under hard-soled shoes, making the entire room feel somewhat like a stage, with the nurse's station at the window a kind of audience, a fishbowl feeling.

In an hour or so a nurse and orderly worked their way into the room wheeling the cumbersome hospital gurney tightly against the bed. They went silently about their business avoiding the eyes of the family.

Michelle lay sleeping in the middle of the big sterile looking cart, her small naked body draped loosely with a sheet. The color had drained from her face and her eyes were closed. They told them she would be under the effects of the anesthesia for some time yet, slipping in and out of dreams.

Stepping to the head of the cart the nurse deftly shifted the IV paraphernalia from the gurney stand to the bed. The only sounds in the room were the occasional clinking of glass and metal and the sound of her rubber-soled shoes squeezing against the floor tiles.

They saw it at the same time. No one wanted to see it at all, but their eyes were drawn to it. The sheet over Michelle dipped vacantly on both sides of her left leg and silently confronted them. Her leg was really gone.

Laura covered a cry with her hand and turned her face into Dick's shoulder. He slowly closed his eyes, shutting out what he could not bear to see. It was so hard to breathe, and there was a tingling sensation in his chest and at the base of his skull. A heavy feeling sank over all of them like a fog settling on a city, cutting off the sun.

Slumping onto the window seat Kim buried her face in her hands crying without a sound. While Rick stood looking at his small sister, the pain he felt surging within mingled with his anger. He turned quickly and bolted from the room. Outside the door he ran a few feet down the hall, then, overcome with weakness he let himself fall against the wall, dropping his forehead against the cold plaster. His arms stretched upward on the wall as he sobbed, "Why, God? Why Michelle? It should have been me, not her. It should have been me." He cried as he once had as a small boy, letting go the walled-in rage, feeling it turn to grief and finally to a vapor of nothingness that covered over the stinging raw feelings inside him.

In the room, at her bedside, the orderly deftly lifted Michelle from the gurney. His shoulders arched slightly, supporting the little girl in his arms. He'd done it so many times before but every one he'd seen, each child he'd touched this way somehow seemed to touch him too. Perhaps it was their helplessness; maybe they just made him remember that he could be the one who was wracked with pain, or had lost an arm or leg. He laid her on the bed. She sleepily looked up as she sank into the cool pillows. Pain shot through her when her stitches bumped the mattress and her face grimaced in protest; then she drifted silently back to sleep.

She slept most of the day as the family dried their tears and resolved they would grow into the changes that lay before them together. They knew it wasn't going to be easy.

Mid-afternoon she opened her eyes to streaks of sunlight coming through the overhead skylight. She watched as tiny particles danced in the warm cylinders of light over her head. Taking a deep breath, she stretched her ribs as wide as she could. She felt like she'd been sleeping a long time.

Laura sat beside her vacantly thumbing through a children's book she'd picked up to give her hands something to do. As Michelle sighed she looked up. "Well," Laura said closing the book and setting it in her lap, "you're awake."

Michelle looked at her mother and sighed again. Then, as if reality had just pushed an unwanted thought into her mind she blinked and looked away, eyes wide. She tightened the muscles in her cheeks and set her jaw. Grabbing the sheet in both hands she lifted the covers, raised her head and painfully drew her eyes to focus on the bandaged stump at the end of her thigh. Her eyes grew dark as she sank back against the pillow and let the sheet settle around her on the bed.

"Oh, Mommy," she cried closing her eyes. Tears squeezed out under her lids and ran down her face onto the pillow. Laura reached between the side rails for the little hand lying limp on the bed. Michelle was trembling as Laura circled her hand with both of her own and leaned forward, her elbows on the bed.

"It's going to be alright, Shelly," she encouraged. "You'll see." Tears swam in Laura's eyes—*if only she didn't have to hurt so on top of everything else*. "It's going to be alright."

Michelle took hold of Laura's hand and watched the shafts of sunlight again for a few minutes. "I heard the voices in the operating room," she said matter-of-factly. "I saw bright lights when I got on the big table." She turned toward Laura and snuggled into her pillow a little more. "It was so-o-o cold in there," she said pulling the blankets around her chin for emphasis. "But the table was warm, real warm."

"The operating table?" Laura questioned a little surprised that Michelle remembered so much.

"I guess so. I wonder if they heat it for you."

"Maybe so."

"Mommy," she confided, "I was so scared."

Laura squeezed Michelle's hand a little tighter. "I know you were, honey. We've all been scared."

"And I was the only little kid in there. I only saw people with masks on their faces. I couldn't even tell if I knew anybody, except Dr. Moor. He talked to me for awhile." She looked past Laura's shoulder into space. She didn't notice the rest of the family nor their concerned expressions. "I really wasn't all alone . . . Jesus was there with me, I knew He was."

In a few minutes she closed her eyes and before long was sleeping fitfully. She struggled with some unseen predator and made mournful groans in her sleep. Without warning she jerked herself awake, seized with searing pain. The leg they had taken was sending signals to her brain that it was knotted into painful spasms, cramping and pulling at muscles that were no longer there, like someone using both hands to pull her toes apart.

Startled and afraid she pulled her leg upward grabbing at it with both hands. "Oh-h-h," she moaned in pain and fright, "oh, it hurts. It hurts! Somebody's pulling my toes apart!"

Laura pushed herself out of the chair gripped with fear. "What is it, Shelly?" she asked over the painful cries. "What's wrong?"

"My leg. My leg," she cried rolling from side to side, her face lined with pain and perspiration.

"Your good leg?" Laura asked trying to calm the child, trying to understand what was happening.

"No," she cried. "It's all cramped up. It hurts, oh, it hurts." Her face wet with tears, her hair damp with perspiration. The pain was relentless. It seared and twisted, burning its way through her body.

Through the viewing window the nurse on duty knowingly assessed the trouble, pushed away from the desk and reached for Michelle's chart. Then she and the medication nurse each used their keys on the double-locked cabinet that guarded the narcotics. Drawing out the prescribed amount into a sterile syringe and locking the narcotics cupboard, she ran into Michelle's room.

"Here's something for the pain, honey," she said pulling back the sheet. She opened the little alcohol sponge and swabbed an area on Michelle's hip then quickly and skillfully slid the needle into her flesh. The clear medication disappeared under the skin and in a few minutes began to dull the pain.

"Remember what Dr. Rosen told you about phantom pain?" the nurse asked, stroking Michelle's forehead, pushing aside her damp curls. "That's what's happening, Michelle. The nerve endings in the leg that's gone are telling your brain something is wrong, all the feelings are different now. But it takes a long time for the parts in your brain that used to get the messages from your leg to understand that it's not there anymore."

"But I really had a charley horse; I could *feel* it all hard and in knots," Michelle justified.

"I know you did," the young woman answered. "Your brain is all mixed up now, and it will tell you you have charley horses, or that your foot itches, or that it's gone to sleep."

"And that's all in my head?" she asked.

"Uh-huh," she nodded, "all in your head."

"Maybe my foot really does itch," she said half wondering. She paused thoughtfully, "What did they do with my leg?" She looked for an answer in the nurse's eyes.

The uniformed woman swallowed hard and sat down beside Michelle. "Sometimes," she began, "they study a leg or arm to discover more things about the disease."

"That's what I want them to do," Shelly said seriously, "then other kids won't lose their legs. They'll have new medicines instead, to make them better."

"That's right," the nurse agreed, "wouldn't that be wonderful?" She studied her small patient's eyes. She could tell Michelle's question was still partly unanswered, so she continued, "And, after they study it as much as they can they'll bury it, or burn it . . ."

"I don't want them to burn up my leg," Michelle said, shocked. "I want it to be buried."

"Then that's what we'll tell them to do." The nurse stood up, slipping her hand into the pocket of her uniform. "I'll tell them we want them to study it first and then bury it when they've finished. OK?"

"OK," Michelle said, then added as the nurse walked through the door, "don't let them burn it." The look on her face was a mixture of hope and fear. She watched the door for a long time after it closed behind the nurse.

The following morning Dr. Rosen ordered the postop IV discontinued. Karen, the nurse removing the confining equipment from Michelle's arm, said without looking at Michelle, "We're going to get you up and walk you to the bathroom."

Michelle looked a little puzzled but waited to see what was coming next. The other nurse came alongside and dropped the railing on the bed. She helped her sit up and swing her leg over the side.

"The room's going around," Shelly said grabbing the bedclothes to steady herself. "I feel funny."

"You're still dizzy from the medicine you've been getting," the nurse said as she wrapped an arm around her tiny patient and eased Michelle to the floor.

Karen moved in close to Michelle's other side, "Just hold onto us. Hold tight."

Michelle wrapped an arm around each nurse's waist trying to gain her balance. The nurses stepped away from the bed and as Michelle tried to catch up to them she automatically shifted her weight to take a step. But she cried out as searing pain shot through her from the newly severed muscles. Without her viselike grip on the nurses she would have fallen. The pain was incredible as she tried earnestly to hop between her escorts; she felt and looked awkward lunging toward the bathroom, clinging tightly to the uniformed women beside her. Frustration and pain filled her eyes as she remembered that only hours before she would have been able to run these few steps from her bed without thinking about it. But she was so limited, so dependent. She felt helpless and embarrassed.

Dick and Laura watched, struggling to hold back their tears. Kim left the room.

"Why don't you and Mom take a walk too?" Rick suggested. "I'll be here if Michelle needs anything."

"Thanks, son," Dick said taking Laura by the hand. "We could use a break. C'mon, honey."

They walked down the hall to the family kitchen. Dick pulled open the refrigerator, took a bottle of pop out and set it on the sink. Laura reached for the paper cups at the bottom of the dispenser and folded her arms holding the cups against her shoulder.

"She looked so . . . awkward, so pitiful," she said looking at the floor, "like a clumsy little bird."

"She'll get better at it," Dick said without looking at her. "It's only her first try."

"I know," Laura said, disagreement in her voice. He took the cups from her and poured them each some of the 7Up he held. "I'd feel awful if she knew how I feel right now," she said, absently watching the bubbles rise and burst at the surface inside the cup. "She'd really be hurt if she knew how hard it is to look at her like that," she added with frustration.

"She doesn't need to know," he said. "She's a strong kid, Laurie." He took her arm gently, "A lot like her mother."

Laura looked at Dick and realized she hadn't focused on him or anything else for a long time. She was glad she had Dick with her in this. They seemed to complement each other most of the time, one was up when the other was down. She wondered how anyone made it through this kind of thing alone, or without God to give meaning to the senseless things that happen.

She set the paper cup on the counter and put both arms around her husband. Neither of them said a word. They didn't need words.

As they walked slowly back into the hall they saw Kim quickly turn the corner into Michelle's room ahead of them. A child's cries met them as they started back down the carpeted hallway.

"Was that Michelle?" Laura asked. They both quickened their pace knowing it was her cry. Pushing open the door on a dead run, they saw Michelle writhing in agony, twisting and turning in a private phantom hell. Sitting beside her talking gently, soothing her little sister, Kim stroked Michelle's back and neck while Rick stood close by, his concern written in his eyes.

"Let's try something," Kim said. "I'm going to rub the leg that's gone."

"You can't," Michelle said squeezing her eyes tightly, then opening them, curious in spite of the pain.

"Let's pretend. Let's play like it's still there, and see if I can rub the pain away."

"It's the back of my leg," she said willing to try anything that would bring relief.

Kim rubbed the back of the imaginary leg, stroking and kneading a badly cramped muscle. Amazingly, Shelly felt some relief. Experimenting in the next few days, they found that when the missing leg itched, scratching the other leg in a corresponding spot sometimes stopped the sensation.

"You've got the magic touch, Kim," Dick said as he watched Michelle relax with Kim's patient massage and quieting influence.

"Yeah," Michelle said, breathing easier, "you're pretty good."

Nurses encouraged her to get up and move around more and more, which Michelle was eager to do. Being sick was never something she took to kindly.

By the third day after surgery she was spending time in the hospital playroom. Bookshelves lining the walls were filled with books for all levels of interest and ability. A blue rug covered the biggest section of the floor; white tiles set apart the game area. The white modern furniture was scaled down to the size of the small-fry patients who used the room, and bright-colored cushions were scattered around on the chairs and floor.

7

Michelle arranged herself at the pedestal table in the center of the carpet and was coloring a springtime scene with an assortment of felt-tip markers on a page of one of the giant coloring books. Laura was curled up on the other side of the table in a comfortable rocker upholstered in a warm blue fabric. She watched as Michelle, absorbed in eliminating black and white, suddenly shifted her attention.

Glancing down at the bandages taped over the end of her stump, Michelle raised her short leg, gently resting it against the edge of the table. With a dark marker she sketched eyes, a nose and a wry little smile onto the white bandage, then laid the marker back on the table. She looked at the little face for a moment then pulled the leg against her, circling it with both arms and rocking back and forth, humming a lullaby as if she held a baby.

"Is that your baby?" Laura asked.

"This is 'little leg,' " Shelly answered. Lifting it high so Laura could see, she pointed to the marks she'd drawn. "I gave it a happy face. It looks like a baby."

Dr. Rosen simply shook his head when Laura told him what Michelle had done. "That's incredible," he said. "It's usually a period of weeks, sometimes even longer before an amputee will even look at himself, let alone begin to *accept* the changes. Three days! It's really hard to believe. She's accepting everything so quickly. It's almost as though she accepted it before it happened."

A smile crept across his lips as he pictured Michelle with her arms gently holding the stump, rocking back and forth, showing her acceptance and courage. "This is one little girl who's going to make it!"

7

A Newborn Sparrow

Five days after surgery Michelle's progress was rated as excellent. The wound was healing well, her spirits were good, she was handling the nearly constant bouts of phantom pain better all the time and was requiring less pain medication. It was a positive picture except for one thing: this was the first day of chemotherapy.

"Usually," Dr. Rosen told Dick and Laura as they shared a cup of coffee, "we administer Methotrexate, the medication Michelle will be getting this time, in milligram doses. We're giving her a gram dosage, a thousand times greater than what we give adults."

"Why so much," Dick asked, understandably worried at the unusual dosage. "Isn't that a lethal amount?"

"The cancer in her body is a killer. It spreads fast and when it strikes it hits hard and quick." Dr. Rosen ran his fingers slowly through his dark hair, carefully choosing the best words to answer Dick's question. "It is a lethal dosage, Mr. Price, but this medication in any amount is potentially destructive. That's why we follow it closely with an antidote to neutralize the effects of the Methotrexate before it has a chance to destroy healthy cells."

"What can we expect?" Laura asked looking steadily into Dr. Rosen's eyes.

He returned her intensity over the top of the little dark-framed Ben Franklin glasses he wore. "You will see her nauseated, and vomiting. She will experience chills and possibly trembling. Later on she may lose her hair."

"Will it grow back again?" Dick asked.

"Sometimes it does, other times it doesn't. It will depend on many things."

"If she's bald she'll look like a little newborn sparrow hopping around the house," Laura said, picturing Michelle without her hair.

The doctor looked at these two people he had spent so many hours with in the past two weeks. Laura and Kim had been there nearly the entire time, while Dick and Rick came as much as possible around their jobs. There were times when they had been afraid but they were always willing to ask questions, to learn what they could to help Michelle. They were grieved and yet able to direct their love to others around them who hurt also. So many families came here and built cocoon-like barriers around themselves. This family worked hard to keep others close to them, to keep their own pain in perspective with the rest of the world.

"Without chemotherapy," Dr. Rosen said compassionately, "we run the risk that wild cells may have broken away from the tumor before we got it. They could attack her lungs, other bone areas, even her brain. We can't take chances like that with Michelle." He added thoughtfully, "We just can't risk it." He did not wait for them to speak, but stood and quickly walked away.

"Michelle," the curly-haired man said pulling a chair closer to her bed later that morning, "I'm Dr. Kramer. We're going to start your chemotherapy today." He took her hand in his and patted it.

"Let me explain how all of this works," he said gesturing toward the IV apparatus brought in a few minutes before he arrived.

"I already know about IVs," she said quickly. "I've had them before."

"Good," he said, nodding approval. "Then all that's different is how the medicine we're giving you works. You're getting a medicine that's going to go through your whole body hunting for bad cells that might have gotten away from the tumor before we took it. The medicine will catch those cells and destroy them."

"Like my cat does with a mouse?" she asked hesitantly, a little puzzled.

"Yes, exactly like that," he agreed. "That's a very good way to put it."

He explained that the first medicine would be given some time to work alone, then she'd get a second medicine which would stop the first one before it could hurt any good cells. "All this is a little bit like a war inside you, and you may feel very sick for a few days. We'll do our best to help you feel better as soon as possible."

"Now," he said walking the equipment over to her bedside, "do you have any questions you want to ask me?"

"How long do I have to have the IV?" she asked sitting up. "I can't use my arm good when it's taped on that board."

"You'll probably feel like resting most of the time, but we'll take it off as soon as we can," he answered, opening a sterile needle. "It's going to be several days though before we can do that."

She shrugged and made a face but did as he asked. He took her hand in his and began swabbing the skin over the vein he'd chosen. "Did I answer your question?"

"I guess," she answered watching him push the needle under her skin. "But I'd rather be riding a horse."

"Do you have a horse?" he asked, attaching the IV tubing and taping it in place.

"Not my own," she said settling back against the pillow, "but I'm going to raise horses someday, and I'm gonna be a famous trick rider."

"You know what," he said, tapping the IV bottle with his index finger to start the drip, "I'll bet you make it too."

He stood beside the bed double-checking the apparatus and timing the drip until it was operating the way it should. Each drip falling through the tubing triggered a small regulator making a sub-dued beeping sound. He set a box of tissue and a blue molded emesis basin beside her pillow in easy reach. "I'll be back to check on you in a little while," he said, winking at her over his shoulder. Then he slipped out the door.

Michelle watched the yellow liquid dripping slowly through the clear plastic tubing from over her head. The beeping was slow and even as the fluid ran slowly into her arm. She lay very still for several minutes before she quietly said, "Mommy, I feel funny."

Laura sat down beside her on the bed just in time to grab the emesis basin and hold it while Michelle lost her breakfast. Then suddenly she was gripped with driving pains in her stomach and chills that ran through her body so strongly she shook the sturdy hospital bed like an earthquake. In pain she drew her knee to her chest and held it tightly against her stomach. Laura was amazed at how rapidly the medication had reacted in Michelle and even though Dr. Rosen told them what to expect she was gripped with panic and fear at the signs of the child's violent illness.

"Dear Lord, help her," she prayed, tears rising in her eyes. "She's so sick, Father. Please help her make it through this. Help me to know what to do to make it easier for her."

The next few days were more of the same. Michelle remained violently ill, vomiting, chills, sieges of trembling. The light hurt her eyes and she asked to have the drapes pulled all the time. As Dick sat beside her in the darkened room she woke from a restless sleep.

"How you feelin', honey?" he asked, moving beside her on the bed and putting his hand on her shoulder. She'd been so ill she was losing weight and her little arms seemed smaller than ever to his big hand.

"Doin' OK," she answered. Always "doin' OK," in case she'd make someone else feel bad.

"Daddy," she said in a half-whisper, "did I ever tell you about my dream?"

"What dream is that?"

"I had a dream for a long time that someday I would be Miss America or somebody." She paused and grimaced as the pains began again in her stomach. "I guess I'll have to find a new dream now," she said sadly. "I don't think Miss America ever has one leg."

"Torture, that's what it is," Laura said, tears spilling down her cheeks. "She just lies there with her eyes closed in that dark room. She's been vomiting four days. It's got to stop. How much more can she take?"

"I know, Mom," Kim said, holding the outside door for Laura to walk through. "It's so hard to watch her lying there. She just takes it. I wish she'd have a fit or throw a temper tantrum. It would be easier for me to handle." Kim's own eyes swam with tears.

"Four days," Laura said again, going back over the long hours in her mind. "If she's not better tomorrow I'm going to . . ." Her voice trailed off as a lump formed in her throat. What could she possibly do?

It always upset Kim to see her mother cry. She glanced at Laura and made an attempt at changing the subject. "She sure seems to brighten when Dr. Rosen or Dr. Moor comes by to see her." She thought for a moment, then added almost under her breath, "If it was me I'm not sure I'd be so happy to see them."

"Yeah, she really seems to love them," Laura added as they walked into the cafeteria, "the very men who took her leg."

They stood in silence, their arms around each other. Kim blew her nose and patted at her eyes with a tissue. Laura was lost in her own thoughts as they selected their salads and took a table. "You know, honey," she said, shaking salt on her lunch, "we asked the Lord to heal Michelle hoping she wouldn't lose her leg."

"But He didn't do that," Kim said wondering where Laura was leading.

"But I think He's done something else we asked Him for," she added sounding excited. "I think He's given her a special ability to accept what she has to go through instead."

"You know, I think you're right. How else would she be able to love the very people who make her hurt?" Kim added in agreement. "In fact, everybody I talk to around here asks about her and they all make some sort of comment about her 'spirit,' how positive she is."

"Uh-huh," Laura said, thinking about it, "I've noticed that too."

Kim tapped her straw on the table pushing it up through the paper wrapper. "Last night one of the doctors wanted to know what you and Daddy did with her to make her take it so well."

"What'd you tell him?" Laura asked.

Kim looked at her mother and made a face, "Well, first of all, *he* was a *she* and I told *her* I didn't think you did anything out of the ordinary. We've all been raised to trust God to take care of everything in our lives, and that's what Shelly's doing."

Laura set her fork on her plate and dabbed the corner of her mouth with her napkin. She looked at Kim, "How'd she take that?"

"Oh, you know," she said, looking out of the corner of her eye to demonstrate the doctor's response. "She was a little skeptical."

They smiled together. "It's funny, isn't it," Laura added, "how just simply trusting God never seems like enough of an answer to be an answer?"

"You know," Kim said, absently stirring her Coke with her straw, "last night I was sitting with her after you and Daddy had gone and I had my eyes closed. I guess she thought I was asleep and she started praying. Remember how you told her about the goldfish being sick at home?"

"Uh-huh."

"Well," Kim continued, "last night she said 'Dear Jesus, will you take care of the disease our goldfish have? If you don't, I'll understand.' " Kim looked away and continued, "Then she got kind of quiet and said, 'And Jesus, about what I have, take care of my disease. If you don't, I'll understand.' "

They sat in silence for several minutes, then Kim said in hushed tones, "I don't know how anybody gets through something like this without Him. I'd go crazy."

Laura reached across the table for Kim's hand. "Honey," she said quietly, "as long as we've got God we can make it through anything we have to. But I'm glad you're here too. Your faith through all this and with Rick has helped keep Daddy and me strong. We love you, Kimmy." Kim squeezed Laura's hand in response. It was good to breathe deeply together.

When they walked into Michelle's room a little later, Dr. Moor, on his evening rounds, was sitting with his legs crossed on the edge of Michelle's bed. He seemed to be enjoying her animated and continuous chatter.

"So you think you're feeling better tonight," he said, listening to her heart with his stethoscope.

"I *know* I am," she assured him quickly. "Know how I know?"

He shook his head looking very serious.

"I've been thinking about *eating* something," she said, dramatically hoping he'd be glad to hear her appetite was returning. Kim and Laura glanced at each other excited by the obvious change in Michelle.

He was indeed glad to hear such good news. Taking the earpieces out of his ears and folding up the apparatus, he asked, "Something like what?"

Michelle slipped the stethoscope out of his hand and moved

closer to listen to the doctor's heart. "Like a Popsicle or a dish of ice cream maybe." Tired from the exertion of sitting up she leaned back against the pillows and slid down under the covers. With the cold chrome disk on her own chest she listened intently.

"Everything OK?" he asked as she handed it back to him.

She nodded looking very important, "And *your* heart is very good too."

"Well, that's good to hear," he responded, standing to leave, and smiling at her warmly. "Maybe even deserves an ice cream celebration. I'll see what I can do."

"I'm not going to have chemotherapy anymore, Dr. Moor," she said looking up at him.

"Oh, really," he said looking a little surprised. "When did you decide that?"

"I don't need it anymore," she continued, "I'm all well now."

"How do you know that, Michelle?"

"Because," she said choosing her words precisely, "Jesus told me I was going to be all well. He's healed me."

The surgeon sat back down on the bed and spoke gently and directly, "Michelle, it's very hard to go through chemotherapy. You don't suppose that you . . ." he searched for the right words, "If you were better you wouldn't need any more treatments, right?"

"Right," Michelle answered. "But, Dr. Moor, I didn't say that because I don't want any more treatments. I said it because Jesus told me I'm well."

"I believe you, honey," he said gently, "but I think we'd better go ahead and finish the chemotherapy anyway, just to make real sure we've done everything we could to help get rid of the cancer. Jesus could have made you completely well already, but I think He'd want you to finish the treatments."

"OK," she said sliding further down the pillow, "but I'm already better, you'll see."

"Have you told Dr. Rosen about this?" Dr. Moor asked, standing again to leave.

"No," she said seriously, "he wouldn't understand."

"Why not?" he asked surprised at her comment.

"Because he wouldn't believe the part about Jesus. He's still looking for the Messiah, you know."

Dr. Moor clung to his composure until he was outside the room but broke into a hearty laugh when he was far enough away. *What a girl,* he thought shaking his head, still smiling. *I hope she has been healed.* Soberly he thought, *We just can't lose this one.*

The lab technician who had come several times a day for the past five days appeared at the door before breakfast one week after chemotherapy was started.

"It's me again," she said flashing a wide grin at Michelle. She was a pretty black girl Kim guessed to be in her early twenties.

"You sure must like blood a lot," Michelle teased, watching the technician tie the rubber tourniquet around her upper arm.

"Well," she said over the needle cap she held between her teeth momentarily, "nobody's supposed to know this, but I'm a vampire." She smoothly slid the sharp needle under the skin and into the vein, then released the band holding back the blood flow. Pulling back on the plunger she looked Michelle in the eye and made a scary face.

"I already knew," Michelle said trying not to laugh. "But I'm gonna call you Dracula from now on."

The syringe was full and the technician moved expertly through the final steps of the test. "Oh, no," she mockingly pled, "if you do that everyone will know my true identity."

"That's what you get for being a vampire, Dracula," Michelle grinned.

"Guess so," she said moving to the door. "See you later."

She stepped outside, then peeked around the door and added, "Oh, by the way, Dr. Rosen said if this is the right flavor you can go home today. How about that?"

The report came through showing that medication levels from the chemotherapy were in a safe range. About 10 o'clock, Dr. Rosen pushed open the door to Michelle's room, smiling broadly.

"How would you like to take your parents and go home for awhile?" he said taking her hand.

"Can I really?" she asked almost afraid to believe what she was hearing. It had been a little over four weeks since all this began. "I feel like I've been here forever."

"I'll bet you'll be glad to see your own room again, won't you?"

Michelle flung back the covers and reached up to the doctor's shoulders. Holding on with both hands she stood on the bed beside him and threw both arms soundly around the man's neck.

"I can't wait," she squealed excitedly. "I can't wait!"

Pulling into the driveway Dick barely stopped the car when Michelle had the door open wide and was standing outside balancing in the wedge of the door.

"Give me my crutches," she pressed in her excitement. "Hurry, Mommy. Lady hasn't ever even seen me. Give me my crutches."

"Just hold your horses, Price," Dick said, pulling the emergency brake into position and getting out his door.

"I'm doing the best I can," Laura said. "You have to be patient."

"I'm *not* a patient anymore," she said pumping toward the front door, her empty pant leg flapping wildly, "*I'm home!*"

"I meant . . ." Laura started to explain, but gave up and leaned against the seat watching Michelle enthusiastically working her way up the walk she had always run before. A sting of loss pierced Laura's happy aura, but only for a moment. Michelle was home and that was all that counted.

"You alright, Mom?" Kim asked, coming back to the car.

"I'm coming," she answered. "I'm just getting my breath."

Lady was excited about meeting Michelle, and from the first minute she was Michelle's dog and faithful friend, a sturdy collie mixture whose favorite pastime was thoroughly licking Shelly's face anytime she got the chance.

"Let's take her for a walk, Daddy," Michelle said, already hopping after the bright new leash.

"Don't you think that's a little bit too much for your first day home?" he cautioned.

"Please?" she begged. "Mommy, tell him it's OK. We won't be gone long, just down to the end of the street and back. Please?"

"You'll take it easy the rest of the day then, OK?" Laura bargained.

"OK!" she chirped, dropping to her knee beside Lady to fasten the leash to her collar. Lady gratefully licked her face and wiggled in anticipation.

"Alright, but just our street," Dick said offering Michelle a steadying hand. "*You* may feel like a hike, Price," he teased as they stepped onto the porch, "but I'm an old man, and I'm tired."

Shelly maneuvered down the path, leash and crutch in her right hand, tugging at Dick's slowness with her left.

As they swung onto the sidewalk and began their way up the street several neighbors were watering lawns or hauling empty trash barrels back into their yards. Friendly hellos were shouted but no one seemed to have the time for the usual chat a walk always produced.

"Daddy," Michelle said on the way back to the house, "I think they feel uncomfortable because of my leg."

Dick responded, a little surprised at his daughter's intuitive comment, "I think you may be right."

Dick listened to the unevenness of the crutch sound and Shelly's one shoe as they walked a little way in silence.

"Daddy," she asked as they neared the house, "will you take a walk with me when you get back from work tomorrow?"

"Sure, honey," he said turning up the walk. Lady slowly followed, unwilling to end their walk so soon. "Lady didn't get enough today."

"It's not for Lady," Michelle said thoughtfully. "I want to go around to the neighbors and tell them what happened to my leg. Maybe they'll feel better then."

He turned to say something but Michelle had dropped her crutch in the entryway and was hopping toward her room with Lady hot on her heel.

"My animals," she cheered loudly, "I've missed you, all of you!"

8
Maiden Flight

As Dick turned off the car ignition the next evening, Michelle burst down the walk toward him.

"Are you ready?" she sputtered. "Can we take our walk now?"

"Does Mom know we're going?" he asked, hoping for at least a short delay. He was not looking forward to this "walk."

"She knows, and she said dinner will wait." She'd covered all the angles as usual. "Come on, Daddy, let's go."

They crossed the street and approached the shrub-lined walk together. The single-story stucco house seemed suddenly unfamiliar and foreign to Dick just now, despite the fact he'd lived across the street some 13 years.

"You don't have to say anything if you don't want," she reassured him, pressing the bell twice.

"Hi, Mrs. Nelson," she called out as the lady opened her front door. The pleasant looking woman stood slowly drying her hands on a kitchen towel as she listened to Michelle.

"I just wanted you to know I had a tumor and they had to take my leg off. But I'm OK now and I'm going to get an artificial leg pretty soon." She smiled at Mrs. Nelson not noticing the look of bewilderment and delight playing across the woman's face. "Oh," Michelle added, "and if you want to ask me any questions it's OK." She smiled at her neighbor as she pivoted and started back down the walk past

We all look a little tired, but it isn't everyday you lose a leg. At least the surgery is over.

Mom and Dad helped me give my "Chemo-completion" party at the City of Hope to say thank you to everybody and to show I was finished with chemotherapy. We had cake and ice cream...it was great!

Joy Sutera, my favorite nurse came.

And Dr. Rosen too.

Even Dr. Moor came to my party. He drove a long way and brought the letter i sent him after he left the hospital. He keeps it framed over his desk.

here's the letter, but i goofed. i drew my picture with two legs, but i erased one when i remembered.

Dr. Moor
I Love You
I miss You
♡
Michelle

i looked like a funny Barbie doll with my wooden leg and bald head but i didn't have to use my crutch. i could hardly wait to show my cousin Jim.

Kim loaned me her hair any time i needed it.

Being bald wasn't so bad!

st to take my family to Las Vegas in June 1978. They were there when i got
e Victor Award. Wayne Newton presented my award and then
urprised me with my very own
rse— i named him Prince
ayne Newton.

Photo by Wayrco

Wayne Newton is a very special
friend to me. He gave me Prince,
but best of all he gave me lots
of love.

i tried skiing and loved it so much that before long...

we were on our way to Winter Park, Colorado to compete in the Handicapped National Championships.

Ready or not, here i come!

Photo by Steve Shuman

Prince is still my big love.

But having a horse means a lot of hard work. He's gotta have a bath...

and my saddle is really heavy (that's why i let 'mom' share in some of the "fun").

Photo by Holly Berry

Training time is important too because we may be going to the 1981 Pentathlon.

Getting up isn't very hard...

He's really special!

As long as Prince doesn't move!

Look hard... can you see m
seat belt?

Sometimes i think i could ride forever!

it took a while to get the hang of skating on one leg...

but once i got it down—
LOOK OUT!

Dad wasn't real happy with my approach to sea-sports. I just wanted to give him a lift!

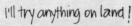

I'll try anything on land!

Tennis is my latest racquet...

and i love it!

Take a good look at my family—they're really special!

My life is full of love and promise, and every time the sun goes down i thank God for one more day.

Back cover photo by Tom Kasser

Dick who smiled quietly back at Mrs. Nelson still standing on the other side of her screen door.

"Well, thank you, Michelle," Mrs. Nelson said pleasantly. "I really appreciate your telling me all this."

"Oh, it's OK," she responded. "I just didn't want you to worry."

"I'm very glad to hear that you're so much better." Mrs. Nelson waved good-bye and stood thoughtfully watching them walk down her path to the sidewalk.

They visited several houses on their block and then turned back toward home. Dick put his arm around Michelle. "Honey," he said with tears in his eyes, "you're OK in my book."

"Daddy," she said looking up at him, "you're not going to *cry*, are you?" There was almost a scolding in her voice.

"Nope," he said composing himself, "but I want you to know I think you really helped some people with your visits. It's going to make it easier for them to accept you and not feel sorry for you."

"I don't want anybody to feel sorry for me," she said shaking her head, "*I* don't feel sorry for me. I'm just the same, only I have one leg now. Daddy," she added in suspenseful tones, slowing her pace, "when Jesus told me He made me well?"

Dick nodded his understanding.

"He told me something else too."

"What else did He tell you?" he asked.

She weighed the words because of how important they were to her, "He told me He has something very special for me to do with my life. Something very important."

They turned up the walk and Lady bounded down to meet them. "I'm sure He does, Michelle," Dick said thoughtfully. "I'm sure He does."

A few days after Michelle came home from the City of Hope, Kim walked by the bathroom and glanced in the open door.

"What are you doing?" she asked Michelle, who stood in front of the sink maneuvering the medicine cabinet mirror and her head back and forth.

"No wonder!" she said emphatically getting a good view of the back of her head.

"No wonder what?" Kim asked. "What are you doing?"

"Aw, Debby just called me Fred."

"Fred? Why?"

" 'Cause she says I look like old bald Fred Mertz on the Lucy show from the back," Michelle explained matter-of-factly. "You know what?" she said, looking at the shaggy ring of hair still hanging on around the bald spot on the top of her head.

"What?" Kim asked.

"She's right, I do look like Fred from the back." She swung past Kim and out the front door to find her friends.

In a few days her hair was gone, completely. Now, hopping around the house, she looked very much like the gangly newborn sparrow Laura had predicted.

Her second Thursday home Michelle propped herself in the bedroom doorway as Laura finished dressing. "You going to Bible study?"

"Uh-huh," Laura said, picking up her hairbrush. "Want to come along?"

"OK," she said, watching Laura's hair fall softly as the brush moved through it.

She moved in front of the mirror beside Laura and turned her head from side to side viewing it from all angles. "I miss my hair sometimes," she said, "but I don't mind being bald. I think I have a nice head."

Laura dropped a bath towel over Michelle's face and said, "It's sure getting big enough. If you're going with me you'd better get dressed."

The women in the Bible study group were delighted to see Michelle. They asked questions and talked with her and Laura, catching up on things they'd missed over the weeks.

"We've been praying for you, Michelle," one gray-haired lady said with tears in her light blue eyes.

"Thank you," she answered sincerely.

"You know, Laura," a younger, red-haired woman said to Laura as though Michelle weren't in the room, "I still have a hard time understanding how God could allow Michelle to be handicapped like this for the rest of her life."

An uncomfortable silence pushed against them as each one dug within herself for some sort of answer.

"But I don't think I'm handicapped," Michelle said surprised to think anyone else saw her that way. "Handicapped," she continued slowly and thoughtfully, "is when you can't do something because you're scared, or when you can't love somebody 'cause you didn't get enough love when you were a kid. Everybody's got handicaps like that. I'm missing a leg, and that just shows more."

As they thought about what Michelle said, expressions of pity and remorse changed to understanding and agreement as the truth of it began to sink in. One heavy-set lady circled Michelle with her large arm and squeezed her tightly.

"You're exactly right, honey," she said, her head bobbing up and down in agreement. "Some of us are handicapped a whole lot worse than you are. Other people just can't see it, that's all."

After a rich Bible study Laura and Michelle headed for the shopping center to treat themselves to lunch. As they walked through the shopping center, Laura began to realize her bald-headed, one-legged little girl with no eyebrows or lashes was attracting a lot of attention from large numbers of shoppers. People stared as they saw her coming toward them, even turning to watch her walk away.

"That little boy's missing a leg," she heard some say.

"Did you see that bald-headed kid back there!" one aghast woman said loudly to her companion.

"He must have had lice," another woman explained knowingly to her friend. "Why else would they shave his head like that?"

Michelle heard the comments and saw the stares but kept her eyes on the restaurant door and never slowed down. Laura felt her face getting warm as embarrassment began to push through her.

"What'd you do to your foot?" the waitress asked, noticing the crutches beside Michelle and making an attempt at pleasant conversation.

"I had a tumor," Michelle answered, "and they had to take my leg off."

"Oh," she gasped dropping a fork. "I didn't know. . . ."

"It's OK," Michelle assured her, shrugging her shoulder and glancing at Laura.

"Don't worry about it," Laura assured the young woman fumbling with her order pad and pen. "Kids with crutches usually have a cast somewhere. You couldn't know."

The waitress took their orders and gratefully left the table. Michelle sat rubbing her hands.

"Do your hands hurt you?" Laura asked.

"Yeah," she answered, pointing to the heels of her hands, "right here. The grips on my crutches rub in the same place all the time."

"That'll probably build up a callous after awhile," Laura encouraged.

"Then my hands will look like my feet," Michelle added, "and I'll have *three*."

"We'll have a hard time finding shoes to fit them," they laughed heartily together enjoying each other's company.

"Michelle," Laura asked, arranging her napkin in her lap, "does it bother you when people stare like they do?"

"I don't like it very much," she shrugged, opening her eyes wide and taking a sip from her water glass.

"I think they haven't seen a little bald kid before," Laura said. "What do you think?"

"Yeah," she said making a face. "If I was a hundred years old and wrinkled up they wouldn't even look at me."

"They might think you're Telly Savalas," she teased.

"Who's that?" Michelle asked.

"Never mind," she said pushing some of the cold moisture down the side of her water glass with her little finger. "I just had an idea."

"Oh-oh," Michelle quipped.

"Would you like to get a wig?" She moved her water glass away from her, watching it pull the ring of moisture after it on the formica tabletop, waiting for Shelly's response.

"A wig?" Shelly repeated leaning forward on both elbows and staring at her mother.

"Yeah, you know, hair."

"I don't know," she said screwing up her face again, "I guess."

They ate their lunch and were standing at the register as Laura paid the bill when a young woman and her small son walked up and stood beside them.

"Who stoled your leg?" the little four-year-old asked Michelle, watching her empty pantleg move as she started to walk away.

Michelle looked back to answer his question but his mother jerked him around and slapped him in the arm.

"Don't say things like that," she growled, apparently suppressing a desire to scream.

The child stood crying against his mother's skirts as Laura and Michelle walked out.

"Why did she do that?" Shelly asked upset because the little boy was punished for his curiosity. "He only wanted to know what happened."

"I know, honey," Laura comforted, "some people don't handle these things very well."

"I'd rather have him ask me questions," Michelle said, "than have people sneak looks and not talk to me."

Things lightened up again when they settled down in front of the mirrors in the wig shop. Michelle's natural "ham" instinct flourished as she tried on wigs that made her look like a pint-sized country western singer. Platinum coiffures piled high over a face that looked like Puck and Shirley Temple rolled into one brought giggles from Laura, Michelle and more than one salesclerk.

They settled on a brown short-haired, feathery style and left the store with it sitting proudly on Michelle's shiny dome. People stared less until the wig pitched low over one eye. She reached up to straighten it and quickly had the bangs fringing her ear.

"Here," she said stopping in the busy shopping mall and grabbing the wig firmly on top, pulling it straight up and off. "Put this in your purse or something."

"I can't believe this," Laura gasped trying to catch her breath. The expressions of horror and delight on people passing by added fuel to her fire. "I can't remember when I've laughed so much."

Laura stuck the fuzzy cap into her purse and Michelle snapped it shut with emphasis. Still laughing they headed for the car.

The three weeks Michelle was home seemed to go too fast. Too soon for everybody, it was time for her to return to the City of Hope for the next course of chemotherapy.

Shelly packed her suitcase quietly, folding things neatly.

Back at the City of Hope, Chris, the Children's Wing admitting clerk, put Michelle in a wheelchair and pushed her down the hall toward her old room. Michelle looked through the open door at the empty bed.

"You won't have to be in there this time," Chris said. "That's only for our surgery patients, when the nurses have to watch them real carefully. You're not going to be one of those this time."

They walked further down the hall past a room where a little blonde girl about Michelle's age was lying on her bed. Michelle smiled at her then remembered she'd seen her here once before. "Hi!" she called cheerfully. They pushed around the turn in the hall and into Michelle's new room.

"It's 158 this time," Chris said as she squatted down and lifted the metal footrest on the wheelchair, helping Michelle step out and over to a chair. The furnishings of the room were similar to her old one but much more cheerful, Michelle thought. There was carpet on the floor and a big window that opened onto some of the biggest, oldest trees on the grounds in a spot called Pioneer Park. The rose gardens Michelle loved were just beyond the trees.

"I like this room," she told Chris looking around, as Dick and Laura came in behind them. On the sliding glass doors at the foot of the bed life-size cartoon characters frolicked across the glass. Yogi Bear smiled back at her.

"That's beautiful!" Dick said walking to the window. "Come see, Shelly," he motioned for her to join him. She hopped to the window seat and climbed up beside him. "Look over there," he pointed.

She pressed her nose flat against the cold window pane. "The rose gardens," she squealed, then added wistfully, "I love those gardens."

She'd barely had time enough to put her pajamas on before Dr. Kramer with his curly brown hair and gentle ways came dragging his IV equipment behind him into the room.

"Hi, Michelle," he greeted her.

"Hi, Dr. Kramer," she said enthusiastically, then paused and quietly eyed his equipment. "We gonna start already?"

"I'm afraid so." He pulled the rack beside him and unhooked it from the stand, pulled the stainless steel pole apart from the wheels and slid it into the IV rack at the head of her bed. She watched his every move, sitting midway down the bed, her robe pulled around her tightly.

"You ready?" he asked quietly turning to face his small wide-eyed patient.

"I guess so," she said. She unbuttoned the top buttons of her robe and slipped it off. Pulling the cover and sheet down she slid under the cover and settled against the pillow, her left arm lying on top of the blanket waiting for the IV.

"You're one of the best patients I've got," Dr. Kramer said. He looked down at her through his thick glasses and she smiled weakly at him. He was awfully nice, but she was not looking forward to another bout with chemotherapy. "This time," he explained as he positioned the IV needle in her vein, "you're getting a different kind of medicine. Last time you got the—"

"Yellow kind," Michelle volunteered.

"Right," he said smiling. "That's called Methotrexate. This time you're getting one called Adramycin. It's red. See?" He held the vial up in front of the window so she could see the clear red liquid. "I'll put this into the bottle of dextrose and water here," he tapped the container at the top of the pole on her bed, "and you'll be done when it's empty. With that part of the medicine anyway.

"After that's gone a nurse or I will come in and give you several injections of another kind of medicine to stop the Adramycin. We'll do that every three hours at first for a couple of days, then every six hours for awhile."

"That's a lot," Michelle said biting her lower lip.

"It is a lot," he agreed. "Do you think we can make this if we try real hard?"

Michelle thought about it, then slowly nodded her head, "I'll try."

"I know you will, Michelle, and I know it's hard to do." He looked at her for a minute, then took a deep breath. "Well, shall we get this over with?"

Michelle nodded and watched while he injected the entire vial of red liquid into the bottle over her head.

"See you a little later, honey." he said at the door.

"Dr. Kramer?"

"Uh-huh?"

"Would you turn the lights off, please?"

Laura stood beside the window seat and began to draw the curtains closed again.

"I like to see the trees, Mommy."

"OK, honey," Laura responded. "Whatever helps."

For a long time Michelle looked out the window and watched the trees moving slightly in the wind outside her window. Jays darted from tree to tree looking as if they were hiding something from each other. Before long the sickness struck again and Michelle lay trembling curled into a ball, holding her stomach. Once in a while she would open her eyes and look longingly at the trees. When she shut them again she seemed a little more relaxed.

Late the next afternoon Michelle's door opened and a nice looking man dressed in a dark blue suit stuck his head into the room.

"Michelle?" he whispered.

She was in the room alone, and opened her eyes slowly. "Hi, Pastor Callen," she said weakly.

He walked into the room and sat on the chair beside her bed. "How are you?" he asked in a quiet voice.

"Doin' OK," she said, then reconsidered. "I feel real sick."

"I'm sorry you feel bad, honey. We just wanted you to know we're all praying for you. We love you, Michelle."

As he stood to go a wave of nausea hit her and she grabbed the emesis basin and vomited as he waited beside the bed. He lightly touched her shoulder, then turned toward the door.

"Pastor," she called after him, "I'm sorry you came all the way out here and I couldn't talk to you." She wearily closed her eyes, then opened them again. "Thank you for coming."

He looked back at her with tears in his eyes as the door closed silently behind him.

The effects of the chemotherapy were violent again this time, but by the end of the fourth day they began to wane. She was sitting up in bed, entering into conversations a little more. Everyone breathed a little easier as she showed signs of getting better.

On the fifth day she thought she felt well enough to pull on her robe and crutch her way up to the desk to "visit." She deeply disliked staying in bed. As she rounded the bend in the hall she saw the little blonde girl she'd remembered from the last time.

"Hi," she said walking into the girl's room and up to the bedside. "I'm Michelle," she said smiling wide. "What's your name?"

The little girl looked at her for a long minute, then looked up at her mother beside her.

"Kaylene," she answered hesitantly in a quiet voice.

Kaylene watched Michelle carefully without responding to her friendliness. Her short blonde hair was thinning and getting shaggy like Michelle's before she lost it. Her eyes were large and searching as she sat propped against the pillows on her bed trying to figure out this bald-headed child with the happy attitude standing beside her.

"How long you been here?" Michelle asked.

"A few days before you," Kaylene answered softly.

"This is my second time here," Michelle said with the air of one who knows the ropes. "I have to come back for chemotherapy, but I don't have to have any more operations."

"Is that what happened to your leg?" Kaylene ventured.

"Uh-huh, I had a tumor on the bone." Her new friend seemed uneasy with what she said so she softened her statement, "But it wasn't so bad. I can do lots of things now I couldn't do when I had two legs."

"Like what?" Kaylene challenged.

"Well," she said using her hands to emphasize the words. "I can put my bathing suit on without taking my pants off first." She grinned broadly, "Can you do that?"

Kaylene's mother put her hand to her mouth to hide her delight.

"And my mom and dad are going to take me to Colorado sometime to learn how to ski."

"You can't ski," Kaylene said emphatically. "You only have one leg."

"People with one leg can ski," Michelle explained evenly. "Lots of people do it, I bet. Well," Michelle said leaning on her crutch, "I gotta go now. I'm visiting. I'll come see you again."

She worked her way to the door then turned and called back, "What grade are you in?"

"Third."

"Me too." And off she went toward the nurse's station.

Kaylene sat looking after Michelle for a couple of minutes. She looked puzzled and confused. "Mommy?"

"Yes?"

"What's she got to smile about?"

Later, after dinner that evening, Dick and Laura were slowly walking the familiar halls while Kim entertained Michelle in the lobby with a game of "Candyland." Kaylene's mother saw them and stepped into the hall as they passed.

"Excuse me, are you Michelle's parents?"

"Yes," Dick said. "We're Dick and Laura Price."

"I'm Dottie Hall, Kaylene's mother," she said motioning toward the room behind her. She was a young looking woman, thin and attractive, a few years younger than they were. "Michelle came in this afternoon while she was visiting and struck up a conversation with Kaylene."

"She wasn't pestering you, was she?" Laura asked concerned.

"Oh, no," Dottie smiled, "just the opposite." She looked from Laura to Dick and decided to say more. "Kaylene has a brain tumor," she began.

"Oh, I'm so sorry," Laura interrupted touching the woman's arm gently. "That must be very hard."

"We're just learning what we're dealing with now that we're here at the City of Hope, so . . ." she paused, and took a deep breath. "Yes, it is hard, not knowing, all the tests . . ." She looked at them again and the worry lines around her eyes softened a little. "But then, you must know exactly what I'm talking about, with Michelle's tumor and all she's been through."

"It's been pretty rough at times," Dick admitted.

"She's got such a positive attitude," Dottie continued, "and she really seemed interested in Kaylene. My daughter hasn't stopped talking about her all afternoon."

"We're glad it helped," Dick said.

"Every little bit makes it easier," Laura added.

"This is the first positive experience she's had since we admitted her to the hospital. She's just gone inside herself in fear. I couldn't thank Michelle enough." She turned to leave, then added, "Will you let her come visiting again? . . . Soon."

"Oh, she'll be back," Laura laughingly assured her. "You can count on it."

Sunday morning Laura left Dick with Michelle and drove to church. It was good to be with their friends again. They asked about Michelle and said that they'd been praying. She wondered if their faithful friends knew how much it meant to them as a family to know that they were being held before God in prayer because of love.

Through some long and difficult nights it was this that kept them going.

Settling into the pew with some friends Laura prepared herself to be encouraged, to be strengthened and prepared again to return to the unknown things ahead of them.

As the pastor spoke he said, "I had a lesson this week in love and what it really is. I drove to the City of Hope on Friday to see little Michelle Price." Laura sat up straighter in her seat. This was the first she'd known of his visit.

"What I saw was a child in tremendous physical pain. She's weak and hurting. Her bed shakes with chills and she's constantly nauseated. Michelle was too sick to talk with me, so I told her how much we love her and about our prayers. As I walked out the door she taught me something about love. 'Pastor,' she said, 'I'm sorry I can't talk to you after you came all this way. Thank you for coming.' "

Laura felt tears stinging her throat. She hardly noticed that people all around her were in tears. "In all her pain," the pastor continued, "she cared enough about me to think how far I'd come to see her. She felt badly that she couldn't talk. What would our homes be like if we loved like that? That's the love of Jesus in action!"

In the car on the way back to the City of Hope Laura pushed an Evie Tornquist tape into the tape deck. As she drove she reflected on what the pastor had said. Michelle seems to give without being concerned whether you can give anything in return, even in her pain she still cares for others.

Then the words of a song caught her attention:

Knowing you'll love me
    through the burdens I must bear,
Hearing your footsteps
    lets me know I'm in your care.
And in the night of my life,
    you bring the promise of day.
Here is my hand. Show me the way.

"It's so clear, Lord," she said out loud, "your care through all of this. You will get us through the burdens we have to bear now—especially Michelle, she needs your strength."

When I think I'm goin' under,
    part the waters, Lord,
When I feel the waves around me,
    calm the sea.
When I cry for help, oh, hear me, Lord,
    and hold out your hand.
Touch my life. Still the raging storm in me.

"The storm that's raging in her body, Lord, hold out your hand to her, give her the calmness in the middle of all this that only you can give. Hear her cry for help and answer her."

Knowing you'll love me
    helps me face another day.
Hearing your footsteps
    drives the clouds and fears away.
And in the tears of my life,
    I see the sorrow you bore.
Here is my pain. Heal it once more.[1]

"That's what the pastor heard wasn't it, Lord? And the doctors and nurses who keep asking why she's accepted all this so well—it's your footsteps, isn't it? Your way of showing us that you're in all of this. Use the pain she's going through to teach her of your special love. Teach all of us."

She rewound the tape and played the song again and again until she turned the car into the long driveway at the City of Hope.

Note
1. Charles F. Brown, "Part the Waters." Copyright 1975 by Word Music Inc. Used by permission.

9
Airborne and Soaring

A full year passed. A year filled with learning and adjustments for all of them. Rick was married to a young woman named Brenda and they were expecting their first child, a documented miracle baby because of the nature and the extent of Rick's injuries. Kim graduated from high school but decided to wait a year before starting college until things with Michelle settled down more.

Michelle was still having chemotherapy treatments every three weeks, and was almost used to comments about her baldness and being taken for a boy. Between treatments she sprouted a little timid fuzz on her head, an encouraging sign that she just might grow hair when all of this was finally over.

Monthly x-rays had become routine for her, regular probing to see whether the disease had spread somewhere else in her body. But reports kept coming back clear. Michelle was doing well.

She tired easily and was quickly bothered by heat, but resumed her usual activities and typical pace very soon after coming home. Her "little leg" slowed her down some, not much.

They had been so busy meeting doctors' appointments and treatment schedules that several weeks after surgery Laura still hadn't been able to get rid of a few things she feared would remind Michelle of her two-legged days. Late one afternoon while Michelle was playing next door, Laura lifted the garage door and went in scanning the contents for Michelle's bicycle, skateboard, skates and other things she wouldn't be able to use now.

A noise behind her drew her attention and her mouth dropped open in amazement. Whizzing past the house, crutches held high at the sides, Michelle sped down the sidewalk on the skateboard Laura couldn't find. Within seconds she returned and passed the garage again, this time squatting on the board with Lady in front as the motor, pulling Michelle uphill.

Laura blinked, then threw her hands up in surrender. "OK, Lord," she said walking back into the house, "you'll just have to keep an eye on her. I can't run that fast."

It was decided at dinner that night that the family ski trip they'd been putting off until Michelle could handle it could probably be safely scheduled. The dates were set, and in a few weeks tightly packed suitcases were sitting at the door ready to be loaded into their camper the next morning. Together they settled in front of the TV to relax before getting to bed. The program they chose was a heart-gripping story dealing with the death of a child. As it progressed Michelle threw herself against Dick and buried her head in his shoulder. "I don't want to die," she sobbed, holding onto her father tightly. He wrapped his arms around her and let her cry for several minutes. She hadn't cried this way since the rose garden, when they told her she would lose her leg.

"That's silly," she said composing herself slowly. She wiped the tears from her face with the back of her hand. "I'm not going to die."

"Michelle," Dick asked gently, "are there things that bother you that you haven't told us about?"

"There's lots of stuff I haven't told you," she said her eyes lowered. "I tell Jesus lots of secrets when I'm having my chemotherapy. It's not stuff you shouldn't know or anything, just . . . sometimes it's easier to talk to Him."

Early the next morning they loaded suitcases, equipment and provisions into their little Chinook camper and took off for a ski weekend at Snow Summit. Chains were required a few hours away from home and new fallen snow covered the landscape with a soft blanket of white as far as they could see.

They found a parking space in the crowded lot at the foot of the slopes with time to spare before they were to meet Michelle's instructor. Before long they were bundled and strapped into everything they needed against the weather and ready for a day of skiing.

"Hi," he called shooshing gracefully up beside them. He moved so easily on skis it was several minutes before anyone noticed he was missing a leg. "You the Prices? I'm Paul." His nose and cheeks were red from the cold and his blue eyes sparkled as he talked about Michelle's background with Dick and Laura.

"Has she skied before?"

"Just once," Dick answered. "We went as a family last year and loved it."

"Great," he said with a big grin. "We'll see you later." Paul handed her two aluminum ski poles with short skis at the bottom, called outriggers. He helped her position her skis and snapped the grips securely on her boot before they took off together for the intermediate slopes.

He sent her down the mountain just ahead of him, calling encouragement and directions about balance and turns as they descended.

"That was great," he commented to her in short gasping breaths. Flipping up the short skis at the bottom of his outriggers he dug them into the snow with a crunching sound. "You sure you're not a professional three-tracker?"

She grinned back at him, "Nope. I only skied that one time before I lost my leg," she said warming her nose with her mittened hand.

Paul looked a little puzzled. "You mean, this is the first time you've used outriggers?"

"Uh-huh," she said nodding.

"And I sent you down the intermediate . . ." He rolled his eyes, grateful she'd made it down unhurt and excited by the expertise she'd shown on her first run. She was a natural.

"She's a natural," Paul told Dick as they took their parkas off beside the fire later that afternoon. "She really did well this afternoon. She learns fast, her balance is great, and she's not afraid of getting hurt. I think she ought to be competing."

"What kind of competition are you talking about, Paul?" Michelle asked nursing a cup of hot chocolate with both hands. She snuggled next to Kim on the couch by a crackling fire.

"Same kind normal skiers do, only you'd be in a class of women and girls who've been skiing about as long as you have. They're all handicapped in one way or another." He pulled his knit red cap off his head, shaking his light brown, tight curls. He flicked his cap and the fire sizzled as bits of snow and ice melted in the flames.

Michelle took a sip of her chocolate and let the warm steam curl up onto her cold nose and cheeks. "I'm not ready to race anybody," she protested. "I'd never make it."

"Yes, you would," Paul assured her, dropping into a chair next to her. "You're good, Michelle, and you've only skied one day. I've seen a lot of handicapped skiers and I'm telling you, you're good."

Late February, 1978, they pulled out of their driveway in Riverside, California with their little white Chinook bulging. Taped along the side was a colorful sign some friends made for Michelle showing Snoopy standing proudly on skis beside bold letters announcing, "MICHELLE IS ON HER WAY TO THE HANDICAPPED NATIONALS, WINTER PARK, COLORADO!"

Two days later, stiff and tired, they pulled slowly up the hill to the center of activity. Stepping from the camper Michelle stood very still, slowly taking in her new surroundings. Like a wide-eyed fawn trying to decide whether it was safe, she leaned forward on her crutches and looked up at the lodge where they would stay.

It was a rambling wooden building, the roof covered with several inches of snow. Icicles hugged the eaves, and snow had fallen not long before they arrived; there was an inch of brand new snow on the stairway and handrail.

She turned to her left and looked down the hill into the little valley below. Several small buildings were scattered around, many with bright red, yellow and blue signs posted against the dark siding. Ski racks opposite the lift area made a dotted line for several feet. The skiers bobbing around in their bright colored ski jackets gave the scene a carnival flavor. Yellow lift chairs silently sailed up and down the mountain, many carrying skiers to the top. Michelle noticed that several of the people sitting in the chairs high above the snow had single skis dangling beneath them flanked with outriggers on either side.

On the other side of the valley, soldier pines stood at attention. It looked like a scene from a bakery store window: everything was dusted with a powdered sugar topping. A haze hung lightly in the valley making the trees seem like part of a movie setting instead of the living landscape.

"Michelle?" Laura called, approaching her daughter through the slippery snow. "You alright, honey?"

Shelly squealed excitedly, throwing her arms around Laura's waist. "It's so beautiful. Thank you. Thank you for bringing me. I can't believe it."

Looking around, Michelle saw a man walking with a limp and a girl about her age who was also missing a leg. Not far away a red-cheeked, laughing man skied past, the stumps of both legs secured inside boot-like structures clamped to his skis. Everyone seemed so comfortable, so *normal*.

Dick crunched through the snow and stopped beside Michelle, his arm on her shoulder. His nose was red and the breath from his mouth fogged his glasses when he leaned forward to talk to her. "Well, Price, what do you think?"

She looked around her briefly then let out a big puff of warm breath that hung in the air. "I think I'm scared."

To qualify, Michelle had to ski the course for placement in a competition division according to her time and ability level. She was assigned a number to be used for all her statistics this week. Laura helped her work the white bib with its black number 143 over her head and secure it with ties at the sides. Michelle pulled it into place over her parka, tugging clumsily at it with both hands stuffed into her black leather mittens. She smiled broadly while Dick snapped several pictures.

It was mid-afternoon and time for her qualifying run. Michelle and Laura caught the lift to the top. They swung in over the landing area and prepared to get off. Michelle quickly pushed off into the snow and Laura followed suit a little slower. The lift nearly swept her right back down the mountain. Laura made a mental note to improve her speed next time around.

She was laughing, a little embarrassed at her lack of expertise when she caught up to Michelle and was surprised that Michelle had nothing to say. She seldom passed up a good chance to tease her mom. "Honey," Laura questioned as they neared the starting point, "what's wrong?"

Michelle kept her head down, running an outrigger back and forth in the snow making a trail. Finally, without looking up she admitted in a small voice, "I'm so scared." Laura reached for Michelle's arm and they stood facing each other beside a snow-crusted pine.

"Honey, you don't have to do this if you don't want to," Laura reassured her. "You know that, don't you?"

"I know," she said, "but I want to." She paused a minute then looked up at Laura, "I'm just afraid I can't."

"Forget about the time then," Laura suggested pulling the child close to her. "When they call you, ski just for the fun of it."

"Maybe that's what I'll do," she said thoughtfully.

Laura faced her squarely and said gently, "We love you no matter what you do here, Shelly. Do you know that?"

Michelle pulled one arm out of the outrigger and circled her mother's neck. "I'm OK now, Mommy," she said. "I'm just scared, but I really want to try."

"Would it help if I follow you down the hill outside the course?"

Michelle nodded, working her arm and the thick blue sleeve of her parka back into the outrigger grip. She pulled her white knit cap further over her ears and started moving the last few feet into her place in the order of entrants.

The haze was becoming more like a light fog and the air was getting colder. Finally Michelle's number was called. She positioned herself on the platform behind the black and white starting arm. She pushed her outriggers back and forth in the snow, nervously biting her lower lip as she glanced up at the starter. He was a small, round, man with a red hunting cap pulled down over his ears. The big fur collar of his navy blue parka stood up around his neck, half hiding his face. She didn't think he looked very friendly.

She searched the faces on her left until she found Laura's, holding her mother's gaze for a moment, as if making some sort of decision. Then smiling weakly she looked back down the course.

Right below the starting platform there was a steep downgrade where she would pick up quite a bit of speed. Then it seemed to quickly level off and become an easier descent that rounded into a wide turn to the left. She couldn't see the finish line from where she stood but the wind was whipping the plastic triangle flags on the red slalom poles.

Laura studied Michelle's back, wondering whether she should pull her from the race. She knew the child was afraid, but also knew that Michelle would not try something she didn't feel strong enough to do. No, she decided, she'd just wait it out and let Michelle take the lead. If she wanted to go down the hill she was going to have the chance to find out how much she believed in herself.

"143, ready?" the starter asked tersely. She nodded her OK without looking back at him. She preferred not to see him again right now. Her heart was beating rapidly and she could feel the pulsing under her goggles on the sides of her face. She closed her eyes briefly. Her eyeballs felt like they'd frozen solid. Her fingers hurt from being so cold and holding the outriggers so tightly.

"GO!" she heard behind her. Her body tensed up and in that split second she committed herself to going down that hill. Nothing else mattered just then. She was going to give it all she had.

She crouched low and pushed herself off the snow-covered platform with a sharp downward thrust on the outriggers. Her ski left the ground momentarily as she pushed open the black and white barrier and jumped into that first steep grade. She picked up speed and could feel the packed snow bumping by underneath her narrow aluminum ski as she shifted her weight, leaning into the first turn around the flag coming rapidly up in front of her.

Laura stood momentarily frozen at the top of the hill. She was a beginning skier herself and as the full slope came into view in front of her it took her breath away. *These were intermediate slopes?* As she stood there she realized she wasn't sure she *could* ski that hill even if Michelle did need the moral support it would give her.

She looked off to her right and down the hill ahead of her. Michelle was already dipping and moving rhythmically in and out between the flags like a dancer. She watched for a brief moment then decided she was going to have to tackle the hill. She'd promised Michelle, and she had to get down somehow, anyway.

She eased over the summit and into the downhill grade. Michelle was yards ahead of her by now, but Laura was no match for the grade of this slope. She began to zigzag back and forth outside the course markings leaving a razorback trail in the snow. She hoped two things, that Michelle would realize she'd tried, and that somehow she'd end up at the bottom safely. It was going to be a long way back.

Michelle quickly skied out of Laura's sight around the bend in the course by this time and Dick and Kim were standing at the bottom straining to see her blue parka somewhere on the white mountainside. Suddenly, at the top of the course a small figure appeared, slipping easily between the poles on the slalom.

"There she is!" Kim shouted excitedly. "Right at the top!"

"That can't be her," Dick said hoping he was right. "That skier is really traveling. Michelle isn't that fast."

As they watched they realized it was, indeed, Michelle and she was, in fact, traveling down that mountain at a very good clip. Dick snapped several pictures and each time he advanced the film his excitement grew a little more. The closer she got to the finish line the bigger his grin became, until, by the time she slipped through the final markers, he was laughing out loud with pride and amazement.

"She made it!" Kim shouted with cheerleader expertise. "Michelle! You did it! You were great!"

Michelle coasted into the safety area across the finish line as the crowd cheered and beat their gloved hands together in a muffled applause. She stood frozen to her outriggers, her eyes glazed, her expression unchanged. Kim could see from a distance that something was wrong and ran the last few feet to her little sister.

"Michelle? Honey?" Kim called putting her hands on the little girl's shoulders. "Michelle, what's wrong? What is it?"

Suddenly Michelle realized Kim was talking to her. "Oh, Kim!" she cried, throwing her arms, outriggers and all, around her, "I was so scared! I was so *scared!*"

Kim pulled her close and let her cry until she felt the little girl's body relax against her. "It's alright," she said. "Don't worry about it honey. Everything's OK."

"Michelle Price, number 143; time 47.80!" the voice sounded over the loudspeakers.

Dick reached the girls realizing something was wrong. "Are you alright, Michelle?" he asked anxiously. "What's wrong, Kimmy?"

"I think she's OK now, Daddy. She was just scared."

"Honey," he reassured her, "you don't have to compete if it frightens you. This is supposed to be fun for you."

"I'm OK, Daddy," she said, pushing her goggles onto her forehead and rubbing icy cold tears from her face with her mittens. "I was just really scared. But I did it!" She smiled at them sheepishly.

Kim and Dick hugged her soundly and agreed, "You did it!"

"And you made good time, Shelly," Dick added. "Hey! Speaking of time, where's your mother?"

They looked blankly at each other, then Michelle said, "She was going to ski down with me on the outside of the course 'cause I was so scared."

They turned toward the fog-covered mountain, looking for a slow-moving blue and yellow figure. "There she is!" Michelle shouted, pointing about halfway up the hillside. "She's right at the second turn."

Before long Laura slid into the trio waiting for her at the bottom of the hill. No one said a word. They simply looked at each other and burst out laughing, wrapped their arms around one another and headed for the warming house, ravenous and ready for something hot to drink.

As they worked their way through the crowd, another skier joined them, moving next to Michelle. He was a nice looking man with dark hair and a small moustache. His sherwood green parka accented his dark eyes. The pant leg and sleeve on his left side were missing but he moved smoothly down the hill on one ski and an outrigger shoulder extension.

"You were great," he said grinning broadly at Michelle. "How long you been skiing?"

"Not very long," she grinned back liking him instantly, "but I sure love it."

"It shows," he said. "There's nothing like that feeling when you're flying down the mountain, is there?"

"I was pretty scared today; that's a pretty steep course," she admitted. "But sometimes I don't even feel the ground. It's like being a big bird."

"Aren't you Jim Stacy, the actor?" Kim asked recognizing the man skiing with them.

He nodded a little self-consciously, "Yeah, I just wanted to tell this little gal what a great job she did up there."

"Wasn't that something!" Dick said shaking Jim's hand. "We're so proud of her."

"Honey, he never would have guessed that," Laura said teasing

Dick about his enthusiasm. "We're the Prices, Dick and Laura," she said warmly to the smiling young man. "And these are our daughters, Kim, and of course, you know Michelle."

"We're proud of Laura too, though," Dick said. "She made it down the mountain in only 12 minutes, 15 seconds."

Laura blushed a little and poked Dick. Jim was one of the family already, joining in the fun. Accepting him as a welcome member, they shared their meal and a growing friendship.

Competition began early the next day and the Prices eagerly watched the people around them. At the starting gate there waited a young man in his late twenties. On his feet, too small for his body, were walking boots. From the waist up Rene Kirby, was normal, and powerfully developed, but his legs were short, misshapen and all but useless to him. His skis dangled at the ends of his arms with his hands inside the ski boots.

When the starter began his countdown, the young man leaned forward, put his skis to the ground and pushed off with his feet, skiing down the mountain on his hands, his face less than three feet from the snow. The final few feet he raised his legs high in the air and skied across the finish line upside down. The expression on his face belonged to a man who would never be accused of giving up.

Crowds of observers, handicapped and normal, cheered the skiers on, encouraging and supporting each one. The handicapped know what it is to be limited, and somehow they share a knowledge that physical limitations are not the worst ones. With determination and fortitude they push past their limits and onto things normal people fear. They stand squarely and master dragons that corner and control others. In their handicaps many find the real meaning of true freedom.

The women's class "C" division in giant slalom was being run now and Michelle waited again at the starting gate. The morning air was cold and clear and the view from the mountain breathtaking. She took a slow deep breath and threw her head back tasting the sweetness of the air. A flawless blue sky was interrupted here and there with small, white clouds and the sun shone brightly, reflecting brilliantly off the endless white snow.

She watched the starter as he signaled the skier before her to begin her descent. The woman, a four-tracker skiing with her prosthesis and outriggers, jumped through the wooden starting arm and down the incline into the course before the starter took his eyes off her. He seemed to lean as she leaned and feel the snow under the skier's blades. From where Michelle stood she could see that under his red hunter's cap were a pair of warm blue eyes. His graying eyebrows were bushy and matched his thick moustache giving him an "old fashioned" look, like a character from *The Music Man* or someone who'd sing in a barbershop quartet on Saturday nights.

The descending skier rounded the turn and could no longer be seen, so the old man straightened up and walked the few steps back toward his lean-to. As he looked up he noticed Michelle watching him and stopped abruptly. He lowered his head slightly, peering out from under his shaggy eyebrows without blinking for a second or two, then he curled one side of his mouth up into a large grin.

"You goin' down as fast today as you did before?" he asked her, resuming his walk and pulling the starting arm across the platform behind him.

"Did I go down too fast yesterday?" she asked a little surprised he remembered her.

"First time jitters, I'd guess." He leaned against the wall of the little shelter checking the time clock before looking back at Michelle. The numbers were still running, the other skier had not finished her run yet.

"I was pretty scared," she said shyly. "I haven't skied very long, just a couple of times since I lost my leg."

"That all?" he said raising his eyebrows and nodding a mute approval. "You're pretty good then. Just make your start a little smoother and relax. You should do real well."

He got his signal that the course was clear. It was time for Michelle. He cleared his timer, "You ready?"

She nodded looking intently down the course, then called back to him, "Thanks."

"GO!" she heard him say as she pushed through the arm in front of her. *Smooth he said,* she thought as she pushed into the downhill slope. She pushed against the knoll and slipped easily down the grade and into the first turn. *Lean into the turn, that's what Paul said. Lean and relax. It's such a long way to the bottom.*

She dipped and swayed evenly and gracefully moving in and out between the red and blue gates of the giant slalom, until the fear she'd felt yesterday was far behind her and she moved easily into the thrill of the downhill descent. The cold wind cut against her cheeks and made her eyes feel cold, even behind the goggles. She could hear the blade of her ski cutting through the packed snow underfoot and a spray of snow shot out from under the outriggers as she slid out of one turn, dipping into the next. It felt good to be flying down the mountain. Her leg ached for a rest and her fingers were like long icicles inside her leather mittens but it was worth it. This was the greatest feeling in the world.

"Michelle Price, number 143, time 35.78"

Cheers of approval and excitement came from the people standing around the finish line. Jim Stacy was there with the family. Everyone was thrilled, especially Michelle. She had conquered her fear and skied a good run. She'd grown up a little bit.

They watched the competition the rest of the day and at one point saw a young man descending the hill while a second skier skied opposite him just outside the course.

"How come there's two skiers, Daddy?" Michelle asked as they watched the figures descend the mountain.

"The man on the course is blind," Dick explained. "The other skier is his spotter. He's acting as the man's eyes."

"You mean he tells him what *he* sees?"

"That's right. He's talking to the blind man all the way through the course, telling him where the pontoons are and when to lean to get around them, and things like that." Dick felt his stomach tighten as he thought what it would be like flying down that hill on skis, unable to see where he was going.

"Is that the way a plane lands in the fog?" Michelle asked beginning to understand the teamwork involved.

"A lot like that," Dick answered putting his arm on her shoulder. "You'd really have to trust the person guiding you in either case, wouldn't you?"

"I *guess!*" she said shaking her head. "I don't think I could do it."

The crowd cheered the blind man on enthusiastically. All around them were onlookers fighting back tears, shouting encouragement to the man skiing down the hill toward them. His courage was contagious, inspiring everyone who watched, whether their handicaps were ones that could be seen or those held tightly within.

Competitors at Winter Park understand about *risk*. For them there's risk in simply being alive, in doing the things "normal" people take for granted, like getting to work and fixing meals. At Winter Park people come face to face with a choice we all make every day—to give up or keep on trying.

The entire week went too quickly for everyone. Michelle competed in the slalom and giant slalom and earned two silver medals and a trophy for best overall in her class, presented with great fanfare at the awards banquet the closing night.

As the little white Chinook worked its way through Colorado toward California the next morning, Michelle realized she'd learned much about herself and her world. She learned a lot about conquering fear and discovered she was capable of dreaming great dreams and then working to make some of them come true. She learned that, as she had suspected, we are truly handicapped most cruelly by our own choices. "If you're going to be brave," she quipped, "you've got to do something that scares you."

Winter Park and the National Handicap Championship stand for so much more than ski medals and competition. It is a place where people reach for a greater prize, where they stretch themselves in the trying. The medals symbolize the best times in events. But all the contestants there are winners because of a belief in themselves and a commitment to never give up.

So as the snow falls silently on the ancient fragrant pines, slowly covering the footprints and ski trails weaving their way through the slopes and valley of Winter Park, it cannot disguise what is there. Days spent there are sweet. Friends met there are special. Even time cannot erase the pungent scent of victory in the air.

10
Swept Off Her Foot

Dick settled back against the fat, cool pillow and drew in a deep breath. He smoothed the top of the sheet over the edge of the light green blanket and crossed his arms on his chest.

"It's been a long day," he said wearily to Laura as she sat down on her side of the bed. She lifted her feet off the floor onto the sheets and looked at Dick out of the corner of her eye.

"You look so comfortable," she said in maternal tones. Then gripping the blanket firmly by the hem she yanked the covers off and flung her arm across him before he had a chance to stop her. Dick laughed with surprise, but wasted no time in a counterattack. Employing well developed ability he defended his title of "fastest tickler in the family," until Laura choked out, "Enough."

For a minute or two they both lay panting against their pillows laughing and gasping for air like two high schoolers at a pillow fight. Then Dick circled Laura's waist with his arm. "You're nuts," he said as if convinced it was the truth, "but I love you."

She turned on her side to face him and lightly touched his face. "I'm glad, 'cause I have some neat news and I'd hate to tell it to somebody who didn't love me."

"What news?" he asked picking up the excitement in her voice.

"Well," she grinned, "when I took Michelle to the City of Hope for her treatment today we saw Dr. Rosen."

"And . . ." he persisted.

"And," she said, pausing for effect, "he told me some great news."

"For Pete's sake, Laurie, what'd he say?" He moved his hand toward her throat in mock agitation. "Say it!"

"He said that Michelle is one of the kids they nominated for the Victor Award this year."

"You're kidding!" he said raising his eyebrows and propping himself up on one elbow. "You mean the Sportsmen's Club thing?"

"I guess so," Laura answered. "I'm really not sure about any of the details. But Dr. Rosen was so excited I figured it had to be pretty special."

"Oh, wow," Dick said dropping back on the pillow and looking up at the ceiling. "It's special alright. The Sportsmen's Club does this every year. I never dreamed Michelle . . ."

"Tell me about it, honey," Laura asked, moving close and resting her head on his shoulder.

He pulled her closer and began to explain, "Every year they choose people from the sports world who've achieved a lot in their area and have acted like winners in other ways too. They've honored people like Roy Campanella, Mark Spitz, Bill Walton . . ."

"Don't they know any women athletes?"

"What are you, liberated?" he teased. "I was just getting to the women . . ."

"That's what they all say."

"Just last year they gave one to Kathy McMillan, and before that Sandra Palmer, and Greta Anderson. Chris Evert's been given a Victor too. I think they've been doing this for 10 or 11 years."

"It sounds great," she said smiling slightly. "Just think, our Michelle . . ."

"The neat part is that she'd hear somebody besides us tell her she's done a great job and been a champ through all this. When are they going to make their final choice?"

"He didn't say," Laura said thinking back over the conversation with Dr. Rosen. "He just said somebody would call in the next week or two to talk to us."

By the end of the week Laura received a phone call setting up an interview time at the house for the whole family. The day arrived and right on schedule the doorbell rang.

"Hi, I'm Rusty Citron," the bearded young man said, smiling and holding out his hand, "and this is Laurie, my assistant. We called—"

"Of course," Dick said opening the door wider, "come on in."

They stepped into the hallway and Rusty eyed a lone cowboy boot standing against the wall.

Following Rusty's glance Dick said, "We can make a pair of shoes last a long time that way. Only wear 'em out one at a time."

Rusty glanced at his partner and they smiled at Dick's easy attitude.

Hearing the voices, Michelle came hopping out of the kitchen and threw her arms around Dick's waist.

"Shelly," Dick said, "this is Rusty Citron and his friend Laurie, from the City of Hope."

"Hi," she said flashing a grin mixed with shyness and fun.

"Hi, Michelle," Laurie said. "We've sure heard a lot about you. I'm glad to finally meet you."

Michelle shrugged self-consciously, quickly asking, "Wanna sit in here?" Before the question was out she was hopping toward the living room. Rusty and Laurie grinned at Dick and Laura and followed the leader.

Laurie was young and her warm eyes were very soft behind the large glasses she wore. Her curly brown hair and easy smile made Michelle relax quickly, answering questions and telling stories like an "old salt."

"Tell me something special that's happened to you this last year, Michelle?" Laurie asked adjusting on her tape recorder.

"Well, there's Lady," Michelle said.

"Lady?" Laurie questioned for more details.

"Yeah, Mommy and Daddy asked what I wanted after my treatments were over. And I told them I wanted a dog, a raccoon and a horse." She reached one hand up and brushed aside a ragged strand of hair. Her chemotherapy treatments had been spaced for every six weeks now, and her hair was growing back in patches, between treatments.

"Well, is Lady your raccoon or what?" Rusty asked teasing Michelle into more conversation.

"Nope, Lady's my dog," she grinned back at the curly-haired man sitting on the couch.

"And what about the raccoon and the horse?" he asked.

"Well, I traded the raccoon in for a different kind of pet. Wanna see him?" she said hopping to a standing position. "He's in the backyard."

"OK," Laurie said shutting off the recorder and taking Michelle's hand.

"Would you hand me my crutch?" Michelle asked her mother.

"What kind of pet did you trade for," Laurie asked, honestly curious.

"Just wait till you see," Michelle grinned, heading at her usual breakneck speed toward the backyard, pulling Laurie by the hand, the other adults in hot pursuit.

"There he is," she said as they stepped into the warm April sunshine. "That's Midnight, my crow." She walked over to a large walk-in cage and opened the screened door. "Come on. Come pet him. He won't bite."

Gingerly Rusty and Laurie followed Michelle into the cage in the middle of the yard and pulled the door shut. Michelle chattered animatedly about the care and feeding of big black crows.

"Don't they look cute," Laura whispered to Dick.

"We should have a picture of them all crowded in that cage," he grinned. "I'm impressed. They're great people."

"And what about the horse, Michelle?" Rusty asked as they stepped back into the cool living room a few minutes later. "Did you ever find a horse?"

"Well, we found a place where we can board one. We can't keep it here 'cause our backyard isn't big enough," she explained. "We just didn't find the right horse yet. But we're looking."

Dick and Laura glanced at each other.

"Can you ride, Michelle?" Laurie asked.

"Of course," she said, matter-of-factly as though every one-legged girl rides horses. "I ride all the time. I get to go over to my friend's house and ride every Monday."

Easy, interesting conversation made the hours pass quickly for everyone.

"You'll be hearing from someone," Rusty said as he and Laurie climbed into his little Toyota. "It was a great afternoon!"

A few days later someone else from the City of Hope paid a visit to the Price's. Sid Keith was warm and friendly as he told the Price family that Michelle had been their final choice to receive the Victor Award for 1977. It took days to call the friends who had prayed so faithfully and share the good news. But it was important to Dick and Laura that those who had so willingly shared in the pain and tears should share in the joy now. The hardest part would be waiting until June when the ceremonies were scheduled in Las Vegas, Nevada. It would seem like forever.

A few days later Kim stood barefoot, dressed in a slip, ironing her dress for work when the phone rang beside her.

"It's Laurie, Mom," she said holding the phone out to Laura. "She wants to talk to you."

"Hi, Laura," the young woman said into the phone. "I've got a kind of odd question to ask you."

"Hardly anything surprises me anymore," Laura said. "What do you need?"

"Good. Then how about this: If we were able to find a horse for Michelle somewhere, would it be alright for her to have one?"

Laura took a deep breath and touched Kim on the shoulder. "Do you really think you could find her a horse?"

Kim's eyes widened as she set the iron down.

"Well, it's a good possibility," Laurie continued, "but we'd have to be sure it was OK with you and Dick before we made any arrangements."

"Oh, yes," Laura said excitedly. "It's just fine with us. That would be so wonderful."

Laura stood with the phone to her ear as Kim hugged her silently, her eyes brimming with tears of joy.

"Well, then," Laurie continued, "there's just one more question. What kind of horse were you looking for?"

"Well, we don't want a rocking horse," Laura said smiling. "Like my mother always says, 'beautiful inside and out.' That's all we care about. It would need to be gentle and good to Michelle—one that would learn to love her as much as she'll love the horse."

"Well, that's a pretty big order. But we'll do our best. Just one more thing, Laura. Can we keep this a secret? In fact, if only you and Dick know that would be best."

"Kim's standing here right now," Laura explained. "But we can make it a secret between us girls. We can even surprise Dick and Rick."

"Sounds like fun to me," Laurie said laughing. "We'll be getting back in touch soon."

For the next few weeks Kim and Laura had a wonderful time keeping their secret. There were times it was hard not to say something but the thought of everyone's delight at the presentation kept them going.

Finally the day came when they were to fly to Las Vegas and early morning found the household in a colorful uproar.

"Michelle," Kim hollered down the hall. "Where's the hair-dryer?"

"I packed it already," she yelled back from her room. "You don't expect me to get my award looking like a scarecrow do you? I have to be beautiful."

Kim left her room long enough to throw a pillow at Michelle who flopped "wounded" on her bed beside her open suitcase.

Before long they were all settled aboard the big yellow Hughes Airwest. The plane trembled as the pilot revved up the engines for takeoff from the California airport. Michelle pressed her nose against the window and watched the runway roll by faster and faster until she was forced back against the seat when the tail of the plane dipped low. She rested her head against the high seatback and smiled slightly listening to the high-pitched hum of the engines. Looking out the window again she could see miniature houses and cars, even tiny little people walking the ribbonlike streets below, so far away.

"It's like dreaming," she said quietly.

"What'd you say, honey?" Rick asked, touching her shoulder as she sat watching the world below her.

"It's like dreaming," she repeated. "Everything looks like somebody painted it. It doesn't even look real."

In what seemed like no time, the Las Vegas airport came into view, and they were in rapid descent over the city.

After they landed the hostess pulled the big door open and a warm breeze pushed into the plane. Michelle grabbed her blue denim cap to keep the wind from snatching it off her head as she started down the stairs, briefly watching a snub-nosed yellow cart with two empty trailers roll under the belly of the plane.

"What's that for?" she yelled back up the stairs to Kim.

"I think that's how they bring the suitcases into the airport," Kim answered, closing the gap between them.

They picked up their luggage and loaded it into a big white limousine the Victor Awards committee arranged for them. With eyes the size of quarters Michelle pronounced it "a block long" as it carried the family smoothly over the desert streets and onto the crowded and flashy Las Vegas Strip.

Finally they made the turn into the drive of the Hilton Hotel. "Is this *our* hotel?" Michelle asked, pressing her cheek and nose against the window straining to see the top.

"Well, we're going to stay here for the next couple of days," Dick teased, "but it's not really ours."

The valet at the entry opened the door for them and Michelle hopped onto the sidewalk. Her face reflected the excitement of what she saw around her. The rest of the family, seeing things through her enthusiasm found that they agreed, this was pretty exciting any way you looked at it.

Pushing through the revolving door, Laura stepped into the lobby and turned to watch Michelle's reaction to the splendor and noise of the Las Vegas crowds just inside.

Michelle pushed the big brass door through its casing and, as if she'd just finished her turn at jump rope, hopped through the opening into the carved marble and brass lobby. Rich colors and ornate styling were everywhere as she stood just inside the entrance looking all around, and overhead.

Her eyes widened as she worked her way to the edge of the lobby, peering fascinated into the noisy casino and the sea of people a few steps below her. The ratchety sound of slot machines and ringing "jackpot" bells played a staccato background for the cheering of people at the playing tables or under the flashing signals of yielding slots. The unmistakable sound of silver dollars falling into hollow metal trays seemed continuous. Everywhere she looked there were people—dressed in shorts and bathing suit tops, evening gowns or tuxedos with the shirts unbuttoned and bow ties clipped to one side of the collar.

"What do you think?" Laura asked her, moving to the railing on the edge of the casino.

"Boy, look at this place!" Michelle said almost in a whisper. "Are we really going to stay here?"

"If I get us checked in we are," Dick said, walking up and patting her shoulder. "Want to help?"

Stepping up to the carved marble registration desk Dick smiled pleasantly at the uniformed man on the other side. "You have a reservation," he said evenly, "for Dick Price."

Nodding professionally the man moved to a rack beside his station and sorted through several slips of paper stacked in a slot marked "P-Q-R." He shuffled through them a second time, replaced them and returned to the window. "I'm sorry, sir. There is no reservation for a Dick Price."

Dick blinked, raised his eyebrows and asked, "How about Richard Price? Or R.C.?"

The man simply shook his head.

Dick looked puzzled as he turned to Laura and Kim beside him. "Would it be under Michelle's name, Daddy?" Kim asked as a wild guess.

"Oh, Michelle Price," the man behind the desk echoed pleasantly. "I have a reservation for a Michelle Price."

• Michelle grinned broadly and threw her chin up in a pose she hoped looked important. Somehow her wooden crutch, one leg and ragged hairdo didn't match the face she made, and everyone including the hotel clerk burst into laughter.

"Michelle," the man said leaning across the counter to see his small patron better, "this is your credit card for your stay with us. Everything is in your name, so you'll have to buy dinner for the family and you'll be the one to pay for the room. It's your treat this time."

"OK!" she said grinning. "I like that idea."

"Well, you can start by signing the register for me if you will," he said smiling back.

The rooms were bright and cheerful, decorated in wood tones and a restful shade of green. Michelle staked "first dibs" on the elegant marble bathroom, claiming a desperate need for a leisurely bath. Before long everyone was freshened up and ready to tackle the penthouse reception for Victor recipients and celebrities. It was scheduled for 5 P.M.

As they stood waiting for the elevator to take them to the top of the Hilton Hotel, Laura made a silent last-minute check of everyone. They all looked wonderful—and excited. She noticed a warm sensation within her as she silently thanked the Lord for His goodness to them, all of them, in honoring Michelle as a Victor. "Let it all count for you, Lord," she whispered as the elevator doors slid open and they filed inside.

Michelle wore a long blue and white peasant dress and stood beside her brother looking straight ahead, discreetly poking her elbow into his ribs every chance she got. Rick said as the car came to a stop, "Just you wait, Price, I'll get you." She landed one last subtle jab as the doors slid open.

The carpeting was a deep peacock blue and seemed to swallow their feet as they stepped into it in the entrance. For a brief moment they just stood taking it all in. No one spoke. Chandeliers sparkled brightly, illuminating the well-dressed, attractive people scattered in pairs and small groups around the room.

People filled the large room, milling, talking, moving slowly around the floor, sitting at small tables, leaning against an ornate railing or the forest green walls.

Barely in the room they heard a friendly voice call out, "Michelle, I'm so glad you're here."

Laurie walked briskly toward them, smiling, her long powder-blue skirt flowing softly around her ankles.

"It's nice to see someone we know," Laura said, hugging Laurie warmly.

"I'll say," Dick said, taking her outstretched hand. "Are we late?"

"Not at all," Laurie assured them. "Come over here and let's get you something to eat."

As they worked their way toward the long white table against the wall they noticed Tom Bosley of "Happy Days" fame talking with a tall gray-haired man with bushy eyebrows. Not far away Marion Ross spoke pleasantly with Rusty Citron and a young girl in her late teens. Rusty looked up and waved as Laurie led the Prices through the room.

At a small table in the center of the room Paul Williams and Alice Cooper talked energetically over small plates of food. And as they zigzagged through the room they passed Dr. "J", Tommy John and Chris Evert.

Suddenly they stood before an enormous table, its clean white linen cloths nearly hidden by a harvest of culinary creations. In the center stood a three-foot ice statue of a thrashing fish poised gracefully erect on its tail, jaws open. Up and down the table were carved-ice clam shells, opened wide, housing hors d'oeuvres of many kinds: clam creations, crabmeat in exotic sauces and vegetables prepared for unlimited enjoyment. Mouth-watering pastries in every shape and flavor imaginable covered gleaming silver trays. Special breads and fancy meats and cheeses seemed to have no end.

Laurie stopped them every now and then to introduce them to different people; Gene and Joyce Klein, the owners of the San Diego Chargers football team; Barron Hilton, president of the Hilton Hotel chain, and others who had turned out for the excitement of the annual Victor Awards.

They settled around a table near the center of the room, and Laurie asked, "How would you like to catch the Wayne Newton Show tonight, Michelle? We've arranged four tickets for you." Michelle looked up and popped a green olive into her mouth, then looked at her mom and dad.

"Sounds wonderful," Dick said.

"That's really a nice extra," Laura said. "I understand his shows are almost impossible to get tickets for."

"You're absolutely right," Laurie said nodding. "He never plays to an empty seat."

"Then the advertising is true?" Dick asked. "He really is Las Vegas's 'Midnight Idol'?"

"He really is," she said grinning. "Wayne Newton is a remarkable performer. He very seldom releases an album and you'll hardly ever see him on TV, but his shows are sold out here, sometimes weeks in advance. He performs more often in Las Vegas than any other entertainer does and he handles just about everything for his shows himself. He chooses the songs he's doing, picks the arrangements; even had the bandstand and stage floor in one of the hotels built to his specifications. He says he loves to perform. Even said he'd probably sing on the street corner if no one paid him to do his shows. I've seen his show a couple of times and I'm crazy about the guy."

"We sure like his music," Laura said. "It would be fun to see him in person."

"Well, good," Laurie said, choosing a piece of carrot off her plate. "Then it's settled. The dinner show, tonight at eight."

Before they left the reception, Laura found Rusty and discreetly asked whether there had been any news on the horse.

"Haven't heard a thing yet," he said shrugging his shoulders. "We just don't know."

Later that night, after finally locating the Wayne Newton tickets (in Michelle's name), they were ushered into a dazzling showroom and shown to a table at the stage.

"When she said tickets," Kim quipped, "I didn't think we'd end up on stage with him."

"These are what you call good seats," Dick said. "Enjoy it. You'll probably never sit here again." They laughed appreciatively and opened the menus.

The stage was concealed behind scarlet velvet curtains, and sparkling chandeliers suspended around the room cast gold and blue hues on the walls and ceiling. They enjoyed their dinner and were talking among themselves when the house lights began to dim and a voice over the loudspeaker said, "Ladies and gentlemen, the Copa Room is proud to present—Mr. Wayne Newton!"

Suddenly an orchestra was playing and the scarlet curtains parted and drew back as the pleasant strains of a man's voice sang out over the applause. From around the still swaying curtain appeared a tall, handsome young man in his mid-thirties in a white suit and red shirt opened at the neck. His deep tan and dark hair added to the brilliance of his smile as he musically greeted his audience, moving easily across the stage looking into their faces. He caught Michelle's eye and his face lit up with a special warmth. He smiled and winked in her direction as he concluded his opening number.

Michelle sat at the very edge of the stage and leaned both elbows on the wooden ledge. Her blue and white dress fell in soft folds onto the plush red carpeting completely camouflaging her "little leg" beneath the skirt. The only outward evidence of illness was the thin, shaggy hair that sparsely covered her head. She watched Wayne Newton intently as he moved through his first number, and enthusiastically banged her hands together showing her approval when the music stopped.

"I thought this show was going to be boring," she yelled across the table to Laura over the applause filling the room.

"How come?" Laura asked in the din.

"I thought he was going to sing old fuddy-duddy music like Daddy listens to," she grinned at Dick. They laughed heartily as the music began signaling another song. She quickly returned her attention to the stage as Wayne Newton lowered his eyes to change the mood. Shelly's brown eyes were clear and dancing with excitement as he slowly raised the microphone and sang softly:

"You are so beautiful to me . . ."

He moved smoothly across the stage in their direction smiling and singing to Michelle. She looked back, barely blinking for fear she might miss something. He walked directly up to her and knelt on one knee as he continued:

"You are so beautiful to me . . ."

He took her hand in his and she just as quickly placed her other hand on top of his, looking intently back into his eyes. She mouthed every word as he sang it and in the middle of the next phrase he looked briefly away to compose himself. Her eyes and attention unnerved him, and he struggled not to laugh out loud.

"You're everything I hoped for, you're everything I need
You are so beautiful to me."

His delight showed on his face as he looked at the happy little girl in front of him. The audience applauded the song and his gesture of kindness, but no one enjoyed it more than he and Michelle. He bent down and kissed her lightly on the cheek.

The rest of the show revealed Wayne Newton as a multi-talented person, playing a number of instruments and singing an expansive variety of songs. In the final portion of his show he came on stage wearing a black, three-piece suit, a white shirt and scarf and an enormous turquoise and silver belt buckle. As onlookers applauded his song he loosened the white scarf and walked back to Michelle. Bending down on one knee he draped the scarf over her head. "This is for you, Sweetheart," he said as he winked and smiled at her, then returned center stage to close the show.

As Laura tucked her into bed that night Michelle raised up on one elbow and straightened the scarf beside her on the bed table one last time. "He was awful nice to me," she said kissing her mother goodnight. "I wish I could see him again. He just swept me off my foot!"

11
Royal Answers

Walking into the Hilton Hotel's Green Room Michelle looked around at the people already there. "There's LeVar Burton," she said, hopping off happily to chat with her new friend. She seemed to be at home with people from any walk of life, never stopping to wonder whether she was welcome. She just loved everyone no matter who they were and figured they loved her just the same way. Dick and Laura looked at each other and smiled.

Rick walked toward them with Kim and Brenda. Dick saw them coming and let out a low whistle. "You guys look terrific!" he said sincerely. "You going somewhere?"

"Thanks, Dad," Kim retorted patting his tummy under his cummerbund. "You look pretty good yourself in your ruffled shirt and tux. I've never seen you so dressed up."

"That's because the only other time I wore one of these things was for my own wedding, and you hadn't even been thought of then."

Laura watched the family banter, enjoying the closeness, happy in the warmth of the evening they were here to share. She still pinched herself every now and then making sure it was for real. But tonight was the night Michelle would receive her Victor Award.

A few minutes later the double doors into the Green Room swung open again and Wayne Newton and his aide, Bear, slipped in unnoticed. Wayne stopped just inside the door and watched Michelle for a few minutes as she animatedly crutched from person to person talking freely with everyone. She spent a little time with LeVar Burton enjoying his questions and teasing, and smiled broadly when pictures were taken. She retrieved autographs and conversation from Pat Harrington, Jr., Valerie Bertinelli, Liberace, Foster Brooks and several other stars. She talked with Marion Ross like an old, dear friend.

"She's really something else," Wayne Newton commented to Bear. "Look at her. She's getting around better on one leg than most people do on two."

"She's got the moves, alright," Bear commented grinning widely, his dark skin showing off his white teeth.

"You know," Wayne said, crossing his arms and shifting his weight, "there's something about her. . . . Maybe it's the way she doesn't seem to feel sorry for herself. She really gets to me. When she sat grinning up at me last night at the show, I told Elaine it was love at first sight."

Just about then Michelle looked up and caught a glimpse of Wayne Newton standing in the back of the room. "Wayne Newton," she said loudly as she bounded toward him as fast as she could go. "Hi!" she said brightly, "I didn't know you were going to be here tonight. I really liked your show last night," she said breathlessly.

Wayne Newton entered enthusiastically into the conversation and the friendship, enjoying himself nearly as much as she was, while Bear stood with an amused expression on his face listening to her rattle on beside them.

"Thank you for the scarf. I tied it onto my crutch for tonight, see?" she said, lifting her crutch into the air for him to see.

"That's really nice, Michelle, I'm glad you like it," he said smiling proudly. "I sure enjoyed having you at the show."

"When I grow up I want to do what you do," she said. "I want to be a singer too, only a lady." She opened her eyes wide and laughing a little she asked, "Wanna sit down?" Plopping into a nearby booth she straightened her pink headscarf.

"I'd love to but I can't," he said in confidential tones. "I think I'd tear my pants if I did." They enjoyed the laugh.

"What's your name?" Michelle asked the strapping black man with Wayne Newton.

"I'm called Bear," he said smiling at her.

"Is that your real name?" she asked with interest.

"That's my real name," he said nodding for reinforcement. "My momma named me after a bear she saw before I was born."

"It couldn't have been a polar bear," Wayne said grinning widely.

"Nope," Bear said enjoying the joke. "It was a big, black grizzly." The three of them laughed heartily.

"Wayne," she asked hesitantly, "are you going to give me my award tonight?"

"No, honey," he said slowly. "I'm here to give someone else their award."

Michelle had so hoped he would say yes that his answer took her completely by surprise. Suddenly she found herself choking back tears. "I gotta go now," Michelle said quickly as she swung to her foot and moved rapidly toward the doors and into the hallway.

"She alright?" Wayne asked Kim genuinely concerned.

"She'll be fine," Kim responded smiling. "I'm sure she's OK. I'll check on her in a minute."

Wayne Newton was surprised how quickly he had come to love this little girl. It wasn't hard, because she was a giver he decided, not a taker. She spent her time giving to those around her, helping them to feel better, making them happy. And in the process she found her own happiness.

"If only more people could be like that little girl," he said reflectively as he and Bear walked across the thick carpet to the dressing rooms. He added thoughtfully, "I wish everyone could meet her. She's the epitome of what we all need to know. She portrays a special kind of hope in the dreams she's got. The world needs the kind of hope Michelle gives."

Out in the hall Michelle paced rapidly working off her frustration. She felt silly being so disappointed over such a silly thing, but Wayne Newton had become a special person in her life and somehow she wanted to share this special award with him.

Kim pushed the double doors open quietly and just watched Michelle for a minute. Finally she asked, "You OK, kiddo?"

Michelle looked up at Kim, stopped pacing and took a deep breath. "Silly, huh?" she said hanging her head.

Kim put her arm around her little sister as they walked back into the Green Room, "I'd never call it silly. This is a pretty important night for you. And I'm proud of you, Michelle." They stopped in the aisle as the doors swung shut behind them and hugged each other soundly.

Finally the showroom at the Las Vegas Hilton was filled to capacity and the Twelfth Annual Victor Awards were under way. The stage was a myriad of lights and rainbows, and at the plexiglas podium a handsome young man who looked like he'd stepped off the list of Best Dressed Men stood waiting for the music and applause to die down. His tuxedo accented his ebony coloring and broad shoulders.

"That's LeVar Burton," Michelle whispered to Kim, proud that she knew his name, happier still that they'd spent some time together.

Celebrities were introduced and they in turn introduced the honored athletes: Rod Carew, baseball; "Dr. J" Julius Erving, basketball; Walter Payton, football; Nancy Lopez, women's golf; Chris Evert, women's tennis; Alberto Juantorena and Francie Larrieu, track and field; and Tommy John, Come Back Athlete of the Year, and many others. Then came a special spot.

LeVar Burton stepped back to the podium and the audience heard him say, "Now we'd like for you to hear a very special story about another kind of inspiring courage. It's about a little girl who's going to be 10 years old next week."

Backstage the cues were given to send Laura, Dick and the family onstage. Laura kissed Michelle lightly on the cheek and whispered, "We'll be praying." Then she lifted her white chiffon skirt and walked up the stairs to the stage with the rest of the family. Michelle went as far as her companion, Jill, would let her, and watched until the family was out of sight.

"Let's fix your sash, honey," Jill whispered hoarsely, "turn around here."

Jill's headset picked up the words of LeVar Burton as he continued, "She was eight years old when she found out she had a malignant bone tumor that was going to cost her a leg. Now, upon hearing this news, most people would have gone into a severe depression. But Michelle Price is no ordinary little girl."

As he spoke he looked out into the audience. Expensively dressed, influential people from all over the country listened intently as he continued. "Her understanding of what was happening to her and the way she handled it is awe-inspiring, and is a great example of what the City of Hope is all about.

"The story should first be told by Michelle's parents, Dick and Laura Price, and their two older children, Kim and Rick who are right here with Wayne."

The cameras picked up Wayne Newton standing with a hand mike beside the Price family. He was pleased to be a part of Michelle's award.

Smiling sincerely, he introduced the Prices to the audience in his resonant voice, "There are questions I'd like to ask you that we've all been wondering about. Dick, when did you first learn of your daughter's illness?"

"We learned of it in November of '76," Dick answered slowly, conscious of the people sitting beyond the lights in the huge hotel showroom.

"And what prompted you to go to the City of Hope?"

"Well," Dick continued, shifting his weight from one foot to the other, and relaxing a little, "we checked many places, about what kind of treatment she would be receiving. We found that the City of Hope reflected what we expected out of a medical institution."

Wayne talked with Dick about Michelle's treatment at the City of Hope bringing out the fact that it is a non-billing institution. As he moved a little closer to Laura the lights glinted off the golden Victor Award he held in his hand. With a tone of understanding coming through his expression Wayne Newton asked Laura, "How did Michelle handle seeing her friends when she came back from the hospital for the first time, if you don't mind my asking?"

"It was hard on her," Laura said softly, remembering the first few days back home. "She was playing with the kids across the street and she knew it was hard on them. So she went to her father and asked if he'd like to take a walk with her. She went door to door and told everyone what had happened to her to put them at ease.

"When she came around to the last house," Laura added, "Michelle said, 'I'm glad it's all over. I think they'll feel a lot better about it.' "

The audience spontaneously applauded expressing their feelings about what Michelle had taken on herself to do.

Wayne's next words were drowned out. When he was able to be heard, Wayne Newton asked Dick, "Have you any advice that you'd like to give parents that might be faced with similar situations?"

Dick briefly looked away then answered, "All I can say is that you can't let fear overcome you. You have to live each day and make the most out of every minute by living on a day-to-day basis." He shifted his weight again and looked out at the audience, his voice filled the room, "And you have to have a lot of faith. Not just in the medical staff, but I believe faith in God helps out too."

The audience applauded their agreement and respect as Wayne Newton laid his hand on Dick's shoulder, "It certainly does," he responded, then turned to the audience and said, "Ladies and Gentlemen, I'd like us all to meet an incredible young lady, Michelle Price!"

Behind him on the stage the rhythmic fountain waters shot their salute into the air as they joyously danced. The orchestra began playing "Michelle" and hearty applause filled the air as the audience strained to see the little girl they wanted so much to meet.

Backstage Jill received her cue and excitedly walked Michelle to the short stairway up to the stage. "Good luck, honey," she said with tears glistening in her eyes.

"Thanks," Michelle shot back earnestly to the young lady urging her on. She stood catching her breath at the foot of the stair when a man with a headset loudly whispered, "Get out there!" The audience was still applauding.

Grabbing her skirt in her hand and hiking it up to her knee she hopped up the step, balanced herself with her crutches and tackled the next step, until she was standing breathless at the top. She dropped her skirt and swung herself forward into the entrance to the stage. As she approached the edge of the open curtain she could hear the wild applause from the audience and felt the warmth from the bright lights cover her arms and face.

Dick and Laura, Kim and Rick turned slightly to see her make her entrance and smiled proudly back at her in her moment of victory. "There she is," Wayne Newton said. His voice was a mixture of pride and tenderness.

She looked like a delicate Dresden doll, her dress a pale pink covered with a gossamer flocking of wildflowers, the organdy sailor bib trimmed in lace, and a matching scarf tied around her head. At the bottom of her long skirt one shiny white shoe swung with her to the mark where she would turn in front of the fountains to walk down the steps and join the family and her new friend.

The already thunderous applause became louder and there were tears in the eyes of the audience. Michelle hesitated at the top of the stage stairway and smiled warmly at her family. She looked radiant, her skin pink, her cheeks rosy, her eyes clear and sparkling. Before descending the stair to the stage floor she smiled at Wayne Newton. He winked back at her.

"You tricked me," she mouthed to him, delighted that he was a part of her big moment.

Dick watched his daughter as she worked her way proudly down the stage stairway under the hot lights. In front of hundreds of people in the showroom and thousands more in the TV audience, she stood tall and held her head high. He thought about her dream to be Miss America and smiled through his tears, *Honey, you're a queen tonight. Your dream is coming true.*

As she rhythmically made her way across the last few feet of stage to Dick and Laura she was almost unaware that the audience was enthusiastically welcoming her and that people all over the room were standing to their feet. The little girl, smiling warmly at everyone around her, touched the hearts of all who watched. Everywhere people were in tears.

Wayne smiled a special smile at his little friend and teased privately, "You thought I was leaving, huh?" The audience's applause began to die.

"Let me ask you a question," Wayne Newton said crouching down on one knee beside Michelle. His voice was full of special secrets as he spoke to this child he'd come to love and respect in the past two days. "Michelle," he asked, "what did you tell the other kids about your leg?"

"Well," she began, opening her eyes wide and tilting her head back slightly, remembering, "sometimes I'd tell them about . . ." She took a deep breath, "Sometimes I would say, I was on a river trip and I fell off the boat and an alligator bit it off, and I got so scared that my hair fell out."

The room immediately filled with a warm, natural laughter.

Michelle and Wayne talked briefly of other interests, then he opened the subject of skiing.

"I hear you're an accomplished athlete, and you like to ski," he began. The bright lights flashed on the award he still held as he moved the hand mike to Michelle for her answer.

With the microphone under her chin she only nodded yes. Her silence tickled Wayne Newton and he looked away briefly collecting himself before pursuing the questioning further. "Was it difficult for you to learn to ski again after your operation?"

He switched the mike back to her again and she looked at it, then self-consciously answered, "Kind of." She looked a little embarrassed as she glanced back at Dick and Laura behind her. They nodded encouragingly and she added, "It was kind of hard, I guess."

"Have you been in any competition since then?" Wayne persisted.

She hesitated, looking at him, "Yeah. I went on the Olympic . . . something." She squirmed slightly, unable to get all the words in the right order, "I forgot what it was called . . ." then remembering part of it, quickly added "the slalom." Her head bobbed up and down as she nodded confirmation of the term.

Obviously amused at her reluctance to tell about her victories on the slopes Wayne Newton continued, grinning broadly, "How well did you do?" The audience was enjoying his difficulty in getting her to tell what he wanted them to know. A muted sound of amusement rose from the attentive audience as they waited.

Dick prompted Michelle quietly from behind and she self-consciously added, "Um, two silver medals." Wayne Newton laughed, the secret finally dislodged. The room filled with a spontaneous applause and the faces around her were smiling encouragement as Wayne Newton presented Michelle with her Victor Award for 1977. They talked about her birthday coming up and the special party she was planning that week to say thank you to everyone at the City of Hope.

"Now," he said, with a sly look, "I happen to know that you love skiing, but it's really not your favorite sport. You want to tell us about your first love?"

"It's horses," she said eagerly. "I love horses."

"How often do you ride?" he asked.

"Every Monday."

"And do you have your own horse?" he prodded.

"No."

"Is there a horse in the future for you?"

"Yeah," she said almost forgetting about the audience and directing her full attention to Wayne, "we're looking for one."

He pulled the mike close to his chin and said almost confidentially, "Can I ask you a question, Michelle? What does the City of Hope mean to you?"

She looked into his dark eyes and said evenly, "Love and faith."

Over the spontaneous applause he commented, "I don't think it could be said any better."

"Tonight, Michelle," he continued, "we've been presenting Victor Awards to athletes who've demonstrated outstanding achievements, and you're one of them. We think extraordinary courage is what you've shown in your fight against one of life's toughest opponents, and that qualifies you to win that miniature Victor you're holding. And we hope you'll enjoy it always, 'cause you're an incredible lady."

Again the audience was on its feet loudly applauding the little girl who'd walked into their hearts just a few minutes before.

"I also know," Wayne Newton said taking a letter from his pocket, and looking at Michelle, "that your favorite star . . . up until last night . . . ?"

They looked at each other, sharing a private joke and Michelle rolled her eyes a little embarrassed, "It's you," she said laughing.

"It's me?" he questioned in mock surprise. Then turning to the audience he explained, "Up until last night her favorite star was Henry Winkler, right, Michelle?" She nodded. Then teasingly he added, "Notice how we changed that around real quick?" They joined in the joke as he opened the letter in his hand.

With her enthusiastic approval he began, "Dear Michelle, first of all, hugs and kisses to you. Last year I spoke to you after you came home from the hospital. This year you're receiving the Special Victor Award in Las Vegas. You must be very proud of yourself, and I'm very proud of you. It is with great regret that I cannot be there with you, but unfortunately, time is not as friendly to me as it once was, and my schedule would not permit my being with you on your special day. Just know, Michelle, that in my heart I'm celebrating your award. Be very good to yourself, and remember, self-respect is joy, and indeed, cool. Love and more love, Henry Winkler."

The audience applauded Henry Winkler's letter and Wayne said, "Now, Michelle, with this Special Victor Award and your tenth birthday coming up this weekend, I went to my ranch and brought along a special gift for you. OK?" he said building the suspense just a little. "I figured if it's personal to me and something I love, you might enjoy it too. I just hope it fits."

Purposely diverting Michelle's attention, he looked over her head and motioned to someone offstage "Uh, if I could get someone to bring it out here." Michelle turned around, straining to see what he was looking at.

Behind her Wayne Newton's trainer appeared leading a regal, cream-colored Arabian gelding. Almost as one body the audience stood, applauding wildly.

Hearing the applause Michelle turned around to see what had happened. There, in front of her stood the biggest, most beautiful horse she'd ever seen. She stared in disbelief, her mouth open as she drew a quick breath and tried to decide whether she could let herself believe what her eyes saw. Could it really be true?

She looked up at Wayne, her face glowing with the joy and ecstasy of Christmas morning. Her eyes were filled with the need for confirmation, assurance that this was not a dream. Wayne stepped beside her and put his hand on her shoulder, nodding the reassurance she sought from him. His eyes brimmed with tears. She looked back at the animal standing like royalty before her and tears filled her eyes. Slowly she leaned forward on her crutches, making her way toward the horse, her shoulders shaking with a trembling joy that pushed out from within her.

"His name is Prince," Wayne said as she crossed in front of him moving toward the animal. His voice cracked. He could not hide his tears.

Standing beside the horse she had prayed for, Michelle reached out her hand and felt Prince's warm breath and velvet muzzle. She seemed almost afraid to touch him, as if it might make him disappear. The trainer held the big animal steady watching the little girl's face. What he saw was all the delight and pure joy anyone could express.

In her eyes danced the dreams and hopes of her young heart. Something deep inside stirred his father-heart and he felt the unbridled joy of the child beside him as she laughed and cried in wonder. The trainer turned his face away from the camera.

The enraptured audience, from every possible walk of life, stood pounding their hands together, tears spilling down their faces—men, women, cameramen, stagehands, celebrities, other Victor recipients, even their tuxedoed host, Wayne Newton. They had been touched by a youngster they would never forget.

Michelle seemed unaware of all of them as she moved slowly toward the horse—her horse. Her eyes danced as she touched Prince again. God works miracles of all kinds. Her prayer had been answered.

12
After the Victor Award

A handsome celebrity on one knee opposite a tired but
beautiful little soldier with one leg—
It was a meeting anointed with honesty and truth:
    a child, simply accepting the star's brilliance
    without pretense,
    a man, with tears in his eyes, reflecting on his
    many blessings—excluding fame.
And eternal love is born between two deserving people.

> From a poem written for Michelle
> by Ken Millett, October 10, 1979

When she'd finally settled in again at home, Michelle turned her
attention to getting things ready for the chemo-completion party she
would be giving soon. She had one last week of treatment at the City
of Hope, and on the last day they would have the biggest party she
could dream up.

When they left for the hospital everything was ready. "Are you
sure you ordered the cake with a rose garden and a waterfall on it?"
Michelle asked, double-checking as they pulled into the familiar
hospital parking lot.

"I'm sure, honey," Laura smiled patiently, reassuring her for the
fourth time that day.

"And pink punch and balloons?"

"Everything. You saw the bags of stuff in the hallway."

"Yeah," Michelle said, leaning back against the seat thoughtfully. "I just want everything to be really special. It's important. I want it to be nice for my friends."

"It will be, Price," Dick said scooping her off the seat and tucking her under one arm like a sack of potatoes. "You have worked so hard on this you can't miss."

Michelle giggled and flailed around in pretend struggle. She wished it were next week already. She'd much rather be going to the party today instead of into the hospital for more chemotherapy. But this was to be the last time. What a wonderful thought! No more chemotherapy. Never, never again!

"Kaylene," Michelle squealed excitedly. "Hi!"

The small blonde girl smiled broadly, just a little embarrassed by Michelle's noisy exuberance. "Hi!" she called back slipping off her bed and into the hallway beside Michelle's wheelchair. "I didn't know you were going to be here this time."

"Me either. Isn't it neat?!" Michelle reached up and took Kaylene's hand. They were comfortable with each other now. They'd seen each other through the months whenever they'd been admitted together and had built a warm and healthy friendship.

"I'm having a party after my treatment this time," Michelle said excitedly. "Can you come? It's for my friends. It's going to be Friday."

"I don't know," Kaylene said, "but I'll ask. I like parties."

"We're going to have rose garden cake and pink punch and balloons and everything."

"Oh," Kaylene said, eyes sparkling, "it sounds so neat."

Before many days had passed the girls were feeling better and were spending as much time together as possible. Sitting across from Kaylene at the white pedestal table in the playroom, Michelle reached across the red and black playing board to move her checker.

"King me," she said happily. "Now I can chase you all over the board."

"Not if I'm chasing you," Kaylene grinned moving her king after one of Michelle's playing pieces.

"I wonder what's taking our moms so long," Michelle said studying the checkerboard, deciding strategy for her next move.

"Maybe somebody caught them and made them take it back."
They looked at each other, wondering whether they should be afraid.

"Nobody would make them take it back. They don't let you
return stuff like that," Michelle said with hopeful authority.

"Boy," Kaylene said, jumping another one of Michelle's men, "I
sure hope you're right."

"Me too," Michelle agreed. "I'll bet our mothers got talking and
forgot to come back. They sure do like to talk."

Finally the playroom door opened and in walked Laura and
Dottie Hall carrying two small packages. Laura peeked down the hall
in both directions, then closed the door quietly behind her, tiptoeing
toward Michelle and Kaylene. Both girls put their hands over their
mouths stifling giggles. Dottie pulled her sweater around her package
hiding it from view, pretending to check for intruders behind chairs
and drapes.

The parcels were set on the table and carefully opened as the
powerful aroma of Italian spices filled the air and Laura and Dottie
pulled their chairs up to the girls' table to split their pizzas.

Morning dawned with blue skies and warm sun as though special-
ly ordered for the party. And Michelle was awake before the birds.

When her breakfast tray arrived she was sitting on the edge of her
bed, washed, brushed and wearing the new dress Kim had made for
the occasion, her first short dress since the surgery.

Her stomach was fluttery but she knew it was just butterflies. The
chapter on chemotherapy had been closed and she was doing her
best to forget it. Today marked a new beginning and pronounced an
end to many painful and frightening days in her young life.

Mid-afternoon, people began arriving in Pioneer Park under the
big blue spruce trees Michelle had found so restful in the long, painful
days of chemotherapy. Bright colored streamers fluttered in the
breeze curling around pine branches and lacing from tree to tree.
Multicolored balloons hung from the rustling boughs in swaying
bunches like giant fruit.

A large, white, paper-covered board greeted guests with cheerful
words of explanation: "Michelle thanks the City of Hope and all her

many friends." The back of the board proudly held mementos of the past 18 months—letters from the White House, newspaper articles about Michelle and the family, her two silver skiing medals and pictures of her skiing, letters from Senator Edward Kennedy, a letter from Totie Fields, a photograph of Wayne Newton and other things of importance to Michelle.

Before long, nurses, technicians, family friends, people from the church, therapists, and others were milling around under the trees.

"Where's Michelle?" Linda asked Laura.

"I don't really know," she said a little puzzled. "She wanted to come on her own. Kimmy went to find her a few minutes ago."

"It looks like some of these folks are on coffee breaks," Linda said looking around at the many uniformed people standing nearby.

"I know," Laura said putting the cake knife down on the table. "I'm going to see what's taking so long."

As Laura moved toward the children's wing the side door opened and Michelle in a wheelchair, Kaylene, Billie and a half dozen more children with assorted medical paraphernalia came toward her, smiling happily. Dressed in party garb, bathrobes and pajamas they made their way toward the trees.

"What took so long, honey?" Laura asked gently, feeling the pressure of people waiting for them to get things started.

"I had to wait for my friends," she said looking back over her shoulder and smiling. "Some of them move kinda slow." Laura looked at the children making their way toward the trees. Little Billie walking just ahead of Michelle's wheelchair, his blue and yellow striped T-shirt pulled across a bulging abdominal tumor, inoperable. Lisa, wearing a head scarf over her sparse and scraggly hair, white tape holding an arm board to her left arm protecting the IV shunt still in her veins. Kaylene, smiling now as she shyly surveyed the festive scene ahead of them, bravely fighting her battle against a brain tumor.

Michelle knew how important a day like today would be to these friends. It's important to share good times; time is so short. What made today special for Michelle was sharing it with others who shared in the same kind of pain. Time to smile is important to those who see how fragile life really is.

Sitting quietly on a folding chair under a weathered old evergreen, Joy Sutera watched the little procession of hospital patients collecting under the trees. Michelle happily checked on her friends like a mother hen, laughing, teasing, making them feel at ease. Joy smiled to herself as she watched the little girl, thinking, *Michelle really enjoys showing love, gets lost in others so easily.*

She glanced at the hem of Michelle's skirt, to the one leg sticking out in front. A runner she had seen that morning came back into her mind and she reviewed the easy, rhythmic movement of his two strong legs as he jogged along the street. The powerful muscles of his thighs, the taut calves straining to meet his demands to push on further, to bear the weight, to move him smoothly along the road. She had watched the man, working his way along the pavement away from her as she pondered the question building inside, "Why, God? Where's the justice? How can anyone face what Michelle has to face?"

She focused on Michelle chattering happily with her friends. Joy's trained nurse's eye saw other things under the cheerfulness Michelle projected so easily. She knew the child's face was thinner, her eyes darker and deeper than usual. Chemotherapy always makes them lose weight; they are so sick for days. Her hair was scraggly and sparse, hardly grown back since the last treatment.

But her spirit! That was radiant. So many of the children she'd seen just seemed to lose their spark. The days and weeks of illness and limitations placed on them so often beat them down, robbing them of their color and personality.

Michelle's spirit soared, her peace and confidence showing through all the outward reminders of the ravages of her illness and the toll it took on her daily. She was a real and challenging encouragement to others. She was living proof of God's gentle care and strong protection in time of greatest need.

That's it, isn't it, Lord? Joy thought silently. *Michelle offers hope. What you've done for her is keep your promise. Anyone who trusts you and takes you at your word can know the same peace. Her peace is so real. Her trust and her dependence on you are strong and genuine—and—it's mine too. I understand that now.*

"Oh, God," Joy whispered as she walked toward Michelle, "thank you."

"Gray elephant!" Michelle chirped. "Stop, Kim!! Let me out of this thing!" She grabbed her crutch from beside her in the wheelchair and bounded toward Joy, using the crutch like a spring. She surrounded Joy with a hearty hug and enormous grin. "You came! I'm so glad!" she whispered.

"So am I," Joy said hugging the little girl tightly. The words came from the depths of her heart.

Soon Michelle was ceremoniously cutting the cake and passing it around. The punch was served and Michelle smiled happily as she looked around at her friends, family, young and old, enjoying her party. Joyce Klein was there; people from the church were enjoying themselves; friends from the neighborhood came; Linda Kurz, Joy, favorites from x-ray and the labs, nurses, Dr. Rosen, Dr. Kramer and others who had touched her life in some way.

As they talked over their cake, Michelle glanced toward a tall man in tan slacks and a short-sleeved shirt strolling toward her. She dropped her cake plate to the ground beside her metal folding chair and, steadying herself on her friend Nikki's shoulder, stood up. Sure now that she recognized the man she loped toward him. He grinned as she called out, "Dr. Moor! You came to my party."

With unbridled enthusiasm she flung her crutch off to the side and hopped the last few feet with her arms open wide. He reached out to catch her as she threw both arms around his middle, hanging on tightly. "I'm so glad to see you," she said breathlessly.

"And I'm glad to see you too," Dr. Moor said sincerely. "If you weren't such a famous TV star I probably wouldn't have heard about your party."

"You heard on TV?" she looked up with wonder.

Laura reached them and warmly welcomed the surgeon. "We're so glad you came," she said, "we tried to reach you but no one here knows your latest address."

"Well, it's funny how I heard about it," he said as they began walking toward the cake table. "I had been reading quite late one night last week and decided to take a little break, so I turned the TV on for a few minutes, and there was Michelle. I couldn't believe my eyes."

"Were you surprised?" Michelle asked hopefully.

"I'll say I was," he answered. "I hadn't heard anything at all about the award. It was wonderful to see that happen after all she's been through," he added sincerely to Laura. "Then you mentioned the party today and I thought I'd just drop by and see what I could see."

Michelle hugged him around the waist again, "I'm so glad you came. I've missed you so much. I was afraid you would forget me."

"Forget you?" he said smiling. "Let me show you something I brought along. Remember the little letter you wrote me when I left here?"

"Sure. I drew pictures on it, too."

He pulled the paper off a small package he'd brought with him, and held up a picture frame for Michelle to see. Under the glass was her letter to Dr. Moor.

"This hangs on the wall just above my desk, Michelle, and every day I remember a very sweet young lady I met at the City of Hope when I was here."

Michelle looked at the letter and then up at Dr. Moor. Her eyes spoke the thank yous her heart felt but couldn't put into words, and the doctor immediately forgot the long, hot drive to the little girl's party.

The air was filled with the sweet song of birds as they flew from tree to tree above the party. The breeze pushed balloons around and the children laughed, enjoying a longed-for break in their hospital routine. Michelle's party was a success. There was just one thing left to do.

With great ceremony Michelle pulled a lovely wooden plaque from its hiding place and approached Dr. Rosen who stood in the shade near the table holding his glasses in his hand. The two lines between his eyebrows deepened as he puzzled over what was happening.

Then Michelle briefly explained that she and her family appreciated so much the care they'd received at the City of Hope that they wanted to present them with a special thank you. He smiled warmly and read each word on the plaque.

"Well," he said still smiling, "you're not the only one who gets to make a presentation today, Michelle." He reached into the front of his lab coat and pulled out a white slip, handed it to Dick and said, "It's Michelle's tomography report. After 18 months her lungs are still clear. There are no signs of any new problems."

Dick and Laura read the report and hugged each other and the doctor. Today was indeed a day for celebration. They'd given her less than four percent chance of survival over a year ago, and God was ignoring their predictions. No man can limit God.

As Dr. Rosen excused himself to return to his duties, he asked Laura, "Would you be willing to speak to our psychological committee next Wednesday morning?"

"What kind of a committee is that?" she asked. "What could *I* tell *them*?"

"It's a group of doctors, psychologists, occupational therapists and other interested professionals. We meet once a month to discuss methods of improving our treatment of the children here, and one area of interest is patient acceptance with catastrophic disease. Michelle was so well prepared and has accepted what has happened to her so positively we'd like to ask you some questions about how you've handled this as a family."

Laura looked at Dick, then back at the doctor. "I'd like to talk to these people as long as I can say what I want to say."

"They will listen, Mrs. Price," Dr. Rosen assured her, nodding his head. "Our purpose is to help others adjust the way Michelle has. There are things you've done as a family we'd like to teach other families to do. We want to know what those things are. No one will challenge what you say."

"Then I'd love to come."

Wednesday morning came and, before long, Laura walked through the door with Dr. Rosen into a small room near the nurse's station. Seated in scattered chairs were seven or eight men and women, most wearing white lab coats. They continued talking quietly among themselves until Dr. Rosen called them to order.

"By way of introduction, I'd like you to meet Mrs. Laura Price," he said gesturing toward Laura. Then opening a large file on his lap he continued, "She and Mr. Price brought their daughter, Michelle, eight years old, to us in . . ." He scanned the sheet in front of him, "November of 1976. She presented with a history of tenderness in the right tibia. Pain was severe, though intermittent, beginning 10 to 12 weeks prior to admission. She saw her family physician who ordered a series of x-rays done which showed suspicion of a tumor. She was subsequently admitted to Children's Hospital where they did a biopsy, and the biopsy showed *osteogenic sarcoma.* The parents requested another opinion and the child was transferred to the City of Hope, where amputation of the right leg above the knee was performed." He closed the chart and laid it in his lap.

"The Prices have done a magnificent job of preparing their daughter for surgery," he continued. "The child faced the reality of what was happening to her before surgery ever took place. Since her adjustment was so smooth and unusual, I have invited Mrs. Price to share with us what she can about what they as a family have done to help their daughter adjust so smoothly and so completely."

Laura swallowed hard as Dr. Rosen turned the floor over to her. She whispered a prayer that God would do the speaking and then she opened her mouth.

"I appreciate the chance to speak to you today, and I hope something I say might help other children in Michelle's position some day. We've been so pleased with the treatment here. It means a lot to us that you care so much.

"First of all, I want you to know that what Dick and I did to help our daughter understand what was happening to her couldn't really be considered unusual. We're not super parents, just simple people with a strong belief in God, and we're not strangers to hard times at our house. Just six months before we found out about Michelle's tumor, our 20-year-old son was run over on the freeway by a semi-truck, and left for dead. The doctors said he could not live, but we kept praying and watched God restore Rick to complete health. Michelle shared in every day of that experience with us and saw God provide for her brother's serious physical needs. She knew He wouldn't let her down. We all share the belief that God cares for each one of us personally.

"That's the basis of our accepting things that take place in our life, as individuals and as a family. We all believe that nothing touches our life that hasn't first passed through the hands of our heavenly Father. Nothing."

Laura looked around the room and was almost surprised at the attentive expressions on the faces looking back at her as she spoke.

"We have always made it a family practice," Laura continued, "to cry *together* when somebody is hurting. That's why one of us stayed here in the hospital with Michelle the whole time. We hurt together, and there's a great deal of strength when you know your hard times are shared by those you love."

The doctors and others in the room asked Laura questions about specific ways she and Dick handled things, for instance, how they told Michelle she would lose her leg. They asked about how they comforted her during chemotherapy, and other common areas the other patients face. Laura answered their questions as completely as she could, reminding them, "When you believe God has a purpose it's easier to accept what comes."

When the meeting was over and people were leaving the room, one woman stopped Laura and said coldly, "You know, no one here believes the way you do, but we've found that people with your kind of faith are the ones who handle these things so well."

Laura looked into the woman's eyes and calmly said, "I was asked to share what we've done with Michelle. That's all I did. I can't do anything at all about what you choose to believe. You have to decide for yourself."

"Well," she said under her breath as she walked through the door, "I don't believe it for a minute."

Lord, Laura prayed silently as she drove along the freeway later, *those educated, intelligent people heard your word today and you promised your word wouldn't return void. Press it firmly into their hearts and use it to touch even one life for you.*

13
Beginning Again

"You gonna wear your wig?" Laura asked Michelle as they scurried around, getting ready for the City of Hope luncheon. In all their 65 years these supporters of the City of Hope had never invited a patient or a family to share their experiences with them. This year they'd made an exception.

"It's itchy," Michelle called back from her room. "It makes my head scratchy, and I feel weird with hair."

Laura looked over her shoulder at Dick and shrugged. "You'd think she could stand it for a few hours for something like this," she said shaking her head.

"Well, honey," he said squinting at a knotted shoelace, "if you think she should wear it why don't you tell her so?"

"No," she said thoughtfully securing a thin strand of beads around her neck. "That's like telling her she's not good enough the way she is. If it doesn't bother her to be bald it sure shouldn't bother me to look at her."

Michelle bounded into the room and backed up to Laura, "Zip my dress, Mommy," she said. "Can I wear my new horse necklace? I'll take good care of it I promise."

"Sure," Laura said pulling on the zipper. "It would look real nice on this." She put both hands on Michelle's shoulders, turned her around and looked at her for a long moment, then pulled her close and hugged her. "We sure love you."

"I love you guys too," Michelle responded brightly.

"I don't know why you want to love the likes of her," Dick teased finally working his shoestring loose. "Price, you're basically no darn good."

Michelle looked at her father out of the corner of her eye, then moved slowly toward him, slipping her arm around his shoulder coyly. "But, Daddy," she protested in a southern drawl, "ah'm *exactly* like you."

"Well, in that case," he said laughing, "I guess you're not so bad after all."

The International Ballroom at the Beverly Hilton Hotel was crowded and buzzing on the hot July afternoon. The luncheon today marked the finish of a weekend conference for the supporters of the City of Hope. Many of those in attendance were among the wealthiest, most influential people in all of California. Everywhere were people in fine clothing in tasteful, classic style. The air was alive with excitement.

The Prices were seated at a round table to the right of the room with easy access to the stage. Dazzling white tablecloths, laid with fine silver settings and lovely china surrounded a centerpiece of pastel carnations and greenery.

Michelle sat beside her mother, taking everything in. "Mom," she asked under her breath, "how come they give you so many forks?"

Laura patiently explained what the forks were for and smiled slightly as she answered Michelle's many other questions that came before the meal.

"Do they have a ladies' room?" Michelle asked.

"I'll show you where it is," volunteered Mrs. Nelson, a finely dressed lady sitting at the table. "I'm just on my way there myself," she added extending her hand and a smile to Michelle as she pushed her chair back and stood up.

They walked together through the double doors a few feet behind the table and were gone only a few minutes when Kim poked Laura and hoarsely whispered, "Look!"

Laura turned around, her mouth dropping open at what she saw. Just inside the double doors, out of the full view of other eyes, stood Michelle. Her head scarf was gone and in its place sat Mrs. Nelson's reddish pompador wig. Kim giggled and Laura covered her eyes with her hand, shaking her head as Michelle turned slowly in the doorway for full appreciation. Pleased with the results, she flashed an impish grin at her mother and sister and disappeared.

"What's Mrs. Nelson doing in the ladies' room all this time without her wig?" Kim said giggling.

"Poor thing," Laura gasped, regaining her composure, "I wonder whose idea that was?" The flush of her cheeks was becoming to her.

Before long Mrs. Nelson and Michelle made their way back to the table. Michelle's head scarf was tied neatly around her head, and Mrs. Nelson didn't have a hair out of place. No one said a word as they began seriously eating their fruit salad.

After the meal and a short introduction the Prices stepped to the microphone. Michelle waited at the table. Trembling, Laura laid her papers on the podium and began to speak.

"I hope you'll excuse me," she said breathlessly, "I'm very nervous." Then, holding her papers tightly in both hands she began, "June sixteenth there was a very special party held under the trees next to the rose garden at the City of Hope. The trees were in bloom with streamers and balloons. There was pink punch and a cake, decorated with a rose garden and waterfall, served by friends. It wasn't a birthday and it wasn't a holiday. It was Chemo-Completion Day!

"There was a large sign: 'Michelle thanks the City of Hope and all her many friends.'

"Chemo-Completion Day marked the end of 18 long months of treatment for Michelle, our daughter. It was a day that she had planned and talked about for months. She wanted to share a special day with the many people who had cared for and visited her, and she wanted to thank God for the strength and inner peace He gave her through it all. Michelle's faith has remained strong and constant.

"The rose garden has a very special meaning for Michelle. It was there that her father and I told her about the malignant tumor in her leg. When we asked Michelle why she picked the rose garden for her party she couldn't put it in words, only that it's special to her and one of her favorite places.

"It must be obvious by the very fact that Michelle wanted to give a party for everyone at the City of Hope that they have indeed become a very special part of our hearts and lives."

She folded her papers in half and leaned a little closer to the microphone to add, "We do love you all and appreciate you for making the City of Hope possible.

"Now I'd like to introduce our daughter, Kim."

Kim stepped to the podium. "As Michelle's sister I'd like to thank you too, and I'd like to read a poem to you that was written for Michelle by a family friend, Ken Millett. It kind of expresses what I feel about my little sister:

> Michelle is in God's ministry
> Proof He really cares,
> Evidence His love exists
> To answer all our prayers.
> She's smiling but it's painful,
> Courage demands a toll.
> Her strength is somewhere deeper
> In the unseen, living soul.
> The courage Michelle gives others
> By using her one leg well,
> Proves Victors aren't impossible.
> She stands where once she fell.

The audience was visibly moved by what had been said so far. Here and there around the room handkerchiefs were appearing.

"Laurie mentioned she was nervous," Dick began as he stepped to the mike. "I'm so nervous I was thinking maybe I'd duck out the back door and send a telegram."

The audience laughed, grateful for a light spot to rest momentarily, but still eager to hear more.

"May 20, 1976 is another date we will remember," Dick continued. "Our son, 20-year-old Rick, was run over by a semi-truck on the freeway." Dick's voice began to thicken, "Every wheel . . ." He paused to regain his composure. "Every wheel on the left side of the truck", he choked on the words, "and trailers passed over Rick's body. He wasn't expected to live. But God intervened and Rick is alive and well today."

Tears glistened in Dick's eyes and the thickness in his throat stopped the words again. He cleared his throat and explained haltingly, "I still relive that once in awhile."

Regaining control he continued, "This experience taught us the importance of faith and a day-by-day relationship with God. Six months later, to the day, we were to draw on that faith again. We learned that our daughter, Michelle, had a malignant bone tumor and was going to lose a leg. Michelle was in a large hospital when we learned the gravity and the nature of the illness. We sought second opinions and were directed to the City of Hope.

"After a warm reception and a complete tour of the facility, we sat down with the doctor and were informed of the philosophy, treatment and prognosis.

"We were greatly impressed with the concept that the family plays an important role in the recovery and well-being of the patient. We at no time were shunted to a remote waiting room and left to wonder what was going on. The consideration shown our family will always be remembered and appreciated. . . ." His voice faded off again as tears pressed against his throat momentarily.

"At the City of Hope the focus is on the recovery of the patient. Money has never distracted family or patient from this goal. This in itself is therapeutic. During this time we learned the meaning of the word *sadaka* —righteous giving.

"We welcome this opportunity as a family to personally thank all of you, and I'm sure these sentiments are shared by all the other families and patients. Thank you."

Dick reached into the pocket of his suit and pulled out a small parcel of blue papers. "Before introducing Michelle I would like to read a letter she received from her cousin. It's another episode from the rose garden which is sort of a focal point for us, a beautiful place where we have shared many good and many tragic times.

" 'Michelle: Remember our games in the rose garden? Isn't it strange that among all the roses we saw, we only wanted to pick maybe one or two? Why did we pick the most beautiful rose that could be found in the whole garden? I don't think we wanted to hurt the rose or punish it for being beautiful. We just wanted to take it to a place where we could show it off. To a place where it could bring more joy to more people. Now all the people who come to visit you who don't have time to take a walk in the rose garden will be able to share its beauty with you.

" 'Remember the other rose in the garden that was so beautiful you wanted to pick just one petal from it? That was a special rose, too. And when it blossoms it will be big and strong and beautiful and different from all the other roses, because, as you and I know, it will have one less petal than the rest.' "

Dick swallowed hard at the lump that would not let him speak, and tears flowed down his cheeks as he finished the last paragraph, " 'Michelle, to me all people are like roses and you are a very special rose who has brought joy and strength to the world around us. You are among the rest of us, the most beautiful rosebud in the rose garden and I love you very much. Your cousin, Jim.' "

Clearing his throat one last time he said, "In the last few months we have heard our daughter referred to in many ways: Miss Wonderful, a powerhouse, cheerful, uncomplaining, funny, special, an incredible young lady. Now here she is, our special rose—Michelle."

As though on cue the audience stood to its feet smiling through tear-filled eyes, applauding as Michelle made her way across the long stage to the podium. She smiled widely as she looked intently into the faces of her family. Each member as valued as the whole, each one caring for the others, together, strengthened because of the unseen member, Christ, the giver of the love they shared.

As the applause died down, people took their seats again, and Michelle said in a clear voice, "I just want to thank you."

Then amid resounding applause the family took their seats at the table once again. The main speaker followed them to the podium and looked quietly after them until they were settled at the table.

"You know," he said intimately into the mike, "maybe we need to change the saying to 'I *did* promise you a rose garden.' "

People sought out Michelle and the family after the luncheon to thank them for coming, to tell how they had been touched. Many shared their own experiences, miracles they'd seen in their own lives.

In the car on the way home as everyone chattered about what people had said, Dick listened quietly for several miles, struggling with his feelings.

God, he prayed silently as they sped along the road, *I'm even ashamed to admit this to you, but I'm—jealous, actually jealous of other people's miracles.* He thought back over the words and sorted through his feelings a little more.

It's like, when I hear about something you've done in someone else's life I compare it with what you've done for us. Like a little kid at Christmas, sizing up everybody else's presents to make sure his were the biggest and best.

That's awful! he thought, genuinely unhappy with what his honesty was revealing in the private corners of his life.

It's wonderful basking in the warmth and comfort of our miracles—Rick and Michelle. I love sharing what you've done for us. Others are so encouraged, so thrilled by your powerful intervention in their lives.

The trouble is I've almost forgotten what it's like to live without being special to other people because of what you've done. He wondered as he drove on, *Why do you perform miracles, Lord?*

You've opened doors for us to tell people about you. That's got to be a part of it. But we've also learned firsthand about how you can work in a person's life.

Thoughts darted through his mind as he pondered this new truth, *Miracles are sent for growth then, a point that requires some kind of action; a place where we can regroup and change directions in our lives. If we just keep looking for miracles we miss the touch of reality, we forget to go where the work waits to be done.* He smiled slightly to himself, *Jealous of someone else's miracles. Thank you, Lord, for growing me a little more today. Help me to encourage others and to share in the joy of miracles you perform in their lives. And thanks for not being small and shortsighted like I am. What a mess this old world would be in if you left me in charge of things. Just keep teaching me, Lord. And be patient. I'm a slow learner.*

The warm weather continued and Laura packed a large sack with goodies. Michelle and a couple of friends piled into the car and they headed for the beach. The sun was warm early and it promised to be a beautiful day. The girls chattered happily all the way to the coast and galloped like young colts across the long stretch of sandy beach to a spot they chose beside the water's edge. Michelle sank her crutch into the sand again and again as she bobbed along keeping stride with the others.

Blankets stretched across the warm sand, Laura suddenly found herself buried under shorts and T-shirts as the girls pulled them off and flung them back toward the blanket on a dead run to the water.

"Last one in the water's a rotten egg," Michelle hollered pushing her crutch into the sand and heading toward the breakers.

"You're gonna be the rotten egg," Cara called back over her shoulder as she raced past Michelle onto the cold, wet sand.

"Oh, yeah!" Michelle said, delight and determination flashing in her eyes as she dropped her crutch and hopped, neck and neck with both friends the rest of the way up to their waists into the Pacific.

Squeals of delight and ripples of giggles harmonized with the sound of crashing waves and calling gulls. Laura smiled from her dry perch on the blanket and watched the girls wrestling and splashing along the edge of the water. She turned, collecting the clothes lying around the blanket, and glanced at the couple beside her.

"Look at that little kid," the young woman was saying to her companion. "She's missing a leg and she's as bald as a cue ball."

"That's gross," he responded. "They shouldn't let kids like that on a public beach."

Laura couldn't believe she was hearing what she knew she heard. She sat there in silence watching these two strangers discuss Michelle like a piece of meat. She wanted to stand up and scream, "How dare you even think things like that about that child. After what she's been through, after the battles she's fought just to stay alive, after the love she's shown to others . . . how dare you!" She wanted to tell them how wrong they were.

She looked back at the ocean and Michelle holding tightly to Cara's arm on one side, Debbie on the other. The three of them worked their way into the breakers and body surfed back to shore laughing and tumbling in the salty water. There was just no way to hide a missing leg when you're wearing a two-piece bathing suit.

Hide? Is that what I want to do? Laura searched her feelings just now. *It is what I'd do if I could. I'd hide her so nobody could hurt her with what they think or say. And I'm the one who wanted her to wear a wig. How fickle feelings are.*

She turned over and lay down on the blanket. It felt warm under her as she reached into the sand and pushed a few tiny grains around with her fingernail. Dropping her hand into the warm sand she pushed against it moving her fingers back and forth until her entire hand was buried under the soft grains. She looked at her arm and realized that it looked as though she had no hand. For several minutes she studied her arm and tried to imagine what it would be like to lose a limb.

God, she prayed silently, *don't ever let me forget these people's faces and somehow teach me to reach out to them in their fear. Help me to make them understand, to help them accept people like Shelly—just the way they are.*

The day was an exhausting success and mid-afternoon they headed home, sandy and sunburned. Michelle pulled the CB mike from its cradle, pressing the button on the side.

"Breaker, breaker, this is Bald Eagle. Anybody got their ears on out there? Come in, good buddy."

The girls laughed as a trucker called "Bushwhacker" responded to her call as they sped toward home. Laura smiled at Michelle's chosen handle, Bald Eagle. *Lord, just let me accept things the way she does.*

14
A Single Step

"OK, Michelle," the physical therapist said as she set the package on the floor. "Here it is."

"My leg?" she asked with anticipation.

"That's right, your new leg." Nancy opened the top of the package and reached inside with both hands pulling the artificial leg out and standing it on the floor where Michelle could get a good look at it. It was already wearing a sock and Michelle's matching shoe.

Her eyes opened wide as she looked the prosthesis up and down. "It looks like a doll leg, Nancy," she commented.

"Want to try it on?"

"I guess so," she answered a little hesitantly. She watched Nancy and did what she was told, and before long she was standing with her stump inside the socket of the artificial limb.

"Now," Nancy continued, "take that strap and wrap it around your waist. . . ."

"Like this?" Michelle asked, pulling it around her left hip.

"Exactly. You're a quick learner," she smiled at her small patient. "Now, hook the strap here and let's get a look at you."

As the therapist backed away a couple of steps for a better look, Michelle caught sight of her own image in the wall of mirrors. She studied what she saw for several seconds. "Maybe with pants on it won't look so ugly," she said, then turned to face her mother. "Well," she said smiling proudly, "what do you think?"

"I think you've gotten taller in the last few months and I didn't notice," Laura said over the lump in her throat. "You look great, honey."

"Well, good," the therapist said smiling. "Now all we have to do is get you to work this thing right and we're on our way. We've got some work to do here, Michelle."

Laura closed the door behind her and breathed a sigh of relief as she walked down the hall into the sunlight. It was so bright it took her a few seconds to adjust, but she welcomed the warmth falling across her shoulders. The sky was clear and blue and there was a light breeze playing in the trees nearby. She settled onto the sweet smelling grass and filled her lungs with the fresh air of another new day.

"Thanks, Lord," she whispered. She hadn't been looking forward to this morning. She'd been concerned that this new leg might be as traumatic for Michelle as the first had been. *That first leg—I'll never forget the look in her eyes when she saw that thing,* Laura thought, *and I didn't blame her. The screws all exposed, leather parts showing—it looked like something an old sailor would have carved for himself at sea.*

It's funny, she reflected, *until I saw Michelle with an artificial leg I didn't realize how natural it had become for her to have only one. But with the prosthesis standing in the corner or flung across her bed it's a constant reminder of the loss.* She straightened her legs out in front of her and leaned back on both arms, turning her face up into the sun. For a few minutes she just concentrated on the warmth, then she opened her eyes and looked into the endless blue sky. "Lord," she said quietly, "keep us from weakening under the daily-ness of all this. Keep us strong, and close to you."

After weeks of practice, the day came when Michelle rode proudly home with her leg on the seat between her and Kim.

"Let's go by and show Jim," she suggested enthusiastically, and before long Laura pulled the car up at the curb in front of their cousin's house.

"Jim," Michelle yelled excitedly bursting through the door of his apartment, "I got it! I got my leg today. Want to see?"

"Of course I want to see," Jim said grinning. "I can't wait. Go put it on."

She felt like all thumbs trying to get into her leg in her excitement. Always before there was someone to help her with it, but this time she wanted to do it all alone. She finally worked the leg into position, snapped the belt around her waist and stood up beside the bed. Her balance was good and she walked through the door smiling to herself.

"Well," she said as she neared the top of the stairway, "what do you think?" Jim and Laura turned to see her smiling broadly down at them.

"Look at you," Kim said walking up behind her on the landing, "you've got two legs." She hugged her little sister tightly. "Well, show us how it works," Kim added.

"I'm coming downstairs," Michelle announced moving to the top step.

Laura started slowly up the stairs toward Michelle, "Honey," she said, "why don't you start with something a little easier?"

"I can do it, Mom," she said clearly disappointed in Laura's cautiousness. "I'm not a cripple."

She took hold of the railing with both hands and started slowly, carefully down the short stairway. Each step was another victory for the little baldheaded girl with the leg like a doll, and as she mastered one step after another she smiled to herself.

Halfway down Jim reached out and touched her hand, his eyes filled with pride.

"How about that, Jim?" Michelle said. "Now I won't have to use crutches."

"It's wonderful, Michelle," he said. "I knew you could do it. Pretty soon you'll be as fast as you are with your crutches."

She just grinned up at him as she stepped onto the carpet at the bottom of the stair. "And now I can wear two shoes again."

She did a few soft shoe steps and then worked her way back up the stairs to take the leg off. Stopping at the top she leaned on the railing. "Mom," she said with a flash of genius, "I just had a great idea!"

"What's that?" Laura asked.

"Remember Matt, the kid at school who used to kick me in the leg all the time?"

"Uh-huh."

"Well," she said hunching up her shoulders and rubbing her hands together like a mad scientist, "I'm going to wear my leg back to school some day and I won't tell him it's fake, see, and I won't snap it on tight. So when he kicks me again, my leg will fly right out of my pant leg and clear across the playground. That'll cure him of kicking anybody ever again," she said triumphant in the thought of such a beautiful plan of revenge.

Later that night as Dick and Laura settled into bed Laura lay staring up at the dark ceiling for several minutes. "Billy died last week," she said quietly.

The words hung in the darkened room. "Oh no," Dick whispered, grateful the darkness hid his tears. "He fought so hard for life."

"You know," Laura said quietly, "I think medicine is a lot like Christianity."

"What do you mean, honey?" Dick asked.

"Well," she said slowly, resting her head against his shoulder thinking it out, "a nurse can give two patients good care and the right medication, and one lives and the other dies."

"Yeah," he said grasping the parallel, "and a Christian can pray for two people, love them as God would, do everything 'right,' and one becomes a child of God and the other goes his way without Christ."

"There isn't any way to tell who will make the choice and who won't."

"You have to give your best to all of them, and let them make the final choice themselves," Dick said.

They moved closer together, into each other's arms and Laura whispered, "I'm so sorry about Billy. I know Billy's with Jesus, but I'm so sorry it ended for him so early. How lonely his parents must be tonight."

Several months later, through an article in a large magazine, Tom Clark of the Arabian Horse Association learned about Michelle's gift from Wayne Newton and extended an invitation to the Prices for Michelle to participate in the 1981 Arabian Horse Pentathlon in Oklahoma City, Oklahoma. It was exciting, and an opportunity for Michelle to develop her riding ability in preparation for the event. But several people involved were concerned about using Prince.

"Honey, you have to try to understand," Laura reasoned with Michelle. "Prince is nearly 11 years old. To try to train him now to do the things he'd have to do in the Pentathlon . . ." She shook her head slowly, "He's too old, Michelle. He won't live forever, honey. He's not a young horse anymore."

A few days later as Dick and Michelle drove home from the stables, she suddenly burst into tears.

"Shelly," he asked, "what's wrong?"

"Please, Daddy," she sobbed, "ask Mommy not to talk to me anymore about Prince getting older."

"But, we're all getting older, honey," he said as they pulled up at a stop light. He looked at her intently, "Mommy's getting older, and me too. Even you."

The light changed and shifting into first gear, Dick started across the intersection.

"But it doesn't bother me to think about you dying," she said.

He almost stalled the car, but managed to shift into the next gear before asking, "It doesn't bother you to think of us dying, but it does when you think about Prince dying? Thanks a lot, Price," he said half teasing.

"No, Daddy," she explained, "it doesn't bother me to think about you and Mommy dying because I know where you'll go when you die. But I don't know what will happen to Prince when he dies."

Dick drove silently for a few blocks. "Michelle," he said, "I don't know for sure either, but I'm sure we can trust God to do what's best. In the meantime, I'll talk to Mommy for you."

Looking out the window Michelle asked, "Daddy, do you know what I picture God like?"

"Tell me, Price."

"Well, I think He's a lover of all His animals. He'll be fun to be around, like He'll play hide-and-seek with me in the clouds when I get to heaven." She leaned back against the seat and thought a moment. Dick glanced at her out of the corner of his eye wishing he could see her full expression.

"I don't think He's like most kings who think they're hotshots and can't be with the regular people," she continued, reaching for her daddy's hand. "I think He'll be like one of us, but we'll really respect Him."

They rode in silence another mile or so, then Michelle patted Dick's hand and added, "You know, it's special the kind of love God has for us because He doesn't just pretend." She paused, watching the children on a playground. "He really loves us."

Dick glanced at the children running on the schoolyard and marveled at Michelle's consistent acceptance of God and life as they came to her.

"Daddy," she said as they pulled in the driveway, "I just want you to know, I'm not afraid to die."

Later that week Michelle called Laura into the bathroom where she was bathing. "Mommy," she said with fear in her eyes, "I think I felt some lumps under my arm."

Laura's blood ran cold at the words but she forced herself to check out the spot Michelle showed her. She felt several lumps on the inside of Michelle's right arm. They would have to be checked.

Sitting on the cold examination table the next afternoon Michelle studied the face of the young man checking her arm. She tried to read his eyes but couldn't penetrate the well-learned, noncommittal veneer. The silence in the room hung like heavy smoke as he slowly prodded and pushed, palpated and studied the small hard lumps under her skin.

Finally he straightened up, folding his arms across his chest. He looked hard at her shoulder from across the room, then raised his right hand to his chin, and slowly bit his lower lip. "Well," he said deliberately, "I don't think it's anything to worry about."

Michelle relaxed visibly at his words.

"We'll have Dr. Rosen take a look too, to be thorough, but I'm sure it's just a couple of glands that have become irritated and infected from the crutches." He patted her knee, picking up the metal chart and tucking it under his arm. "You put your shirt back on now and I'll tell Dr. Rosen you're on your way over."

When the door closed behind the doctor, Laura unfolded Michelle's shirt and handed it to her. She looked into her daughter's eyes and asked, "Were you scared, honey?"

"Worse than that," she answered pulling her T-shirt over her head and letting out a deep sigh, "I was terrified!"

"Were you afraid it might be cancer again?" Laura asked, moving beside Michelle and smoothing down the short brown hair that was coming slowly back.

"Yeah, but that part doesn't scare me so much." She studied her hands in her lap. "It's the treatments," she said quietly. Then raising her eyes to meet her mother's, she softly added, "I don't think I could ever go through those treatments again."

Laura pulled her daughter close and held her for a moment. In 18 months of chemotherapy, Michelle had never once asked not to be taken for a treatment. She had never complained about the pain and violent sickness, or losing her hair; she was a model patient. God's grace was truly sufficient to her need.

She sat quietly beside her mother as they waited outside Dr. Rosen's office, tracing the pattern of the rug with her foot, sighing quietly.

"What're you thinking about?" Laura asked, softly touching Michelle's short brown hair.

"Just stuff," Michelle answered without looking up.

"Good stuff?" Laura continued, gently probing. "Or bad stuff?"

"Not really bad. . . ." Michelle pulled her leg into the chair, curling around to face her mother. "It's just . . ." she paused, thinking her words through, "it's just that, well, I'm afraid the boys aren't gonna like me." She searched her mother's kind eyes for reassurance or a little hope.

"You mean because of your leg?" Laura asked, trying to understand Michelle's real fears.

Michelle shifted in the chair, looking down at her fingers and nodded. Without looking up she added, "I try to look nice all the time. I comb my hair and I don't wear clothes with holes, and all that stuff, and I try to be friendly to everybody. But sometimes . . ." she paused thinking it through, "sometimes I think they just don't want a one-legged girl around." Tears filled her eyes as she looked to her mother for comfort.

Laura reached around Michelle and pulled her close. "Honey," she said gently, "I think only part of what you're feeling is because of your leg. A lot of it is just plain growing up. Sometimes that happens around your age.

"Almost-12-year-old girls feel kinda uncomfortable about boys, and boys feel the same way about the girls."

"Really?"

"Really," Laura assured her. "I remember thinking the boys didn't like me when I was your age, and I've got both legs."

Michelle thought about her mother's words, "But some of it is because of my leg, I know it is. At school there's lots of stuff I can't do now, at least not as good as I used to. So I get picked for a team just 'cause I'm the only one left and somebody *has* to pick me. They really don't want me on their side 'cause I can't help 'em win very much." Tears squeezed past her lashes and rolled down her face. "I don't blame 'em."

She rubbed her hand across her cheek abruptly wiping the tear away, wanting to wipe away the unfairness, suddenly angry that she hurt so much over something she could not control.

"I feel like quitting," she said, momentarily giving in to her frustration. "Even Maria picks Patty or Beth before me now. She used to say they couldn't play as good as I could." She looked off in space, remembering for a minute. "I miss my leg. Sometimes I really miss it."

As Michelle cried in her arms, Laura's thoughts drifted back to the day over three years before when this had all begun, the day she and Dick found out Michelle had a tumor.

The doctor had scheduled Michelle for a biopsy the morning after they'd found the tumor. On the way home from his office they'd stopped by the high school to get Kim.

Kim and her friends were practicing pom-pom drills on the football field when they found her and as soon as Michelle saw her sister she broke loose from Dick and Laura and ran down the green grassy slope, arms open, welcoming life inside. Kim turned and scooped Michelle up, whirling her round and round in circles. Their laughter echoed in the bleachers and poured across the deep pain that Dick and Laura bore.

Could it be possible that this would be the last time their little girl would run again? they had wondered that day. *Would the joy of being a child, of playing games and sharing with her friends be marred with tragedy? Would Michelle really be handicapped the rest of her life? How could this happen to a child? Their child?*

The questions were frightening and it had been far too soon for any of the answers, but fear lay like rocks at the bottoms of their stomachs in a dull ache. Dick stood behind the bleachers out of the girls' view, his shoulders heaving in great, deep sobs. Laura remembered now how he'd cried that day, as if his heart would break with its burden.

She looked at Michelle sitting beside her now. She was older, over three years older. She was tall and slender; a thick, lovely head of brown hair; deep, penetrating dark eyes; an infectious grin; and a faith that could move mountains. She was drawing on that faith again now, and today she struggled with an enemy Laura could not help her subdue, no matter how her mother heart ached to make things right for Michelle.

"I feel bad about feeling bad," Michelle said thoughtfully, interrupting Laura's thoughts. "God's gonna think I'm not grateful for what He's done. I think I'm looking at the bad too much, and not enough at what's good." She pondered her thoughts another minute, then added, "If I didn't have *any* arms or legs, I'd still have a mouth to praise God with."

"Now," Laura said smiling, "that's the Michelle I know and love." Then patting Michelle's hand gently she added, "Honey, no matter what happens, God isn't finished working His miracles in you. Nowhere near finished."

A Note from the Prices

When faced with the impending death of a loved one, fear and anxiety can be overwhelming. The message we hope will come through in this book is that regardless of the circumstances, God is *a very present help in time of trouble.* He does give *a peace that passes all understanding.*

We are ordinary people caught up in extraordinary circumstances. We live our ordinary lives through the grace of God. Our days are very similar to those of our friends and neighbors, though they face different lives, different struggles. Many people have said to us, "We don't know how you can do it. We don't think we could face what you've faced." Not only could you face our situation, but you could face it with peace and confidence—as long as you face it with God. He has already given us the solution to any problem; we only need to accept and act on His promises.

The lessons we've learned and continue to learn, all point to one thing—God means what He says. We only have to believe Him. In our situation—the near death of two of our three children—options were reduced to zero. God was the only alternative. That made the choice simple for us. The difficult part for us is applying this same principle—letting God do it *His* way—to our daily lives and receiving His help where we haven't exhausted all the alternatives. We're still growing!

We pray that you will be encouraged as you read, to place your faith and trust in God. He specializes in little problems and impossibilities. God has been the source of incredible joy in our lives—He loves *you*, and *cares* what happens in your life. That's what we hope we've shared with you in the pages of this book.

We would love to hear from you. Please write to us, Dick and Laura Price, c/o Regal Books P.O. Box 3875, Ventura, CA 93006.

Epilogue

Ending Michelle's story is the next best thing to impossible. She keeps meeting new challenges—*gold* medals in skiing, riding a float in the famed New Year's Day Rose Parade (1979), Grand Marshall in another, being asked to give the invocation at the Celebrity Equestrian Benefit, being part of the 1978 American Cancer Society success flier, and on and on. Collectible stories are endless—like the emergency room doctor's reaction when he heard that the little amputee had broken her hand rollerskating.

Michelle's story *has* no end. It will go on and on and as she is used of God she will encourage and challenge others with her faith.

One of Michelle's special friends, Ken Millett, has written a poem that says it all. It's called, "Perspective"

> I suppose I'm supposed—
>   To keep winning in life,
> With me, the "gold" is expected.
> A little girl from the City of Hope
> Whose courage the world respected.
>
> I suppose I'm supposed—
>   To be impressed with myself,
> For the way I coped with cancer.
> But I'm really impressed with medicine
> And with God for allowing the answer.

I suppose I'm supposed—
To be always first
In skiing the downhill race.
But victors sometimes are second—or last,
Despite the smile on their face.

I suppose I'm supposed—
To be humble and shy,
Instead of repeating my story.
But if telling about me gives others hope,
Then I give God the glory!